Gandhi's Passion

GANDHI'S PASSION

The Life and Legacy
of Mahatma Gandhi

STANLEY WOLPERT

OXFORD
UNIVERSITY PRESS

2001

OXFORD
UNIVERSITY PRESS

Oxford New York
Athens Auckland Bangkok Bogotá Buenos Aires Calcutta
Cape Town Chennai Dar es Salaam Delhi Florence Hong Kong
Istanbul Karachi Kuala Lumpur Madrid Melbourne Mexico City
Mumbai Nairobi Paris São Paulo Shanghai Singapore
Taipei Tokyo Toronto Warsaw

and associated companies in
Berlin Ibadan

Copyright © 2001 by Stanley Wolpert

Published by Oxford University Press, Inc.
198 Madison Avenue, New York, New York, 10016

Oxford is a registered trademark of Oxford University Press

Library of Congress Cataloging-in-Publication Data
Wolpert, Stanley.
Gandhi's passion : the life and legacy of Mahatma Gandhi / Stanley Wolpert.
p.   cm.   Includes bibliographical references and index.
ISBN 0-19-513060-X
1. Gandhi, Mahatma, 1869–1948.
2. Statesmen—India—Biography.
3. Nationalists—India—Biography.
DS481.G3 W64 2001   954.03'5'092—dc21
[B]   00-045298

1 3 5 7 9 8 6 4 2
Printed in the United States of America
on acid-free paper

for
John Kenneth Galbraith
who has so generously shared
his love of India, his friendship
and his wisdom

PREFACE

F OR MORE THAN half a century, from the day I first set foot on Indian soil, February 12, 1948, the day one-seventh of Mahatma Gandhi's ashes were immersed in waters off Bombay, I have been fascinated by the remarkable life and tragic death of the man Indians call "Great Soul" (*Mahatma*) and "Little Father" (*Bapu*).

Stepping ashore at Bombay's bustling gateway to India I found myself surrounded by more people than I had ever seen, millions of white-clad mourners headed to Chowpatty beach, where a glistening white ship bore the urn filled with a portion of Gandhi's remains. As that bright vessel weighed anchor, thousands waded after it in the bay, hoping to touch the Mahatma's ashes before they were swallowed by the sea.

At that time I knew no more about Gandhi than that he was called the Father of India yet had been murdered by an Indian of his own Hindu faith. The many questions raised by what I saw and heard that day changed the course of my life from marine engineering to Indian history. A decade later, when I began teaching at UCLA, I wrote my first book about Gandhi, a fictionalized story of his assassination, published as *Nine Hours to Rama*.

Over the next four decades I periodically considered writing the history of Gandhi's life and his leadership of the Indian National Congress. After a year or two of trying in vain to plumb the ocean of Gandhiana with its conflicting currents, however, I returned enthusiastically to teaching, opting to tackle other subjects and less enigmatic lives. Though invariably daunted by Gandhi's elusive personality and the extent of his archive, I kept hoping that greater maturity and deeper knowledge of India would help me to understand the Mahatma's mentality and reasons for his often contradictory behavior.

Preface

After completing my *India, A New History of India, Morley and India, Jinnah of Pakistan, Zulfi Bhutto of Pakistan,* and *Nehru: A Tryst with Destiny,* I decided it was time to return to the challenge of Gandhi. That was five years ago, when all ninety volumes of *The Collected Works of Mahatma Gandhi* had been published by Navajivan Press, in Ahmedabad, where Gandhi had founded his first Indian ashram. On my first visit to the famous Satyagraha Ashram, fewer than five volumes of his letters and papers were in print, though all letters written by or to him were then being indexed and filed chronologically by his disciples.

The daily diaries and biographical works of Gandhi's faithful secretaries, Mahadev Desai and Pyarelal Nayar, were by then also in print, as was D. G. Tendulkar's exhaustive eight-volume chronicle, entitled *Mahatma*. After Mahadev's early death, Pyarelal took up his task and published two massive volumes called *Mahatma Gandhi: The Last Phase*. He was still working on another two, called *Mahatma Gandhi: The First Phase*, when he died. Pyarelal's sister, Dr. Sushila Nayar, one of Gandhi's most intimate disciples, completed her brother's labors the year I dined at her home in Delhi four years ago. I almost decided then to abandon my "Gandhi" once again, feeling that perhaps I had nothing new to add to what was known about the amazing man who called his life an "open book," and fearing that at age sixty-eight, completing my research and writing might take longer than my lifetime.

Then, on May 11, 1998, I flew into Delhi to speak at India's International Center and learned that India had just exploded three underground nuclear bombs in Pokhran. A few days later Prime Minister Vajpayee announced, following several further successful explosions, that India had "a very big bomb" and was a "nuclear weapons State."[1] The popular response in New Delhi and throughout most of India was euphoric. Much to my amazement, hardly any Indian voices were raised against so complete a departure from everything Mahatma Gandhi believed in and had tried to teach throughout his mature life. His total faith in nonviolent love (*ahimsa*) as the surest path to peace, as well as Hinduism's "highest Religion," seemed forgotten by most of his newly militant, prideful heirs. "Hatred can be overcome only by love," Gandhi argued, insisting, "Let us keep our hearts and hands clean. Then we can ask for justice before the whole world. . . . [A]rms have to be given up. We cannot protect ourselves with arms."[2] When asked by several Americans whether the atom bomb might not help to universalize *ahimsa* as "nothing else can?" Gandhi replied: "So far as I can see, the atomic bomb has deadened the finest feeling that has sustained mankind for ages. . . . Mankind has to get out of violence only through non-violence."[3]

I resolved that May to write my book on the life and legacy of Mahatma Gandhi. I am deeply indebted to many wise friends for sharing their memoirs of and insights into the life of Gandhi with me. My Sanskrit guru and friend, Professor W. Norman Brown, was the first of my teachers to tell me how singularly wise a man Gandhi was. A few years later, when I returned to India in 1957, I was privileged to meet and walk with Mahatma Gandhi's foremost follower, Vinoba Bhave. Our neighbors in Poona, Rao Sahib and Pama Patwardhan, were close friends of Vinoba and thanks to them, my wife and I were welcomed to join Vinoba's entourage during his *Gramdan* ("Gift of Village") pilgrimage of Southern Maharashtra State on December 23, 1957, my thirtieth birthday. I vividly recall Vinobaji's unadorned frail body and totally unaffected, unpretentious spirit as well as the brilliance of his mind, and I have always felt that meeting and listening to him was as close as I ever came to meeting Gandhi himself. The Patwardhan brothers often reminisced about Gandhi in our nightly conversations and helped dispel some of the myths and much of the mystery that still shrouds his memory. Jaya Prakash (JP) Narayan, another good friend of Rao Sahib and Achyut Patwardhan, volunteered to join Vinoba's *Jivandani* ("Gift of Life") movement while I was still in India, and I also met him as well as his good wife, who had long been an intimate disciple of Mahatma Gandhi.

Dr. Sushila Nayar, the only other lifelong follower of Mahatma Gandhi with whom I met in Delhi in 1996, thanks to our mutual friend and Gandhian disciple, D. C. Jha, was much like Vinoba Bhave, totally devoid of pretense, her mind as sharp in its memory of her greatest patient as was her tongue in its defense of his unblemished character. Madame Vijaya Lakshmi ("Nan") Pandit, with whom I enjoyed several teas during the last decade of her life, in New Delhi, once told me that Mahatma Gandhi's "influence for the good" in her life was "as great" as her adored older brother Jawaharlal Nehru's influence had been. I never met any of Gandhi's sons, but I have recently had the pleasure of speaking at some length with Mahatma Gandhi's two most brilliant grandsons, Dr. Rajmohan Gandhi, whose *Good Boatman* sketches a sensitive illuminating portrait of Gandhi's personality and mind, and Ambassador Gopal Gandhi, who was then assisting President K. R. Narayanan, in whose Rashtrapati Bhavan I met with him in January 2000, thanks to our good friend, former prime minister Inder Kumar Gujral.

Over the last four decades I have learned so much about Gandhi from so many scholars and friends that I could not possibly mention or adequately thank all of them for contributing to my understanding of his life and legacy but must rest content to name just a few. My dear friend, Professor Stephen Hay of the University of California–Santa Barbara, who has devoted so much of his life to a meticulous study of Gandhi's early life and times, has been most generous and helpful, sharing his excellent published papers and entire library of Gandhiana with me. Thanks to Steve, I have come to appreciate the importance of Jainism to Gandhi's philosophy and have learned many hitherto unknown facts of Gandhi's youth, including the very early age of his marriage. My now departed old friend, Professor Raghavan Iyer, whose seminal work on Gandhi's philosophy first introduced me to him and his brilliant wife, Professor Nandini Iyer also helped me to understand better many of Gandhi's complex ideas and his remarkable foresight. I also thank my friend Professor Judith M. Brown for her luminous work on Gandhi's life, focusing so carefully on his political activities and each of his Satyagraha campaigns. Soon after I first joined UCLA, I had the pleasure of meeting Professor Joan Bondurant and Margaret Fisher at Berkeley and enjoyed their fine studies of Satyagraha. My good friend, Professor Sibnarayan Ray, visited our campus shortly before editing and publishing his excellent international symposium, *Gandhi India and the World*, and I still recall with pleasure several illuminating discussions about Gandhi and his global impact with him and our mutual friend, Professor J. Richard Sisson. The only time I met Dr. Martin Luther King, Jr., was a few years before his assassination, when he visited UCLA and we lunched together, after his talk, at our University Religious Conference. I knew then, as I better understand now, just how vital and important the influence of Mahatma Gandhi's methods and teachings were to Martin Luther King's life and his faith in nonviolent struggle and love for the liberation of all mankind.

I owe a special debt of gratitude to Professor J. Kenneth Galbraith, who encouraged me to continue to pursue this study when I had all but abandoned it, and to his dear wife, Kitty, for her warm hospitality in Newfane as well as in Cambridge.

I thank my wonderful typist, Jane Bitar, for magically transforming my messy holographs into electronic files. To my original brilliant editor at Oxford, Thomas LeBien, who was unfortunately lured to Princeton's Press prior to my book's completion, I can hardly express strongly enough how much I appreciate his creative editorial labors and constructive criticism. I also thank my new editor, Susan Ferber, for her kind assistance, and Oxford's production editor, Joellyn Ausanka, for her expeditious cooperation.

I must thank my most youthful friend Mimi Perloff, for her unfailing loving kindness. Thanks again to my sons, Daniel and Adam, each now practicing in his own way Gandhi's practical philosophy of selfless service, who perhaps inadvertently taught this old man the unique powers of Ahisma and Satyagraha.

Finally, to my soulmate, Dorothy, who for almost half a century has taught me, long before I ever realized it, to understand Mahatma Gandhi's passion, through her unselfish love, infinite patience, and silent acceptance of every variety of pain, I offer this book as her disciple's gift of love.

Los Angeles, July 2000   S.W.

CONTENTS

Contents

Gandhi's Passion

Introduction

"SUFFERING" and "the suffering of pain" are the primary definitions of *passion*. The first example of the word *passion* in the *Oxford English Dictionary* is "the sufferings of Jesus Christ on the Cross." The story of Mahatma Gandhi's life may be read as a pageant of his conscious courting of suffering. Gandhi's life of passion also ended in martyrdom.

Gandhi's passion has Indian historical roots that predate Jesus by more than two thousand years. Hinduism's Great God Shiva, yogic Lord of Beasts and of the Dance, was first depicted on an Indus Valley seal dating back to the third millennium B.C. Among the skills honed by yogis, including breath and mind control, none is more potent or important than *tapas*, a Sanskrit word meaning "suffering." When first used in the *Rig-Veda*, *tapas* meant "heat," the self-incubating creative power that gave birth to ancient India's first monistic neuter god, *Tad Ekam* ("That One").[1] In subsequent sacred texts, *tapas* refers to yogic powers of contemplation and meditation whose laserlike beams were, it appears, hot enough to awaken even a neuter divinity to life.

Soon after launching his monumental *Satyagraha* ("Hold fast to the Truth") movement in South Africa, Gandhi resolved, as he wrote in 1906, that "sacrifice" was the "law of life." He gave up his pleasures as a British barrister, his Saville Row suits, and sexual relations with his wife, vowing to focus all the heat of his passion toward helping India's emigrée and indentured community, living in Natal and the Transvaal, win freedom from racial prejudice and discrimination. Gandhi's elder brother felt betrayed and abandoned by the young man he had so generously supported for three years while he studied law in London. Gandhi's wife and eldest son found it impossible to understand his courting hatred and violent contempt in his selfless service to the Indian community. They could not fathom his eagerness to give up his fortune and every comfort of home and hearth to break "evil" laws and then warmly welcome long prison terms. Gandhi's passion turned each prison cell he occupied into a self-proclaimed "temple" or "palace," even as he taught his self-sacrificing yogic spirit to relish the "delicious taste" of fasting, taking pleasure in every pain he suffered for the "common good."

Gandhi early won the admiration and active support of the greatest liberal leaders of India's National Congress, a body that also included a radical revolutionary wing whose members were repelled by his scrupulous insistence on nonviolence. Other more conservative Anglophile Indians, of course, found Gandhi's rejection of Western garb and his prison record abhorrent. But after twenty years of successfully leading the Indian struggle in South Africa, Gandhi returned to India during World War I to widespread acclaim for the passionate courage he displayed during a series of Satyagraha campaigns against injustice in Gujarat and Bihar. Soon after the war ended, he was ready to assume supreme command of the Congress, rewriting its constitution and transforming its mostly moderate political reform lobby into a mighty mass movement demanding freedom for India from British imperial exploitation and domination.

But after acquiring more political power than any other Indian of the previous century of British rule had enjoyed, he rejected all the power perquisites coveted by others the world over. He refused to travel any way but by foot or in third-class railway carriages and retreated to the spartan simplicity of remote village ashrams he founded whenever he was not jailed in a British prison. Gandhi's seemingly eccentric or at any rate curiously contradictory behavior, his rejection of all "normal" pleasures, acquisitive and sensual, and his oft-repeated retreat from the brink of victory can best be understood in light of his passionate resolve to suffer and experience in daily life all the pain and deepest sorrow sustained by India's poorest peasants and outcastes. He shivered naked in winter as they did and bore the scalding heat of central India's summers without complaint. When the Congress offered him complete control over its national machinery and the crown of its presidency, he invariably declined, grooming younger men to wear what he called the "crown of thorns." He abandoned the organization he had revitalized when it became too high and mighty, too rich and greedy, for his passionate nature.

By re-creating himself, through the power of his passion, in the humble, vulnerable image of India's poorest starving naked millions, Gandhi could, when moved to do so by his "inner voice," call upon that unarmed ragged army, whose pain he mirrored and magnified in his own naked body, to follow him barefoot up India's Via Dolorosa to freedom. And countless millions unhesitatingly did follow him, not as a modern political leader, nor as a medieval native prince or martial maharaja, but as their own *Mahatma*, India's "Great Soul," the only title he ever enjoyed, until even that became too burdensome an honorific for his passionate spirit.

"The purer the suffering (*tapas*)," Gandhi believed, "the greater the progress. Hence did the sacrifice of Jesus suffice to free a sorrowful world. . . . If India wishes to see the Kingdom of God established on earth, instead of that of Satan which has enveloped Europe. . . . [w]e must go through suffering."[2] Brilliant yogi that he was, Gandhi resolved to pit the passionate powers of his sublimated suffering spirit against the world's mightiest empire. His creative religious genius allowed him to unite the mainstream of Western passion with India's traditional *tapas*, synthesizing both forms of suffering within his Great Soul. He turned himself into a cauldron of pain so brilliantly illuminating as to endow him with an aura of goodness and light, magnetizing millions to enter prison without flinching when he called, and to die for him, if ever he asked.

But the meaning of Western *passion*, much like the semantic evolution of *tapas*, which shifted nuance from "heat" with "hellish connotations" to "suffering," soon came to embrace opposites of emotion, feelings like "desire" and "aversion," "hope" and "fear," "love" and "hatred."[3] Gandhi's passion proved similarly ambivalent. He struggled throughout his mature life to subdue his strong sexual drive, believing that intercourse with his wife for any reason other than procreation was evil. His antipathy to every form of violence, moreover, made him most acutely sensitive to the potential violence of sexual brutality. Here too he probed ancient India's deep roots for a remedy, finding it, he felt, in *Brahmacharya* ("celibate studenthood"), the first stage of a traditional upper-caste Hindu's life, prior to his sexual initiation through marriage. Gandhi strove to return to and remain in that chaste first state for more than the last four decades of his life, struggling most passionately to adhere to his vow of total abstention.

Gandhi equated *Ahimsa* ("Non-violence"), or as he preferred to define it, *Love*, with God. He also believed that "Truth (*Satya*) is God," devoting most of his life to the passionate quest of "seeing" God by living in perfect harmony with His golden attributes. Gandhi's passionate embrace of *tapas*, moreover, taught him to forget fear. He incorporated that fearless mantra into his life's mission to liberate his followers from fear's self-imposed shackles, as well as those more easily visible chains forged by foreign tyranny. Armed with *Ahimsa*, *Satya*, and *tapas*, Gandhi transformed his frail, naked body and fearless soul into an all but impregnable fortress. In choosing the subtitle for his *Autobiography* (*The Story of My Experiments with Truth*), however, and as evident throughout that book, Gandhi readily revealed how often he erred in his personal as well as his public life. Whenever he detected some imperfection or sensed he had made a strategic mistake (what he called a "Himalayan blunder" in prematurely launching Satyagraha), he never hesitated to admit his error and to reverse his course, obeying his "inner voice," which he believed was the voice of God.

Reaching so ideally high, adhering so adamantly to noble principles and what he called "purity of means," Gandhi failed to achieve all he hoped for India. But the passion of his life was the legacy he left to his country and to the world, inspiring millions with the grandeur of his dream and some few disciples with an ardent love of suffering on their own painfully narrow road to martyrdom. In Gandhi's passion lies the key to his inner temple of pain. He suffered joyfully, guarding his dream to someday restore the epic "Golden Age" of goodness and truth to Mother India. And through the multifaceted prism of his passion, Gandhi's tragic weakness is revealed as the other side of his singular strength, helping to account for his final failure to win that for which he worked hardest and suffered most.

1

Midnight in Calcutta

MAHATMA GANDHI fell into "darkest despair" on the eve of India's independence in August 1947.[1] Savage fighting spread from Punjab and the North-West Frontier to Eastern Bengal and Bihar. Brutal violence unleashed a year earlier by Muslim thugs in Calcutta had triggered Hindu counterattacks and the murder of more Muslims in Bihar. Mayhem, rape, and murder spread to the villages of Bengal as well, each report inciting more massacres of innocents as communal hatred raged across most of South Asia's subcontinent.

On July 17, 1947, acting on the advice of India's prime minister-in-waiting, Jawaharlal Nehru, and the consent of Pakistan's governor-general-to-be M. A. Jinnah, Viceroy Lord Mountbatten won his government's final approval to partition Punjab and Bengal along religious lines prior to Great Britain's withdrawal from India. Their plan to carve up British India was never approved of or accepted by Gandhi, however, who realized too late that his closest comrades and disciples were more interested in power than principle, and that his own vision had long been clouded by the illusion that the struggle he led for India's freedom was a nonviolent one.

"Who listens to me today?" a despondent Gandhi muttered. "And why should anyone?" To disillusioned devotees, the *Mahatma* ("Great Soul") freely confessed his "bankruptcy," admitting that he lived in "a fool's paradise."[2] Nonetheless, the seventy-seven-year-old little Father (*Bapu*) of his nation did not surrender to sorrow. Great Soul that he was, Gandhi carried on, passionately ignoring daily threats to his life, refusing to silence his criticism of the government, and rejecting appeals to remain in New Delhi to celebrate the dawn of India's freedom at midnight on the Fifteenth of Au-

[7]

gust 15, 1947. "What is there to celebrate?" This "vivisection of the Mother," as he called partition, was fit only for prayer and "deep heart-searching," not for fireworks, proud speeches, and songs.[3]

Gandhi had tried to win Nehru over to his faith in the virtues of simple living, urging his aristocratic Anglophile heir to give up India's democratic throne, abandon the great house he planned to occupy, and instead move into a "village hut." He argued: "I believe that if India, and through India the world, is to achieve real freedom, then . . . we shall have to go and live in the villages—in huts, not in palaces."[4] Gandhi feared now that India was approaching its doom, whirling mothlike round the hot light of power till its wings would burn. His duty was to save India from that sad fate, though he well understood it might take his last passionate breath. As Delhi draped itself in miles of festive electric lights and the saffron, white, and green bunting of India's bright national flag symbolizing wishful Hindu-Sikh-Muslim unity, Bapu entrained for Bengal on his lonely pilgrimage of prayer for peace.

"What to do?" was the mantra he muttered daily that November as he walked barefoot through the blood-soaked mud of Noakhali District's scorched villages in Eastern Bengal's anguished Delta.[5] He had gone there in response to his old Quaker friend Muriel Lester's personal plea, made after she had met Hindu widows who had watched their husbands butchered by Muslims. Before their husbands could be cremated, those widows were dragged off to be "converted" and "married" to the same killers. "These women had a dead look," Muriel wrote him, a look of "utter blankness."[6] Gandhi soon saw worse things in Noakhali. Believing as he did that "Truth is God," he could not understand how so much he thought true about India turned out to be so violently false.

Lured back to Delhi by appeals from the new viceroy seeking Gandhi's wise advice on how to stop the killings, Bapu offered it. But Mountbatten was staggered by what this naked "old fool" told him. He consulted Nehru, who explained that the "old boy" was "out of touch" and could hardly be taken seriously when he urged the viceroy immediately to replace his own Congress ally and heir with their most hated Muslim League enemy, Jinnah.[7] Mountbatten agreed, understanding little more about India than what Nehru, Nehru's closest comrade, V. K. Krishna Menon, and his own clever wife, Lady Edwina, explained to him. They all agreed that Gandhi was a saint, but saints should never indulge in practical politics or govern nations, should they?

Gandhi realized soon enough that it was all a charade, a polite royal brush-off, once the tea party ended, the carriages were called, and the servants escorted him down the garden path. That was when he decided to leave Delhi and return to Noakhali, where he was at least listened to, if not worshipped, by villagers too uneducated to be insincere, too timid for flattery or duplicity, too poor to fear that he wanted anything from them. These were the people he loved best and felt most at ease and at home among. Mostly naked, with no possessions to worry about losing, they had nothing to hide; they were as remote from regal Mountbattens and Nehrus as Noakhali was from New Delhi.

But before reaching Noakhali, his train steamed into Calcutta's noisy, bustling station, arriving five hours late in that smoky magnificent "City of Dreadful Night."[8] Imperial bullies later hammered her into the richest, sexiest, sickest capital of the grandest empire on earth, built along the wrong side of a river named Hughli atop dung-filled mud at whose ancient womb worshippers of the Mother Goddess Kali laid petals of puja and slaughtered sacrificial goats and lambs. Gandhi considered all modern cities satanic, the ugliest fruit of Western civilization. He had long sought refuge from their soul-crushing noise, industrial speed, and poisonous air, preferring the harmony of India's ancient village community. And the train ride (he adamantly refused to fly) was exhausting. Noisy crowds awaiting his arrival at every stop, shoving, shouting, banging at his carriage windows; even a glimpse of the Mahatma—his darshan—was considered a blessing to devout Hindus. He tried to wave them off and to spin or pray in peace, but they never left him alone, testing his patience, causing him often to lose it, making him shout angrily at them through toothless gums. Too tired to move on immediately to East Bengal, he got into a car that was waiting at Calcutta's station to drive him to suburban Sodepur, where his Bengali disciple Satish Chandra Das Gupta had established a retreat for the handspinning of cotton.

He never planned far ahead. "One step enough for me," he often said, quoting the last words of the hymn he loved best, "Lead, Kindly Light," by Cardinal Newman.[9] He waited at all times for instructions from his "inner voice" before making his next move. Only now he heard many voices, mostly those of anxious Muslims importuning him to stay in Calcutta. The Muslim minority there feared that the transfer of power to a Hindu Congress government in West Bengal would revive riots that had started a year ago, on August 16. That was proclaimed "Direct Action Day" by *Quaid-i-Azam* ("Great Leader") Jinnah, president of the Muslim League. Of all his failures, the one Gandhi regretted most was not convincing Jinnah of the error of his insistence on partition, the dreadful operation that was to bring Pakistan to birth by virtually bleeding Mother India to death. If only Mountbatten and Nehru had agreed last April to tempt Jinnah by offering him the premier crown of thorns! Now it was too late, and the sole penance Gandhi could perform was to spend the remaining days of his life in Pakistan, trying to protect minorities there from extortion and violence by the Muslim majority. He resolved to leave India, moving either to Karachi or Lahore on that final pilgrimage, but first he would visit Noakhali once again to bring what little comfort his unarmed presence could to Hindus living there in daily fear of death.

Calcutta's anxieties that the previous year's orgy of terror would be repeated, however, inspired him now to launch one of his most creative initiatives in problem solving. The man most widely blamed for the mass murder of Hindus and the torching of their property in the days and weeks following Direct Action Day was Bengal's Muslim League Chief Minister Huseyn Shaheed Suhrawardy. Every British officer, including Governor Sir Frederick Burrows and Chief of the Eastern Command Lt. General Sir Francis Tuker, pointed to Suhrawardy as the villain of the terror that exploded after he gave Calcutta's police a special holiday to "celebrate" Direct Action.[10] What those self-righteous British officers failed to explain, of course, was why the army they commanded was kept in barracks until the rioters had done their worst work. As soon as troops did show themselves, marching through the streets up Garden Reach, Metia Bruz, Beliaghatia, and along the Lower Circular Road, the killers slipped away. Calcutta's Marwari Hindu merchants and bankers also pointed fingers at Suhrawardy. So did their sycophants in every court and bazaar, who soon hired their own thugs to wreak vengeance on Muslim quarters of the city, gutting homes and shops there for months.

Suhrawardy by now was stripped of Calcutta's chief ministership, replaced by Dr. Profullah Chandra Ghosh, leader of West Bengal's Hindu Congress majority provincial government. Nor would Suhrawardy be picked to become chief minister of East Pakistan; his less popular Muslim League rival Khwaja Nazimuddin had been selected instead by Jinnah to take that post in Dhaka. Jinnah knew that Suhrawardy's dream had been to preside over an independent nation of Bengal—Bangladesh—a new nation state he had lobbied hard to have carved out of the Eastern quarter of British India. His vision was to integrate Hindu majority West Bengal and Muslim majority East Pakistan into a single unified land of Bengali speakers, whose language and culture would transcend any differences of religious doctrine or practice. Mountbatten, however, refused even to consider Suhrawardy's brilliant plan, just as he had ignored Gandhi's proposal to replace Nehru with Jinnah. Though Suhrawardy's dream of becoming the king of Bengal was thus aborted, he lived to emerge less than a decade later (but only briefly to remain) as prime minister of Pakistan. He was removed by martial coup and died a few years later in Beirut.

Gandhi had long known and liked Suhrawardy, who for three decades had admired him as well. So when Muslim friends pressed him to stay on in Calcutta, at least until after Independence Day, the Mahatma agreed to do so, on one condition—that Shaheed Suhrawardy share the same roof with him so that they could appeal to Muslims and Hindus alike to live in peace in this greatest of all Indian cities. "Adversity makes strange bed-fellows,"

Gandhi told his prayer meeting that August 11.[11] Suhrawardy agreed, and they moved into the abandoned Hydari House, a once-splendid residence whose terrified Muslim owners had fled, leaving it to be robbed and ruined by looters and hoodlums. They seemed an odd couple, the almost naked Bapu and Bengal's Big Daddy dressed meticulously in his white linen or beige silk suits. But Gandhi's genius for symbolic gestures was never wiser than this experiment in Hindu-Muslim cohabitation. It visibly demonstrated to Calcutta's millions of angry and fearful Hindus and Muslims alike that a Mahatma and the Muslim League leader most often blamed for instigating the worst of last year's riots could peacefully live under a single roof. They stayed there together for almost a week, answering the most hostile, angry questions as honestly as they could, as fearlessly as both of these remarkable men had lived all their lives. It proved to be a potent lesson in the practical possibility of peaceful coexistence, cooperation, and the powers of love. Of the lessons Gandhi had labored most of his life to teach, this was one of the most important. The interlude with Suhrawardy, however, was his last demonstration of the miraculous force of love and the value of trust and faith in one's fellow man as well as in truth. Pacifist Horace Alexander, whose leadership of the Society of Friends had first brought him to India in 1929, was invited by Gandhi to join them in Hydari House, where Alexander proved useful in helping to keep crowds of irate Hindus from breaking in that first night. "Why have you come here?" they shouted at Gandhi. "Why did you not go to places from where the Hindus have fled?"[12]

"I have come here to serve not only Muslims but Hindus," he explained. The hooligans told him to "go away," but Gandhi was never easily dissuaded or intimidated from doing what he believed to be right. "You can obstruct my work, even kill me. I won't invoke the help of the police. You can prevent me from leaving this house, but what is the use of your dubbing me an enemy of the Hindus? I will not accept the label." The Mahatma then asked them what good it would do now to "avenge" the wrongs committed in 1946.

On August 14, Gandhi argued again with the young Hindus who had so angrily challenged him the previous day. By evening he had won their hearts and minds. "What a spell-binder this old man is!" one of them cried. "No matter how heavy the odds, he does not know . . . defeat."[13] That same convert volunteered to help guard Hydari House against any future attacks. An estimated ten thousand people gathered to hear Gandhi's prayer that evening. "If the flames of communal strife envelop the whole country," Bapu asked, "how can our newborn freedom survive?"

He awoke at 2 A.M. on August 15, having slept through Nehru's "Tryst with Destiny" speech at midnight. When he left Hydari House for his morning walk, crowds followed him, keen for just a glimpse of the Mahatma. Soon after he returned, West Bengal's new cabinet arrived, seeking his blessings. "Wear the crown of thorns," Gandhi told them. "Strive ceaselessly to cultivate truth and non-violence. Be humble. Be forbearing . . . beware of power; power corrupts. Do not let yourselves be entrapped by its pomp and pageantry. Remember, you are in office to serve the poor in India's villages."[14]

How obvious it seemed to him now, that simple prescription for using power most wisely, and yet how long it had taken him to learn. And how difficult it was to avoid life's lures and traps, the pomp and the wrong passions.

2

Dawn in Gujarat

T HE MAHATMA'S father, Karamchand ("Kaba") Gandhi, was a man of power and pomp, prime minister of the princely Indian state of Porbandar in Gujarat. Kaba was also a man of passion, taking his fourth wife (the previous three had died), Putlibai, then only fifteen, "when he was over forty."[1] Their youngest child, Mohandas Karamchand, the future Bapu, was born on October 2, 1869. Gandhi was over fifty when his autobiography, which he called *The Story of My Experiments with Truth*, was published, and though he wrote of his father as a man "given to carnal pleasures," his recollection of his mother was of her saintliness and deeply religious nature. Young Moniya, as she called him, was mother's darling. He had three older sisters (two of them half-sisters) and a doting aiya (nanny), named Rambha, to help mother pamper her "little prince." He also had two brothers. Lakshmidas, who was six years older, eventually took an Indian law degree and entered Porbandar's financial service; Karsandas, three years older, at maturity enlisted in the police force of the neighboring state of Rajkot. Karsandas's best friend was the son of the Muslim chief of police, a tall, handsome boy named Sheikh Mehtab, who became young Mohan's (short for Mohandas) first hero, and later his nemesis.

When Moniya was seven, the Gandhis moved inland from Porbandar's Arabian Sea coastal city to Rajkot State, which was more than a hundred miles to the north. His father now served a more powerful Hindu prince, and Moniya would soon be enrolled in Rajkot's Alfred High School, where he learned English and cricket. He was also married that first year in high school, at age eleven, to the child bride chosen for him five years earlier by his parents, Vaishnava priests, and astrologers.[2] Kasturba, the daughter of wealthy Porbandar merchant Gokuldas Makanji, remained his mate for life, until she died sixty-two years later in the Aga Khan's old malaria-infested Poona palace, where they were both incarcerated by the British for most of World War II.

Merchants of the Modh Vania Hindu caste to which the Gandhis belonged were famed for their wealth, frugality, shrewdness in business, and honesty. Gandhi's father and uncle had only three unmarried children left: Mohan, brother Karsandas, and one male cousin. They decided to pool resources by holding all three weddings at the same time, under the same festive pandal (tent) in Porbandar. "Less expense and greater éclat," Gandhi noted. "My father and my uncle were both old, and . . . they wanted to have the last best time of their lives."[3] But racing back for the wedding from Rajkot in the royal coach, Kaba almost lost his life when the coach overturned, tossing him out onto sharp stones, breaking several bones, and forcing him to remain seated and witness the grandly festive wedding through facial bandages.

"I was devoted to my parents. But no less was I devoted to the passions that flesh is heir to. . . . Little did I dream that one day I should severely criticize my father for having married me as a child. . . . And oh! That first night. Two innocent children all unwittingly hurled themselves into the ocean of life . . . we were too nervous to face each other . . . too shy. . . . We were the same age. But I took no time in assuming the authority of a husband."

Spoiled from infancy by his adoring mother, sisters, and aiya, Gandhi naturally assumed that all women, including his young and equally willful bride, would obey his merest wish as regal command, doing exactly what he desired, without hesitation or argument. Kasturba, however, proved more than a match for his male chauvinism, petulance, and egotism. Like him, she had been reared as a Vaishnava princess. Though she lacked formal education, she was braver than her young husband, who had never slept in the dark without nightmares, fearing attacks from demon ghosts or giant snakes. She could be just as stubborn and long-suffering as he was. In some ways, especially concerning the rearing of children, she was much wiser and more compassionate.

Mohan, with absolutely no reason, as he later admitted, was a jealous husband as well as a tyrannical one. Kasurba "could not go anywhere without my permission."[4] He went wherever he liked, and thanks mostly to his friend Mehtab soon started indulging in strange and unsavory experiments. The Gandhis had always been strict vegetarians, as are all devout Hindus. Mohan's mother, however, was particularly strict about her diet, often undertaking prolonged as well as regular daily fasts in the more monastic Jain tradition to which she personally was attracted.[5] Gandhi's later use of fasting as a political weapon was one of his mother's legacies.

In Mehtab's company, however, Mohan not only ate meat but smoked purloined cigarettes or purchased them with coppers stolen from house servants. Kasturba warned him to stay away from Mehtab, but "I was too proud to heed my wife's warning."[6] For about a year Gandhi surreptitiously enjoyed "meat-feasts" specially prepared for them both by Sheikh Mehtab and the state's chief cook in a secluded house, to whose dining hall they had access. After those feasts, Mohan had no appetite, of course, for his mother's cooking, and when she anxiously asked why, he lied that something was "wrong with my digestion." The lying troubled him more than the eating forbidden meat, so that he finally told his friend he could indulge in no more meat feasts.

Mehtab also took him to a local brothel and "prepaid" for his guest and himself. "I was saved by the skin of my teeth. . . . God in His infinite mercy protected me. . . . I sat near the woman on her bed, but I was tongue-tied. She naturally lost patience with me, and showed me the door, with abuses and insults. I then felt as though my manhood had been injured." He admits, however, that "the carnal desire was there," thanking "Divine mercy for the escape." His adventures with his best friend may be viewed as little more than adolescent rebellion against the strictures of tradition.

"One of the reasons of my differences with my wife were undoubtedly the company of this friend [Mehtab]," Gandhi concluded in the chapter entitled "Tragedy" in his autobiography. "I was both a devoted and a jealous husband, and this friend fanned the flame of my suspicions about my wife. I never could doubt his veracity. And I have never forgiven myself the violence of which I have been guilty in often having pained my wife by acting on his information."[7] Gandhi gives no details of the angry confrontation with Kasturba or the clearly false accusations, based on whatever Mehtab whispered insidiously into a jealous husband's ears. Two decades and many pregnancies were, moreover, to pass before he finally resolved never to sleep with his wife again. Yet, significantly enough, he links that *Brahmacharya* (celibacy) vow in his autobiography to the "tragedy" of his experiences with Mehtab.

"The canker of suspicion was rooted out only when I understood . . . the glory of *Brahmacharya* and realized that the wife is not the husband's bond-slave, but his companion . . . an equal partner in all his joys and sorrows—as free as the husband to choose her own path. Whenever I think of those dark days of doubts and suspicions, I am filled with loathing of my folly and my lustful cruelty, and I deplore my blind devotion to my friend."

Despite Gandhi's retrospective loathing of the folly and cruelty of his *"negative identity,"* Sheikh Mehtab, their intimacy continued for decades.[8]

Gandhi even brought Mehtab to South Africa to live with him for a while, only to expel him from their Eden after catching him naked with a prostitute in his house. Gandhi's profound problems with his eldest son, Harilal—who would convert to Islam, change his name, and become a drunkard as well as a wastrel—were attributed by psycho-historian Erik Erikson to the boy's identification with Sheikh Mehtab, his "saintly" father's "murdered self."[9] Gandhi's ambivalence toward the powerful influence of his "friend" certainly remains one of the most puzzling questions about the formation of his complex personality. Young Gandhi's ambivalence toward his own father, of course, was at least equally seminal in nourishing the roots of his remarkable evolution from Moniya to Mahatma.

Moniya was only fifteen when "I stole a bit of gold out of my meat-eating brother's armlet."[10] Brother Karsandas had run up a debt of some twenty-five rupees for the meat-eating habit he, Moniya, and Mehtab all enjoyed. The soft solid gold of Karsandas's armlet was "not difficult to clip," Gandhi recalled, and the small bit of gold he clipped, paid off their debt but left its weight in growing feelings of guilt. "I did not dare to speak. Not that I was afraid of my father beating me. No, I do not recall his ever having beaten any of us. I was afraid of the pain that I should cause him." So he resolved to make a "clean confession," in written form, trembling "as I handed the confession to my father. He was then suffering from a fistula and was confined to bed." Kaba did not rebuke his son, but after reading the note "pearl-drops" of tears "trickled down his cheeks," wetting the paper, which he tore up. "I also cried," Gandhi recalled. "I could see my father's agony . . . still so vivid in my mind."

To Gandhi those paternal pearl-drops were an "object-lesson" in Ahimsa, the nonviolence or pure love that was to become equated in his heart with God, the greatest force for good. "There is no limit to its power," Gandhi believed, but indicative of how surprised he was to find it in Kaba, he added: "This sort of sublime forgiveness was not natural to my father."[11] The reason, he finally decided, "was due to my clean confession . . . combined with a promise never to commit the sin again . . . the purest type of repentance."

Soon after that incident Mohan was nursing his sick father, massaging his legs, having just given him medicine. Suddenly, he felt feelings of "carnal lust" for his then-pregnant wife. Kaba was so sick that his brother had come especially to see him that night and relieved young Mohan at about 11 P.M. "I was glad and went straight to the bedroom. My wife, poor thing, was fast asleep. . . .I woke her up. In five or six minutes, however, the servant knocked. . . .'Father is very ill.' I knew of course . . . so I . . . sprang out of bed. 'What is the matter? Do tell me!' 'Father is no more.' I felt deeply ashamed and miserable. I ran to my father's room . . . if animal passion had not blinded me, I should have been spared the torture of separation from my father during his last moments. . . . It was a blot I have never been able to efface or forget."[12] Worse, Mohan's child lived no more than four days.

Erikson, following Kierkegaard's analysis of the lives of "spiritual innovators," calls this "the curse" of Gandhi's life. The "account" with his father could never be settled, leaving a lifelong "existential debt."[13] That "double shame" as Gandhi called it, linking his father's death to that of his first child, always remained in his mind the product of carnal lust, helping to explain his passionate preoccupation with *Brahmacharya*, upon which he focused intently during the last years of his life.

"My meaning of brahmacharya is this," Gandhi wrote an anxious old disciple who had inquired nervously about strange reports she'd heard of his behavior. "One who never has lustful intention, who by constant attendance upon God, has become capable of lying naked with naked women, however beautiful they may be, without being in any manner whatsoever sexually excited. Such a person should be incapable of lying, incapable of intending doing harm to a single man or woman, free from anger and malice and detached."[14]

Mohan was eighteen when he finished high school in 1887, two years after the birth in Bombay of the Indian National Congress he was destined to lead and revolutionize. To take his matriculation examination, the young man had to travel from little Rajkot State to Ahmedabad. British India's Gujarati capital city, Ahmedabad had more than 100,000 people, most of them Hindus; even so, it was a far cry from its heyday of great Mughal power in the seventeenth century, when half a million Muslim soldiers and Hindu merchants lived there. To the young graduate, reared between tiny Porbandar's port of fewer than 15,000 and Rajkot's slightly larger provincial princely capital, Ahmedabad was the busiest, most exciting city he'd ever seen. Its marble palaces—regal homes of Gujarati and Marwari merchants, purchased with profits from the opium trade and sales of gold, jewels, silks, and saffron—were rivaled only by the multistoried British bungalows surrounded by lush gardens, through whose high gates rolled broughams bearing pukka sahibs in pith-helmets, and their flower-decked "mems" sporting long white gloves. He had never seen so many people: among them were elegant long-coated, stiff-turbaned Parsis, bearded Jews, and white-collared Christian missionaries, mingling with India's wealthy cloth merchants and people dressed as simply as himself. Camels hauled bulging bales of cotton, and rickshaw coolies dragged ladies in silk saris.

He had come here alone and was so enchanted by this first sight of multifaceted Ahmedabad that years later he would choose one of the suburbs along its river, Sabarmati, as the venue of his first Indian ashram, soon after he returned from South Africa. "I had a predilection for Ahmedabad. . . . Being a Gujarati I thought I should be able to render the greatest service to the country through the Gujarati language. And . . . as Ahmedabad was . . . the capital of Gujarat, monetary help from its wealthy citizens would be more available here."[15]

After high school, Gandhi felt obliged to go to college to prepare to succeed his father as premier advisor to one of Gujarat's princes. He personally would have preferred to study medicine. His experience nursing his sick father, despite its traumatic end, appealed strongly to his ardent desire to serve the ill and disabled, a passion he never lost. But when he told his oldest brother of his professional preference, lawyer Lakshmidas "interrupted me: 'Father never liked it. . . . [H]e said that we Vaishnavas should have nothing to do with dissection of dead bodies. Father intended you for the bar.'"[16] Their senior family advisor, "a shrewd and learned [Maharashtrian] Brahman" named Mavji Dave Joshi, added his weight in favor of legal studies; "a medical degree will not make a Diwan [Prime Minister] of you. . . . It is the wisest thing . . . to become a barrister."

Becoming a barrister, however, meant going to London, where no member of his family had ever gone. "I began building castles in the air," Gandhi recalled, excited by the very prospect. If Ahmedabad was almost like London compared to Porbandar, what on earth could real London be like—Queen Victoria's fabled world capital with its population of more than five million? "I had a secret design in my mind of coming here to satisfy my curiosity of knowing what London was," Gandhi confessed in the first lines of his "London Diary," written soon after he'd arrived.[17]

To reach London, however, he first had to go to Bombay, British India's commercial capital and Western gateway port, to and from which the giant P&O liner steamed each month. London via Southampton was less than a month from Bombay, but only over seas, called "black waters," forbidden to be crossed by any devout Hindu, fearing loss of caste from distant pollution. The elder members of Gandhi's Modh Vania caste, whose council met in Bombay, were shocked by the proposal of one of their young men, who dared express his wish to cross the dark and polluted waters to so "sinful" a destination of beef-eaters and wine-drinkers as London. They threatened to ostracize him from the community if he dared to disobey their strict prohibition. Neither Gandhi nor his brothers feared such ancient superstitions, however, and knew that the worst caste councils could do during this era of British rule was to demand acts of prayerful penance or impose limited fines upon disobedient members of their community.

Gandhi's mother was worried more about the potential danger of such a journey to her darling son's health than to his soul, for "someone had told her that young men got lost in England. Someone else had said that they took to meat; and . . . liquor."[18] Perhaps she had a premonition that she would not live to welcome her son home. Yet she knew how excited, how eager he was to explore the world, venturing to see for himself what

London, embodying all the pomp, power, and glory as well as the danger and challenge of the British Empire, really *was*. So she consulted her trusted saintly Jain adviser, Becharji Swami, who reassured her: "I shall get the boy solemnly to take . . . three vows, and then he can be allowed to go."[19] Gandhi vowed never to touch "wine, women or meat" in London, after which his tearful mother gave him her farewell blessings.

To Mohandas Gandhi's provincial eyes, London would open up the world. Without living in London he may well have succeeded to his father's political power over princely states like Rajkot and Porbandar. He might even have climbed a rung or two higher in Gujarat or Bombay, but hardly more than that. After London, however, the entire world, including all of Westminster's mighty towers, would open wide, accessible to his curious mind, eager heart, and great soul.

3

The Impact of Victorian London

G ANDHI REACHED Southampton on a Saturday. It was September 29, 1888, three days before his nineteenth birthday.[1] The S.S. *Clyde* tied up at the new Tilbury Docks, and young Mohandas was the only one of its more than a hundred passengers to disembark in white flannels, handing keys to his luggage kit to Grindlay and Company's waiting agent, who failed to warn him that nothing would be delivered to his room at the grand Hotel Victoria until Monday. Dressed as he was for Bombay's summer rather than London's fall, Gandhi felt cold and exasperated.

He had written ahead to several of his father's friends, however, and one of them, Dr. P. J. Mehta, called on him Saturday soon after he reached his elegant hotel on Northumberland Avenue. Fascinated by Mehta's gleaming top hat, Gandhi "passed my hand over it the wrong way and disturbed the fur." Mehta angrily took his hat away, cautioning the new arrival never to "touch other people's things" in England, and never to ask personal "questions as we usually do in India." That was "my first lesson in European etiquette." Gandhi soon learned many more. He was dazzled by London's elevators and electric lights and shocked at the cost of its comforts. He very quickly moved out of his grand room, when he learned its exorbitant price. Mehta located cheaper accommodations for him in Richmond, at a friend's place, but finding suitable food remained a serious problem for the avowed vegetarian.

Except for "fairly filling" breakfast oatmeal, "I always starved," Gandhi recalled.[2] He had resolved never to break his vows and repeated Lord Rama's name whenever pangs of hunger or well-meaning Indian friends tempted him with a rib of beef or a steak. His Aiya Rambha had taught him the refuge of reciting Rama's name (*Ramanama*). The last word Gandhi would utter after he was shot would be "Ram."

After suffering hunger for a month in Richmond, Gandhi moved to an Anglo-Indian's house at 20 Baron's Court Road in West Kensington.[3] "The landlady was a widow. I told her about my vow. . . . Here too I practically had to starve."[4] The widow had two daughters, who kindly offered their shy young boarder an extra slice or two of bread, but his autobiography makes no further reference to either girl. Gandhi had not yet begun his studies. He did, however, quickly become addicted to London's newspapers. His favorites were the *Daily News*, the *Telegraph*, and liberal John Morley's *Pall Mall Gazette*.[5] He also wandered far and wide in search of a vegetarian restaurant, which he finally found on Farringdon Street, enjoying "my first hearty meal since my arrival in England."[6] There were books on vegetarianism for sale as well at that oasis restaurant, including H. S. Salt's diatribe, *A Plea for Vegetarianism*, and a weekly journal, *The Vegetarian*, to which Gandhi subscribed and would contribute several articles (his first published work) before leaving London.[7] The Vegetarian Society, which Gandhi joined and to whose executive committee he was soon elected, became his most vital link to London's Victorian social life. Vegetarianism introduced him to many English friends who opened their homes and hearts to this shy young man. Several of them would remain in touch with him years after he left London in 1891, supporting his political passions as well as the culinary faith they shared.

More than twice the size of Paris and New York at this time, London was the world's largest, most modern metropolis, housing people from every nation on earth, including some two hundred Indians, most of whom studied either business or law. Gandhi could have confined himself to the society of fellow Gujaratis like Mehta and his friend Shukla and might have spent time with that "Grand Old Man" of India's National Congress, Parsi Dadabhai Naoroji. (He carried a letter of introduction to Dadabhai, but chose to use it only on the eve of his departure from London.) Popularly known in England as "Mr. Narrow-Majority" after his three-vote majority election to the House of Commons in 1892, Dadabhai would preside over India's National Congress no less than three times.[8] Young Mohammad Ali Jinnah, who was to reach London just two years after Gandhi left it, would volunteer to help Dadabhai's campaign, keenly cultivating his friendship and support, becoming his political secretary. But Gandhi showed little interest in politics as yet, preoccupied as he was with vegetarianism and religious philosophy.

His vegetarianism was rooted in the Hindu reverence for cows. Much later, when asked to define Hinduism, Gandhi said that it was "cow-worship." He called the cow "a poem of pity" and, as did all devout Hindus, considered it divine. His delight in finding a whole society of British allies in protecting cows can hardly be exaggerated. In London, Gandhi remained in daily touch with his vegetarian friends, as ardent an advocate of the salubrious values as well as religious virtues of their faith as any among them. In 1891, when he moved to 52 St. Stephen's Gardens, Bayswater, Gandhi started a new local branch of the Vegetarian Society, serving as its secretary; his friend and roommate, Dr. Josiah Oldfield, editor of *The Vegetarian*, agreed to preside over all meetings of their West London Food Reform Society.[9] "Good Christian" that Dr. Oldfield was, he tried to convert his young Indian friend to the Anglican faith, urging him to read the Bible.[10] Gandhi found the Old Testament much less appealing than the New, attracted on first reading to the Sermon on the Mount, which "went straight to my heart." He thus received scriptural validation for nonviolence from Christian sources even before reading much about it in India's literature.

Two vegetarian bachelor "brothers" who had been studying the Hindu *Bhagavad Gita* ("Song of the Blessed One"), using Edwin Arnold's poetic rendition, *The Song Celestial*, invited Gandhi to read and translate the original Sanskrit version of that epic poem with them. Edwin Arnold would later agree to serve as vice-president of Gandhi's Bayswater Food Reform Society, and Mohan found his *Light of Asia*, a life of the Buddha, just as compelling as his work on the *Gita*. The unnamed bachelor "brothers" were both Theosophists, and they tried to convert Gandhi to that esoteric sect. At one point they brought him to Blavatsky Lodge in London, where he met the mysterious founder of Theosophy, Madame Helena Blavatsky, then mortally ill. Her *Key to Theosophy*, Gandhi recalled, "stimulated in me the desire to read books on Hinduism and disabused me of the notion fostered by the missionaries that Hinduism was rife with superstition."[11] At London's Theosophical Society he first met Madame's recent convert, her most brilliant disciple, Annie Besant.[12]

Annie had gained notoriety, long before meeting Madame Blavatsky, as atheist radical Charles Bradlaugh's lover, helping him lift a ban imposed on a book advocating birth control, leading the first women's strike (of matchmakers) in London, joining George Bernard Shaw's Fabian Socialist Society, and campaigning as vigorously for Irish Home Rule as she later would for Indian Home Rule. She was to be the first woman, and the only Englishwoman, ever elected to preside over India's National Congress. Annie tried her eloquent best to lure Mohandas into Theosophy, as she would later convert Motilal Nehru and his only son, Jawaharlal, but Gandhi remained impervious to all her allures, as he was to Dr. Oldfield's attempts to bring him "up" to Christ.[13] "It was only after I came in contact with . . . Christians, that I resolved . . . I should be termed a Hindu," he later reflected.[14]

Shamed by his new-found Theosophist friends into studying the *Gita*,

Gandhi viewed it through the lens of his prior reading of the Sermon on the Mount, resolving to try to reconcile Hinduism's misnamed "New Testament" with the message of his favorite Christian sermon.[15] A singular challenge! He read again Hindu Lord Krishna's teaching to the noble warrior Arjuna, who lost courage facing his own guru and cousins just before an epic battle. Krishna instructed Arjuna to fight and kill without fear or malice, dispassionately, as a true warrior's sacred caste "duty." The *Gita's* key message of "disinterested action" (*karma yoga*) was most effectively used by revolutionary nationalists like Bal Gangadhar Tilak to provide ideological validation to young Indian assassins, who later gunned down or bombed British officials, even as it helped to inspire Gandhi's own assassin, Nathuram Godse.[16] Krishna was the most popular earthly emanation of Lord Vishnu, Hinduism's powerful solar divinity.

Gandhi's amazingly imaginative reading of the *Gita*, which allowed his syncretic mind to reconcile its potent advocacy of violence with Jesus' message to turn one's other cheek to "whomsoever shall smite thee," was to argue that the epic *Mahabharata's* "field of battle" around old Delhi was really a struggle between good and evil in the field of man's "soul." Rather than convert himself to the idealistic Christian faith he loved and admired, to which his sensitive spirit so strongly resonated, Gandhi thus tried to reinterpret Hinduism's most famous philosophic justification for murder into a paean of Christian passivity. Like ancient Hindu logicians, he sought to reconcile opposites and hoped by the sweet optimism of his analysis to disarm his staunchest opponents, whether British, Muslim, or Hindu. Ironically, his method was to prove most effective against Christians and least acceptable to a fanatical fringe of Brahmans of his own faith.

While remaining staunchly Hindu at heart, young Mohandas transformed himself during his years in London into a proper English gentleman. He bought his evening clothes on Bond Street, wore a "chimney-pot" hat and winged collars whenever he dined out, and taught himself "the art" of knotting his black bow tie. "I wasted . . . ten minutes every day before a huge mirror . . . arranging my tie and parting my hair."[17] He paid for private lessons in dancing, French, elocution, and violin. He quickly abandoned the violin, though he had purchased one, and gave up dancing classes as well, finding it "impossible to keep time."

Two months after reaching London, Gandhi paid his fees and enrolled to begin his legal education at London's Inner Temple, the most expensive as well as the largest of London's four ancient Inns of Court. The major prerequisite for becoming a barrister at this time was "keeping terms" by paying for and attending (not necessarily eating!) at least six dinners per term in the Temple's grand dining hall. There were four terms per year, and each aspiring barrister was obliged to remain in London no less than three years and was required to be at least twenty-one years old when called to the bar. Written tests in Roman Law, and English Common Law as well as Equity, also had to be passed.

"I could not see then, nor have I seen since," Gandhi reflected three decades later, "how these dinners qualified the students better for the bar. There was once a time when only a few students used to attend these dinners and thus there were opportunities for talks between them and the benchers, and speeches were also made. . . . No such thing was possible in my time."[18] Hundreds of students would fill the hall's floor, four at a table, with black-robed barristers, who presided over the Inn ("Benchers") seated at their own raised high table in splendid isolation. Though, as Gandhi concluded, the "institution" of keeping terms had "lost all its meaning . . . conservative England retained it nevertheless." English barristers were jokingly referred to as "dinner barristers." Wealthy Indian families, like the Gandhis, Jinnahs, and Nehrus, were eager to send their brightest young men to dine in London's Inns of Court set amid lovely garden grounds north of the Thames Embankment. There they breathed the sweet air of liberty, imbibing such revolutionary concepts of the Common Law as the presumption of innocence and the freedom to express one's ideas and opinions in speech or writing, whatever one's color, creed, or caste might be. Those London Inns (the Inner Temple for Gandhi and Nehru; Lincoln's Inn for Jinnah) proved inadvertent cradles to the nationalist leadership of India and Pakistan, educating those brilliant barristers to voice English demands for justice and teaching them most effectively to speak, petition, and act in rallying millions of their followers to demand freedom.

Like most Indian students in London, Gandhi never spoke of his wife or son (Harilal had been born a few months before he left home) to any of his English friends. He felt ashamed of having married so young and pretended instead to bachelorhood. Another "reason for dissembling," he confessed, was that for married students it would be "impossible" to "flirt with the young girls of the family in which they lived."[19] Mohandas obviously "saw" that "our youths had succumbed to the temptation and chosen a life of untruth for the sake of companionship. . . . I too caught the contagion." But he never "took advantage" of any English women he met, though several seemed quite interested in penetrating his "armor" of "shyness," tempting him to break at least one of the sacred vows he had made to his mother.

He generally met with temptation on short holidays at watering places, like Ventnor and Brighton. In his hotel dining room at the seaside resort he met an old widow, who kindly helped him read the French menu. Their acquaintance ripened into friendship, and soon he dined at her London home every Sunday. To help him "conquer my bashfulness" the old woman invited young ladies to join them. She seemed to have "thought of an engagement" between Gandhi and one of them, he recalled, much to his dismay at not having earlier mentioned his wife and child. Too embarrassed to speak of it, he wrote her a letter confessing his falsehood. "I have been unworthy of your affection. . . . But I am glad God has now given me the courage to speak out the truth. Will you forgive me? I assure you I have taken no improper liberties with the young lady."[20] Both ladies enjoyed "a hearty laugh" over his chagrin and apology, urging him to return for Sunday dinner whenever he wished.

At a vegetarian conference in Portsmouth, late in 1890, Gandhi met another young English woman, with whom he played a rubber of bridge in a boarding "house," which he describes as one containing "women of ill fame . . . not actually prostitutes, but at the same time, not very scrupulous about their morals. . . . Just when I was about to go beyond the limit, leaving the cards and the game . . . God through the good companion [at bridge] uttered the blessed warning: 'Whence this devil in you, my boy? Be off, quick!' . . . I took the warning. . . . Remembering the vow I had taken before my mother, I fled from the scene. To my room I went quaking, trembling, and with beating heart . . . the first occasion on which a woman, other than my wife, moved me to lust. I passed that night sleeplessly."[21]

By the start of his third year in London, Gandhi had grown so interested in Christianity's good works that he took a visiting Indian poet, Narayan Hemchandra, with him to meet Cardinal Henry Edward Manning, whose personal intervention had been instrumental in settling the crippling London dock strike of 1889. Manning, then over eighty, greeted the young visitors at his residence. "I do not want to take up your time," Gandhi told him. "I had heard a lot about you and I felt I should come and thank you for the good work you have done for the strikers."[22] "I am glad you have come," the Cardinal replied. "I hope your stay in London will agree with you. . . . God bless you."

Perhaps it was Manning's energetic example of strike intervention that inspired Gandhi later to take such pains in resolving a number of important labor disputes and helping to organize India's first trade unions. Personal contact with such socially conscious leading Christians at any rate helped him to appreciate their commitment to Britain's impoverished workers and may have contributed to the evolution of, if not directly inspiring, Gandhian Socialism, which he named *Sarvodaya*, "The Uplift of All." Perhaps the greatest gulf between Gandhi and Nehru was to emerge over different forms of social action that appealed most powerfully to each man: Gandhi's inspired by early Christian and ancient rural Hindu ideals of love and communal sharing; Nehru's by Marxist-Leninist concepts of inevitable class conflict and violence, leading to victory by the proletariat.

During his last years in London, Gandhi also met industrialist Arnold Hills, whose editorials in *The Vegetarian* had inspired him to appreciate the Christian spiritual connections of their common faith in vegetarianism.

Hills, like William Morris, Edward Carpenter, and John Ruskin, was a vigorous Victorian critic of the monstrous horrors of modernity's urban industrial pollution and human degeneration. His work and words inspired Gandhi to seek a simpler, more truthful ethos for India and all of humankind. "When he who is impure has learned to loathe the sensual sins which war against the soul, when he has learned to love that heavenly chastity which is a sign and seal of God's abiding presence," wrote Hills, "then for him the process of salvation is begun—for in the body he has begun to know God."[23]

Gandhi's life in London, remote from the "carnal temptations" of his wife and bound by the threefold abstinence demanded by his mother, was in many ways more nearly like that of a Christian monk than the Hindu husband and father he was. By leaving for London he had thus left the second "householder" (*gryhasta*) stage of a traditional Hindu's ideal four-staged life, returning instead to stage one, *Brahmacharya*, "celibate studenthood." Apprentice barrister Gandhi appears to have found celibacy much more congenial to his shy, sensitive personality and spirit than the life of "lust" thrust upon him perforce by his very early arranged marriage.

With no conjugal distractions or obligations, young Mohandas decided to take required courses and examinations to qualify as a matriculate from London University while completing his final terms for the Bar. He studied Latin and chemistry, in addition to French and physics ("Heat and Light"). Though he first failed both examinations in Latin and chemistry, he did not lose heart, resolving to try again, passing the Latin at second try, taking physics instead of chemistry to fulfill the science requirement.

On the eve of his departure for home in 1891, Gandhi was interviewed by a *Vegetarian* reporter, who asked what had induced him to come so far. "In a word, ambition," he replied.[24] Ambition to become a barrister was his youthful incentive. Yet once he arrived in the imperial capital of so many Inns of Court, built around their "Temple" of Justice, he embarked upon an eager spiritual search for deeper understanding, stimulated by London's plethora of sects and spires, temples of Parliament, and parliaments of religion, all challenging him to question every axiom of his faith. Ambition may have lured him to London, but self-awareness sustained him there. Every day in that capital of the world he was stimulated to learn more about faith and philosophy as well as the law, about India and Mohandas Gandhi as well as Great Britain and the roots of British power.

On June 12, 1891, the day after he was admitted to the Bar, Gandhi left London and started his passage back to Bombay. At Liverpool Street Station he took the express train to Southampton's docks, but "I could not make myself believe that I was going to India until I stepped into the P. & O. steamship *Oceana*." In less than three years he had grown "so much attached" to London and its environment, he confessed to his *Vegetarian* friends. "Who would not be? London with its teaching institutions, public galleries, museums, theaters, vast commerce, public parks and vegetarian restaurants, is a fit place for a student and a traveler, a trader and a 'faddist'—as a Vegetarian would be called by his opponents."[25]

The first part of his voyage home was luxurious, the more than six-thousand-ton *Oceana* seemed a "vast floating island" to Barrister Gandhi, who relished his "gratis" tea and enjoyed a rich variety of vegetarian food on board, from vegetable curry and rice to fresh fruit and brown bread brought down from the first-class saloon to Gandhi's second-class cabin by a kind and "obliging steward." After reaching the Red Sea, however, temperatures rose so high that "for the first time, we felt we were going to India." And at Aden he and the other Bombay passengers were obliged to transfer to a smaller old boat named *Assam*.

"It was like leaving London for a miserable village," he recalled. "Misfortunes never come single; with the *Assam* we had a stormy ocean, because it was the monsoon. . . . Many were sick. If I ventured out on the deck I was splashed. . . . In the cabin you cannot sleep. . . . Your bags begin to dance. You roll in your bed. . . . Thus tossed up and down, we reached Bombay on July 5th. It was raining very hard. . . . How hopeful, yet how often disappointed, is the human mind!"[26]

4

Brief Interlude at Home

BROTHER LAKSHMIDAS welcomed him on the rain-drenched dock in Bombay and drove with him to Dr. P. J. Mehta's grand house, where they spent the night. Mohan first learned now of his frail mother's last illness and recent death. He stoically accepted the sad news, shedding no tears, taking "to life just as though nothing had happened."[1]

His wife and son had remained in Rajkot, but before returning to them Gandhi accompanied his elder brother on a purification pilgrimage to the Hindu city of Nasik, where he washed away his pollution, acquired from crossing "dark waters," in the mud-yellow meandering streams of the temple-lined Darna River. The Modh Vania caste council had ordered Lakshmidas to take his excommunicated rebel sibling to Nasik for a ritual bath as the first step toward his readmission to their caste. He would also be required to host a feast for all the Vania elders of Rajkot, each of whom Barrister Gandhi was obliged personally to serve bare-chested (except for his sacred thread), bowing low as he humbly begged forgiveness. Finally, there was a rather exorbitant fine he was expected to pay. Mohandas reluctantly accepted the first two conditions, but refused point blank to pay any fine.[2] His refusal left him excommunicated in Porbandar, where Kasturba's entire family resided. He would never again step inside the grand homes of any of his wealthy in-laws in their Arabian seaside city. "I would not so much as drink water at their houses. They were prepared secretly to evade the prohibition, but it went against the grain with me."[3]

Kasturba's reaction to her stubborn husband's adamant refusal ever again to enter her father and mother's home, or that of her sister or brother, may well be imagined, though no mention is made of it by Gandhi. She had after all been deprived for almost three years of her husband's supportive presence and love, left under his mother's protection in his brother's home with her infant son, who had barely glimpsed his father's face. No sooner was Gandhi reunited with his wife, moreover, than clouds of lust and jealousy again darkened their days and nights. "Even my stay in England had not cured me of jealousy."[4] He was suspicious of Kasturba's every excursion out of his sight. Sheikh Mehtab continued to do his insidious worst to exacerbate such foolish, baseless fears, but Mohandas was as yet still more of a passionate young husband than a Mahatma. "Once I went the length of sending her away to her father's house," thus "excommunicating" her much as her father's caste had done to him. He took her back "only after I had made her thoroughly miserable." Much later he could dispassionately appreciate that sad event as "pure folly on my part."

The self-righteous barrister now resolved to "reform" his illiterate wife and son, as well as his brother's children, who all shared the same large house, into literate reflections of Victorian London. He tried to teach Kasturba English and insisted that the children do regular daily physical exercise to make them hardy. He also taught them to dress like Englishmen and to use Western utensils at the dinner table, where tea and coffee were banished, replaced under his ever-watchful eye by cocoa and oatmeal porridge. He even introduced English shoes and European dress, all of which proved expensive and painfully frustrating.

"Friends [doubtless including his poor wife and puzzled brother] advised me to go to Bombay for some time." His exotic experiences and studies in England obviously made him too grand and exalted a barrister for backward little Rajkot! Bombay had its own High Court, moreover, so the friends suggested he should try to get briefs there, for despite his own high opinion of himself he was slow to win gainful legal employment of any kind in Rajkot.

Bombay failed, however, to offer him any more lucrative opportunities to use his costly British title of Bart-at-Law, though he walked daily from the flat he found in Girgaum to the High Court, vainly waiting with other briefless barristers in the crowded corridors of legal power, hoping to be tapped by some litigant in need of representation. "I found the barrister's profession a bad job," he reflected, "much show and little knowledge."[5] He learned from colleagues that it was not unusual for a new barrister to vegetate up to seven years before earning enough of a reputation to support himself. His brother, who had invested a small fortune in funding him abroad, now tried his best to help Mohan get briefs.

Gandhi felt as fearful and helpless he oddly confessed "as the bride come fresh to her father-in-law's house!"[6] And when at last he actually "stood up" in Small Causes Court, "my heart sank into my boots." He could think of no question to ask and feared that the judge was secretly laughing at him. Ashamed of his impotence, Gandhi left the court, turning the case and its fees over to a Mr. Patel, for whom it was child's play. Unlike Jinnah, who would soon rocket to the top of Bombay's Bar by his unflappable courtroom presence and rhetorical brilliance, Gandhi proved himself an utter failure at the profession his brother had chosen for him. His was a prophetic failure, however, which compelled him to move on, conquer other worlds, and answer other callings.

But first he returned to Rajkot, setting up his own office there, drafting applications and memorials brought to him primarily by his brother's partner. He barely earned as much at such drudgery, however, as his father's salary had been decades earlier. It was hardly the sort of life young Gandhi had dreamed of when shivering in Victoria, starving in Richmond, or declaiming to his Vegetarian Society in Bayswater. The barren boredom of reading and drafting reams of legal boilerplate in mercantile memorials made him wish he had never come home. Then one day his brother asked him "to put in a word" on his behalf with the British Political Agent Sir Edward Charles Ollivant, the Viceroy's representative in the Princely States of Rajkot and Porbandar.[7]

Lakshmidas had been accused of "advising" the young Rana of Rajkot to remove some of that state's precious jewels from its treasury without the requisite prior permission of the British agent. The myth of Princely State independence had long been understood by India's 570 puppet potentates as a political shadow game played to help each state's subjects remain calm and loyal. Those hereditary "native" princes enjoyed their palatial comforts and pleasures only as long as they never conspired against Great Britain's foreign suzerain power. British martial leaders and Western weapons had trained Indian soldiers to crush and conquer all of South Asia's princes over the past century, even after the "Sepoy Mutiny," which had launched the last great Anglo-Indian War of 1857–8.[8] British officers were then sent by Victoria's viceroys from Calcutta to reside at every Indian prince's court—men like Sir Edward. With British troops under their command, these officers were ready to blow away any prince or his advisors foolish enough to ignore orders or venal enough to try to liquidate the state's valuable treasures without prior permission from the agent, who was, in fact, the real sovereign.

Mohandas had briefly met Ollivant in London and naturally mentioned it to his brother, who considered that "trifling acquaintance" enough to "influence" the mighty British agent in this embarrassing matter of purloined princely jewels. Barrister Gandhi, of course, understood that if his brother was innocent he hardly needed any influence to exonerate himself, but should simply "submit a petition."[9] Lakshmidas, however, had not spent as much as he had on his brother's travel and education merely to be told that the family barrister could be of no use in so vital a matter.

So despite misgivings, Gandhi felt obliged to ask for and, indeed, was quickly granted an appointment to meet with Rajkot's shadow monarch. Forty-eight-year-old Ollivant was a big man and a busy one. Having taken up his "White Man's burden" of high office and grave imperial responsibility a quarter century earlier, he had no illusions about any of the "Natives" he met, harbored little expectation of thanks from the princes he managed, and enjoyed no sense of humor or great pleasure in the daily work he did with earnest self-righteousness. "Your brother is an intriguer," he told Gandhi, who had barely started his argument. "I want to hear nothing more from you. I have no time." Then he stood up, towering above the tiny barrister, whose single virtue, of course, was that he dressed like an Englishman.

Gandhi refused to believe that his audience was over. He had been given more time in the palace of Cardinal Manning. He had roomed, after all, with Dr. Josiah Oldfield. His vegetarian friends had hosted an elegant and very well-attended farewell dinner in his honor in one of London's finest restaurants, and *The Vegetarian* had published no fewer than seven of his articles! How could this political agent be so peremptory in dismissing him? Surely good English manners dictated more dignified patience. Pleading to be heard out, Mohan was instead shown the door. Ollivant "called his peon [who] placed his hands on my shoulders and put me out. . . . The *sahib* went away . . . and I departed, fretting and fuming."[10]

It was the most humiliating experience of his life since he had left London. Much like the curse of his father's death, this violent expulsion from Ollivant's office instantly altered the glowing image he'd painted in his mind of English honor, justice, good manners, and friendly behavior. "You have insulted me," he wrote at once to Sir Edward. "You have assaulted me through your peon. If you make no amends, I shall have to proceed against you." Mohan was outraged, mad enough to rise in court himself and shout those words seared into his mind by the agent's voice and his peon's hot hands—*insult* and *assault*! Clearly such gross conduct must be actionable.

Yet Ollivant's swift written answer sounded even colder than his voice had to Gandhi's sensitive ears. "You were rude to me. I asked you to go and you would not. I had no option but to order my peon to show you the door. . . . He therefore had to use just enough force to send you out. You are at liberty to proceed as you wish."[11]

"I had heard what a British officer was like" Gandhi later confessed in his autobiography, "but up to now had never been face to face with one." It had proved a rude awakening. But for his years in London, Mohandas should never have approached so exalted an officer, at least not for any favor. Yet traveling to and from England had taught him how kind, gentle, gracious, and generous Englishmen and women were to everyone everywhere, except in India. The Raj seemed to turn some of those same human beings into despots and monsters. No Englishmen ever spoke so harshly, so rudely to him in their own domain. It was doubly humiliating to hear one speak to him this way in his own home state! Ollivant never imagined, of course, how much he personally did to help convert a timid barrister, deeply loyal to Great Britain's Imperium, into India's greatest revolutionary nationalist leader.

Gandhi's impotent fury and rage at Ollivant's rudeness was, moreover, compounded by his own understanding of how wrong he had been to approach such an official "in such a false position." He knew that his brother had been wrong—at least according to the rules of the game created and enforced by foreign umpires. He had learned enough, merely from dining at the Inner Temple, about British officious mentality to intuit that when his brother first asked him for the favor, it was doomed to failure. But he was Indian enough not to be able to refuse an elder brother's request.

Sir Pherozeshah Mehta, the "Uncrowned King" of Bombay, whose wealth and hauteur were much greater than those of most English officials, came by sheer coincidence to Rajkot shortly after Mohan's rude expulsion from Ollivant's office. "If [Gandhi] would earn something and have an easy time here," Mehta advised, "let him tear up the note and pocket the insult. He will gain nothing by proceeding against the *sahib*, and . . . will very likely ruin himself."[12] It was the first time Gandhi ever solicited advice from Sir Pherozeshah Mehta, and he chose not to follow it. He did not tear up Ollivant's note nor did he pocket the insult, nurturing it instead, trying to make some sense of such arrogance and irrational contempt on the part of a single representative of one national entity for every member of another, much larger, much older, much more civilized nation.

"This shock changed the course of my life," Gandhi reflected. He was still indebted to Lakshmidas, but he had now learned that he could never pay off that debt as his elder brother might wish him to. Speaking the Queen's English and wearing proper English clothes had not sufficed to shield him from humiliation or from the rough dirty hands of an illiterate peon, who mastered neither English nor Latin and would never be called to any Bar. The insult he'd sustained less than a year after having returned from England searingly convinced Gandhi that he could never be content to live out his life in the provincial princely backwater to which he'd been born. He had seen too much of the wider, greater world to rest content in the shadow of impotent indigenous royalty and arrogant foreign despots, served by stooges, who included his own brothers and countless other peons ready to do anything *sahib* ordered.

"He [Ollivant] could have politely asked me to go," Gandhi reflected, unable to stop thinking or writing about this traumatic incident. "But power had intoxicated him to an inordinate extent . . . most of my work would naturally be in his court. It was beyond me to conciliate him. . . . Princes were always at the mercy of others and ready to lend their ears to sycophants. Even the *sahib's* peon had to be cajoled . . . here the *sahib's* will was law. I was exasperated."[13]

Anxious to escape, Gandhi would have jumped at any opportunity of gainful employment virtually anywhere other than Rajkot. Just at this time, his brother learned from a Meman Muslim merchant friend that the firm of Dada Abdulla & Company needed a barrister to handle a "big case" for them in South Africa. They were offering first-class passage to and from Natal, with all living expenses paid for one year's stay, as well as a fee of £105.

"This was hardly going there as a barrister. . . . But I wanted somehow to leave India," Gandhi noted. "I closed . . . without any higgling, and got ready to go to South Africa."[14] So in April of 1893, less than two years after returning home, the twenty-three-year-old barrister set sail again, destined this time for Durban and his own rebirth to a career of community service and a life of religious and political leadership.

5

Early Traumas and Triumphs
in South Africa

"WHEN STARTING for South Africa I did not feel the wrench of separation . . . I had experienced when leaving for England," Gandhi confessed. "I only felt the pang of parting with my wife. Another baby had been born to us. . . . 'We are bound to meet again in a year,' I said to her, by way of consolation."[1]

Their second son, Manilal, had been born in October 1892, barely six months before Gandhi so cavalierly steamed off again from Bombay, leaving him, Kasturba, and their four-year-old Harilal at home in Rajkot. Gandhi was no more of a chauvinist than most of his equally affluent Indian contemporaries, nor was he any less. Though Gandhi prided himself on having become his wife's teacher and guide, he also admitted that "our love could not yet be called free from lust."[2] Kasturba may well have felt more relieved to see him go than he was eager to be off again.

Dada Abdulla, Natal's wealthiest Gujarati merchant, was waiting on the quay in Durban to welcome Gandhi, personally taking his frock coat-clad "white elephant" (as Gandhi later called himself) to his firm's warehouse office building. Indian "coolie" labor, mostly indentured Tamils from the south, had since 1860 been shipped to work on that "Garden Colony's" tea and sugar plantations as virtual slaves. After their five-year indenture contracts expired, they could sail home free or stay on in South Africa. Most Indians chose to remain, many drifting North, from Natal's colony to the Republic of Transvaal.[3] Gujarati merchants had quickly followed the poor laborers and prospered by selling them every variety of good, from cottons to pots and matches. Natal's white rulers watched the growing influx of Indians, who by 1893 slightly outnumbered them, with alarm, anger, and racist revulsion.

A week after reaching Durban, Gandhi was sent by his employer to Pretoria in the Transvaal to meet his solicitor there and to discuss the case against Dada Abdulla's merchant cousin, Tyeb Haji Khan Muhammad. He was to travel first class by train, and since it was a long journey he had brought his own bedroll. The train reached Maritzburg station at around 9 P.M., when another passenger entered Gandhi's compartment.

"He . . . looked me up and down. He saw that I was . . . 'coloured.' . . . Out he went and came in again with . . . two officials."[4] They told Gandhi to go to the van compartment, where all the coolies were. He refused to budge. They searched for a constable, who "pushed me out. My luggage was also taken out. I refused to go to the other compartment and the train steamed away." He then spent a long cold night seated in the waiting room of that empty station thousands of miles from home. "Should I fight for my rights or go back to India, or should I go on to Pretoria without minding the insults?" Gandhi recalled reflecting. He decided, "It would be cowardice to run back to India without fulfilling my obligation."[5] No peon this time, but a constable, had assaulted him, and the reason for this expulsion was much more heinous than Ollivant's rude impatience. The British agent, who had been impolite and short-tempered, was, Gandhi knew, quite right in rejecting his attempt to use influence on behalf of his guilty brother. The indignity to which he had been so violently subjected in Natal, however, was "a symptom of the deep disease of colour prejudice."

Gandhi had to travel to South Africa to experience one of life's meanest, most irrational prejudices. Reared as he was in princely India, a child of privilege and power, enjoying as he had Christian friendship and support in England, but for the single trauma he'd sustained at the hands of Ollivant and his peon, Gandhi might have escaped racial prejudice for the rest of his life had he not taken this job in Africa. The arrogance of British Imperial officials paled beside that of white Afrikaner settlers and their police. His youth, once again, inspired him to resolve to fight rather than run or silently swallow such insults to his dignity and human rights. "I should try, if possible, to root out the disease [of colour prejudice] and suffer hardships in the process. Redress for wrongs I should seek only to the extent that would be necessary."

He took the next train to Pretoria, after wiring the general manager of the railway as well as his employer. Dada Abdulla met with the manager, but the latter stood by his guards. Abdulla also alerted his friends and relatives, however, all along the line, urging them to help Gandhi in every possible way. All those kind friends who awaited him tried to comfort him by telling Gandhi similar tales of prejudice they had suffered and opted meekly to accept, much as Mehta had advised him to do in Rajkot. Had he been older, meeker, or more interested in enjoying an easy time of it and earning more money, Gandhi could have silently lowered his head and kept his mouth shut. But that was hardly young Barrister Gandhi's idea of how to deal with injustice.

He could, however, take a more pragmatic approach when he saw that one of his just demands would not be met. The next day, in fact, after the train took him to Charlestown he was obliged to board a stage coach to Johannesburg, since no track had as yet been laid there. His first-class ticket entitled him to a comfortable seat inside the coach, but the "white man in charge" ordered him to sit on the side of the coachbox instead. "I knew it was sheer injustice and an insult, but I thought it better to pocket it. I could not have forced myself inside, and if I had raised a protest, the coach would have gone off without me . . . the loss of another day. . . . So, much as I fretted within myself, I prudently sat next to the coachman."[6]

Still flexible enough to bend, Gandhi was willing to stoop only so far in accommodating racist despotism. When that same white man decided he wanted to taste the fresh air from Gandhi's seat, calling him "Sami" [for *Swami*] as he ordered him to come down to the footboard, the "insult was more than I could bear. . . . trembling I said to him . . . 'I will not . . . but I am prepared to sit inside.'"[7] The bully boxed his ears and tried to "drag me down," but Gandhi tenaciously "clung to the brass rails . . . determined to keep my hold even at the risk of breaking my wristbones." His courage and fierce resolve aroused the sympathy of other passengers, who denounced the bully and invited Mohandas to sit next to them inside. Shamed by such human shouts, the bully let him be, banishing a "Hottentot servant" from the coachbox instead, while Gandhi sat silently praying "to God to help me." At the next stop Dada Abdulla's friends were waiting to take him quickly to comfort and safety for the night. He wrote the coach company to complain of his treatment on their vehicle and was assured a good seat in the larger coach that took him the next day to Johannesburg.

In busy Johannesburg, however, Gandhi missed Dada Abdulla's agent, so took a cab to the Grand National Hotel and asked for a room. The Manager "eyed me for a moment. . . . 'I am very sorry, we are full up.'" So he told his cab driver to take him to Abdulla's friends' shop and found them expecting him, enjoying a good laugh when they learned he had asked for a hotel room. "Only *we* can live in a land like this, because, for making money, we do not mind pocketing insults," the smiling Muslim merchant explained. "This country is not for men like you."[8] He advised Gandhi to travel third class to Transvaal, but the haughty barrister was not as yet a Mahatma, insisting on the first-class ticket he'd been promised. Abdulla's friend did as requested, but warned, "I am afraid the guard will not leave you in peace." Sure enough, a guard came to order him to third class.

This time, however, an English passenger accompanied him in the first-class coach. "'What do you mean by troubling the gentleman?' he said. 'Don't you see he has a first-class ticket? I do not mind in the least his traveling with me.'" To which the bigoted guard muttered, "If you want to travel with a coolie, what do I care?"[9] So Gandhi journeyed to Pretoria in comfort.

No one awaited him at Pretoria's station, which he reached quite late on a Sunday. Afraid to go alone to any hotel and unsure of where to spend the night, he was approached by "an American Negro," who offered to take him to Johnston's Family Hotel near the station.[10] Mr. Johnston agreed to rent him a room for the night. What exactly had brought Gandhi's American helper to Pretoria in 1893 remains uncertain, though he "may have been connected with the Ethiopian Church movement."[11] Thus, the first man to greet and assist Gandhi in Pretoria was an African-American, who took him to a hotel run by a man who instantly reassured Gandhi that "I have no colour prejudice."[12]

The next morning Gandhi went to Abdulla's Pretoria solicitor, A. W. Baker, who first of all told him there was really no work for a barrister in this matter, then worked very hard at trying to convert him to his own Christian faith. "I am a Hindu by birth," Gandhi answered. "And yet I do not know much of Hinduism. . . . I should not think of embracing another religion before I had fully understood my own."[13] As a director of the South African General Mission, Baker devoted most of his time and energy to building a church in Pretoria, where he preached every afternoon, and invited Gandhi to attend his prayer meetings.

More important than the missionary Christian contacts Gandhi made in Pretoria, however, was his awakening to the Indian community there and to the role he might play in helping to organize and activate them. Dada Abdulla's wealthy disputant, Tyeb Haji Khan, the acknowledged leader of Pretoria's Indian merchants, liked Gandhi at first meeting and invited him to address all the leading Indian merchants in the Transvaal at a meeting held in the spacious house of Haji Muhammad Haji Joosab. In "the first public speech in my life," Gandhi talked about the racial discrimination he'd observed and experienced and urged his listeners always to be truthful in business, to improve their sanitary habits, and to forget debilitating caste and religious distinctions, which generally weakened the community in its struggle for justice and equality with whites. "I suggested, in conclusion, the formation of an association to make representations to the authorities . . . in respect of the hardships of the Indian settlers."[14] He made "a considerable impression" on his audience and during the discussion that followed, offered to teach his new friends the English language. Though he'd come to work as a barrister, he thus early began to transform himself into a community leader and teacher.

Satisfied with the result of that meeting, Pretoria's Indian community leaders decided to hold such meetings weekly, and soon Gandhi found "no Indian I did not know," which "prompted me in turn to make the acquaintance of the British Agent," who agreed "to help us as best he could."[15] Next, Gandhi wrote to the railway manager to inform him that from his careful study of railway regulations he saw no reason why properly dressed Indians who purchased first- and second-class tickets should not be allowed to ride in those carriages. The manager agreed to leave it up to the station master to decide who was properly dressed. Gandhi, the patiently persistent agitator-negotiator, was thus well on his way to becoming the spokesman for Indian merchant interests. He inched his way, one step at a time, toward finding remedies to inequities, first for the elite Indian community, later for the entire community, including its lower-class ex-indentured workers. He had thought of returning home by the end of one year, or even a bit earlier, "but God disposed otherwise."[16]

South Africa became his proving ground, the launching pad for Gandhi's rise to premier leadership of its emigré Indian community during the next two decades. By the time he would return permanently to India he would have totally transformed himself, in dress and manner of daily life as well as in thought, speech, and ultimate goal. Unrecognizable to those who once thought they knew him, the frock-coated "white elephant" would be reborn a Mahatma.

First, however, he resolved to settle the legal dispute that had lured him to South Africa. Gandhi's mind had never been predisposed to the fiercely disputatious side of legal argument. He favored the resolution of conflict through negotiation rather than litigation whenever possible. The traditional Hindu proclivity to find consensus, in social and political affairs as well as religio-philosophic argument, was the matrix of Gandhi's approach to legal problems. Dada Abdulla's suit was for the substantial sum of £40,000, which he claimed was owed to him based on promissory notes and the failure of specific performance by his merchant cousin, who was equally convinced that he had done nothing improper. After hearing both parties argue their points, Gandhi was convinced that the case would take years to litigate, costing a fortune in legal fees. He advised arbitration, and soon afterward an arbitrator was appointed.

Gandhi's sweet reasonableness, frugal Vania nature, and abhorrence of the waste of resources thus helped him at the very start of his legal career to recognize and reject the grossest aspects of litigation, its fee-grinding, hatred-generating qualities. His failure as a barrister was in great measure a reflection of his human strengths and values, his preference for negotiated settlement rather than Pyrrhic victory after prolonged battle. In this case, moreover, his client actually won, and thanks to Gandhi's persuasive powers, Dada Abdulla agreed to accept modest annual payments over a long period of time, thus saving his opponent the ignominy of bankruptcy. "My joy was boundless. I had learnt the true practice of law . . . to find out the better side of human nature and to enter men's hearts . . . to unite parties riven asunder."[17]

Gandhi was later to call his first year in South Africa "a most valuable experience in my life."[18] His public work was launched, and his religious spirit became "a living force." Legal work was to him of tertiary interest, despite having learned much about the law and having won his client's suit. By year's end he was eager to stay on, less as a lawyer, more as the friend, advisor, organizer, and spokesman for the Indian community in every public matter. Initially, of course, that meant representing its mercantile elite, for they had paid to bring him and were the friends who continued to sustain him.

Dada Abdulla hosted a farewell party for Gandhi on the eve of what was to have been his return home to his family, in April 1894. That same month, Natal's first independent Parliament had introduced a new Franchise Amendment Bill that would discriminate against most "Asiatic" Indians, except for the tiny percentage who had previously voted. "This Bill, if it passes into law . . . is the first nail into our coffin," Gandhi warned Dada Abdulla. "It strikes at the root of our self-respect."[19] His affluent merchant friend was, however, hardly concerned over the loss of a franchise right he never used. But he liked and respected Gandhi, so he asked his advice. Others at the party who overheard them immediately suggested to their young friend, "You cancel your passage . . . stay here a month longer, and we will fight as you direct us." This marked the birth of Gandhi's new job—as a lobbyist-advisor-lawyer-at-large for Natal's merchant Indian community. The month turned into years.

"Thus God laid the foundations of my life . . . and sowed the seed of the fight for national self-respect."[20] He stayed up all night writing a draft and the next day circulated a petition, which by June of 1894 was submitted to Natal's Council and Assembly over the signatures of nearly five hundred resident Indians. That petition "Humbly Sheweth: That your Petitioners are British subjects," many of them registered as electors qualified to vote, who with "greatest deference to your Honourable House, beg to dissent entirely from the views of the various speakers, and feel constrained to say that the real facts fail to support the reasons adduced in justification of . . . the unfortunate measure."[21]

He then put to good use the English he had learned in London, at the same time teaching the expatriate community he mobilized, as well as Natal's new parliamentary leaders, much about Indian history. "The Indian nation has known, and has exercised, the power of election from times far prior to the time when the Anglo-Saxon races [did]. . . . Every caste in every Indian village or town has its own rules . . . and *elects* representatives. . . .

The word *Panchayat* is a household word throughout . . . India, and it means . . . a Council of Five elected by the class of the people to whom the five belong."

Gandhi's petition cited many sources and quoted representative speakers who had misrepresented the facts. He also used British authorities who had written about ancient India's civilization, including Oxford professor Max Muller, repeating his most famous encomium, "If I were asked under what sky the human mind has most fully developed some of its choicest gifts . . . I should point to India."[22] After no fewer than twenty-five such persuasive paragraphs, Gandhi concluded "And for this act of justice and mercy, your Petitioners, as in duty bound, shall for ever pray."

Natal's Parliament did not, of course, retract the proposed discriminatory legislation after this first shot fired by young Gandhi across its floor. Nor did Durban's newly hired spokesman-draftsman for its Indian merchants expect immediate capitulation. He understood the self-righteous mentality of the racists he confronted and carefully laid his plans for a long and arduous struggle. To mobilize his community more effectively, Gandhi knew that a standing political association was required, similar to the Indian National Congress, which had been started almost a decade earlier in Bombay. "I recommended that the organization should be called the Natal Indian Congress."[23] On the evening of May 22, 1894, seventy-six of Natal's well-to-do merchants met at Dada Abdulla's house, most of them Muslims, but many Christians and Parsis as well as a few Hindus, convened by Honourable Secretary M. K. Gandhi. The Congress was formally established three months later, by which time over two hundred members promised to pay five shillings in monthly dues.

The first object of this new Congress was to "promote concord and harmony among the Indians and Europeans residing in the Colony."[24] Second, it was to inform people in India of what was happening in Natal, by writing to newspapers and delivering lectures. Third, Gandhi urged all "Colonial-born Indians to study" Indian history and literature. After those publicity, consciousness-raising objectives, the new Congress would "inquire" into the conditions of all Indians and take steps to remove their hardships. Finally, Gandhi's list called for helping "the poor and helpless" to improve their "moral, social and political conditions." In June, Gandhi led a deputation to call with his petition upon Sir John Robinson, Natal's premier. "We beg to present this petition . . . with greatest respect to your Honour, (and) we beg to point out that both the Anglo-Saxon and the Indian races belong to the same stock."[25] Gandhi was unconcerned about white discrimination against Africa's black majority at this time, invoking arguments of respected Western scholars to prove ancient Indo-European linguistic bonds between Aryan Vedic Indians and Caucasian tribes. "Max Muller . . . and a host of other writers with one voice . . . show very clearly that both the races have sprung from the same Indo-European Aryan stock."

A week later, in early July 1894, Gandhi led the same deputation to call on Natal's governor Sir Walter Francis Hely-Hutchinson, leaving another copy of their petition with the governor. Appealing to him on the basis of their common "British" tie, Gandhi begged him not to sanction a measure so unjust as to deny the franchise in Natal to "any Indian British subject of Her Majesty."[26]

In addition to their discriminatory Franchise Act, Natal's newly independent Parliament tried to impose a £25 tax on every ex-indentured Indian who opted, at the end of his five-year contract, to remain in South Africa. "The proposal astonished me," Gandhi recalled, and he then launched an opposition that proved effective enough to reduce the tax to £3, "due solely to the Congress agitation."[27] It would, however, take another two decades of agitation before that opprobrious tax was completely removed.

During his second year in South Africa, Gandhi "set up a household" in one of the better parts of Durban overlooking the sea "in keeping with my position as an Indian barrister . . . and as a representative."[28] Instead of inviting his wife to join him, he called for Sheikh Mehtab and paid his old friend's fare. Gandhi later confessed in his autobiography that his old "companion was very clever and, I thought, faithful to me. But in this I was deceived. He became jealous of an office clerk who was staying with me, and wove such a tangled web that I suspected the clerk." Again playing the role of Iago, Mehtab aroused innocent Mohandas's jealousy and doubts, finally going too far in his insidious behavior. He brought a prostitute home to the house at midday; alerted by his loyal cook, Gandhi caught them naked and expelled them both.

To Sheikh Mehtab he shouted, "From this moment I cease to have anything to do with you. I have been thoroughly deceived and have made a fool of myself. That is how you have requited my trust in you?" Instead of humble apologies, Mehtab threatened to expose Gandhi. Having nothing to conceal, Gandhi told his erstwhile friend to "expose" whatever he wished, "But you must leave me at this moment."[29]

After that, Gandhi decided that he had left his family alone much too long. So in 1896 "I made up my mind to go home, fetch my wife and children, and then return and settle" in Africa.[30] He requested and received permission from his patron-clients to take six months leave to return to India, sailing out of Durban in mid-1896 aboard the S. S. *Pongola*, headed not to Bombay, but for Calcutta. It would take them twenty-four days at sea to cross the Indian Ocean and travel up the Bay of Bengal and the Hughli River to British India's capital city. The same day Gandhi disembarked in Calcutta, he took the train for Bombay.

6

Between Two Worlds

G ANDHI REACHED Bombay in 1896, shortly after the first wave
of devastating sea-borne bubonic plague had arrived from China.
Amid a general panic he returned home and immediately offered
his services to the state. He was appointed to Rajkot's sanitation committee, embarking upon what would become one of his lifelong compulsions,
the inspection and cleaning of latrines. His interest in nursing, of course,
harked back to his daily care of his ailing father, but his compulsion to do
work ordinarily reserved by Hinduism for "untouchables" may have had
powerful social reform implications as well as deeper psychological roots.

"The poor people had no objection to their latrines being inspected.
. . . But when we went to inspect the . . . upper ten, some of them even refused us admission." Gandhi recalled finding latrines of the richest inhabitants of Rajkot "dark and stinking." His committee had to inspect the
untouchables' quarters also. Only one member of the Hindu committee
agreed to accompany him there, though "the entrances were well swept,
the floors were beautifully smeared with cow-dung, and the few pots and
pans were clean and shining."[1]

Gandhi's transition from Anglophile barrister dress and high style to
peasant simplicity and minimal possessions began first in his heart and
mind, though not as yet in his dress or home furnishings. The decade from
1896 to 1906 marked that most remarkable metamorphosis from Mohandas to Mahatma. His aptitude for nursing became a positive passion
and during his few months at home in 1896 he brought his dying brother-
in-law to his Rajkot residence, where he nursed him around the clock, en-
gaging not only his wife but the whole household in such service. Kasturba

was by now quite used to her husband's strange compulsions but hardly found nursing as appealing as he did, perhaps because she had done so much of it while he was far away. "Such service can have no meaning unless one takes pleasure in it," Gandhi wrote, insisting that "all other pleasures" paled before "service which is rendered in a spirit of joy."[2]

The day after his brother-in-law's death, Gandhi left for Bombay. He was to address a public meeting, convened at his request, to inform the leaders of India's National Congress of the plight of their brethren in Natal and the Transvaal. Sir Pherozeshah Mehta presided over the meeting in Bombay's historic hall and fortunately insisted that Gandhi write out his speech, as his voice was too weak to articulate it. Gandhi asked an old friend with a stronger voice to read for him, but the audience wanted silver-tongued Sir Dinshaw Wacha instead, shouting "Wacha, Wacha" until that small man, who usually hid himself in Mehta's shadow, rose to speak.

From Bombay, Gandhi journeyed over the Western Ghats to Poona, former capital of the Chitpavan Brahman prime ministers, who in pre-British times ruled Maharashtra. There he met first with *Lokamanya* ["Revered by the People"] B. G. Tilak. Tilak was the leader of the radical wing of India's nationalist movement who would soon be jailed for "sedition," British judges insisting that his editorials incited violence among young nineteenth-century Maharashtrian Brahmans. Tilak seemed to Gandhi as foreboding as the "ocean," whose dark waters were always potentially dangerous and destructive. Tilak was, however, young India's first great populist leader. His Marathi language newspaper *Kesari* ("Lion") brought his weekly messages of Hindu nationalism to millions of Maharashtrians never reached by any of the more moderate Anglophile leaders of Congress, like Mehta, Wacha, or Gokhale.

Gopal Krishna Gokhale also lived in Poona and would later be honored by Gandhi as "My Political Guru." After their first meeting, Gandhi compared Gokhale to the healing waters of "Mother Ganges" rather than the stormy ocean. "He gave me an affectionate welcome, and his manner immediately won my heart."[3] Gokhale's total honesty, brilliance, and integrity inspired Gandhi's public work and political action, as did the sweet reasonableness of his demands and the fearless moderation of his language in appealing to British officials of every rank. At the same time, it was from Tilak that Gandhi learned the potent power of using Hindu religious symbols, sacred places, and festive celebrations, enlisting mass support by employing vernacular tongues understood by India's ordinary people, most of whom never learned a word of English. Annie Besant tried without success to reconcile Tilak and Gokhale, whose distrust of each other would tear the Congress apart. Gandhi's unique capacity to integrate opposites, finding something of value in every person or party, would later allow him to rise above the political factionalism represented by those two greatest pre-

Gandhian nationalists. After they both died, he led a reunited Congress committed to both "mainstreams" of cultural nationalism and nonviolent reform.[4]

During his six months in India, in the latter half of 1896, Gandhi also addressed audiences in Madras and Calcutta and wrote a powerful "Green Pamphlet" about Natal's racist discrimination.[5] That piece was quoted by several Indian English newspapers and roused the ire of South African white leaders and settlers when Reuters reported Gandhi's claim that the South African treated Indian merchants and indentured laborers "unfairly" and "harshly."

In December 1896, Dada Abdulla wired Gandhi first-class return tickets to Durban for Gandhi, his wife, and children, all on the company's new steamship *Courland*, an offer that was gratefully accepted. Another, older steamship owned by Abdulla's company, the *Naderi*, sailed from Bombay at the same time. The ships reached the port of Natal on the same day, and since they had both come from Bombay they were detained for five days at quarantine, to be sure they had brought no plague. But Gandhi and most of the eight hundred Indians aboard believed that the long quarantine was ordered because the white residents of Durban had been agitating for the repatriation of all newly arrived Asiatics. White leaders were even ready to indemnify Abdulla's company if he agreed to send both ships back. But Abdulla was determined to "disembark the passengers at any cost."[6]

Gandhi believed that he was the real target, for having written his "Green Pamphlet." And as soon as he stepped ashore in Durban, after the quarantine lifted, he was chased by an angry mob. "They pelted me with stones, brickbats and rotten eggs. Someone snatched away my turban, whilst others began to batter and kick me. I fainted and caught hold of the front railings of a house and stood there to get my breath. . . . They came upon me boxing and battering. The wife of the Police Superintendent, who knew me, happened to be passing by. The brave lady came up, opened her parasol . . . and stood between the crowd and me. This checked the fury of the mob."[7]

Mr. Alexander, the superintendent, was quickly notified of the assault and led some of his men to the rescue, offering Gandhi refuge inside his station. But Gandhi felt sure the mob would leave him alone now, so he went instead with a police escort to the home of his wealthy Parsi friend, Rustomji, where his wife had immediately gone with the boys. A doctor came to dress his wounds and bruises. When night fell, an angry lynch mob gathered, shouting for Gandhi, ready to break into the house if he refused to come out. The superintendent tried to humor the mob, but warned Gandhi to disguise himself in an officer's uniform to escape quietly from the rear alley, saving his life and his friend's property, both of which Alexander judged to be in jeopardy.

"I put on an Indian constable's uniform and wore on my head a Madrasi scarf, wrapped round a plate to serve as a helmet. Two detectives accompanied me, one of them disguised as an Indian." They reached a neighboring shop by a by-lane and in a carriage that had been kept waiting drove off to the same police station Alexander had earlier offered him for "refuge."[8] Gandhi thus proved flexible enough to elude danger much the way Kipling's *Kim* might have done, yet believed firmly enough in nonviolence to refuse, in writing, Colonial Secretary of State Joseph Chamberlain's offer to prosecute his "assailants." Instead, he wisely thanked the secretary of state and told him that he desired no vengeance, requiring no white settlers to be brought to book. "I am sure that, when the truth becomes known, they will be sorry for their conduct."[9] His reputation and that of Natal's Indian community, which he represented, were clearly enhanced by such sweet restraint.

Four days later, Gandhi and his family moved into their home on the palisades overlooking the port. His fame and professional practice, both enhanced by his narrow escape, made him the most celebrated member of his community. He raised a permanent fund for the new Natal Congress, renting an office to house his secretariat. He hired "an English governess" to care for his boys, nine-year-old Harilal and five-year-old Manilal.[10] Their third son, Ramdas, would be born before year's end; the fourth, Devadas, would be delivered by Gandhi himself in May of 1900.

His passion for home nursing by the latter date included midwifery. He tried to care for everyone himself, in home education as well as prescribing healthful routines and remedies. But his oldest son never appreciated his father's teaching and subsequently deeply resented Gandhi's refusal to allow him to study abroad and train for a profession as Gandhi had done.

"I could not devote to the children all the time I had wanted to give them . . . [and] they seem to feel the handicap of a want of school education," Gandhi confessed.[11] Claiming not to regret his experiments in home education, however, he blamed "undesirable traits" he discovered in his eldest son on his own "undisciplined" early life, as well as on his youthful "lust" and "self-indulgence." Harilal, not surprisingly, considered his father's refusal to permit him to enjoy the privileges and pleasures he himself experienced in London sheer hypocrisy. Gandhi was never able fully to answer his eldest son's charge, other than to suggest, perhaps too vaguely and optimistically, that "the ultimate result of my experiments is in the womb of the future." Harilal's tragic and dissolute life would prove to be one of Gandhi's most poignant failures.

In his public life, Gandhi became the most articulate Indian supporter of British imperialist expansion before and during the Boer War. Most Indians viewed the Boers as a "small nation" much like the Indian community itself, fighting to retain their hard-won independence in the Transvaal in the face of blatant attempts by Great Britain and its raiders to steal their gold mines and assault their republic. Jameson's Raid in 1895 was sponsored by Joe Chamberlain, and after 1897 by "Forward" imperialist Alfred Milner, Britain's High Commissioner in South Africa. "The British oppress us equally with the Boers," most Indians argued, urging support for President Paul Kruger's brave band of Afrikaner fighters.[12]

"Our existence in South Africa is only in our capacity as British subjects," Gandhi counterargued. "We have been proud of our British citizenship . . . and what little rights we still retain, we retain because we are British subjects. It would be unbecoming to our dignity as a nation to look on with folded hands at a time when ruin stared the British in the face . . . if we desire to win our freedom and achieve our welfare as members of the British Empire, here is a golden opportunity for us to do so by helping the British in the war by all the means at our disposal."[13]

Gandhi would use the same basic argument at the outbreak of World War I, as would all the leaders of India's National Congress, including Tilak. But for Gandhi this opportunistic position was perhaps more startling since he himself recognized the Boer War's imperialist roots, admitting that "justice is on the side of the Boers. But every single subject of a state must not hope to enforce his private opinion in all cases. The authorities may not always be right, but so long as the subjects own allegiance . . . it is their clear duty . . . to accord their support to acts of the state."[14]

Gandhi was struggling to define himself, trying to tie the realities of ambivalent daily life to some anchor of coherent belief, tossed about as yet by shifting tides of political pragmatism, while seeking deeper rocks of religious philosophy. He tried to strengthen his position by arguing against those who feared possible Boer revenge as "a sign of our effeminacy. . . . Would an Englishman think for a moment what would happen to himself if the English lost the war . . . without forfeiting his manhood?" Gandhi's participation in the Boer War was to raise and run an ambulance corps of Indians, recruiting no fewer than 1,100, many of them still working off indentures. Clergyman Dr. Booth was put in charge of first-aid training as medical superintendent, and the Indian Ambulance Corps worked side by side with the European Ambulance Corps under the overall direction of General Buller. Indians acquitted themselves so bravely that almost forty of them, including Gandhi, won medals. "No matter how timid a man is," Gandhi noted, "he is capable of the loftiest heroism when he is put to the test."[15] Since his ambulance corps saved lives, rather than taking any, he saw no contradiction in what they did with his faith in Ahimsa.

The Indian Ambulance Corps was disbanded long before the Boer War ended, however, and Gandhi decided to return to India in 1901, hoping to find a place in the Congress, possibly as Gokhale's full-time assistant. Feeling that his "work was no longer in South Africa but in India," he wanted to expand his field of service, knowing how much more remained to be done in India.[16] Wacha had been elected to preside over the Congress session to be held in Calcutta that December, and Gandhi was invited to join him in the first-class carriage in which he, Sir Pherozeshah Mehta, and Gokhale journeyed together across India from Bombay. Gandhi had drafted a resolution in support of equality for South Africa's Indians and the abolition of the £3 tax. He hoped to win strong National Congress support for it, but Mehta responded without enthusiasm: "Gandhi . . . so long as we have no power in our own land, you cannot fare better in the Colonies."[17]

His ardor for reform and revolution was further dampened as he became more familiar with the Congress, which "would meet three days every year and then go to sleep," he recalled. "And the delegates . . . would do nothing themselves."[18] He had abandoned South Africa, feeling cut off from the center of India's national agitation, whose famed leaders he had glimpsed during his visit five years ago. But seeing them up close, their petty prejudices and vanities disillusioned him. He felt at a loss to know where or how to begin the revolution required to wash away all the pomp and lethargy, to let in cleansing waters of true national service, currents of selfless commitment to the uplift of India's millions. His disillusionment at that Calcutta Congress included finding caste segregation and Hinduism's cruelest prejudice against the "untouchables" poisoning what should have been the nation's noblest institution.

To the Tamil delegates even the sight of others, whilst they were dining, meant pollution. So a special kitchen had to made for them . . . walled in by wicker-work." He noted no limit to the filth and pollution inside the Congress grounds, left uncared for by upper-caste volunteers, who viewed all cleaning as "scavenger's work." Gandhi shocked them, finding a broom and cleaning his own latrine, yet hundreds of others were left to fester and stink. Another week of that Congress session, he feared, would lead to the "outbreak of an epidemic."[19]

At thirty-two, Gandhi was impatient, eager to effect change wherever he went. "I am here to do anything that is not beyond my capacity," he told both Bengali secretaries of Congress, who lauded his spirit. Soon he was put in charge of sorting out and answering a "heap of letters." Next he volunteered to button Secretary Ghosal's shirt, noting later that he "loved to do it, as my regard for elders was always great."[20] He also taught himself to iron and took special pleasure in carefully ironing Gokhale's silk scarves.

The resolution he proposed to Congress's Subjects Committee was "unanimously passed," but only after Gokhale seconded it and Wacha supported it. Once again when Gandhi rose to read his brief motion he found that his head reeled and he could barely speak. "The procedure was far from pleasing to me. No one had troubled to understand the resolution, everyone was in a hurry to go."[21] He was disillusioned with virtually everything he learned about Congress procedures and politics, and even found his guru Gokhale "wasting" time by frequently going to the posh India Club to play billiards. He accompanied Gokhale there and recorded his distress on seeing how rich Indians decked themselves out. "How heavy is the toll of sins and wrongs that wealth, power and prestige exact from man!"[22]

For a month he apprenticed himself to Gokhale, admiring his diligence and integrity but disliking the way he always attended the Viceroy's Legislative Council in a horse-drawn carriage. Gentle Gokhale was "pained" by his disciple's reprimand and tried to explain how high office brought certain duties that could not be shirked. "When you are the victim of as wide a publicity as I am, it will be . . . impossible for you to go about in a tramcar,"[23] Gokhale explained. But Gandhi's own habits were to become more austere, as he would reject all the elegant trappings of the mechanized modern world. He was still clad at this time in a long "Parsi coat and trousers"; soon he would wear nothing more than a scant hand-woven dhoti, or loincloth.

During his winter visit to India in 1901–2, Gandhi began what was to become his most famous means of long-distance travel, journeying from Calcutta to Rajkot as a third-class railway passenger. He wanted to acquaint himself with the "hardships of third-class passengers."[24] What he learned was depressing, finding that third-class passengers were "treated like sheep" and that the compartments were not only overcrowded but also filthy. The passengers themselves threw rubbish of every variety on the floor, smoking and chewing betel nuts, spitting blood-red juices, turning the entire carriage into "a spittoon . . . yelling, and using foul language."[25] It proved a painfully instructive journey for the young barrister training to become a Mahatma.

He went back to Rajkot to practice the profession he had been certified to pursue in London. He was helped in getting briefs by his father's old friend Dave Joshi and no longer felt too shy to stand and speak in court. But Rajkot was still too much of a backwater, so Dave urged him to venture to Bombay rather than allow himself to be "buried" in Gujarat.

He rented chambers in the busy Fort area of Bombay, near the high court, and found a house in Girgaum, to and from which he walked from chambers. Low-lying, mosquito-infested, polluted Girgaum all but killed his son Manilal, who suffered an acute attack of typhoid compounded by pneumonia. Gandhi nursed the boy day and night, wrapping his fever-wracked body in wet sheets, keeping him on a diet of orange juice and water, refusing to allow him to touch either the eggs or chicken broth prescribed by their doctor. In addition to the wet sheets, Gandhi gave his son hip baths and prayed, repeating *Rama's* name all night. "Who can say whether his recovery was due to God's grace, or to hydropathy, or to careful dietary [*sic*] and nursing?"[26] Soon after Manilal recovered, however, Gandhi moved his family to a fine bungalow in suburban Santa Cruz, where the air, water, and light were less contaminated.

For Gandhi, the trip to his chambers was too long a walk, so for several months in 1902 he relapsed to riding first class on the commuter train, buying a round-trip "season ticket" at reduced price from Santa Cruz to Churchgate. There were, however, slim pickings for fresh barristers in the high court, so he spent much of his time in the library there, rather than auditing the courtroom arguments of senior barristers. Just as he was starting to feel neglected and a bit bored, a cable came from South Africa. Now that the British had defeated the Boers in Transvaal and the Orange Free State, taking control of those former republics, Colonial Secretary of State Joe Chamberlain was headed for Durban to review the situation in South Africa personally. Dada Abdulla and his friends requested that Gandhi return immediately to press the Indian community's case with the crown minister on their behalf.

"I had an idea that the work there would keep me engaged for at least a year, so I kept the bungalow and left my wife and children."[27] He took "four or five" of his cousins and nephews, however, including Maganlal Gandhi, who was soon to become one of his staunchest disciples and closest confidants. Prolonged separation from his wife would only help him keep the vow of sexual abstinence which he had been trying for several years to observe, though with little success. He blamed his early failures on his "weak will" and "lust," reflecting: "To be fair to my wife, I must say that she was never the temptress."[28] The prospect of a year's separation, therefore, hardly daunted either of them. It would, however, be another four years before Gandhi was finally ready to keep his vow never again to have sexual relations with his wife.

"The separation from wife and children . . . was for a moment painful, but I had inured myself to an uncertain life . . . all else but God that is Truth is . . . transient."[29]

7

Satyagraha in South Africa

GANDHI RETURNED to Durban on the eve of Joe Chamberlain's visit to South Africa to celebrate Britain's victory over the Boers late in 1902. Dada Abdulla and his friends welcomed their barrister home and immediately put him to work drafting the Indian deputation's memorial to be presented to the colonial secretary the day they met with him. Chamberlain had, however, come primarily to "get a gift of 35 million pounds" from British settlers who now had free access to Transvaal gold, Gandhi recalled, "So he gave a cold shoulder to the Indian deputation."[1]

Never easily discouraged, Gandhi resolved to press Indian demands for more equitable treatment by following the indifferent crown minister from Natal to Pretoria. Britain's victory in replacing Boer rule with its own did not open the Transvaal to Indian settlers, only to white Englishmen. Indians were required to obtain special permits to enter the Transvaal, and unless they were prepared to bribe officials in the new Asiatic Department to the tune of thousands, permission was denied. Gandhi, however, appealed to his old friend Police Superintendent Alexander and was soon on his way to Pretoria. Transvaal officials, angered at his having managed to procure a permit "by mistake," flexed their petty muscles, preventing his meeting once again with Chamberlain, arguing that the Pretoria deputation should only include "resident" Indians. His friends were insulted enough to suggest they cancel the meeting, but Gandhi insisted they go without him, having drafted their strong memorial. "I smarted under the insult, but as I had pocketed many such in the past I had become inured to them."[2] No longer the thin-skinned young barrister Ollivant had ordered thrown out of his office, he never again would allow disappointment to defeat him.

The arrogance of Pretoria's autocratic Asiatic Department served only to convince Gandhi to settle in the Transvaal rather than return to Durban. "I could see that the Asiatic Department was . . . a frightful engine of oppression for the Indians. . . . I saw that I had to begin my work from the very beginning."[3]

He had gone home the year before with high hopes and every intention of staying on in India, either in Rajkot or Bombay. His plan had been to re-establish residence there and find legal work enough to support his family while serving Gokhale and Congress in the greater national interest. But Mehta's aloof indifference and all the glaring flaws he saw during the Calcutta Congress and his month with Gokhale, not to speak of his failure once more to find work at Bombay's Bar, gave him renewed appreciation of the loving support and trust lavished upon him by Dada Abdulla and his loyal friends in Natal's Indian community. Now that he was back among them, he could "clearly see that if I returned with the vain fancy of serving on a larger field in India while I was fully aware of the great danger which stared the South African Indians in the face, the spirit of service which I had acquired would be stultified."[4]

His work was in the Transvaal, not in Bombay or Calcutta, and his admiring, trusting, devoted Gujarati mercantile friends implored him to remain in South Africa. Ten of them were eager enough to contribute funds on an annual retainer basis for his legal services. So he enrolled as a barrister in the Transvaal's Supreme Court in Johannesburg and opened his office in the heart of the frontier capital of Britain's newest gold rush colony. He organized a Transvaal British Indian Association, pressed charges against the "corrupt" Asiatic Department officials, and led a deputation to call upon the British governor of the Transvaal, Lord Milner. He also wrote a cogent summary of "The Indian Question" in South Africa, copies of which he sent directly to Dadabhai Naoroji and Sir William Wedderburn, who ran London's British Committee of the Indian National Congress. Wedderburn passed his copy on to Whitehall's secretary of state, the latter sending it to Viceroy Lord Curzon in Calcutta.

Gandhi also kept Gokhale informed with weekly letters and copies of all documents and wrote as well to the editor of *The Vegetarian* in London. He thus kept very busy as lawyer, publicist, organizer, and official lobbyist for the Indian community of Natal and Transvaal, which now numbered well over 50,000. "Indians are entitled to equal privileges with Europeans in this British Colony," Gandhi argued to *The Times of India*, "on the ground, firstly, that they are British subjects, and, secondly . . . desirable citizens . . . industrious, frugal and sober."[5]

On June 4, 1903, Gandhi launched his first newspaper, *Indian Opinion,* devoted to the Indian community and its needs. In his first editorial Gandhi sounded more like an Englishman than an Indian nationalist, denouncing "prejudice in the minds of the Colonists . . . and the unhappy forgetfulness of the great services India has always rendered to the Mother Country ever since Providence brought loyal Hind under the flag of Britannia."[6] He appealed both to members of the Indian community and to those of the "great Anglo-Saxon race" for support of his paper, created to "promote harmony and good-will between the different sections of the *one* mighty Empire." In the next issue, however, Gandhi was more caustic in his criticism of his imperial brethren.

Gandhi was harshest in his criticism of Lord Milner for his defense of the Asiatic Office and the £3 tax on all ex-indentured Indians and restrictions on Indian entry to and property rights in Transvaal, merely "because the Indian is a coloured man!"[7] What angered him most was that Milner advised the government of India to ship many more indentured Indians to South Africa to help develop Transvaal mining, but insisted that all of them must be required at the end of their indentures to return directly to India. "If you must introduce Indian labour," Gandhi reprimanded Milner, "be just, be fair, do unto us as you would be done by."[8] Thus drawing upon his knowledge of the Bible, Gandhi became the hero of his community and the bane of British officialdom from Johannesburg to Durban.

By the end of June 1903 Gandhi knew that the public work he'd started would not end in one year, nor in two. He wrote to his lawyer friend, in Rajkot, Haridas Vora, to ask illiterate "Mrs. Gandhi" if she would agree to remain there without him for another "three or four years. . . . If she does not . . . of course, she must come here at the end of the year, and I must be content quietly to settle down in Johannesburg for ten years or so." He hoped she would consent to remain in India, since that would "enable me to give undivided attention to public work. As she knows, she had very little of my company in Natal; probably, she would have less in Johannesburg. However . . . I place myself absolutely in her hands. If she must come, then she may make preparations . . . and leave in . . . November."[9]

He clearly preferred by now to live a celibate life of work rather than being attached to Kasturba, distracted day and night by his wife and young children. But his sense of responsibility was too deep-rooted to allow him to break his promise to bring her to South Africa in a year, unless she agreed, which, of course, she did not. For Kasturba, living with her husband's relatives but without him, hardly ever able to see her own parents or siblings, was the worst of all possible arrangements. Gandhi tried his best to dissuade her from joining him, however, sending a copy of his letter to Haridas Vora to his nephew Chhaganlal in Rajkot, urging him to "try to convince . . . your aunt . . . that it will be best for her to remain in India."[10] Kasturba had always been stubborn, however, and she resolved to join him after one year's separation, as he had promised on the eve of his departure.

Gandhi's law office in the booming, noisy heart of Johannesburg kept no fewer than four Indian clerks as busy as he was from early morning until late at night. A handsome painting of Christ hung on the wall above his own desk, with photos of Dababhai Naoroji, Gokhale, and Annie Besant adorning the other walls. He attracted two full-time assistants, both English Jews: twenty-three year old Henry S. L. Polak, who would remain one of his most loyal followers for the next decade, and Theosophist Louis W. Ritch, another enterprising idealist, lured to the Transvaal by gold fever but who chose to remain on the Rand in the service of the budding Mahatma.[11] Polak and Ritch proved eager to fight for minority rights and the dignity of all humans, whatever their ethnicity, color, or religion. Gandhi's secretaries in Johannesburg were two lovely young Western women. One was a Scottish beauty he called "Miss Dick," who "immediately prepossessed me," and "before very long . . . became more a daughter or a sister to me than a mere steno-typist."[12] A few months after she started working for him, however, Miss Dick married. Then Gandhi found another more remarkable young female steno-typist-bookkeeper-office manager, Sonja Schlesin, a seventeen-year-old Russian Jewess whose dark-eyed beauty was as radiant as her brilliance. Miss Schlesin, like Henry Polak, remained at his side throughout the ensuing decade of struggle. Gokhale would later marvel at "the sacrifice, the purity and fearlessness" of Miss Schlesin, ranking her "first" among all of Gandhi's "co-workers."[13]

By the end of 1903, though his legal earnings of £5,000 annually were more than enough to support his large residence on the outskirts of Johannesburg, as well as his spacious office across the road from the High Court, Gandhi remained restless, searching for a better base on which to develop and integrate his life of community service as an active agent of social reform. He soon found a cause, when torrential rains in 1904 drenched the gold mines and Indian bazaars of Johannesburg, triggering an epidemic of pneumonic plague. Poor Indian mine workers were particularly hard hit, restricted as they were to bazaar ghettos, living in overcrowded quarters with garbage-infested alleys. Germ-bearing rivers of rain spread the plague with such intensity that Gandhi shut down his office, turning himself and all four of his Indian clerks, as well as his legal assistants, into a volunteer nursing corps.

"Sacrifice is the law of life," he wrote that month in *Indian Opinion*. "We can do nothing or get nothing without paying a price for it. . . . Christ died on the Cross of Calvary and left Christianity as a glorious heritage. . . . Joan of Arc was burned as a witch to her eternal honour and to the everlasting disgrace of her murderers. . . . The Indians in South Africa . . .

Transvaal in particular, are undergoing many troubles . . . unless we are prepared to stand and work shoulder to shoulder without flinching and without being daunted by temporary disappointments, failure would be the only . . . reward, or rather punishment."[14]

He was bracing his community for its fiercest struggles, sensing as he did so that all of his earnest appeals to British officials, from Chamberlain and Milner down to the lowliest functionary in the Asiatic Department, even when met with smiles and gracious promises, were doomed to failure. The greatest self-sacrifice, he well knew, was made in one's self-interest. Gandhi's self-interest now embraced the entire Indian community of Natal and the Transvaal, all of whom he was ready to serve in court or out. He now wrote his articles in Gujarati, so that more Indians could understand his passionate message, while virtually no English eyes could comprehend it.

Transvaal inspectors blamed Indians for bringing "bubonic plague" to Johannesburg from Bombay, but Gandhi insisted that the plague had broken out "entirely owing to the unsanitary and overcrowded conditions" in which Indians were forced to live, aggravated by the recent bad weather. The only way to keep hundreds and thousands more from dying, he argued, was to burn the entire infected area to the ground and resettle its inhabitants in a temporary camp.

"People were in a terrible fright," Gandhi recalled, "but my constant presence was a consolation to them."[15] Many poor Indians had buried all of their savings of silver and copper under their homes, and they frantically dug up those coins before the location was burned down. Gandhi now became their banker. He kept careful records of each person's savings, had all the coins "sterilized," and deposited nearly £60,000 into his own bank, returning their savings to each individual a few years later.

Indian Opinion had by the fall of 1904 become the most important publication for the Indian community of South Africa, keeping its members informed on issues of current interest to all. But the publication and distribution of the weekly papers remained a growing drain on Gandhi's own resources, so much so that in October of 1904 he decided to take the overnight express to Durban to reorganize the journal, which was being published there. Henry Polak saw him off at Johannesburg station and handed him his copy of John Ruskin's *Unto This Last*, urging him to read it. Ruskin's interest in social reform, based on his artistic sensitivity, made him reject Manchester's industrial ugliness, degradation, and pollution; it echoed Gandhi's own concerns and strong feelings. Ruskin's idealism, inspired in part by Jeremy Bentham's utilitarianism and Robert Owen's utopianism, stressed the equal value of all manual work and the importance of craftsmanship to each human being's creative growth.

"The book was impossible to lay aside," Gandhi recalled, reading it all that night. "I was determined to change my life in accordance with the ideals of the book."[16] Those ideals, as he understood them, were first of all that "the good of the individual is contained in [the] good of all," that "a lawyer's work has the same value as the barber's," and that "the life of the tiller of the soil and the handicraftsman is the life worth living." He later translated this seminal work of Ruskin, which helped to transform his life, into Gujarati, abandoning its biblical title for the Sanskrit compound *Sarvodaya*, literally "The Uplift of All," which he adopted as the name for Gandhian socialism.

Gandhi hastened to implement Ruskin's burning ideals by acquiring his hundred-acre "Phoenix" farm within a month of reaching Durban, the first of several rural communes, *ashrams*, he would found during his life. Another English vegetarian friend, Albert West, came to work with him on the *Indian Opinion*, joining Henry Polak and Chhaganlal, now in South Africa with his family. As did all the press workers, they agreed to limit themselves to subsistence salaries of £3 a month while living and working on the new "settlement," which had "a nice little spring and a few orange and mango trees." Before year's end the Phoenix had become a vital and healthy community, and a model of the social transformation Gandhi would devote his life to propagating.

"The plan was . . . a piece of ground sufficiently large and far away from the hustle of the town . . . each one of the workers could have his plot of land . . . healthy conditions, without heavy expenses. . . . workers could receive per month an advance to cover necessary expenses. . . . Living under such conditions and amid the beautiful surroundings which have given Natal the name of the Garden Colony, the workers could live a more . . . natural life, and the ideas of Ruskin and Tolstoy [would be] combined with strict business principles."[17]

Eight years earlier Gandhi had been "overwhelmed" by Tolstoy's *The Kingdom of God Is Within You* when he first read it during his initial visit to the Transvaal. "It left an abiding impression on me," he recalled, admiring Tolstoy's "independent thinking, profound morality, and . . . truthfulness."[18] His second ashram, founded half a decade later, would be called Tolstoy Farm. To remain closer to his work, Gandhi continued for more than a year to live in Johannesburg, leaving his nephew in charge of affairs in Phoenix and West to edit the newspaper there.

For South Africa's Indian community, as for India, 1905 and 1906 proved to be years of great historic significance. The first partition of Bengal, that "cruel wrong" as Congress President Gokhale called it in his Benares Congress address, awakened India's nationalist movement, initiating mass boycotts of British imports in Calcutta and Bombay, raising cries of "Sva-raj" ("Self-rule") or "Freedom!" from millions of Indians furious over British imperial paternalism and its "divide and rule" policy.[19] In the name of administrative efficiency British bureaucrats partitioned India's oldest and largest province, dividing the heartland of its Bengali-speaking core and creating the new province called Eastern Bengal and Assam with a Bengali-speaking Muslim majority and a new capital of Dhaka. The outspoken Calcutta-centered Hindu Bengali-speaking leaders of India's National Congress were left a minority in their own province of West Bengal, which included millions of Bihari- and Oriya-speakers in regions only later to be carved away into the separate provinces (now states) of Bihar and Orissa. Surendranath ("Surrender Not") Banerjea led the boycott opposition, and *Gurudev* ("Divine Guru") Rabindranath Tagore wrote the music for what would become India's first national anthem, *Bande Mataram*, or "Hail to Thee, Mother!"

"Bengal seems to have truly woken up at this time," Gandhi wrote in his Gujarati edition, hailing the "mammoth meeting" of Bengalis in Calcutta to protest partition, and noting how the boycott of British cloth had "rapidly" increased sales of Indian-made goods (*swadeshi*).[20] The Muslim majority of Eastern Bengal, however, rallied less than a month later in Dhaka to welcome the birth of their suddenly booming provincial capital, which after 1971 would emerge as independent Bangladesh's capital. Since most of Gandhi's supporters were Muslim merchants, he was constrained yet surprised to report mass Bengali Muslim support for the "cruel" partition. "We cannot . . . believe that the movement could possibly be spontaneous. It is absurd on the face of it. Assuming that there was any oppression on the part of the Hindus, relief could be obtained without partition, because the might of the British power was there to protect one community against another."[21] It appears paradoxical that a nationalist as ardent as Gandhi would argue in favor of even-handed British "protection" as the best way of avoiding communal conflict or unfair Hindu-majority discrimination against the weaker Muslim-minority, as in Calcutta. It was also prophetic. Four decades later, of course, rivers of blood would flow when provincial Bengal's partition was reincarnated as partition of the subcontinent.

The startling defeat suffered by Russia's Baltic Fleet in the Sea of Japan in 1905 fueled Gandhi's hope that India, too, might similarly surprise the world by overcoming imperial tyranny. "The power of the Viceroy is no way less than that of the Czar. Just as the people of Russia pay taxes, so also do we . . . as in Russia, so in India, the military is all-powerful," Gandhi wrote. "The movement in Bengal for the use of *swadeshi* goods is much like the Russian movement. Our shackles will break this very day, if the people of India become united and patient, love their country, and think of the well-being of their motherland. . . . The governance of India is possible only because there exist people who serve."[22] More than a decade before he would launch his first nationwide multiple boycott against British rule, Gandhi not only appreciated its revolutionary powers but shared his thoughts with South African compatriots.

While thinking far ahead of how best to break "our shackles" in British India, Gandhi led a merchant deputation to address the new British governor of Transvaal, Lord Selborne. Gandhi appealed to the governor to allow more Indians to enter Transvaal, explaining that his merchant friends "have constantly to draw upon India for confidential clerks . . . reliable men," currently excluded under the harsh Immigration Restriction Act.[23] He further requested that local boards or town councils be empowered to issue new trade licenses to expedite that intolerably slow process. Finally, he urged repeal of the £3 tax on ex-indentured Indians and all new immigrant Indians. "What we want is not political power; but we do wish to live side by side with other British subjects in peace and amity and with dignity and self-respect . . . which we have learned to cherish as a priceless heritage of living under the British Crown."[24]

To the end of 1905 Gandhi remained His Majesty's loyal subject. But Lord Selborne listened in stony silence to all that Gandhi and his British Indian Association deputation had to say, promising nothing. Yet 1906 began, it seemed to Gandhi, with reason to hope for beneficent changes, first, because the "Indian cause is just," and also because a new Liberal government was voted into power in Great Britain, bringing "Honest" John Morley to the helm of London's India Office as its secretary of state. "His sympathies for the weaker party are well known," Gandhi assured his readers. "A moderate appeal to him, therefore, . . . cannot fail to obtain a good hearing."[25] Two months later, however, Morley spoke of Bengal's partition as "a settled fact," leaving Gandhi to conclude that "the people of Bengal will not get justice." Nor would the Indians of Transvaal without the "requisite effort."[26]

What began as "Natal Native trouble" in March of 1906 escalated a month later into a full-scale "Zulu Revolt." Gandhi responded much the way he had to the Boer War. "We are in Natal by virtue of British power. Our very existence depends upon it. It is therefore our duty to render whatever help we can."[27] Gandhi proposed another Indian Ambulance Corps at a meeting of the Natal Indian Congress in Durban. His proposal was sent to the colonial secretary and accepted.

In April of 1906, brother Lakshmidas wrote angrily to chastise Gandhi for having stopped sending his monthly savings to Rajkot and for appearing no longer to be attached in any respect to his extended family and for neglecting the traditional duties of a younger Hindu brother. "You are prejudiced against me," Gandhi replied. "All that I have is being utilized for public purposes. It is available to relations who devote themselves to public work. . . . You may repudiate me, but still I will be to you what I have always been. . . . I have no desire for worldly enjoyments of any type what-ever. I am engaged in my present activities as . . . essential to life. If I have to face death while thus engaged, I shall face it with equanimity. I am now a stranger to fear."[28]

Gandhi led his corps of some twenty Indian stretcher-bearers in pledg-ing "true allegiance to His Majesty King Edward the Seventh, His Heirs and Successors," promising "faithfully" to "serve in . . . the Active Militia Force of the Colony of Natal."[29] He wrote a few weeks later in Gujarati that "this has produced a very favourable impression on . . . prominent whites," encouraging more Indians to volunteer, adding "It can be looked upon as a kind of . . . picnic. The person joining . . . gets enough exercise and thus keeps his body in good trim and improves his health. . . . People love him and praise him."

At this very time, when actively engaged in removing wounded bodies from fields of battle, Gandhi's thoughts turned "furiously in the direction of self-control. . . . It became my conviction that procreation and the con-sequent care of children were inconsistent with public service. I had to break up my household at Johannesburg. . . . I took my wife and children to Phoenix and . . . the idea flashed upon me that . . . I must relinquish the desire for children and wealth and live the life of . . . one retired from household cares."[30] The vow of celibacy which he took now he viewed as one that "opened" the "door to real freedom. . . . I vow to flee from the ser-pent which I know will bite me."[31] He had feared serpents as a child, hardly surprising in rural India, yet in this context the use of serpent seems more an echo of Christianity's symbol of temptation. He would attempt a much deeper analysis near the end of his life, some forty years later, involv-ing more dangerous experiments with the Brahmacharya celibacy vow. Now he had no difficulty in abstaining from further physical contact with Kasturba, noting "where . . . desire is gone, a vow of renunciation is the natural . . . fruit." Kasturba silently accepted his avowed wish, apparently relieved at his decision to abstain from sex with her.

Sergeant-Major Gandhi worked bravely with his corps for six weeks in the summer of 1906, but by the end of July each of the Indian stretcher-bearers was presented a silver medal by the Natal Indian Congress when the corps disbanded. Gandhi advised the Congress to try to organize a per-manent corps, and "in the process white prejudice against Indians might al-together disappear."[32] But instead of disappearing, the prejudice intensified so the community voted to send a deputation, consisting of Gandhi and one of its leading merchants, to London to lobby on behalf of South Afri-can Indians. Winston Churchill, colonial under secretary of state at this time, arrogantly tried to "justify" the "deprivation of the franchise from British Indians," Gandhi reported, arguing that all "non-European Na-tives" were "coloured people," and therefore unsuited to representative or responsible rule.[33] Thus began the bitter feud between Gandhi and Churchill, which was to intensify over the next four decades, much to the misfortune of Great Britain as well as India.

The Legislative Council of the Transvaal now introduced an Asiatic Ordinance Bill that would require registration of all Indians, including women and children, who would then be fingerprinted and forced always to carry identification cards. Gandhi's first editorial reaction was to call it "abominable!" A week later he termed it "criminal."[34] All Indians would be subject to "indignities" at the hands of "arbitrary" officials, who would be empowered even to banish those whom they disliked.

On September 9, 1906, Gandhi addressed Johannesburg's Hamidiya Islamic Society, speaking against the ordinance he labeled a "Black Act" and urging his audience to prepare "cheerfully" to "suffer imprisonment. There is nothing wrong in that. The distinctive virtue of the British is bravery. If therefore we also unite and offer resistance with courage and firmness, I am sure there is nothing that the Government can do."[35] Two days later he organized a mass meeting, at which he proposed that all of them take a solemn oath against "The Government," which "has taken leave of all sense of decency." Not to oppose such an evil government would be "cowardice," Gandhi argued, but everyone must "search his own heart, and if the inner voice assures him that he has the requisite strength to carry him through, then only should he pledge himself."[36] This was the birth of Gandhi's revolutionary method of *Satyagraha*, or "Hold Fast to the Truth," which would be replicated in India many times, beginning with a sacred vow, taken only by those who had considered the full implications of their solemn oath. This was his first public reference to his "inner voice," the voice he later defined as God that was Truth. If a majority of the Transvaal's Indian community took the oath, he told them, the ordinance might not be enacted, but he warned against excessive optimism.

"We might have to go to Gaol, where we might be insulted. We might have to go hungry. . . . We might be flogged by rude wardens. We might be fined heavily and our property might be attached. . . . We might be deported. . . . some of us might fall ill and even die." The risk of death did not deter him, however, and he argued that "even if every one else flinched leaving me alone to face the music, I am confident that I would never violate my pledge. Please do not misunderstand me. I am not saying this out of vanity."

Was there not just a touch of vanity, however, in that public declamation that he was ready to die rather than surrender? This was, after all, but two months since he had risked death daily without flinching in order to bear wounded soldiers from fields of carnage. Sergeant-Major Gandhi, who fearlessly led his ambulance corps into the center of battle unarmed, would hardly tremble were he now faced with prison or flogging in so righteous a cause. Like the bravest of British officers he admired, he would do his duty. Bravery, as he told them, was the "distinctive virtue of the British," and much of Gandhi's psyche had indeed by now become *British* to the core. The rest of him, which remained Hindu and Indian, had also changed. His April 1906 letter to Lakshmidas made that clear: "I have no desire for worldly enjoyments of any type. . . . If I have to face death . . . I shall face it with equanimity." He had steeled himself, like a true yogi, impervious to personal family feelings or to any pleasures of the flesh, devoid of desire, material or sexual, living simply to serve the community, whose spokesman and foremost advocate he had become, working only for public purposes. Thus uniting within his battle-hardened body the rock of British martial courage and the steel of a naked Sadhu's yogic indifference to heat and cold, beds of nails or burning coals, Gandhi sublimated all his powers and potent sexual energy, pitting himself against discriminatory anti-Indian laws enacted by racial bigots. Fearing nothing, loving no one, neither wife, nor eldest son, nor older brother, he had made himself invulnerable to physical coercion of any kind and to human temptations that so easily lured men of weaker resolve from their sacred vows.

Three thousand Indians attended the mass meeting in Johannesburg's packed Empire Theatre, where Gandhi so forcefully spoke, unanimously passing resolutions, calling upon the Legislative Council to withdraw its ordinance, and warning that if so "tyrannical" a law was passed the entire Indian community would "prefer gaol" to abiding by it. The Council was not moved to change its ordinance, however. Nor was Victor Alexander Bruce, the Earl of Elgin, former viceroy of India, now colonial secretary of state, moved to withhold Great Britain's approval. Indeed, the Transvaal's governor, William Waldegrave Palmer, the Second Earl of Selborne, conveyed the news of Lord Elgin's approval to Gandhi's association in mid-September. That news came as a bombshell on the very eve of Gandhi's planned departure for England. Many members of the community feared that if he left them they might "waver" and take out registration certificates under the Black Act.[37] Others insisted, however, that Gandhi must go and voted to provide him with funds to do so, even as Lord Elgin, through Lord Selborne, informed Gandhi that no useful purpose would be served by sending a deputation to him. Gandhi immediately replied that his community must adhere to its "resolve to resist the Ordinance."[38] So on October 1, 1906, Gandhi and Haji Ally, president of Johannesburg's Hamidiya Islamic Society, boarded the Cape Mail and two days later sailed from Cape Town aboard the S.S. *Armadale Castle* for London.

To help prepare his community for resistance to the ordinance, when it came into effect on January 1, 1907, Gandhi wrote from shipboard an article about the principled courage of Wat Tyler, John Hampden, and John Bunyan. Tyler had lost his life leading the fourteenth-century Peasants' Revolt against heavy royal taxation, inspiring many farmers to join him before his beheading by the lord mayor of London. He also lauded Oliver Cromwell's cousin, Hampden, who led the opposition to Charles I's extortionist demands for "ship money" in the Commons. Imprisoned by that despotic king for nearly a year, Hampden's principled opposition "sowed . . . [the] seed of the struggle for freedom" leading to the English Civil War, which brought in Cromwell and real parliamentary power for the people.[39] John Bunyan was "a saintly man," whose devout faith made him oppose the "religious oppression" of the bishops in his time. Locked up in Bedford Prison for twelve years, he wrote *The Pilgrim's Progress*, hailed by Gandhi as "the most beautiful book in the English language." If enough Transvaal Indians also went to jail, the fruit of their suffering, he assured them, would be to break their chains, to overcome tyranny and persecution, and one day allow them to emerge as free as the English.

Gandhi's deputation reached Southampton on October 20, 1906, and entrained for Waterloo Station, from which they were driven to the Hotel Cecil. Dadabhai Naoroji and his Parsi colleague in Parliament, Sir Muncherji Bhownaggri, agreed, together with Sir Henry Cotton and Sir George Birdwood, to accompany their deputation to Lord Elgin. Haji Ally, who suffered badly from rheumatism and too many cigars, developed a high fever as soon as they reached London and was immediately taken to Lady Margaret Hospital in Bromley, where Gandhi's old friend Dr. Josiah Oldfield promised to attend to him every day.

Lord Elgin agreed to receive the deputation on Thursday, November 8, 1906. The day before, Gandhi and Ally addressed a meeting in the House of Commons' Grand Committee Room, attended by one hundred members of the Liberal, Labour, and Nationalist Parties, all of whom were sympathetic. A resolution supporting the deputation's objects was unanimously adopted. Upon meeting Elgin, Gandhi presented his memorial, arguing that the recently passed ordinance assumed that every Indian was a criminal guilty of dishonest, unlawful actions and accentuated "colour prejudice in the most offensive manner. . . . it undoubtedly reduces Indians to a level lower than . . . Kaffirs [blacks]."[40] Elgin listened patiently to all that the deputation had to say and was cordial but unmoved in his reply. Gandhi then pressed for another minute of His Lordship's time, urging that a special commission be appointed to look into the grievances of the deputation and requesting a second appointment in order to correct the misinformation Lord Elgin had received from the Transvaal.

Gandhi made the most of every hour he spent in London, writing to everyone he knew or could contact, granting interviews to every reporter he could reach, and visiting every member of Parliament or official at Whitehall, who was willing to see him. He rarely went to sleep before 3:30 A.M. and was up before dawn, carrying out a more rigorous routine than he ever had in South Africa. At thirty-seven he was physically in his prime and drove himself with relentless intensity.

The day after he met Elgin, he sent a copy of the petition he had drafted and submitted to him to "every Member of Parliament with a courteous covering letter."[41] His legal training and growing skills at public relations allowed him to amplify every action he took to the largest, most influential audience, making the most of each precious moment. He wrote to India's secretary of state, John Morley as well, requesting an audience with him, and was invited to bring his deputation to the India Office shortly before he sailed back to Africa. He urged Sir Muncherji and other friends to establish a "permanent committee for the South African Indians" in London so that the work he had started would not be "frittered away."[42] Indefatigable, inexhaustible, he pressed on, urging everyone he met to do whatever was possible to help him in seeking to redress his community's many grievances. Louis Ritch agreed to act as that committee's permanent secretary and remained his man in London.

Gandhi wrote to the editor of the *Times*, urging that a commission be appointed to investigate and report on conditions in the Transvaal, pending whose report "Royal sanction for the Ordinance in question" be withheld. "If the Colonies persist in their policy of exclusion, they will force on the mother country . . . a very serious problem. . . . 'Is India to remain a part of the British Dominions or not?' He who runs may read that England will find it difficult to hold India if her people, immediately they migrated to British Colonies, are to be insulted and degraded as if they belonged to a barbarous race."[43] The importance of this brief, intense return to London for Gandhi's strategic thinking and the evolution of his revolutionary movement of peaceful protest can hardly be exaggerated. His mind raced decades ahead, spinning off ideas of effective agitation and creating inchoate organizations to carry forward demands he and his growing army of followers would articulate over the next four decades.

He even wrote to Winston Churchill as colonial under secretary, requesting a private interview to place the whole position before him and was granted an audience shortly before leaving London. Churchill had answered a question in the Commons a few days earlier, arguing that "it is very desirable to keep the White and Coloured quarters apart."[44] Gandhi tried to convince Churchill of the inhumanity of his viewpoint, but the century's two greatest leaders of India and England rarely agreed on any issue, Winston later maligning the Mahatma as a "fraud" and "scoundrel."

Liberal John Morley, on the other hand, not only warmly welcomed Gandhi and his deputation to the India Office but was so supportive of all he heard that he swayed Elgin and their Liberal Prime Minister Campbell-Bannerman, as well as the rest of Great Britain's Cabinet to veto the Transvaal Ordinance. In his half decade at the helm of London's India Office,

Morley labored mightily to open British India's narrowly despotic administration to representative and responsible change. But Morley saw little value in the idea of appointing another royal commission, which usually took so long in gathering evidence that its report proved hopelessly irrelevant.

Gandhi appreciated Morley's kind words and sympathy, as well as those of others, but in his own "Deputation Notes" penned the next day he reflected with penetrating political insight that "we would get no redress until we acquired strength like the Whites . . . we should realize that our salvation lies in our own hands."[45]

The deputation sailed back to Cape Town on the R.M.S. *Briton* and welcoming receptions cheered them there and in Johannesburg before year's end. On January 1, 1907, Gandhi addressed his Natal Indian Congress in Durban, informing them that "British rule is essentially just. . . . But we should not be elated by our success. Our struggle has just begun. Now . . . we have to explain things to the politicians here."[46] This would not, of course, be easy.

Two days later Gandhi told Durban's Mohamedan Association that he felt certain the reason they succeeded in turning Britain's government around was thanks to "the perfect accord that obtained between Mr. Ally and myself. . . . We acted with love and in concert. . . . though following different religions, we remained united in our struggle. Secondly, truth and justice were on our side. I believe God is always near me. He is never away from me."[47] It was his first public profession of constant proximity to God, but it would not be his last. Though still dressed as a British barrister, Gandhi now began to sound more like a Mahatma.

The suffragette movement was on in force during Gandhi's brief visit to London, and he reported to his community the reply of Chancellor of the Exchequer Herbert Asquith to "the women of Great Britain" that "if all of them demanded the franchise, it could not but be granted." Gandhi told his followers that "under British rule, justice is often not to be had without some show of strength, whether of the pen, of the sword, or of money. For our part we are to use only the strength that comes from unity and truth. That is to say, our bondage in India can cease this day, if all the people unite in their demands and are ready to suffer any hardships that may befall them."[48] The remaining forty years of his life would be spent in explaining, in reiterating, and in implementing this passionate, inspired prescription for winning freedom for the people of India, or, indeed, for any enslaved or politically oppressed people.

Gandhi was moved to write about the eight hundred English women who marched on Parliament in February, fearlessly courting imprisonment. "We believe these women have behaved in a manly way."[49] He was bracing his community for the struggle ahead, knowing that though he'd convinced

Britain's Home Government to reject the Transvaal Colony's ordinance, that same government had now given the Transvaal full responsible rule, which meant they could reintroduce the same ordinance on their own. Their deputation's victory thus offered his community but a brief respite. In March of 1907 General Louis Botha, who had fought the British, capturing Churchill, among others, during the Boer War, was elected first prime minister of independent Transvaal, and three years later of the Union of South Africa. Botha's greatest assistant and successor was General Jan Smuts, South Africa's foremost legal mind, statesman architect of South Africa's Union, and Gandhi's most brilliant South African adversary.

The Transvaal's new Boer Parliament reintroduced and passed the Asiatic Registration Ordinance as its first order of official business, leaving Indians "staggered" by the swiftness of that action.[50] Gandhi immediately responded by calling a mass meeting and reminding his community of their promise to refuse to obey that "Black Act," and instead to welcome entering the "palace" of prison. He cabled Lord Elgin, of course, urging him at least to postpone any Royal decision on the act passed by the new dominion. And, in early April, Gandhi led a deputation to Pretoria to call on Colonial Secretary Smuts and argue against the new act.

Royal assent was granted in May to the Transvaal Asiatic Registration Act. Gandhi repeated his earlier pledge never to register and called upon all members of the Indian community not to "swerve," not to fail in doing their duty.[51] Many of his friends, however, asked "How?" Gandhi's answer had long before been supplied by Martin Luther: We have now earned the freedom to burn old permits, together with the new ones. Not a single person must enter the Permit Office. . . . a final date will be fixed for taking out new permits. Only after that date can the doors of prison-palace open for us.[52]

The new act requiring Indians to register was gazetted to be enforced starting on July 1, 1907. On Sunday, June 30, Gandhi's community turned out in numbers too great to fit inside any home in Pretoria. "If any Indian, big or small, should accept the title-deed of slavery under the law," Gandhi told that enormous crowd, "others would not follow. . . . Those who kept themselves free would win in the end."[53] Indians in Pretoria started to picket outside the Permit Office to keep Indians tempted to enter it from doing so, and Gandhi soon urged them to extend that boycott to Durban. A week later, however, several Indians appealed to Jan Smuts, asking him not to require those who registered to give their mother's name or to be fingerprinted by Kaffir [black] police. Smuts sent a long and "very ingenious" reply, which made Gandhi's blood boil. He agreed to withdraw the mother's name requirement, most obnoxious to Muslims, and also to promise that no black policeman would ever fingerprint any Indian. "After reducing us to a living death . . . could there be a fresh amendment in order to kick at the dead?" an outraged Gandhi cried. "It should be noted that on no single point has Mr. Smuts given up his obstinacy. . . . With God as our witness, we have pledged opposition to the law. With the same God as witness, let us prove our courage."[54]

Braced as he was for martyrdom, this was one of the few times in his life that Gandhi lost his temper, shifting his tone from calm reasonableness to heated anger, a clear tribute to Smuts's negotiating skills. "BOYCOTT, BOYCOTT, PERMIT OFFICE! BY GOING TO GAOL WE . . . SUFFER FOR OUR COMMON GOOD, AND SELF-RESPECT," Gandhi wrote on a poster hammered up Luther-like onto the door of the Permit Office in Pretoria. "LOYALTY TO THE KING DEMANDS LOYALTY TO THE KING OF KINGS. INDIANS BE FREE!"[55]

"Indians in the Transvaal will stagger humanity without shedding a drop of blood," Gandhi later explained in his weekly journal: Gentle Jesus, the greatest passive resister the world has seen, is their pattern. . . . Was not Jesus rejected and yet did He not resist the blasphemy that His persecutors would have Him utter on pain of suffering what was, in their estimation, an inglorious death, side by side with thieves and robbers? But the crown of thorns today sits better on that bleeding head than a crown bedecked with diamonds. . . . He died indeed, yet He lives in the memory of all true sons of God. . . . So, too, will Indians of the Transvaal, if they remain true to their God, live in the memory of their children . . . who will be able to say . . . "Our forefathers did not betray us for a mess of pottage."[56]

The British Committee worked hard in London to rally support for Gandhi's struggle, and its secretary, Louis Ritch, kept him informed daily by cable of all those he contacted in Parliament and the Cabinet and sent him every newspaper report as well. Gokhale, of course, worked even harder to win support for South Africa's Indians, not only from every member of India's National Congress but also from colleagues on the Viceroy's Legislative Council, including Jinnah, who was at this time still a leader of Congress. "Surrender-not" Banerjea also cabled his "warmest sympathy" from Calcutta, as did William Wedderburn from London. Gandhi's valiant efforts thus were applauded by the best and most principled leaders of three continents by the fall of 1907. Nonetheless, some Indians were registering in Johannesburg; Gandhi cautioned his pickets not to assault them, for any such assaults would "turn our success into failure."[57]

The first Indian to be prosecuted in the Transvaal under the new act was Hindu "priest" Ram Sundar Pundit, arrested in Germiston on November 8, 1907. Gandhi appeared on Ram's behalf in court, but offered no defense, since his client admitted he had no permit and wished to offer no bail, though "scores of Indians had offered to bail him out."[58] Thanks to Gandhi's appeal Ram was released without bail. Ram was later sentenced to one month imprisonment under the Asiatic Act. Mass protest meetings were held, and Gandhi addressed them. "If, after sending Pundit to gaol, any Indian submits to the obnoxious law, we do not think he deserves the name of man. . . . Hindus and Muslims have become completely united . . . this work concerns all Indians," Gandhi wrote for *Indian Opinion* that November.[59]

Gandhi was arrested and first tried on December 28, 1907, in Johannesburg's Criminal Court. Accused and found guilty of having no "registration certificate,"[60] he was ordered to leave the colony within forty-eight hours. He refused to obey, however, and on January 10, 1908, was called back to court, where he was to be sentenced to prison, together with several other leaders of the community. He was now charged with contempt of court for having disobeyed the order to leave and sentenced to "two months' imprisonment without hard labour."[61] The police led him off to a prison cell and shut the door.

His first incarceration distressed him more deeply than he had imagined it would. "I was somewhat agitated and fell into deep thought. Home, the Courts where I practiced, the public meeting—all these passed away like a dream. . . . Would I have to serve the full term? If the people courted imprisonment in large numbers . . . there would be no question of serving the full sentences. But if they failed . . . two months would be as tedious as an age. . . . How vain I was! I, who had asked the people to consider the prisons as His Majesty's hotels . . . and the sacrifice of one's . . . life itself. . . as supreme enjoyment! Where had all this knowledge vanished today?"[62]

Passive resistance was the English term generally used for the struggle that Gandhi first launched in South Africa. He wanted to find an Indian word for it, however, and invited suggestions through *Indian Opinion*, finally receiving the one he liked best from his own cousin, Maganlal Gandhi, a Sanskrit compound of *Satya*, meaning "truth," and *agraha*, meaning "hold fast to." *Satyagraha*, "Hold fast to the Truth," could alternately be rendered "Truth-force," and since Gandhi equated Truth with "Love" (*Ahimsa*), which literally meant "Non-violence," it might also be called "The force of Love." "Such is the miraculous power of *satya agraha*," he wrote on the eve of going to prison. "I seem to hear it whispered in my ear that God is always the friend and protector of truth. Our success in bringing this campaign to this stage is a triumph for truth."[63] But his struggle had only just begun.

8

Victory through Suffering

FTER LITTLE MORE than two weeks in jail, Gandhi, and friends
arrested with him, agreed to the "voluntary registration" of the entire Indian community of Transvaal, if General Smuts would agree
to withdraw the Asiatic Registration Act, with its element of "compulsion."[1] To Gandhi's way of thinking the dishonor in the act lay in its en-
forcement by the government, not in the issuing of permits, nor even in taking fingerprints, a point that many members of the community would
continue, however, to consider obnoxious.

"The substance of the proposed settlement was that the Indians should
register voluntarily, and not under any law," Gandhi explained. On January 30, 1908, the superintendent of police took him to meet General Smuts.
They had a good talk, Smuts congratulating him on the Indian community's having "remained firm" even after Gandhi's imprisonment.[2]
Gandhi then caught the next train back to Johannesburg and went directly
to inform his friends of the agreement, suggesting that a meeting should be
called. It was held on the grounds of the mosque that very night and despite
the short notice nearly a thousand Indians turned up.

Not everyone attending that meeting, however, was pleased with what
Gandhi reported. Though all were surprised to find him a free man again
and hear that he had spoken with General Smuts, skeptics doubted if they
could take the general at his word. Some posed even harsher questions,
asking if Gandhi had been "paid" anything by Smuts to "change" his
mind. "We have heard that you have betrayed the community and sold it to
General Smuts for 15,000 pounds," one giant Pathan in his audience
shouted. "I swear with Allah as my witness, that I will kill the man who

takes the lead in applying for registration," another charged.[3] It was the first but would not be the last time that some of Gandhi's followers doubted his integrity.

Gandhi never hesitated to reverse his position, particularly if he learned that his followers used violent tactics or sensed that his opponent underwent an honest change of heart, as he now believed true of Smuts. To those who feared treachery, Gandhi argued "A Satyagrahi bids good-bye to fear. He is therefore never afraid of trusting the opponent . . . for an implicit trust in human nature is the very essence of his creed."[4] Nor did he pay heed to threats.

"It is God in whom I placed my trust while launching on this struggle," he softly explained; "it is He who has given us this unexpected victory, and it is Him therefore that we must give our thanks."[5] Undeterred, he left for the Permit Office the next morning, resolved to be the first to register voluntarily, as he had promised Smuts. Gandhi found a tall powerful Pathan waiting at his own Satyagraha office to follow him toward the Permit Office that morning. Before they reached the registration office, the man knocked Gandhi to the ground with a series of heavy blows, the "words *He Rama* (O God!)" on Gandhi's lips.[6] Forty years, less one day, later he would utter that same cry again, after three bullets pierced his heart. This time he sustained only scalp wounds and bruised ribs. He pressed no charges against the arrested Pathan but reiterated his faith in Smuts, insisting that "it is the sacred duty of every good Indian to help the Government and the Colony to the uttermost."[7]

Gandhi recuperated from his beating in the home of Johannesburg's Baptist minister, the Reverend Joseph J. Doke, and his wife, who cared for their friend for weeks. "Those who have committed the act did not know what they were doing," Gandhi wrote in February. "I request that no steps be taken against them. Seeing that the assault was committed by a Mahomedan . . . Hindus might probably feel hurt. . . . Rather let the blood spilt today cement the two communities indissolubly—such is my heartfelt prayer."[8]

Many Transvaal Indians were confused when Gandhi told them they had won a "victory," viewing it instead as a defeat. He wrote at length trying to explain the deep and basic differences between voluntary and compulsory behavior. In expounding the "Secret of Satyagraha," Gandhi quoted Henry David Thoreau's arguments in his "Duty of Civil Disobedience."[9] He also referred again to Luther, thanks to whom "Germany enjoys freedom." And "there was Galileo who opposed society," and Columbus, who "acted like a true satyagrahi" when threatened with death by his sailors, who wanted to turn their ship back, saying: "I am not afraid of being killed, but I think we ought to go on." Deriving his inspiration from many heroic figures, Gandhi went on to explain, "Satyagraha is really an attitude of mind. . . . He who has attained [it] . . . will remain ever victorious . . . irrespective of whether it is a government or a people that he opposed, whether they be strangers friends or relatives."[10] Had he not recently waged and won such battles, after all, with Lakshmidas, Harilal, and Kasturba, as well as with Sheikh Mehtab and Smuts, and the "Devil within" himself?

Though Gandhi tried his best to gloss over the growing Hindu-Muslim conflict and communal mistrust among South African Indians, the problem became so serious before the end of February 1908 that he felt obliged to write a letter to *Indian Opinion* explaining that, though Hindus stood with him in implementing the compromise, Muslims wrote "condemnatory letters." The founder-president of the Hamidiya Islamic Society, Haji Ally, who had accompanied him to England, was foremost among those who no longer fully trusted him, "because I was a Hindu," Gandhi sadly reported. Ally cabled his concerns about Gandhi to Privy Council Muslim member, Syed Ameer Ali, whom he had met in London, expressing his mistrust of Gandhi and his own opposition to Satyagraha. Ally's fear was that Gandhi's boycott would "ruin thousands" of Muslim merchants, like himself, without harming any South African Hindus, all of whom were "hawkers" and peddlers.[11] Ally's fears were not unfounded: he lost so much of his once prosperous trade that he moved back to India just before Satyagraha started. The Pathans eventually sent a telegram complaining of Muslim fears to Jinnah, which Gandhi considered a most regrettable sign of weakness. It was the first time anyone ever told Jinnah of Gandhi's "Hindu" bias, but for most of the rest of his life he would accuse Gandhi of precisely such bias and "anti-Muslim prejudice."

When Gandhi recovered enough to travel again, he took a train to Durban in order to explain the agreement he had reached with Smuts to the troubled Indian community of Natal. Once again he was almost killed by an angry Pathan, armed "with a big stick." Luckily, he was surrounded by volunteers and escaped without injury. He had felt no fear, passionately noting that "nothing better can happen to a Satyagrahi than meeting death all unsought in the very act of . . . pursuing Truth."[12]

Three months after Gandhi's agreement with Smuts, however, he felt "betrayed." Gandhi believed Smuts had promised faithfully to repeal the "Black Act" as soon as most Indians registered themselves voluntarily. In late May, however, with more than 7,000 of 9,000 Indians having completed voluntary registration, Smuts warned that after June 9 all unregistered "Asiatics" would be subject to enforced registration under the old act or be expelled immediately. Asked why he had trusted Smuts, Gandhi now replied, "That is how political affairs always have been and will be conducted. . . . General Smuts' falsehood will prove unavailing."[13] He called upon his community to prepare again for Satyagraha. In the interim, he wrote as many people as possible, giving interviews to every reporter willing to listen to him. Ever willing to discuss matters with his adversary, he also returned to Smuts but found him "obstinate" and called him "dishonest." In late June, Smuts offered to repeal the obnoxious act, but only "on certain conditions," which Gandhi deemed "unacceptable."[14] The community united behind Gandhi's adamant position, and Indians started going back to prison, after brief courtroom appearances, where Gandhi represented them and requested that they be sentenced to maximum punishment at "hard labour." Satyagrahis, he argued, must always welcome the harshest punishment, never plead for leniency.

Among those Indians jailed in late July of 1908 was his son Harilal, then living in South Africa and for this period at least willing to follow in his father's footsteps. Gandhi requested "a severe sentence" for his son and co-accused, arguing that "it would be better for the sake of their health if they had a sustained term."[15] The magistrate sentenced Harilal to just seven days at hard labor. In response to inquiries as to why he sent his son to jail, Gandhi explained: "It will be a part of Harilal's education. . . . every Indian, whatever his status, must go to gaol for the sake of his country."[16]

"In every great war, more than one battle has to be fought," Gandhi informed his community. "The same is true of the Transvaal Indians' satyagraha. . . . General Smuts has now provided the opportunity to complete what was prematurely abandoned. . . . Those who were angry with the leaders for having prematurely called off the campaign have now an opportunity . . . to lay down their lives for the sake of the honour and rights of Indians. . . . [B]rave Indians, arise . . . draw the sword of satyagraha and fight unto victory! . . . The people of the East will never, never again submit to insult from the insolent whites."[17]

Tilak's "New party" of revolutionary nationalism, born with the partition of Bengal, had gained popularity throughout India by this time. Breaking away from the moderate old Congress party, the New party advocated the use of "amulets" like bombs and pistols, as well as the boycott of all things British, in their race toward the goal of *Swaraj*, or "Self-rule." But Gandhi cautioned against the illusion of ends won by violent means. "Real swarajya consists in restraint," he wrote. "Many people exult at the explosion of bombs. This only shows ignorance. . . . If all the British were to be killed, those who kill them would become the masters of India, and . . . India would continue in a state of slavery. The bombs with which the British will have been killed will fall on India after the British leave."[18] He thus rejected violence in all its forms, even as he did the accumulation of gold and silver with its glittery allures.

"Let it be remembered that western civilization is only a hundred years old," he cautioned. "We pray that India may never be reduced to the same state as Europe. The western nations are impatient to fall upon one another. . . . When [that] flares up, we will witness a veritable hell let loose in Europe." Six years before the outbreak of World War I, from distant South Africa, the budding Mahatma shuddered at the thought of such "hell" waiting to be "let loose."

By mid-August of 1908, with some sixty Indians in Johannesburg jail, Gandhi wrote Smuts, urging him to repeal the Asiatic Act at once or face the consequences of a mass Satyagraha against it. Two days later he addressed a meeting of his community, advising all assembled there to burn the identification certificates they currently held, explaining that he had not "come out of the gaol before my time was up . . . to avoid any hardships." He would rather spend his whole life behind bars, than see Indians "subjected to indignity."[19] Hundreds of certificates were burned that day, and a week later at a larger meeting 525 more individuals cheerfully burned their Asiatic identification cards. "I do declare that our fight, my fight," Gandhi thundered, "has always been for a principle. . . . General Smuts has been saying that we claim partnership. We do. . . . I claim it now, but I claim it as a younger brother. Their Christianity teaches them that every human being is a brother. The British Constitution teaches us, it taught me when yet a child, that every British subject was to be treated on footing of equality in the eye of the law, and I do demand that equality."[20] By thus taking his stand atop pillars of Christian brotherhood and British equality under the law, Gandhi reminded Smuts and the entire British establishment of their most cherished ideals, challenging his adversaries to live up to principles they themselves professed.

The "coming struggle," Gandhi anticipated, would be "a bitter and extended one." Though 2,300 Indians burned their certificates by the end of August, Gandhi had hoped for at least twice that number. But some Indians were "secretly" applying for certificates in Johannesburg and elsewhere, while others were being sentenced to months at hard labor in the Transvaal. Gandhi himself was locked up in Volksrust jail in October of 1908. From his cell he sent a message, lauding "passive resistance" and passionately arguing that "suffering is our only remedy. Victory is certain."[21]

Kasturba fell so dangerously ill three weeks after he was jailed that the government offered to release him to go to her bedside. But Gandhi refused, writing his wife a rare letter in Gujarati, which was read to her by their nephew. "I am very much grieved but I am not in a position to go there to nurse you. I have offered my all to the satyagraha struggle. . . . If you keep courage and take the necessary nutrition, you will recover. If, however, my ill luck so has it that you pass away, . . . there would be nothing wrong in your doing so. . . . I love you so dearly that even if you are dead, you will be alive to me. . . . I will not marry again."[22] Kasturba survived and Gandhi was released from prison on December 12, 1908. The next day he addressed Johannesburg's Islamic Society: "We have won because of the suffering of our people. A community, 1,500 members of which have been to gaol, must certainly be considered . . . victorious. . . . The echoes of this campaign have already been heard in India and in the rest of the world."[23] He left for Natal on Christmas Day and was at Kasturba's bedside on December 26. Four days later Harilal was rearrested, and five more Indians joined him on New Year's Eve.

Gokhale and Pherozeshah Mehta convinced Congress to pass a resolution denouncing the "harsh" and "cruel treatment" of British Indians in the Transvaal. Gandhi now wrote of the "third phase" of the Transvaal struggle, reminding the readers of *Indian Opinion* that to climb "the last steps" was always hardest. "The main object of this fight is that we should learn to be men, to be a nation, to cease being the goats that we are and be lions, and to show the world that we are one people . . . children of India ready to lay down our lives for her."[24] It marked a most significant change in Gandhi's goal: no longer did he urge Indians to prove how they could be proper Englishmen; instead he focused on rallying them to become brave, united Indian lions.

To help build national pride, Gandhi now stressed the importance of using Indian languages only when Indians wrote or spoke among themselves. "Any nation that cherishes its individuality must love its own language and feel proud of it," he wrote in Gujarati. "The learning of English must come second to learning one's mother tongue."[25] A few years later when Gokhale visited South Africa at Gandhi's behest, Gandhi insisted he address the community only in Marathi, Gokhale's mother tongue. Gokhale tried in vain to persuade Gandhi to permit him to speak in English, the language he knew best, but finally gave up in frustration, muttering, "You will have your own way in this—as in everything." Virtually no South African Indians had come from Maharashtra, so Gandhi translated whatever Gokhale said into Gujarati, understood by every Indian merchant who attended en masse the meetings Gokhale addressed.

Before the end of February 1909, Gandhi was sentenced again to three months in prison, going cheerfully, repeating Thoreau's admonition that in a tyrannical state the only appropriate place for a free man was prison. He was arrested along with Henry Polak and taken first to Volksrust, but transferred a week later to Pretoria Central Gaol. On March 10 he was brought to court in handcuffs, looking "thin and unhealthy." The Reverend Doke protested the manacles and felt "ashamed . . . that a man of the character and position of Mr. Gandhi should be . . . insulted in this way."[26] Gandhi was released on May 24 and addressed a meeting that day at Pretoria's mosque: "He who has tasted the sweetness of gaol life will never shrink from it. . . . I find no happiness outside gaol. While in gaol, I could devote myself regularly to prayers."[27]

Gandhi was now hailed in Johannesburg as "King of the Hindus and

Muslims." He insisted, however, "That is not right. I am a servant of the community, not its king. I pray to God to grant me the strength . . . to lay down my life in the very act of serving."[28] He was so overwhelmed with emotion as he uttered those words that he could not continue for several moments, but then regained his voice. "If any Indian talks of defeat, that will mean that he himself is defeated. If a person going to gaol is firm in his resolve, he is ever victorious." The internal transformation of Gandhi that had begun more than three years earlier was now fully realized. The British barrister emerging from prison in iron cuffs had been reborn as the passionate leader of his community, not as their king but in an even more exalted role in the eyes of millions of Hindus who were soon to worship him as Mahatma.

A satyagrahi gives "no thought to his body," the transformed Gandhi explained. "Fear cannot touch him at all. That is why he does not arm himself with any material weapons." In his constant "pursuit of truth," a satyagrahi "must be indifferent to wealth," Gandhi argued, though "this does not mean that a satyagrahi can have no wealth. Money is welcome if one can have it consistently with one's pursuit of truth."[29] A satyagrahi would be obliged, moreover, to break free of family attachments, walking alone on the edge of truth's sharp sword, indifferent to any temptations, fear, or tyranny, single-pointedly focused on his faith in God. "If we learn the use of the weapon of satyagraha, we can employ it to overcome all hardships originating from injustice . . . not here alone . . . more so in our home-country."[30]

The universal efficacy of Gandhi's spiritually inspired method of non-violent struggle against any form of injustice was thus for the first time clearly articulated by its remarkable author. He had not only transformed himself through the soul-tempering fires of suffering and hardship but had turned his particular grievance over the "Black Act" from a struggle launched on behalf of his tiny community in the Transvaal and Natal into a mighty message. It became a torch destined to light countless paths to freedom for millions suffering from discrimination and oppression, whether perpetrated by imperial or provincial tyrannies, in every dark corner of the earth.

Gandhi was appointed to lead another Indian deputation to London in mid-June and he reached Southampton on July 10, 1909. Tragically, shortly before Gandhi arrived, Lord Morley's political aide-de-camp, Lieutenant Colonel Sir William Curzon-Wyllie was assassinated by a Punjabi student terrorist. Recalled as a singularly "kind, genial, unselfish, and helpful creature," Curzon-Wyllie was known for his "sympathy for all things Indian."[31] From his Westminster Palace Hotel, Gandhi wrote to Henry Polak of the "terrible tragedy about Sir Curzon Wyllie," which "complicates the situation here."[32] Lord Ampthill agreed to assist Gandhi, but only after being reassured that South Africa's Indians had neither any connection with nor sympathy for India's extremist party, to which the assassin belonged. Gandhi wrote again as exhaustively as possible on the history of his community's struggle and met with everyone willing to see him, answering all questions and granting interviews to all reporters.

Gandhi sought a meeting with Colonial Secretary of State Lord Crewe, but to his disgust, he was not immediately welcomed. He no longer had the patience or optimism that had energized his first deputation to London. "Those who occupy positions of power show little inclination to do justice. Their only concern is to hold on. . . . I think it will be far better to submit to still further suffering than exhaust ourselves in such efforts and waste so much money. . . . Suffering is bound to bring redress."[33] He had lost most of his faith in the old liberal-moderate methods of political petitions sent up to viceroys, secretaries of state, and prime ministers by the Gokhales and Mehtas of Congress. Though he rejected Tilak's violent speech and all terrorist action, Gandhi, on the eve of his fortieth year, preferred incarceration and passionate suffering to polite pleas in a language attuned to the eyes and ears of British barristers. He feared nothing, but was weary of waiting for justice long overdue.

His most important interview on this visit was with Lord Morley, then in his final year at the helm of the India Office in Whitehall. Morley listened carefully and, as Gandhi reported soon after their meeting in late July, "promised to help." Still Gandhi urged his friends in South Africa to "fill the gaols," insisting that "no force in the world can compare with soul force, that is to say, with satyagraha."[34] Smuts was in London at this same time, working out the details of South African integration into a union, over which he would soon preside. Lord Ampthill did his best to bring Smuts round to accepting Gandhi's position, as did Sir Muncherji, who also met with Gandhi. While in London, Gandhi attended a "great" suffragette rally at the end of July and met Mrs. Emmeline Pankhurst. "We have a great deal to learn from these ladies and their movement," he wrote Polak, enclosing Mrs. Pankhurst's *Votes for Women* and other pamphlets sent on to Phoenix. In his next Gujarati article for *Indian Opinion*, Gandhi quoted suffragette Mrs. Pethick-Lawrence, who said there could be "no building for progress unless . . . some men do the building with their blood."[35]

"These words should be pondered . . . by every lover of India. If we want freedom, we shall not gain it by killing or injuring others but by dying or submitting ourselves to suffering. The Transvaal struggle is for the defence of our honour . . . for freedom. To lay down one's life to achieve this is as good as remaining alive. To go on living without it is no better than being dead."[36] It was more than three decades before he would launch his last great Satyagraha campaign, the "Quit India" movement in 1942, whose mantra, *Karega ya marega*! meant "Do or die!" Yet for Gandhi, as early as mid-1909, the only honorable alternative to Indian freedom, whether in the Transvaal or in India, was death.

To Gandhi's mind, London had lost most of its earlier appeal. As he wrote to son Manilal in August: "The more I observe things here, the more I feel that there is no reason to believe that this place is particularly suited to any type of better education. I also see that some of the education imparted here is faulty."37 Not that he was against allowing his boys to visit London "for a while," but he felt more certain of the value of educating them himself or through teachers living at his ashram. His ideas about marriage and sex also hardened. He felt strongly opposed to any early marriage and wrote, "I believe very few Indians need marry at the present time. . . . A person who marries in order to satisfy his carnal desire is lower than even the beast. For the married, it is considered proper to have sexual intercourse only for having progeny. The scriptures also say so." It is not clear which scriptures he had in mind, though they were probably Catholic, and certainly not Hindu or Dharmashastra, or the more ancient Vedic Aryan texts.

He went on to warn his son against procreation as well as marriage, arguing: "All the progeny . . . born now are mean and faithless and continue to be so. Do not . . . think that I want to bind you not to marry even after the age of 25 [Manilal was eighteen]. I do not want to put undue pressure on you or on anyone. . . . I just want to give you advice . . . though you are but a child." He continued to think both of Harilal and Manilal as children, despite their maturation, plagued as he was by feelings of guilt over his "carnal lust" that led to the birth of both older sons. Harilal had already married and fathered a daughter, for which Gandhi viewed him as "mean and faithless." Even from the distance of London, he attempted to "save" Manilal from a similar "fall."

Regrettably, despite his saintly goodness and brilliance, Gandhi never managed to probe the dark roots of his irrational Puritanism, which haunted and obsessed him until the end of his life. That it poisoned his relations with at least one of his loving sons is certain. He never congratulated any relatives on the birth of a child. To his nephew Chhaganlal's wife Kashi, who had just given birth to a daughter, Gandhi wrote from London: "What shall I write . . .? If I say that is good, it would be a lie. If I express sorrow, it would be violence. . . . I would only say and wish that you learn to control your senses."38

Gandhi's growing disillusionment with London and Western civilization reached its peak soon after Louis Bleriot completed the first flight from France over the English Channel and American Dr. Frederick Cook claimed he had reached the North Pole, a claim refuted by Admiral Peary. While the world applauded, Gandhi remained unimpressed. "I have grown disillusioned with Western civilization. The people whom you meet on the way seem half-crazy. They spend their days in luxury or in making a bare living and retire at night thoroughly exhausted. . . . I cannot understand when they can devote themselves to prayers. Suppose Dr. Cook has, in fact, been to the North Pole, what then? People will not, on that account, get the slightest relief from their sufferings. While Western civilization is still young, we find things have come to such a pass that, unless its whole machinery is thrown overboard, people will destroy themselves like so many moths."[39] Gandhi's negative assessment of Western civilization would never change, and though he continued to travel by train and ship, he would never fly and always abhorred the pollution and violence of urban industrial machinery.

Smuts refused to yield to Gandhi's demands and Crewe refused to do more to pressure his colonial colleague than to suggest that he consider the Indian arguments more sympathetically. To Gandhi's mind, therefore, this mission had yielded precious little at a very high price in sterling and time. On the eve of Gandhi's departure on November 12, the Reverend F. B. Meyer hosted a farewell dinner at his Westminster Palace Hotel, to which, among others, Motilal Nehru came, having visited with his twenty-year-old son, Jawaharlal, who had just completed his studies at Harrow School and was now enrolled at Trinity College, Cambridge. Gandhi thanked the Reverend Meyer and all who came to cheer him along, informing them that as long as he was alive he would continue the "passive resistance" struggle for equality and partnership in the Empire. The meeting then expressed "earnest sympathy with the Transvaal British Indians in their peaceful and selfless struggle for civic rights."[40]

The deputation left for South Africa on November 13 and reached Johannesburg on December 2, 1909. Those weeks at sea proved to be one of Gandhi's most fruitful fortnights, for he wrote his first major book, *Hind Swaraj* ("Indian Home Rule"). Written in Gujarati, the book was published that year in two issues of *Indian Opinion* and was translated into English for publication as a book early in 1910. As with many Gujarati works and ancient Indian philosophic expositions, Gandhi wrote his first opus as a dialogue between himself, the "Editor," and a constantly questioning "Reader." He modestly disclaims any originality for his brilliant work, attributing its inspiration to Tolstoy, whose life and book, *The Kingdom of God Is Within You,* profoundly impressed him, and to Ruskin, Thoreau, and Emerson. However, his critique of Western civilization and British rule in India was original enough to lead to the book's immediate seizure by British Indian authorities. Gandhi later noted: "To me, the seizure constitutes further condemnation of the civilisation represented by the British Government. . . . The British Government in India constitutes a struggle between the Modern Civilisation, which is the Kingdom of Satan, and the Ancient Civilisation, which is the Kingdom of God. The one is the God of War, the other is the God of Love."[41]

Victory through Suffering

The "Reader" of the *Hind Swaraj* dialogue asks why, if civilization is such a disease, the English afflicted with it have been able to conquer India? To which Gandhi's wise Editor answers: "The English have not taken India; we have given it to them. . . . Who was tempted at the sight of their silver? Who bought their goods? . . . In order to become rich . . . we welcomed the Company's officers with open arms. . . . The sword is entirely useless for holding India. We alone keep them. . . . [W]e keep the English in India for our base self-interest. We like their commerce; they please us by their subtle methods. . . . We further strengthen their hold by quarrelling amongst ourselves."[42]

One question the Reader asked, however, was not easily answered by the otherwise self-assured Editor. "How can they be one nation? Hindus and Mahomedans are old enemies. Our very proverbs prove it. Mahomedans turn to the West for worship, whilst Hindus turn to the East. . . . Hindus worship the cow, the Mahomedans kill her. . . . How can India be one nation?" "India cannot cease to be one nation because people belonging to different religions live in it," Gandhi's optimistic Editor replied. "If the Hindus believe that India should be peopled only by Hindus, they are living in [a] dreamland." He insisted that the enmity between Hindus and Mahomedans had ceased long before the British arrived. The British, he argued, stimulated communal conflicts to help them "divide and rule" over all the peoples of India. Those were, however, hardly adequate answers to questions that would echo much louder each subsequent decade, eventually rising in crescendos of hate-inspired pain that reverberated forty years later in the prelude to and aftermath of partition.

Gandhi finished his book before he stepped ashore in Johannesburg, and three days later addressed a meeting of 1,500 Indians in the great Mosque. Their "life and death" struggle, he argued was "on behalf of the whole of India, indeed, on behalf of the whole Empire."[43] The mass meeting resolved to "carry on the struggle by means of self-suffering in the shape of imprisonment and otherwise." The next day Gandhi cabled Gokhale, who had sent him a gift of 25,000 rupees from India's richest Parsi industrialist Ratanji Jamsetji Tata, thanking him and reporting that he expected "imprisonment" before month's end. Much to his own surprise, however, he was not arrested on December 22, when he entered Transvaal from Natal with Manilal and several others. Clearly having learned while in London how many friends Gandhi had in the highest as well as lowliest of places and how potent an appeal his passive prison martyrdom made upon the conscience of the world, Smuts ignored Gandhi's return.

Having steeled himself in preparation for returning to the prison "Palace" with his son Manilal, Gandhi was disappointed. Instead, he found himself welcomed and his newspaper bolstered by adulation and financial support. For the first time since starting *Indian Opinion*, he was free of debt; and for the first time since its founding, his Phoenix ashram was functioning without major personnel or financial problems. Despite his resolve repeatedly to defy the Transvaal Act, he was, moreover, still a totally free man, allowed to come and go across the borders of Natal and the Transvaal with impunity. The angst or ennui of success, the discontent induced by newfound safety, plagued and disturbed him. How could such affluence and security of "modern life" be *right*, after all?

In March 1910 Gandhi led a "respectable number" of passive resisters into the Transvaal. The government again disappointed them, however, refusing to arrest anyone. This "non-arrest . . . means a great deal of waste of money and energy to the Indian community," *Indian Opinion* reported: "The Transvaal Government intend to exhaust our resources. . . . we must be prepared to meet them . . . undaunted."[44]

On June 1, 1910, the Union of South Africa was born, integrating the Transvaal, Natal, Orange Free State, and Cape of Good Hope, and administered from Pretoria, its Union parliament meeting over a thousand miles south in Cape Town. Louis Botha was elected first prime minister of the Union, retaining nominal premier power until his death in 1919. Smuts, who succeeded him, was, however, the major architect behind the creation of the Union and remained its guiding political force.

In March 1911 Smuts piloted a new bill through the Cape Parliament that repealed the hated Asiatic Act of 1907. Though Gandhi asked several questions about the new bill's convoluted legalisms, he recognized, as he wrote Maganlal that "the struggle will definitely come to an end."[45] Gandhi believed throughout most of 1911 that Smuts would convince the Union Parliament, when it next met, to delete all discriminatory measures against Asiatics and thus avert further Satyagraha suffering. "Theirs alone is victory who follow truth and religion," he assured friends. "A great campaign such as this could not have been waged without faith in God."[46] But Smuts also believed God was on his side, and most South African whites still despised Indians and referred to them as "coolies." In February of 1912 when Smuts's new Asiatic Immigration Bill went through Parliament on its first reading, Gandhi considered it "more an Asiatic Expulsion Bill," preparing himself and his community for renewed Satyagraha. Gandhi kept his political guru Gokhale informed of his plan to launch a new protest movement. Gokhale tried to defuse that confrontation by stopping off in South Africa for a brief stay on his way home from England. Gokhale reached Cape Town on October 22, 1912, and was welcomed by Gandhi, who hailed selfless Gokhale's "life's work." Harry Hands, the mayor of Cape Town, presided over the welcoming reception. The banquet given for Gokhale at Kimberley four days later was the first recorded occasion when Indians and Europeans dined together. With Gokhale's arrival, moreover, much-needed rains finally came to South Africa, convincing "superstitious Indians" of his remarkable powers. Gandhi cautioned all who gathered at these meetings, however, against expecting too much of Gokhale's visit. Though briefly up-lifted, South Africa's Indians knew after Gokhale departed that they faced continued discrimination and a long, painful struggle.

On April 27, 1913, a mass meeting was held at Vrededorp, near Jo-hannesburg, at which Gandhi explained why the new immigration bill must be resisted with Satyagraha. Those gathered resolved to do so, and all were prepared for further suffering, including incarceration. Gokhale now returned to London, trying to solicit support from the imperial government to assist Gandhi in his struggle against the Union, inviting Gandhi to join him there. By July, however, the battle lines were sharply drawn. Nearly a hundred Indians were in jail by late October, and Gandhi himself was ar-rested on November 7, 1913, near Palmford, released on bail, and rear-rested the next day at Standerton. He was charged with "aiding . . . pro-hibited persons to enter the Transvaal." He had arrived with some 2,000 passive resisters, eighty-five of whom were Indian miners. He was released again on £50 bail and "motored to rejoin the marchers." Gandhi caught up with the "Great March" a little beyond General Botha's farm. They cheered him on and saluted, calling out *"Bapu"* as he passed.[47] Arrested for the third time that week, Gandhi was taken to Dundee Gaol, before which he announced: "We have reached the limit now. The courage that the in-dentured labourers have shown and the suffering they have gone through have been boundless. . . . Women have walked in the heat of the noon . . . bags in arms and bundles on head. . . . To what end? For India. Such sac-rifice will no doubt result in repeal of the £3 tax but what is more, it will enhance India's prestige."[48]

At Dundee, Gandhi, found guilty of advising Indians "to strike" and "deliberate contravention of the law," was sentenced to fines of £60 or nine months' imprisonment at "hard labour." Gandhi announced in a "clear and calm voice" that "I elect to go to gaol."[49] Three days later he was brought to trial on his initial arrest at Volksrust and sentenced to three more months. A month later he was released, and a special commission was appointed to consider the Indian question. He was not thankful for his release and told his friends he considered the commission a "fraud," since it was appointed without consulting the Indian community.

Several indentured Indians on the Great March were shot dead by white soldiers, who claimed to do so in self-defense. In the aftermath of his release, therefore, feeling "those bullets" had gone through his own "heart," Gandhi abandoned the barrister's clothing he had worn for the past twenty years and adopted instead the scant simplicity of an indentured laborer's garb, shaving his head and never again reverting to Western dress or tonsure.[50] Gandhi passionately warned his community to prepare them-selves now for "still greater purifying suffering" unless government accepted their demands for appointing Indians to the commission. He set January 1, 1914, as the deadline for acceptance or resumption of do-or-die Satyagraha. On Christmas Eve, Smuts offered to meet with Gandhi, seeking to avert bloodshed. Gandhi agreed to postpone the deadline at Gokhale's cabled request. On New Year's Day of 1914, Gokhale's messengers of peace, the Reverends Charles Freer Andrews and William W. Pearson, arrived in Durban from India. Two years younger than Gandhi, Charlie Andrews was soon to become one of his closest friends and staunchest supporters. Pearson went off to investigate Indian labor problems in Natal's sugar estates, but Charlie stayed with Mohan for a week at his Phoenix ashram.

On January 9, 1914, Gandhi and Andrews journeyed to Pretoria together to meet with Smuts. South Africa was then in the midst of a crippling general strike by English workers, which had taken a high economic toll. If Indian passive resisters would now join them, it could prove devastating to Botha and Smuts. Gandhi was asked if Indians would "join the General Strike" by the editor of the *Pretoria News*, who greeted him outside Smuts's office. "No, certainly not," he replied. "We are out for a clean fight. Passive resistance will be suspended." "May I publish that?" the news editor asked. "No—there is no need to do so," was Gandhi's initial reply. Then the editor asked of Andrews: "Do persuade him, Mr. Andrews. . . . There will be Martial Law within twelve hours."[51] Charlie explained to his friend that he was "Of course . . . right to suspend the struggle . . . but if no one knows till afterwards, all the good effect will be lost." They paced back and forth until Gandhi agreed, and the message of his reasonable cooperation was wired by Reuters to Cape Town as well as to London and India.

In their meeting, General Smuts was "patient and conciliatory," retaining "sympathetic interest in Mr. Gandhi as an unusual type of humanity, whose peculiarities, however inconvenient . . . are not devoid of attraction," a confidential report noted.[52] That document helped explain Gandhi's skills in negotiating with "Europeans." "The workings of his conscience are inscrutable to the occidental mind. . . . His ethical and intellectual attitude, based as it appears to be on a curious compound of mysticism and astuteness, baffles the ordinary processes of thought." Gandhi reached a "provisional agreement" with Smuts on all points of conflict before the end of January. The £3 tax was finally to be repealed, South Africa–born Indians would be allowed to enter freely the Cape and Orange Free State, and several other "rights" would be restored or guaranteed. A mass meeting in Durban unanimously endorsed the agreement as Gandhi reported it to them on January 25, 1914.

Gandhi hoped for a permanent settlement by March, but the process of reconciling minor points of disagreement took longer than anticipated. He was keen to return to India in April of 1914, hoping to take about twenty men, women, and children to live with him. "I do not know whether you still want me to live at the Servants of India quarters in Poona," he wrote Gokhale. "I am entirely in your hands. I want to learn at your feet."[53] Gokhale had invited him, pledging him to one year of "silence," however, upon returning to India, knowing how outspoken his impulsive disciple could be, how unpalatable to older Indians his revolutionary program could sound. "I shall scrupulously observe the compact of silence . . . as I have understood it does not include the South African question and may be broken at your wish for furthering any project about which both of us hold the same view. My present ambition . . . is to be by your side as your nurse and attendant."[54] Since ailing Gokhale was then still in London, Gandhi decided to go there directly from South Africa, planning to return to Poona with his political guru later.

9

The Impact of World War I

GANDHI REACHED London in August of 1914, just a few days after the outbreak of World War I. As did most Londoners, Gandhi also optimistically thought that the war would end in just a few months. He immediately offered, as he had done in South Africa, to raise an Indian Ambulance Corps to serve Britain on the Western Front. Kasturba's health improved dramatically in London, but Gandhi suffered sharp pains in one leg and eventually a total breakdown. However debilitating, it proved fortunate, since it kept him from the murderous front. He took classes in nursing for his first six weeks in London and spent as much time as he could fruitlessly trying to nurse diabetic Gokhale back to health. By mid-September, Gandhi was sick of London, calling it "poison. My soul is in India."[1]

Colonel R. J. Baker was appointed to command Gandhi's medical corps on October first, and two weeks later Gandhi was ready to resign. Baker had appointed the "section leaders" of the corps without consulting him, and since Gandhi was "entirely a cripple," he invited Baker to his room for "a mutual discussion."[2] The colonel refused, however, to call upon Private Gandhi, or to allow *his* corps to "elect" its corporals. "I assure that nothing can be further from my thought than to undermine your proper authority," Gandhi replied, "but if you desire to train us . . . there is no other way than the one I have ventured to suggest . . . and may I say that, by accepting my humble advice, you will add to your popularity and prestige."[3] The colonel, not amused, proved adamant, so Gandhi finally felt obliged to resign from the corps he had raised. By mid-October he started to cough blood and was "under strict medical orders not to leave my bed at least for a fortnight."[4]

By mid-November Gandhi was "longing to go to India," but his health would not permit it. He suffered a relapse at month's end and was still confined to bed in December. Emaciated and weak, at this time fearing the worst, he wrote: "If only we learn to maintain ourselves by agriculture and manual labour, there will be nothing more for us to earn or learn. That is what I too must learn. I may, however, pass away without doing so."[5] At forty-five, having firmly resolved how to live, he feared he would die. A week later, however, he felt strong enough to attend a farewell dinner given for him and [Kastur-]Ba at the Westminster Palace Hotel. He was returning to India, returning home, where he hoped to be "restored to strength."[6]

"Wonderful is the sport of God!" Gandhi wrote Chhaganlal from the S.S. *Arabia* five days later. "I have been able to leave London unexpectedly early. . . . We are both keeping good health. . . . Let us see whether I regain my former strength." Keeping to a diet of banana biscuits and dry fruit soaked in water, they disembarked in Bombay on January 9, 1915, "exceedingly glad to see . . . the dear old Motherland."[7] His health continued to improve and in mid-January he and Ba left Bombay for Rajkot, to visit his family there, whereupon his health went "down very badly." But the cordial receptions he received were heartening, and before month's end he felt strong enough to venture back to Porbandar, calling on his widowed sisters-in-law. He returned to Bombay in February, leaving for Poona on the seventh.

Gandhi reached Gokhale's Servants of India Society in what was then a rural suburb of Poona on the Deccan plateau. He stayed there only for a few days but immediately busied himself by cleaning out and polishing every urinal and night soil pot he could find. Gokhale and his old friend Professor M. R. Jayakar of Poona University were sitting and chatting on the shaded verandah one morning when a troubled sweeper hesitantly approached "Baba Sahib" (Gokhale), saluting and timidly reporting that the "new visitor" had taken away his work, Jayakar recalled. Gokhale angrily shook his head and firmly told the poor fellow to inform Gandhi that he must "stop doing that." Then Jayakar, who had heard others complain about Gandhi's "strange hobbies," asked Gokhale why he put up with him, if he was so troublesome? "He is stubborn and very difficult at times," Gokhale responded, "but one day he will be the leader of our Congress and our nation!"[8]

Less than a week before ailing Gokhale died, Gandhi and Ba left Poona and journeyed across India from Bombay to Bengal, where they joined Maganlal and some fifty South African pilgrims, all of whom went to live at Rabindranath Tagore's rural Santiniketan school. There Gandhi received the cabled news of Gokhale's death.

"We should seek the company of those who have suffered and served," Gandhi told those who gathered to hear his passionate eulogy. "One such was Mr. Gokhale. He is dead, but his work is not dead, for his spirit lives. . . . His last words to those members of the Servants of India Society who were with him were: 'I do not want any memorial or any statue. I want only that men should love their country and serve it with their lives.' This is a message for the whole of India."[9]

Gandhi returned with Kasturba to Poona later that month, hoping to live at the Servants of India Society and to inherit Gokhale's mantle of leadership. But the other members were fearful of his radical ideas and lifestyle. V. S. Srinivasa Sastri, who took charge of the society after Gokhale's death, was a competent administrator but lacked Gandhi's greatness. Instead of welcoming him with open arms, he fearfully drove him from Poona soon after Gandhi returned there. "I am left without shelter through revered Gokhale's death," Gandhi wrote an old friend in March.[10] He was not without funds, however, and soon would start his ashram on the outskirts of Ahmedabad, on the banks of the Sabarmati. But first he journeyed back to Bengal, where, in Calcutta, he had a bitter "misunderstanding" with Harilal, who thereafter "parted from me completely."[11]

In April, Gandhi and Ba went to Hardwar for the great Kumbh Mela celebration there and to pay "respects" to Mahatma Munshiram (later Swami Shraddhanand), who after seeing Gandhi and blessing him, called him "the beacon light of India."[12] From there they proceeded to Madras, where Gandhi was hailed by a welcoming crowd of Tamils, shouting "Long live our hero."[13] At a reception in Madras he spoke reverently of Gokhale as "my *rajya guru*" and that "saintly politician."[14] By May of 1915 he was back in Gujarat, ready to launch his ashram, preparing a detailed list of needs and an estimate of anticipated expenses. "I have understood it to be the desire of the leaders that we should merely experiment for a year in Ahmedabad" he wrote Sheth Girdharlal. "If that is so, Ahmedabad should bear the whole of this burden. . . . As we have now changed the basis, I think Ahmedabad should bear the entire burden for a year."[15] He was always careful about money matters and ever firm in negotiating any contractual agreement. Despite his uniquely developed spirituality and idealism, Gandhi never lost his innate bargaining skills or acquired legal brilliance, using both most effectively when appropriate.

Gandhi's Satyagraha Ashram, as it was first called, was inaugurated at Kochrab, near Ahmedabad, on May 20, 1915. The ashram's constitution, which Gandhi drafted, required all members, including novitiates and students, to take six vows: truth, nonviolence, celibacy, control of the palate, nonstealing, and nonpossession. Three "subsidiary vows" followed from the first six: *Swadeshi*, that is, using clothing made by hand and never wearing or purchasing imported cloth of any kind; fearlessness, keeping all ashramites "free from the fear of kings or society, one's caste or family, thieves, robbers, ferocious animals . . . and even of death";[16] and finally, a vow against untouchability, which Gandhi called "a blot on Hindu religion" and viewed as so dreadful a "sin" that all his ashramites were encouraged to "touch" anyone so designated and to work for "the eradication of the evil of untouchability."

That September, Gandhi admitted his first "untouchable" (*Dhed*) family to the ashram, and Kasturba became so upset at living with Dudabhai, wife of this Gujarati outcast, that she threatened to leave Mohandas. "I have told Mrs. Gandhi she could leave me and we should part good friends," he wrote Srinivasa Sastri. "The step is momentous because it so links me with the suppressed classes mission that I might have at no distant time to carry out the idea of shifting to some *Dhed* quarters and sharing their life. . . . It is of importance to me because it enables me to demonstrate the efficacy of passive resistance in social questions and when I take the final step, it will embrace swaraj [freedom]."[17]

By November of 1915 Gandhi had enlisted thirty-three residents in his busy ashram, three of them *Dheds*. Ahmedabad's upper-caste leaders were so outraged by his embrace of that hitherto untouchable family that they threatened to declare the entire ashram "outcast."[18] Gandhi was undeterred.

That December, Gandhi attended the thirtieth annual meeting of India's National Congress in Bombay. He also attended the Muslim League meeting in Bombay and in early February 1916 spoke at the gala inauguration of Banaras Hindu University, at which Annie Besant, president of the Theosophical Society, also spoke. "Friends, under the influence of the matchless eloquence of [Mrs. Besant]," Gandhi said following her address, "pray, do not believe that our University has become a finished product. . . . It is a matter of deep humiliation and shame for us that I am compelled this evening under the shadow of this great college, in this sacred city, to address my countrymen in a language that is foreign."[19] After all he had suffered and struggled so valiantly to achieve in South Africa, Gandhi found it impossible to speak without caustic criticism before so many bejeweled maharajas, the princely puppets of British imperial rule, who prided themselves on their English, clad in imported silks and satins. Mrs. Besant squirmed as well in increasingly nervous discomfort on her cushioned chair on the stage behind this homespun-clad bare-legged little man, who spoke so fearlessly and truthfully.

"Congress has passed a resolution about self-government. . . . But . . . no paper contribution will ever give us self-government. . . . It is only our conduct that will fit us for it. (Applause.). . . . His Highness the Maharajah . . . spoke about the poverty of India. Other speakers laid great stress upon it. But what did we witness in the great *pandal* in which the foundation ceremony was performed by the Viceroy? . . . an exhibition of jewellery. . . . I compare it with . . . the millions of the poor. And I feel like saying to these noblemen: 'There is no salvation for India unless you strip yourselves of this jewellery and hold it in trust for your countrymen.'" Shouts of "Hear, hear" came from the student audience, moved to applause each time Gandhi paused for breath. He had found his voice now on Indian soil, in the ancient city most sacred to his Hindu faith, Varanasi (Banaras).

"If we trust and fear God, we shall have to fear no one," Gandhi assured them, teaching his passionate message of "love of the country," and the value of "bravery" and *tapas* to all the bright-eyed young men, who felt uplifted, instantly inspired by his fearless simplicity, his dauntless courage. "I hope I would be prepared to die," Gandhi told them, in defense of India's freedom. "That would, in my opinion, be an honourable death."[20]

At this point Mrs. Besant stood up and shouted at him, "Please stop it." Gandhi turned to face her and the maharaja chairman, saying, "I await your order. If you consider that by my speaking as I am, I am not serving the country and the Empire, I shall certainly stop." Cries of "Go on!" from the student audience encouraged him to continue. "I want to purge India of the atmosphere of suspicion on either side; if we are to reach our goal, we should have an empire which is . . . based upon mutual love and mutual trust . . . much better that we talk these things openly. . . . If we are to receive self-government, we shall have to take it. . . . Learn your lesson if you wish to from the Boer War." Mrs. Besant and the chairman maharaja and all other princes abruptly left the platform, putting an end to the program and Gandhi's passionate revolutionary speech, which his student audience very much enjoyed.

The next day Gandhi informed the ceremony's chairman, the Maharaja of Darbhanga: "My sole object . . . was to express the very strong views I hold against all acts of violence. . . . My mission in life is to preach and assist in securing the utmost freedom for my country but never by violence."[21] The maharaja, however, and all his princely colleagues who had attended the event, expressed "disapproval" of what Gandhi had said. They rightly recognized from his austerely unadorned attire, as well as from his comments regarding their jewels and the needs of India's poor, that their days of lazy luxury would be numbered if ever he came to power. The Banaras "incident," as India's press soon called it, only confirmed Annie Besant's fears about Gandhi's revolutionary fervor. When he reprimanded her for interrupting him and leading all the princes off the platform, she angrily replied: "How could we sit still when you are compromising everyone of us on the platform?"[22]

Gandhi continued to travel around India, speaking everywhere he stopped, unveiling statues and portraits of Gokhale, inaugurating schools, addressing Gujarati merchant societies from Madras to Karachi. His

thoughts about the sins of untouchability evolved at this time, and he forcefully argued that this orthodox Hindu discrimination must stop. "For the
sake of our souls, our own good, must we repent. . . . what is the practical
solution? . . . First, we must clearly realize that we have to attain not their
salvation but ours by treating them as equals, by admitting them to our
schools, etc."[23] He had not as yet coined his brilliant new name for them,
Harijans ("Children of God"), but he insisted on integrating them into all
his ashram families and hoped that when India finally won freedom a Harijan would become its first president. That visionary dream was fulfilled
only after fifty years of independence, when Harijan-born K. R. Narayanan
was elected India's tenth president in 1997.

Gandhi attended the annual Bombay Provincial Conference, held in
Ahmedabad, in late October 1916, and supported the election of Jinnah as
its president. "It has chosen as President a person who holds a respected
position . . . a learned Muslim gentleman. . . . I know the President's job is
like walking on the edge of a sword. . . . I pray to God to grant him the necessary strength, wisdom and ability to guide the work of this conference."[24]
Gandhi spoke in Gujarati but Jinnah understood him very well. Immaculately attired as the successful Lincoln's Inn barrister he was, looking and
sounding far more British than Indian, Jinnah, though seven years younger
than Gandhi, had also been Gokhale's political disciple and two years earlier had led a Congress deputation to Secretary of State Lord Crewe in London. His provincial Congress election and his brilliant success in uniting
Congress and the Muslim League, the biggest Islamic association, over
which he presided, on a joint platform of national demands by year's end
positioned him uniquely as India's candidate to lead the nation to full dominion status after the end of World War I.

That December Gandhi presided over the All-India Common Script
and Common Language Conference, insisting that Hindi should be India's
common language, feeling now that whenever he spoke English, "I am
committing a sin."[25] He also attended the Lucknow Congress and argued
that unless Congress business was conducted in Hindi, rather than English,
Swaraj was not possible. "In provincial matters, the provincial languages
may be used," he conceded. "But national questions ought to be deliber-
ated in the national language only."[26] That change alone would suffice to
eliminate leaders like Jinnah from the national spotlight. Gandhi also attended the Muslim League meeting to move a resolution protesting ill-
treatment of Indians in the colonies, and when President Jinnah called
upon him to speak, Gandhi told him and his followers that they should all
speak only in Urdu. He also urged them to take greater interest in reading
"Hindu literature" and "not be afraid of the Government because it was in
the nature of Englishmen to bow before the strong and ride over the
weak."[27] For Jinnah, who was more of an Englishman than Gandhi had

ever been, the last two bits of gratuitous advice must have sounded singularly offensive.

Gandhi spent most of his time, however, at his ashram. His second son, Manilal, had been living with him at the Sabarmati Ashram, but early in 1917 they argued over Manilal's inability to adhere to all of his vows, so Bapu sent him back to Africa. "It was more painful for me to let you go than it was, perhaps, for you to go," he wrote his twenty-four-year-old son. "But I have often to make my heart harder than steel, for I think that to be in your interest."[28] Soon after a despondent Manilal reached Phoenix he got so sick that he could do no work. So Gandhi wrote again, this time to prescribe "proper treatment for your cough. . . . deep breathing and a teaspoonful of olive oil will suffice. . . . It can be taken . . . mixed with a tomato. If you can give up tea, coffee and cocoa, that will help. . . . Keep up your studies in the way I have shown you. Do not give up doing sums. . . . The same about Sanskrit. . . . It is also necessary to form the habit of reading Gujarati books. . . . All this will be easy if you . . . get over the habit of day-dreaming."

Several indigo laborers and their lawyers had appealed to Gandhi during the Lucknow Congress, begging him to come to Champaran District in what is now Bihar State to help the miserably exploited peasants there, who cultivated the rich blue dye plant indigo in the shadows of the Himalayas. Gandhi decided to undertake the long railway journey east, across most of north India, from Ahmedabad to Champaran, in late March of 1917. He then met the indigo workers and heard their complaints of violent treatment as well as shameless exploitation by brutal indigo planters. He was granted an interview by the Division's Commissioner Barrister L. F. Morshead, who "proceeded to bully me . . . and advised me forthwith to leave."[29] Inured to such treatment, Gandhi wasted no more time with that narrow-minded official.

Soon after leaving Morshead's office, Gandhi wrote to cousin Maganlal: "An order to leave the District has been served upon me and I have refused to obey. . . . It is likely that a warrant of arrest . . . will be served upon me any moment."[30] He was arrested on his way to a village to carry out his interrogation of aggrieved peasants there. "To go to jail here under such circumstances is a great joy to me," he wrote Maganlal again. "It suggests an auspicious outcome." He informed District Magistrate W. B. Heycock that he had no intention of leaving his district or paying any fine. Then from the district magistrate's office he wrote Viceroy Lord Chelmsford's Private Secretary Maffey:

"I have come to this district to learn for myself whether there is truth in the allegations of the ryots [peasants] against the planters." Gandhi explained that his motive was humanitarian national service. The evidence he had been given to examine convinced him that the planters had used "illegal force to enrich themselves at the expense of the ryots."[31] He asked Maffey to place this matter before the viceroy, requesting that he appoint an independent commission of inquiry to investigate this matter.

Thus Gandhi launched his first Satyagraha campaign on Indian soil. Before he could be jailed, however, instructions from the lieutenant governor of Bihar were sent to the district magistrate to release Gandhi and offer him facilities and official assistance in carrying out his investigation. Charlie Andrews and Pearson as well as Henry Polak had all been hard at work, talking to their friends in Calcutta, Allahabad, and Simla, and both Congress and Muslim League leaders were active on his behalf. "The work here is enormous," Gandhi wrote to Mahatma Munshiram, who had just changed his name to Swami Shraddhanand. "Tyranny, by God's grace, will end."[32] He now expected to remain in Champaran for at least four months. Each day he visited indigo workers in their village homes, and he and his assistants recorded their statements about the hard working conditions they were forced to suffer.

What Gandhi soon discovered, of course, was that this exploitation of Indian peasants by planters and large landowners was hardly limited to one district of Bihar. He was not ready, however, to lead a nationwide Satyagraha against rural inequities and violations of law. Adhering to the fixed rule of Satyagraha he had established in South Africa, he never expanded his original goal, focusing his yogic powers instead on the single target he had chosen. "No stone is being left unturned," Gandhi reported, even as he acknowledged his limited goal in doing so.[33] "The desire is, by inviting the Government to deal with the planters firmly, to avoid the publication of a report which is bound to stagger India." But when he turned over those heavy "stones" in Bihar, multiple social problems swiftly emerged—from starving children forced to work all day instead of receiving minimal education, to women suffering every indignity of the poor and helpless, to misshapen men, bent low and disfigured by goiter growths, too timid to complain of the virtual slavery in which they were kept.

The indigo planters did their worst to "quash the mission," intimidating their ryots, warning them not to testify, bullying most, bribing some. Yet they were unable to stop the full revelation released by Gandhi's presence and personal fearlessness. As he had suggested to the viceroy, an independent commission to be chaired by Sir Frank Sly was soon appointed by Lieutenant Governor Sir Edward Gait, who invited Gandhi to be a member. Gandhi naturally agreed to serve, and though physical intimidation, including arson, was used by several of the worst planters to derail the commission's work, the findings were fair, abolishing the system of exploitative "slavery" (*tinkathia* system) that for almost a century had forced ryots to work without compensation for their planter landlords.

"Here, I am being showered with love," Gandhi reported to Maganlal from Bihar.[34] This early adventure in remote, rural Bihar induced Gandhi to return there in the final anguished years of his life, seeking again that shower of love, those glorious highs he experienced in his first victorious struggle, waged in India's epic heartland of Rama and Sita, where the mythical golden age of righteousness, *Ram Rajya* ("Rama's Rule"), was born.

In the summer of 1917, the governor of Madras arrested Annie Besant, who had started her own Home Rule League. The charge against her was sedition, and by arresting her the governor turned her from a nuisance into a martyr and national hero. Shortly after her release, Mrs. Besant was chosen to preside over the annual session of Congress that December. Gandhi's reaction affords a glimpse into his own evolving strategy. In July Gandhi wrote to warn the viceroy that Mrs. Besant's arrest was "a big blunder." He stated, "Many of us have respectfully differed from Mrs. Besant but all have recognised her powers and devotion. . . . I plead with all the earnestness I can command . . . to acknowledge the blunder . . . withdraw the orders of internment and to declare that the country has the right to carry on any propaganda that is . . . totally free from violence." Failure to reverse her internment, Gandhi feared, would result in the spread of a "cult of violence," which, he said, his life was dedicated to preventing. "I have presented to the youths and to Indians in general . . . a better and more effective method and that is the method of soul force or truth force or love force. . . . It involves self-suffering and that alone. . . . No government in the world can afford continually to imprison or molest innocent men."[35]

In a letter to his Danish Christian friend Esther Faering, Gandhi expanded on this argument while answering questions she raised concerning Jesus' nonviolence: "I think the command of Jesus is unequivocal. All killing is bad. . . . He who is filled with pity for the snake and does not fear him will not kill him. . . . This state of innocence is the one we must reach. But only a few can reach it. . . . A nation to be in the right can only fight with soul-force. Such a nation has still to be born. I had hoped that India was that nation. I fear I was wrong. The utmost I expect of India is that she may become a great restraining force."[36]

That August Gandhi met young Mahadev Desai, who was to become his personal secretary and disciple for the next quarter century. "I have found in you just the type of young man for whom I have been searching for the last two years," Gandhi told him, after watching him for three days. "I have spoken like this only to three persons before . . . Mr. Polak, Miss Schlesin, and Shri Maganlal . . . for I have found three outstanding qualities in you. They are regularity, fidelity and intelligence."[37] Thirty-three-year-old Mahadev was so amazed and flattered that he barely knew what to say, whispering that Gandhi had as yet seen nothing he had written or "done." But Gandhi confidently replied that he could "judge people in a very short time." He was, of course, quite right about Desai, who from November of

1917 until his sudden death in 1942 remained Gandhi's trusted secretary and virtual "son," his "right and left hands" as Kasturba emotionally called him when she learned of his death.

After his success in Champaran, Gandhi returned to his Gujarat Ashram, and in November 1917 presided over the first Gujarat Political Conference at Godhra. "Only when men, fired with the belief that service is the highest religion, come forward in great numbers, can we hope to see great results," he told his large audience. "Fortunately, India is richly endowed with the religious spirit, and . . . when sages and saints take up this work, I believe India will achieve her cherished aims."[38]

Recent events gave him cause for sounding optimistic. Annie Besant had just been released from jail, and Morley's protégé at the India Office, the new secretary of state, Edwin Samuel Montagu, was on his way to India for a personal visit to decide how Britain's Cabinet might try to satisfy Indian demands for dominion status after the war. It must be remembered that to British liberals, as to all Indian moderates, Swaraj meant dominion status, not total independence or home rule. A joint Congress-Muslim League deputation, led by Jinnah, with whom Montagu was most impressed, would call upon him and Viceroy Chelmsford. Gandhi also met Montagu, who however, found him too "unworldly" and too ill-clad to take seriously. Gandhi did not, of course, consider Jinnah's Lucknow Pact to be Swaraj, only "a great step towards" it. Yet even the Swaraj that Mrs. Besant and Congress radicals like Tilak talked about was "foreign" to Gandhi, a Western import, replete with a modern army and heavy industry. "I feel that India's mission is different from that of other countries. India is fitted for the religious supremacy of the world [and] has little use for steel weapons," he stated. "Other nations have been votaries of brute force. . . . India can conquer all by soul-force."

At the Gujarat Social Conference, also held in Godhra, Gandhi declaimed most forcefully against the "sin," the "great crime," as he called it, of untouchability. "The untouchables must not be considered as falling outside Hinduism. . . . This religion, if it can be called such, stinks in my nostrils. . . . I shall put up a lone fight, if need be, against this hypocrisy."[39] He would later launch Satyagraha against untouchability and undertook a fast unto death rather than accepting the idea, insisting that *Harijans* were pure Hindus.

Monetary contributions flowed into Gandhi's Sabarmati Ashram throughout 1917, and in January of 1918, while he was back in Champaran, trying to better educate the peasants there, especially in caring for their cattle, he suddenly thought of how potentially dangerous it might be to keep so much money in his own name. He knew the British government could become vindictive when faced with political challenges to its survival. As he wrote to Maganlal, "Its fury then will be almost unbearable. . . . I mention this to remind you to be careful that in the storm that will follow we do not lose, whether in our wisdom or folly, the money that we have received for the Ashram. . . . there should be nothing in my name, at any place. Keep everything in your name. . . . The amounts that will be transferred to your name will not become your property, but will be treated as donations in aid of our activities."⁴⁰ Gandhi's practical wisdom and economic shrewdness is rarely revealed as clearly as in this letter to his cousin—manager of the ashram. Indeed, in that same letter he comments on the importance of this ashram's focus on its hand loom production of cloth. Wartime inflation had more than doubled the price of cotton cloth in the preceding six months, more than justifying focusing so intently on the value of hand spinning and weaving.

Gandhi now contemplated launching three different Satyagraha struggles: one in the Kheda (or Kaira) district of Gujarat over excessive land revenue demands by the British collector there; another on behalf of the mill hands in Ahmedabad; and a third to convince the viceroy to release two outspoken radical Muslim brothers, Shaukat and Mohamed Ali, jailed for "seditious" writings and soon to be adopted by Gandhi as his own "brothers." Gandhi hoped by his fragile bond of brotherhood with Shaukat and Mohamed Ali to bridge the deep doctrinal differences dividing Hinduism from Islam and forge a single nation, uniting the some 300 million adherents to India's two great religions. But his bridge of brotherhood so carefully constructed with Shaukat and Mohamed collapsed just a few years later, when they both lost faith in him.

Gandhi would have better luck at adopting sons than brothers: in such a spirit did Mahadev Desai join the ashram, as did Vinoba Bhave, "India's Walking Saint."⁴¹ Vinoba had taken the Brahmacharya vow at the age of ten and was a genius at mastering languages as well as his own passions, first conquering Sanskrit and memorizing the *Bhagavad Gita*, then learning a new language every year of his long life by reading the *Gita* in various translations. "A hercules, a Samson!" Gandhi called young Vinoba, who was to remain his most saintly disciple.⁴² "Your love and your character fascinate me," Gandhi wrote Vinoba in February of 1918. Calling him "son," Gandhi went on to state, "In my view a father is, in fact, a father only when he has a son who surpasses him in virtue. . . . This is what you have [done]. . . . May God grant you long life, and use you for the uplift of India."⁴³ Vinobaji devoted his three decades after the assassination of his Mahatma to *Sarvodaya* ("The Uplift of All"), launching a series of socially revolutionary movements across India, from his "Gift of Land" (*Bhoodan*) to "Gift of Life" (*Jivandan*) reforms. His saintly life and the impact of his social reforms remain one of Gandhi's greatest legacies to modern India.

Gandhi thus inspired younger leaders and prepared them for the coming struggle, leaving Kasturba in Champaran to help organize village schools there and distribute medicines to ryots for diseases like malaria. His mind was focused on the Satyagraha about to begin first in Ahmedabad, next in Kheda District.

His compassionate friend and ashram benefactor, Anasuyabehn Sarabhai, the unmarried sister of Ahmedabad millionare mill owner Ambalal Sarabhai, urged him to help her brother's poor employees to earn fairer wages. Those workers, faced with wartime inflation, found it impossible to feed their families adequately, even working full time. "Why should not the mill-owners feel happy paying a little more to the workers?" Gandhi questioned Ambalal in a letter dated December 1917. "There is only one royal road to remove their discontent . . . binding them with the silken thread of love," Gandhi argued, adding that Anasuyabehn's suffering placed her brother "under a double obligation: to please the workers and earn a sister's blessings."[44] Ambalal did not quite see it Gandhi's way, considering him a double "meddler," intruding in his business as well as his family affairs, wishing he would keep his protruding ears and intruding nose out of both.

On February 8, 1918, Gandhi told the workers who wanted an increase in wages from 50 percent to 60 percent not to expect that much "all at once." He advised them to be patient and to wait for an arbitration committee, upon which he agreed to serve, to investigate the matter and propose an appropriate solution to this labor dispute. After addressing their economic concerns, he gave them more personal advice. "Learn to be clean" and get rid of your "various addictions," Gandhi told the workers, urging them to see that their children all got an education.[45] He and two others—one a fellow Gujarati lawyer, Vallabhbhai Patel, who was to become his strongest Satyagraha lieutenant and most devoted political disciple—agreed to serve on the arbitration committee. Comparing the Ahmedabad wages to pay earned by comparable mill workers in Bombay, they concluded that a raise of 35 percent was appropriate. Ambalal and his fellow mill owners disagreed. Offering only 20 percent more, they promptly locked out all their weavers after they rejected that offer as insufficient. The lockout began on February 22, 1918, and continued for twenty-one days. Gandhi spoke daily to all the striking workers, reminding them of their pledges never to resort to violence or seek alms, training them in the techniques of self-suffering essential to waging Satyagraha and the peaceful resolution of any dispute. Addressing them under a giant *babul* tree on the bank of the Sabarmati, he argued, "Workers have no money but they possess a wealth superior to money—they have their hands, their courage and their fear of God."[46]

He taught them how best to busy themselves during the strike, so as not to weaken or turn to harmful habits like gambling or sleeping all day. He urged them to learn cabinetmaking or tailoring, or some subsidiary occupation to help them earn a livelihood, to study languages, and to repair and clean their own houses or compounds. Such occupational therapy helped to lift their sagging spirits. Gandhi vowed to help "feed and clothe" the striking workers if any or all of them were "reduced to starvation" during the lockout. Anasuyabehn remained faithful to her promise to stand by the strikers as well. On March 1, 1918, he wrote a "Dear Friend" letter to Ambalal Sarabhai:

If you succeed, the poor, already suppressed, . . . will be more abject than ever and the impression will have been confirmed that money can subdue everyone. . . . Is it your desire . . . that the workers be reduced to utter submission? Do you not see that in your failure lies your success, that your success is fraught with danger for you? . . . Kindly look deep into your heart, listen to the still small voice within and obey it, I pray you.[47]

He would much later address several viceroys and prime ministers in exactly the same way, always treating those opposing him in any struggle he launched as a "Dear Friend." Gandhi never tired of pleading with the opposition to change course or abandon stubborn adherence to falsehood and evil ways. The sweet reasonableness of his arguments softened the hardest of hearts, and if it did not immediately lead to victory, it often diminished the length of each struggle and at times even achieved conversions to goodness and a recognition of the truth of his arguments.

As the strike went into its third week Gandhi visited the homes of the locked-out workers, finding filth and improper ventilation in all and dirt in the narrow alleys of the impoverished quarter near the closed mill. The weavers' children wore ragged and filthy clothes and none of them went to school. Pained at the extreme poverty he witnessed, Gandhi realized that even if the workers' wages were doubled, their lives would remain wretched. These Gujarati Hindus he served in his own beloved Ahmedabad were as poor and miserable as many he had seen in Champaran. The deeper he probed into the subsoil of India's society, the more seemingly incurable the illnesses he uncovered.

On March 12 the owners lifted their lockout and tried to lure the striking workers back to their mills by repeating their offer to raise wages by 20 percent. Gandhi firmly rejected the offer, again insisting on 35 percent, keeping the oath he had asked every striker to take. In another attempt to divide and conquer, Ambalal invited Gandhi to move into his house that same day; Gandhi refused even to consider doing so as long as the struggle continued. Some workers, of course, were tempted to return to the now open mills and Ambalal charged that they were being forcibly prevented from doing so, supposedly intimidated by bullies. But Gandhi offered personally to escort any striker to work, if he asked for such protection. None did; all remained faithful to their pledges.

Three days later, Gandhi heard that some of the strikers complained that he and Anasuyabehn came and went in "their car; they eat sumptuous food, but we are suffering death-agonies; attending meetings does not prevent starvation."[48] That evening he announced his decision to fast until the strike ended. Three days later, on the morning of March 18, 1918, the mill owners agreed to raise their workers' wages by 35 percent. At a meeting attended by thousands of workers and held under the same tree where they had met daily for three weeks, Gandhi announced the settlement. That evening Ambalal invited Gandhi to a celebration in the huge compound outside his house. Sweets were distributed to workers, and Gandhi, as did Ambalal, spoke briefly: "I hope you will always maintain peace. All I ask is that both [owners and workers] should utilize my services to the full."[49]

No sooner had he finished with Ahmedabad than he focused his full attention on Kheda. The annual crops had partially failed, and famine conditions were approaching, but the government had for the most part refused to suspend revenue demands. Only one village out of 600 was granted full revenue suspension, and only 103 villages were allowed to pay but half the crop share assessed by collectors. In early February Gandhi appealed to Bombay's governor to suspend revenue collection in the entire district until a proper investigation of the crop yield could be assessed by representatives of an "independent committee" made up of the people as well as officials. In mid-February he visited Kheda, first informing the British commissioner of his intention to do so. "If you wish to send any representative of yours with me during my inquiry, I shall have no objection."[50] The British commissioner F. G. Pratt sent no escort with Gandhi, nor did he agree to suspend the collection of revenue. A month later, four days after ending his struggle in Ahmedabad, Gandhi wrote the commissioner one last time, requesting the suspension of revenue collection prior to launching Satyagraha in Kheda. The commissioner again refused.

On March 22, 1918, Gandhi announced Satyagraha at a meeting attended by some 5,000 peasants in Nadiad. "The occasion which has brought us here is so important that it will be enshrined in your memory forever," he passionately told them. "All nations which have risen have done so through suffering. If the people have to sacrifice their land, they should be ready to do so and suffer. . . . To refuse a thing firmly . . . in the name of truth—that is satyagraha."[51] He drafted a pledge for those who agreed to take it, cautioning them to remember that a pledge once taken, in God's name, must never be broken. Some two hundred people signed the pledge that day, more later. A struggle was thus launched that would not end until early June.

That March he spoke again on the virtues of India's ancient civilization, contrasting it to the evils of the West. "That European civilization is Satanic we see for ourselves. An obvious proof of this is the fierce war that is going on. . . . If we can ensure the deliverance of India, it is only through truth and non-violence. . . . Love is a rare herb that makes a friend even of a sworn enemy and this herb grows out of non-violence. . . . We should love all—whether Englishmen or Muslims. . . . So long as we do not have unshakable faith in truth, love and non-violence, we can make no progress."[52]

As Satyagraha intensified in April Gandhi urged Kheda women to stand by their husbands, following them, if need be, into prison. "Our goods are being attached and buffaloes taken away," he acknowledged, arguing that "hardships such as these purify us as fire purifies gold."[53] To his friend Henry Polak, now in London, Gandhi confessed, "A series of passive resistances is an agonizing effort. It is an exalting agony. I suppose the agony of childbirth must be somewhat like it."[54] He spoke every day to different village groups, encouraging them by his presence as well as his words, promising that their salvation would come from fearlessly clinging to truth, that freedom was "bound to follow."

"This is not a struggle merely to escape payment of the revenue this year," he told his brave band of satyagrahis that April. "No king can remain in power if he sets himself against the people. I have taken it as the chief mission of my life to prove this."[55] The British soon tested his resolve. They started to confiscate movable property and land belonging to those peasants and landowners of Kheda who had refused to pay the demanded revenue, and most of them opted to pay out of fear of losing everything they possessed. "If we give way to this fear, we shall become incapable of any manly effort," Gandhi told the staunch peasants of Nadiad, who remained firm. "About eighty per cent of the farmers have paid up the dues out of this fear and, therefore, it is for the remaining twenty per cent to redeem the honour of all."[56]

His speeches to the peasants of Gujarat were given not only in their own language but were enriched by countless references to Hindu epic lore, which they knew and loved, and to recitations from the *Bhagavad Gita*, and ancient tales of the struggles and miracles of Hindu gods taken from the *Puranas*. He brought the folk wisdom and religious philosophy of India's Vedic and Upanishadic, pre-Christian, eras to life for these adoring, mostly illiterate audiences, who waited long hours in the blistering sun just to catch a glimpse of him. They were prepared to listen to him "till the sun burns itself out."

When he wasn't touring villages, he went to Bombay as well as Ahmedabad and met with British governors and heads of the Revenue Department as well as commissioners, much as he had done during earlier Satyagrahas in South Africa. This April, moreover, he journeyed to Delhi to attend the war conference called by Viceroy Lord Chelmsford, leaving in his absence Vallabhbhai Patel in charge of the Kheda struggle. Since neither Tilak nor Annie Besant was invited to the conference, nor could the imprisoned Ali brothers join it, Gandhi had last-minute misgivings about attending.

Chelmsford met with him on the eve of the April 27, 1918, conference to reassure him. "In fear and trembling I have decided as a matter of duty to join the Conference," Gandhi wrote the viceroy's private secretary, who replied: "The Viceroy does not believe in your 'fear and trembling.' Nor do I! His Excellency is very glad indeed to hear that you will join."[57] Gandhi seconded "with all my heart," the conference resolution supporting the war effort and recruitment in every possible way.[58] He then freely offered his other services to the viceroy, "because I love the English Nation, and I wish to evoke in every Indian the loyalty of the Englishman."[59]

Early in June 1918 the Kheda struggle ended in compromise, the government agreeing to suspend the collection of revenue from poor peasants, taking payments only from well-to-do landowners, of whom there were quite a few in Kheda District. "Thus the people's prayer has at last been granted," Gandhi publicly announced, though he felt the settlement was "without grace" and "lacks dignity."[60] Yet the struggle brought attention to Gujarat and "an awakening among the peasants," he argued, "the beginning of their true political education . . . that the salvation of the people depends upon themselves, upon their capacity for suffering and sacrifice."[61]

A week later Gandhi spoke to the peasants of Nadiad to urge them to enlist in the army. "Half a million men were required from India," he explained, "and . . . [t]o receive military training was the stepping-stone to acquire Home Rule."[62]

Gandhi thought these peasants, trained as satyagrahis would respond with enthusiasm to his call to arms. He was quickly disillusioned. "My optimism received a rude shock. . . . 'You are a votary of Ahimsa, how can you ask us to take up arms?' 'What good has Government done for India to deserve our cooperation?'"[63] Such questions troubled his sleep and though he tried to rationalize what he had agreed to do in the heady atmosphere of the viceroy's palace, he could not add conviction to his appeal, and obviously felt so ambivalent about it that he stayed awake sickening himself as well as those peasants who now berated and humiliated him. "We are regarded as a cowardly people," he wrote to friends in Kheda District, trying to justify his contradictory behavior, to rationalize his opportunistic abandonment of Ahimsa. "If we want to become free from that reproach, we should learn the use of arms. Partnership in the Empire is our definite goal. . . . Hence the easiest and the straightest way to win Swaraj is to participate in the defense of the Empire. . . . If the Empire wins mainly with the help of our army, it is obvious that we would secure the rights we want."[64] It was not, however, convincing enough to recruit any of the peasants who listened to him with lowered eyes.

"I very nearly ruined my constitution during the recruiting campaign," Gandhi recalled of those depressing days and sleepless nights. "The devil had been only waiting for an opportunity. . . . [D]ysentery appeared in acute form. . . . Whilst I was thus tossing on the bed in pain in the Ashram, Sjt. Vallabhbhai [Patel] brought the news that Germany had been completely defeated, and that the Commissioner had sent word that recruiting was no longer necessary. The news that I had no longer to worry myself about recruiting came as a very great relief."[65] Gandhi now recovered swiftly from what he recalled as the "first long illness in my life," during which he felt "I was at death's door."

With the Allied victory in November 1918, Indians naturally expected something close to freedom as their just reward for all the support, in men and materiel, rendered to Great Britain. Instead of dominion status, however, an extension of martial law was carried through the viceroy's legislative council over the opposition of every Indian representative serving on it. Justice Rowlatt, the viceroy's legal member, had completed a study on the dangers of "sedition" and terrorist action. In consequence he requested a six-month extension of Defense of India Acts passed in 1915. Those "Black Acts" as Gandhi would call the Rowlatt Bills were indeed passed roughshod over all opposition, as Jinnah so eloquently put it before resigning, "by an overfretful and incompetent bureaucracy which is neither responsible to the people nor in touch with real public opinion."[66]

"If the [Rowlatt] Bills were but a stray example of lapse of righteousness and justice, I should not mind them but when they are clearly an evidence of a determined policy of repression, civil disobedience seems to be a duty imposed upon every lover of personal and public liberty," Gandhi wrote. "For myself if the Bills were to be proceeded with, I feel I can no longer render peaceful obedience to the laws of a power that is capable of such . . . devilish legislation."[67] He marshaled his strength, preparing himself now to "fight the greatest battle of my life." The war was over; yet Britain's victory brought no offer of dominion status, only renewed repression. So Gandhi, along with most outraged Congress leaders, girded themselves for what would surely be but a short struggle to complete Swaraj. None of them imagined it would take almost thirty more arduous years.

10

Postwar Carnage and
Nationwide Satyagraha

O N FEBRUARY 24, 1919, Gandhi cabled Viceroy Chelmsford, offering him the opportunity to reconsider his government's decision to enact the Rowlatt Bills, or so-called Black Bills, extending martial law. If enacted, Gandhi promised to launch Satyagraha, personally encouraging his followers to "commit civil disobedience of such laws." Gandhi noted he was well "aware of the seriousness of the proposed step."[1] Fifty of his followers signed a pledge the next day to disobey the bills. At about the same time, Gandhi also started his Satyagraha Sabha [Society], daily recruiting more volunteers to help him launch an effective protest and gathering signatories to the Satyagraha pledge.

In sending copies of his pledge to the press, Gandhi wrote that this was "probably the most momentous [step] in the history of India."[2] Gandhi went to Delhi in early March for a last meeting with the viceroy. Neither man changed the other's mind. "An Englishman will not be argued into yielding. . . . [H]e recognizes moral force and . . . perhaps even against his will, yields to it. It is this moral force we are employing and, if it is genuinely moral, we shall win."[3]

On March 30, 1919, police in Delhi opened fire at anti-Rowlatt protesters, leaving several dead. This tragedy was but a mild portent of the carnage to come. Sunday, April 6, 1919, was proclaimed by Gandhi a day of national humiliation on which to protest enactment of the Black Bills. That morning Gandhi went to Bombay's Chowpatty beach to pray and fast. He was soon surrounded by devout Hindus. He exhorted them to take the Satyagraha Pledge on Lord "Rama's birthday," which would fall on April 9. Devout Hindu Swami Shraddhanand had led the crowd on which Delhi's

police opened fire. Gandhi announced to the gathering that he had a telegram from the Swami reporting that nine "corpses" had been recovered
from that Delhi massacre site. "[N]o nation has ever been made without
sacrifice," passionate Gandhi told his followers that morning on the beach.
"This is satyagraha . . . not a bad beginning."4 The only thing the Swami's
followers had done wrong in Delhi, however, was to demand the release of
prisoners arrested at the station for their picketing. "It is arrest and imprisonment that we seek," taught Gandhi.

After prayers, he left the beach with some disciples to attend a mass
meeting of Muslims being held at Grant Road in front of the mosque there.
He was escorted up to the balcony, and appealed to his "Mahomedan
brethren to join the satyagraha movement in large numbers."5 Satyagraha
was their best hope to unite India's two great communities, Gandhi told
them, thanking his Muslim comrades for inviting him to speak at their
sacred place.

While Gandhi's enthusiasm grew as his new Satyagraha campaign
gathered in popularity and momentum, most other leaders of the Congress
watched cautiously and did not join him. Home rule leader Annie Besant
and moderates like Wacha and Srinivasa Sastri feared further violence. Jinnah also remained unconvinced by Gandhi's rhetoric, though he felt just as
negative about the Rowlatt Acts and had been the first member of the viceroy's legislative council to resign his seat in principled protest against them.
Gandhi's revolutionary mystic methods, however, were so foreign to his
temperament and approach to political problems that he could only view
them with growing alienation and trepidation. So when Gandhi invited him
to join his Satyagraha Sabha, Jinnah refused. Gandhi's "extreme program"
attracted the inexperienced and the illiterate, and caused further division
everywhere in the country. "What the consequence of this may be, I shud-
der to contemplate. . . . I do not wish my countrymen to be dragged to the
brink of a precipice in order to be shattered."6

Gandhi's faith in his method, however, only increased as protest after
protest was mounted in defiance of British laws. On April 7, 1919, he published an unregistered newspaper, *Satyagrahi*, in which he issued instructions on how best to court arrest. He urged his followers never to object to
punishment, nor "resort to surreptitious practices."7 Defiance must always
be nonviolent and open. It was in the *Satyagrahi* that Gandhi called upon
all Indians "to destroy all foreign clothing in our possession."8 He called
swadeshi "a religious conception" and a "natural duty" for all Indians, and
the boycott of British goods was its counterpart, to remain in full effect until the Rowlatt Acts were withdrawn. Here, too, he published his "vow of
Hindu-Muslim unity," which called upon members of both great communities to unite in "one bond of mutual friendship." The vow reflected
Gandhi's philosophy and read in part: "With God as witness we Hindus

and Mahomedans declare that we shall behave towards one another as children of the same parents. . . . We shall always refrain from violence to each other in the name of religion."[9] A noble dream. Unfortunately, a futile vow.

On April 8, 1919, Gandhi took the train from Bombay to Delhi and on April 9 was served with an order not to enter Delhi or Punjab at Kosi. He refused, of course, to obey the order, was arrested, and brought back under police guard to Bombay. As the news of Gandhi's arrest spread through Bombay, however, riots broke out; crowds threw stones at British buildings and violently obstructed tram-cars.

"This is not satyagraha," Gandhi warned as soon as he learned of the violence. "If we cannot conduct this movement without the slightest violence from our side, the movement might have to be abandoned."[10] The violence of his followers, however, paled in comparison to the response of British India's police and soldiers. Gandhi went from Bombay to his Sabarmati Ashram on the outskirts of Ahmedabad, where more serious riots broke out as word of his arrest spread. Before he could calm the crowds some fifty people were killed and 250 wounded. That was April 13, 1919, the day of India's worst massacre. As the sun started to set on Amritsar's Jallianwala Bagh, British Brigadier Reginald Dyer ordered fifty of his toughest Gurkha and Baluchi troops to open fire without warning on an unarmed gathering of Punjabi peasants celebrating their spring harvest.[11] Four hundred were murdered, another 1,200 wounded. As their ammunition ran low, the troops withdrew without caring for any of the wounded or calling for any medical assistance. Martial law was imposed over the entire province of Punjab, and so news of the Amritsar atrocities was slow to escape, leaving Gandhi and the rest of India oblivious of its magnitude for many months.

With no reference to Jallianwala Bagh's butchery, therefore, on April 14 Gandhi wrote his apology to Maffey, the viceroy's secretary. He had found Ahmedabad a city of "lawlessness bordering . . . on Bolshevism . . . a matter of the deepest humiliation and regret for me."[12] Later that day, addressing 10,000 people who walked to his ashram to hear him speak, Gandhi said he was "ashamed" of the violence that had "disgraced" Ahmedabad for the past few days. "Satyagraha admits of no violence, no pillage, no incendiarism; and still in the name of satyagraha, we burnt down buildings . . . stopped trains, cut off telegraph wires, killed innocent people and plundered shops and private houses."[13] Gandhi passionately decided as "penance" for these violent insults to Satyagraha to fast for three days and confessed that unless the violence in Ahmedabad stopped he would no longer find life "worth living."

He returned to Bombay on Friday and found the situation there so volatile that he announced his decision temporarily to suspend civil disobedience on April 18, 1919. Three days after his scrupulous act of suspension he learned of the savage behavior of the Punjab's martial authorities, where the public whipping of men caught walking rather than crawling to their homes on certain streets in Amritsar had been ordered in the ugly aftermath of Dyer's horrendous massacre a week earlier. "Such whipping would rouse gravest indignation," Gandhi wired Maffey. "Hope there is some explanation that would remove all cause of anxiety."[14] There was, however, none. More and more details trickled out, slowly informing Gandhi and India's leaders of the inhumane actions ordered by Dyer and his supporting Lieutenant Governor Michael O'Dwyer during that blackest spring of Indian history.

By the end of May, Gandhi could no longer keep silent. "I have refrained from saying anything in public because I had no reliable data," he wrote the viceroy. "I was not prepared to condemn martial law as such. . . . But . . . [t]he secrecy that has surrounded the events in the Punjab has given rise to much hostile criticism. The complete gagging of the Indian Press has created the greatest resentment."[15] He urged the viceroy to appoint an "impartial and independent committee of inquiry." That would take a while longer, coming only after the secretary of state intervened, with Congress later appointing its own committee and Gandhi himself as its chair.

Lord Hunter, former solicitor-general of Scotland, was appointed to head a special Punjab Committee that fall, whose six members included two Indian judges, Sir Chimanlal Setalvad, and Sahibzada Sultan Ahmed. The viceroy announced the special inquiry at the opening session of his Imperial Legislative Council, and Gandhi welcomed the inauguration of a full judicial investigation of the Punjab atrocities. It soon seemed clear, however, that the official committee would not conduct as extensive an investigation of Indian claims and charges, or the needs of indemnity of survivors, as hoped for. Gandhi readily supported Congress's cry for the appointment of an independent Indian Committee to inquire into the Punjab atrocities. "The people's case is this," he wrote in his "New Life" Gujarati weekly, *Navajivan*, "that Sir Michael O'Dwyer proved himself unfit as Governor . . . If he had not prevented me from going to Delhi, the disturbances would not have taken such a violent turn."[16] The people's case, Gandhi argued, "is so sound that it requires little adorning . . . it is spoilt . . . only through our anger or our apathy."

Gandhi asked the viceroy to lift the restraining order issued in April that prevented Gandhi from visiting Punjab, and on October 15, 1919, he was permitted to enter that province. "The scene that I witnessed on my arrival at Lahore can never be effaced from my memory," Gandhi recalled. "The railway station was from end to end one seething mass of humanity. The entire populace had turned out of doors . . . as if to meet a dear rela-

tion after a long separation, and was delirious with joy."[17] Pandits Malaviya and Motilal Nehru, as well as Swami Shraddhanand, were waiting to
welcome him to Lahore. It was his first "close personal contact" with Jawaharlal Nehru's father, who presided over the Congress that December in
Amritsar and was soon to become one of Gandhi's major supporters,
though never a disciple, as Jawaharlal was to be for a decade. The decision
was then taken by both Pandits, the Swami, and the Mahatma to boycott
the Hunter Committee. They appointed instead a nonofficial committee of
inquiry on behalf of the Congress. Gandhi was to chair the Congress Committee, on which Motilal Nehru and C. R. Das, the great lawyer leader of
Bengal and Subhas Chandra Bose's guru, agreed to serve, along with several others. Charlie Andrews was also there, his "ceaseless work" continuing, as Gandhi wrote "unobtrusively. . . . his service is the purest charity
given in secret."[18]

In mid-November Gandhi and Charlie Andrews went together to Amritsar. The need for and popularity of the independent committee, headed
by Gandhi, was evident. "The entire area outside the station was packed
with the citizens of Amritsar. Their cheers and shouts almost overwhelmed
me. . . . Thousands stood on all sides."[19]

It was at this time that Gandhi began his tactical, principled appeal to
India's Muslim community. He joined pan-Islamic leaders whenever possible, from the Punjab to Delhi, where he spoke to a large audience of Muslims assembled to attend the Khilafat Conference to protest the Allied dis-
memberment of the Ottoman Empire, despite Anglo-French promises to
the contrary throughout the war. "[B]orn of the same mother, belonging to
the same soil," Hindus and Muslims must love one another, Gandhi insisted. "When it is said that Hindus should join the Moslems in regard to
the Khilafat question some people express surprise, but I say that, if Hindus
and Moslems are brothers, it is their duty to share one another's sorrow."[20]
It was one of Gandhi's most brilliant and controversial strategies, recognizing as he rightly did that without Hindu-Muslim unity there could be no independence for India as a whole. But his orthodox Hindu comrades were
shocked, even outraged, by his sudden warm embrace of this pan-Islamic
cause, for Swami Shraddanand and millions of his Hindu-first followers
viewed cow-killing Muslims as enemies of their faith, seeking only to "re-
convert" them to Hinduism or forcibly to stop them from slaughtering
sacred cows. Gandhi insisted, however, that the best way for India to
achieve freedom was for all Hindus and Muslims to unite in serving their
motherland. His speech was greeted with "loud cheers" and "long and
continued applause."

Gandhi's work with the Congress on the Punjab atrocities inquiry, and
his commitment to the Khilafat cause of the brothers Shaukat and Mohamed Ali and the Muslim masses who followed them, won him greater

national popularity than was enjoyed by any other nationalist leader. As a *Mahatma*, moreover, thanks to his dedication to service, his propagation of swadeshi, and the limited though well-published success of his Champaran, Ahmedabad, and Kheda Satyagrahas, Gandhi was uniquely prepared, or so at least it seemed at the end of 1919, to lead India to freedom's promised land of Swaraj.

Fifteen thousand Indians attended the National Congress meeting in Amritsar that December. Moderate conservative Motilal Nehru thundered in his presidential address: "India has suffered much at the hands of an alien and reactionary bureaucracy, but the Punjab has in that respect acquired a most unenviable notoriety. . . . But repression and terrorism have never yet killed the life of a nation; they but increase the disaffection and drive it underground . . . breaking out occasionally into crimes of violence. And this brings further repression. . . . It is due to the perversity of the executive which blinds itself to the causes of the discontent and, like a mad bull, goes about attacking all who dare to stand up against it."[21]

Gandhi found too much "bitterness" in Motilal's speech, but nevertheless eagerly seconded several of the Congress's resolutions on swadeshi and the Khilafat issue. He also accepted an invitation to serve on a small committee that would entirely rewrite the Congress Constitution, aiming to transform that still mostly moderate organization into a mass revolutionary national party, one that would reflect for the most part Mahatma Gandhi's ideas and leadership on the road to Swaraj.

The complexity of Gandhi's life requires careful attention to both his public and personal trials. At fifty and on the eve of his greatest nationwide success in 1920, Gandhi experienced an intensely personal passion for a young, golden-haired, blue-eyed Danish beauty, Esther Faering. Devout Christian missionary Esther fell in love with Mahatma Gandhi's spiritual commitment to selfless service and left her Danish mission the day he agreed to permit his "Dear Child" to join his Sabarmati Ashram. Acutely aware of how jealous Kasturba was of several of his adoring disciples, Gandhi tried at first to disarm his wife of such feelings by asking Esther "to help Ba in the kitchen." But he warned his Dear Child that "Ba has not an even temper. She is not always sweet. And she can be petty. . . . You will therefore have to summon to your aid all your Christian charity to be able to return largeness against pettiness . . . to pity the person who slights you. . . . And so, my dear Esther, if you find Mrs. Gandhi trying your nerves, you must avoid the close association I am suggesting to you."[22] It didn't work, of course. Kasturba treated *his* Dear Child so harshly in her kitchen that Esther soon broke down. "You were with me the whole of yesterday and during the night. I shall pray that you may be healthier in mind, body and spirit," Bapu wrote to console Dear Child Esther "with deep love." A few days later Esther wrote to report that it was too difficult to please Ba, who would always look upon her "as a stranger." Gandhi was "glad you have opened out your heart" about his "difficult" wife. He immediately insisted that Esther must have a "separate kitchen" for herself. "My heart is with you in your sorrow."23

Obsessed with thoughts of her wherever he was, Gandhi wrote a few days later, "'Resist not evil' has a much deeper meaning than appears on the surface. The evil in Ba, for instance, must not be resisted, i.e., you or for that matter I must not fret over it or be impatient and say to ourselves, 'why will not this woman see the truth or return the love I give her.' She can no more go against her nature than a leopard can change his spots. If you or I love, we act according to our nature. If she does not respond, she acts according to hers."24 He pleaded with her to "write to me daily."

Shortly thereafter, piqued that Esther had attended a party without requesting his permission, he wrote her another "love-letter," as he called his daily missives. "You have been a bad child to keep me without a line for so many days. I do however hear about you from others. You are at a marriage party. I have felt a little disturbed. What is it all about? How could you have fared in the midst of strangers? It was wrong. . . . Where did you have to sleep? Who suggested your going? It seems all so strange to me. I do not want you to make experiments in the dark. . . . I am filled with anxiety about you. I know it is stupid to be anxious. God is above us all. . . . But give me the privilege of calling you my child. 'Rock of ages, cleft for me; let me hide myself in Thee.' With deep love."25 Never had he written so anxiously to any of his four sons. And of all the biblical sermons he might have chosen to inflict on her at the end of the strangest letter, what ever made him opt for "'cleft for me; let me hide myself in Thee'"?

That same night he wrote her: "My heart weeps for you . . . you must not prick yourself in your waywardness. A disciplined conscience is one to obey. It is the voice of God. An undisciplined conscience leads to perdition, for the devil speaks through it. I wish I was with you. . . . I shall pray for you and love you all the more for your waywardness."26 Shortly thereafter she wrote to inform him of how eager she was to return to her Danish mission's convent. "I see I have hurt you," he responded at once, "forgive me . . . I wrote as I did because I love you so."27

He was working round the clock in Lahore, finishing his committee's long report on the Punjab atrocities of the year before. Throughout this arduous period he was plagued by possessive fears and anxieties for his Dear Child, sending her prescriptions for her dysentery, including many "hip baths," coyly asking her "Are you an unworthy child?" Gandhi was completely unconscious of Freud's luminous work, had read no psychoanalytical literature, and would for the rest of his life remain virtually unaware of his own sexual passions toward a number of Western women drawn to him as disciples and for several virginal Indian women who lived in his ashrams as well. "You have made yourself dearest to me by your wonderful love and conscientiousness," he wrote to reassure Esther. "You do not for one moment think that your waywardness can make any alteration in my estimation of your worthiness. If the body is the temple of the Holy, it requires the utmost care . . . with deep love."[28]

Two days later she resolved to return to Denmark to care for her sick father. "To express purest love is like walking on the edge of a sword," Gandhi replied to that unhappy news. "We never know when we are not selfish even when we fancy we are all love. . . . Love and truth are two faces of the same coin and both most difficult to practice and the only things worth living for. . . . I shall therefore pray that both you and I may realize this to the fullest measure."[29]

Gandhi felt more tortured each day as the prospect of losing her became more real to his confused and enraptured mind and heart. "You are constantly in my mind . . . are you happy and joyful? How are you in body? I would like you to return . . . With love."[30] She had returned to her convent in Madras, trying to cure her ailing body in prayer and trying to decide whether or not to marry Dr. E. K. Menon, who had proposed. Gandhi continued writing to her daily, sending poems by Tennyson, Lowell, and George Herbert, adding his own poetry, ending always with love, or "Another evening has come to fill me with thoughts of you."[31] Day and night he traveled from Lahore to Bombay, to Delhi, Banaras, and back to Ahmedabad, yet found no respite, no escape from her or from his own unrequited longing.

When Gandhi first learned of her plans to marry Menon, he replied: "Your letter grieves me beyond words. . . . But true joy will come to the godly. . . . With love."[32] Falling ill, he retreated from his ashram to the lofty and isolated "Fortress of the Lion," *Sinhgadh*, high above the sea on the Deccan plateau of Maharashtra. After a busy fortnight of fasting and prayer in memory of the previous year's turmoil and Punjab tortures, he wrote again, explaining his silence, which "does not mean that I have thought any the less of you. . . . I am quite resigned to your marriage. I will not argue against it. . . . do exactly as God guides you. Only always be sure it is the voice of God."[33]

Before she left India Esther agreed to come to visit him atop Sinhgadh, for he was much too weak now to see her off at Bombay. "I did not at all like to part with you," he confessed after her two-day visit. "But I know it was good for your health's sake."[34] She left Bombay on the S.S. *Berlin* on May 20, 1920. "As for my health, there is nothing in particular except weakness," he wrote his youngest son that same day. "I am so weak that I cannot walk at all. The legs have lost all strength. I cannot understand the cause."[35] But he was soon to recover the strength necessary to lead his first nationwide Satyagraha, a movement of mass civil disobedience mighty enough to rock the world's most powerful empire.

By the summer of 1920 the Allied Powers' resolve to dismember the Ottoman Empire in the aftermath of World War I proved so harsh and humiliating to Turkey as well as Germany and Italy that Gandhi wrote to express his shock and disappointment in his Gujarati newspaper. "To say that there is peace where one party forces the other to agree to something against its will, crushes it under its brute strength, is a grave offense against God in the form of Truth."[36] The 1920 Treaty of Sèvres violated all the noble pledges given during the war by the British and French governments to the Turkish Empire—namely, their promises that not only Mecca and Medina and other holy cities of Islam but the entire Near Eastern littoral and Arabian peninsula would remain under the control of the Ottoman Empire's Caliph (Khalifa). Instead, the Caliph was deprived of his prewar control of those holy places, rousing Muslims of India, as well as everywhere else in the Islamic world, to righteous indignation and fervent pan-Islamic protests. India's viceroy urged angry Muslims to show restraint and remain peaceful, but Gandhi joined the Khilafat cause, arguing, "If the Muslims sit still, all that they have done during the last four years will be proved to have been hollow. If the Muslims have no peace, Hindus can have none. . . . [S]uch is the law of friendship." Nonetheless, he cautioned Muslim comrades against violence, urging them to join his Satyagraha campaign.

"The Peace Terms and Your Excellency's defense of them," Gandhi wrote the viceroy on June 22, 1920, "have given the Mussulmans of India a shock from which it will be difficult for them to recover. . . . In my humble opinion their cause is just. . . . Muslim soldiers did not fight to inflict punishment on their own Khalifa or to deprive him of his territories. . . . Mussulmans and Hindus have as a whole lost faith in British justice and honour. The Report of the Majority of the Hunter Committee, Your Excellency's Despatch thereon, and Mr. Montagu's reply have only aggravated the distrust. . . . It is . . . because I believe in the British Constitution that I have advised my Mussulman friends to withdraw their support from Your Excellency's Government, and the Hindus to join them, should the Peace Terms not be revised in accordance with solemn pledges of Ministers and the Muslim sentiment."[37]

In July, Gandhi prepared his followers for the advent of Satyagraha planned for August 1, 1920. He urged lawyers to abandon their practice in all courts and litigants to settle their disputes entirely through arbitration. "I have believed for many years that every state tries to perpetuate its power through lawyers."[38] The same was true of schools, all of which were used by government to distort the minds of "children on whom the future of India rests." He called upon all school children to "boycott," relying entirely on national education learned either at home or in ashrams, like his own, in which a school continued to function. Congress leader Lala Lajpat Rai had returned to Punjab and already announced his intention to boycott the elections planned to be held under the Montagu-Chelmsford Government of India Act of 1919. Gandhi warmly endorsed Lala Lajpat's boycott. "I would not have the best attention of the country frittered away in electioneering," Gandhi wrote. "The issue is clear. Both the Khilafat terms and the Punjab affairs show that Indian opinion counts for little in the councils of the Empire. It is a humiliating position, we shall make nothing of reforms if we quietly swallow the humiliation."³⁹

Gandhi returned the medals he had been given for his work in South Africa to the viceroy on August 1, 1920, "in pursuance of the scheme of non-co-operation, inaugurated today in connection with the khilafat movement."⁴⁰ Wealthy Bombay Muslim Mian Mohamed Chotani sponsored Khilafat Day meetings throughout Bombay that first week in August, and on every platform Gandhi appeared with Shaukat and Mohamed Ali, as well as other Muslim leaders like Punjab's Dr. Kitchlew and the League's Hasrat Mohani. Most of the Congress moderates now urged their followers to ignore Gandhi's call for noncooperation or else asked him to suspend its implementation until after the special session of Congress was held in Calcutta that September to vote on it. But Gandhi insisted that "the still small voice within me suggests otherwise." He argued that it was not possible for him to wait on Congress's vote and decision, since "I had in my hands a sacred trust. I was advising my Mussulman countrymen and . . . I hold their honour in my hands. I dare not ask them to wait for any verdict but . . . their own conscience."⁴¹ Gandhi now rallied all those who listened and agreed with him to attend the Congress in Calcutta and vote as he would. His major Muslim supporters, like Chotani, paid the fare for trainloads of Muslims to cross the subcontinent from Bombay in order to reach Calcutta in early September, packing the Congress pandal and voting for Gandhi and the Khilafat noncooperation movement.

On September 5, 1920, he expressed his complete distrust of British bureaucrats to the Subjects Committee of Congress, urging them to support his noncooperation resolution. British constitutional reforms, he warned, were nothing but a "trap," which would leave them at the "mercy of unscrupulous men."⁴² Then he urged them to boycott elections under the new act. Most of the senior statesmen of Congress, including C. R. Das and Jinnah, now opposed him, warning that his actions would dangerously divide the Congress and the nation. Nevertheless, on September 8 he moved his resolution on noncooperation and won, despite a "large number" of the Congress leaders arrayed against him, who considered his movement too revolutionary and bound only to stimulate more violence and divisiveness in the country. He promised them Swaraj in one year if they faithfully followed the course he proposed without fear or violence.

"Is the country ready?" he asked. "Are the title-holders ready to surrender their titles? Are parents ready to sacrifice literary education of their children for the sake of the country? . . . If you have the same feeling burning in you as in me for the honour of Islam and the Punjab then you will unreservedly accept my resolution."[43] He promised that if they all worked to implement the program and traveled far and wide gathering public grievances to bring to the notice of officials that government's "eyes will be opened." His passion, his conviction, and his firm resolve carried the Congress by more than two to one, thanks in some measure to Pandit Motilal Nehru's support. Father Nehru was swayed to Gandhi's side by his more radical son, Jawaharlal, soon to follow the Mahatma into village India's crowded heat and then for nine years to the cold isolation of British prison cells.

Vallabhbhai Patel resigned from the Viceroy's Council the following week and together with Gandhi drafted noncooperation boycott instructions for the Congress to be circulated to all provincial and local committees. Swadeshi instructions were included and not only Lancashire cloth but Japanese and French silks as well were all to be shunned by every patriot. Classes in hand spinning and weaving were begun throughout the land, and "ladies of high-station," including Lady Tata and Saraladevi Chaudhrani, Rabindranath Tagore's grand-niece, who traveled with Gandhi and whom he called "my spiritual wife," were assiduously spinning.[44] A special "Swaraj Fund" was to be raised as well as a "Volunteer Corps."[45]

The physical weakness that had followed Esther's departure had left him and his mind focused on the forthcoming revolutionary December session of Congress to be held in Nagpur. Meanwhile he embarked on another tour, stirring up hope for freedom. Wherever he went and spoke, or simply showed himself, crowds chanted "*Mahatma Gandhi ki jai!*" "Victory to Mahatma Gandhi!" He soon began to find it impossible to rest, for at every station were noisy crowds, insistent and assertive. "In vain did Mrs. Gandhi and others plead with the crowds for self-control and silence. . . . It was a unique demonstration of love run mad. An expectant and believing people groaning under misery and insult believe that I have a message of hope for them." As always, Gandhi sounded a cautionary note: "There is no deliverance and no hope without sacrifice, discipline and self-control."[46] But those who could read such prudent imprecations were hardly the illiterate millions, who fought to bow and touch his bare feet or his naked legs, and worshipped this Mahatma as their living god, walking all day and all night just for a glimpse of his bald head. He had wakened the slumbering tiger of India's long-neglected, abandoned, ignored millions by daring to jump upon its sleeping form. Now the ride left him reeling, but as yet he could not, or dared not, get off.

Most of the old Congress leaders, however, now distanced themselves from him, as Annie Besant and her friends had done much earlier. Jinnah and M. R. Jayakar of Bombay both resigned from the Home Rule League, which they had led, once Gandhi was elected its president, changing its name over their protests to Swarajya Sabha ("Swaraj Society"). Barrister Jinnah was not amused at having the Home Rule League's laws and constitution, which he had carefully helped to draft, overruled by this upstart. In his letter of resignation from the Sabha, Jinnah called Gandhi's new constitution "unconstitutional and illegal," which echoed Viceroy Chelmsford's reaction to Gandhi's noncooperation: "the most foolish of all foolish schemes."[47] But it was only the first blow Mr. Jinnah would have to sustain that fateful year in crossing legal swords with Mahatma Gandhi and his ardent host of youthful supporters, so many of them Muslims, thanks to the Khilafat cause Gandhi embraced and from which Jinnah always remained aloof.

Elections were held throughout British India in late November and December of 1920. In Bombay, voter turnout was so light that Gandhi could claim it "demonstrated the success of noncooperation about Councils."[48] Gandhi visited Banaras University again, urging students to leave and winning over many of them with every speech he made. When he spoke to women's associations he was showered with gold jewels to use in his campaign, gaining money and momentum every day. And wherever he went he was surrounded by chanting crowds eager to touch him or simply to gaze upon this remarkable man, whom they called Mahatma. "Freedom merely means that, unafraid of anyone, we should be able to speak and act as we feel."[49] Then seeing the worshipful look in their eyes as they watched and listened to him, he anxiously added: "I am not asking you to shake off Government's slavery to be slaves to me afterwards."

In mid-December Gandhi reached Nagpur, located almost equidistant from India's four compass points, where he was welcomed by wealthy disciple Jamnalal Bajaj and his reception committee, and he was pleased to see delegates arriving daily from every direction. At Nagpur, Gandhi moved for adoption of the new Congress creed, which changed "The object of the Indian National Congress" from "Responsible Colonial Government" to "the attainment of swaraj by the people of India by all legitimate and peaceful means."[50] He spoke in support of this creed he had drafted in Hindi, insisting it should be India's national language and the language of every Congress meeting. "I know, before we are done with this great battle on which we have embarked . . . we have to go probably, possibly, through a sea of blood, but let it not be said . . . that we are guilty of shedding blood, but . . . that we shed . . . our own." In proposing the new creed at the plenary Congress session that evening, Gandhi cautioned, "We cannot save anything, ourselves or our dharma or the Empire, by using force."[51]

The new creed and Congress Constitution passed by acclamation and with a prolonged standing ovation from the more than 14,500 delegates inside the pandal. Two days later Gandhi proposed as the last resolution to this historic Congress a reaffirmation of his noncooperation motion, adopted in Calcutta three months earlier. Jinnah had tried in vain to amend that resolution in committee, fearing it would only provoke illegal activities and prolonged violence. After failing in committee, however, he tried once again to propose his changes from the floor of the final plenary session of Congress. But no sooner did he mention "Mr. Gandhi's resolution" than he was "howled down with cries of "shame, shame" and "political imposter" and louder shouts of "*No. Mahatma Gandhi.*"[52] Jinnah repeated "Mister" but the irate audience yelled "*Mahatma.*" He waited for the noise to subside, turning toward Gandhi to say, "Standing on this platform, knowing as I do that he commands the majority in this assembly, I appeal to him to pause, to cry halt before it is too late." But Gandhi did not respond, leaving Jinnah to step down from that platform, followed out of the crowded Congress by ugly hisses and catcalls, this chapter of his career as India's "Best Ambassador of Hindu-Muslim Unity" shattered by Gandhi's honorary title.

Gandhi's resolution that final day in Nagpur was also carried by acclamation, again followed by cries of "*Mahatma Gandhi ki jai.*" He then told his eager followers that if they "show no violence in thought, deed or word whether in connection with the Government or . . . with ourselves . . . we do not require one year, we do not even require nine months to attain our goal."[53] It was a bold, proud, and impossible promise.

As early as February 1921 Gandhi felt "ashamed" to write that "Swaraj will be delayed" after he learned of the looting of shops in Bihar. In Punjab that February, 150 unarmed Sikhs were slaughtered by guards hired by a corrupt Hindu Mahant (temple manager) as they tried to enter and reclaim for Sikhism the *gurdwara* (temple) at Nankana, the birthplace of Guru Nanak, founder of the Sikh faith. The massacre of those nonviolent members of the devout Sikh *Akali* ("Immortal") Party vitalized and united hitherto disparate Sikhs much the way Dyer's earlier massacre at Jallianwala Bagh had energized and unified India's National Congress. "I am so constituted that the sufferings of others make me miserable," Gandhi told his Sikh friends when he visited Nankana in early March. "So when I heard of the tragedy of Nankana I felt like wanting to be among the victims."[54] From this time on Sikhs remained in the vanguard of India's nationalist movement, many of them joining the Congress as well as their Akali party. They were among the first ardent supporters of Gandhi's future Satyagraha campaigns, and younger Sikh revolutionaries readily risked their lives to help liberate India from foreign domination.

At the approach of the second anniversary of "Satyagraha Week," from April 6 to 13, Gandhi toured all of India, urging mass implementation of the multiple boycott movement he had launched in 1919 and continuing to call for hand spinning and weaving. To a huge meeting of students and lawyers in Orissa's capital he asked: "What can be nobler than to die as free men of India?"[55] The "era of talking" should now end, Gandhi insisted, and a new "era of action" must begin, if they were to achieve Swaraj. Such action included recruiting men and women from every province and village for the restructured Congress, raising enough money to sustain local Congress committees, and working to transform India into a totally self-governing society of peaceful, harmonious, industrious people. Everywhere he went he called upon those who listened to stop drinking liquor and start spinning cotton. Gandhi believed that, if every peasant family had a spinning wheel and used it regularly, India's "grinding poverty" would soon disappear.

Since launching his Satyagraha in concert with the Khilafat movement, Gandhi embraced the brothers Shaukat and Mohamed Ali as his own "brothers" on every platform upon which they appeared together. The Ali brothers, who often spoke alone, however, were reported by government agents to have been inciting Muslim audiences to violence and welcoming an Afghan invasion of India. When Viceroy Lord Reading informed Pandit Malaviya that his government would have to initiate criminal proceedings against the Ali brothers, Malaviya asked the viceroy to postpone any such action until he could meet with Gandhi. Gandhi went to Simla and the viceroy met with him four times, showing him the objectionable passages from many reported speeches. Gandhi "admitted" they could warrant the violent interpretation the government had given to them, but he said he was "convinced that it was not intended" by the Ali brothers "to incite the audience to violence."[56] He got the brothers to agree to a disclaimer, which he later published, but it was only a holding action. In truth, the Ali brothers never really believed in nonviolence as Gandhi did, and their brief interlude of Khilafat cooperation was little more than a political marriage of convenience, doomed to early dissolution and growing Hindu-Muslim disillusionment and communal antipathy.

Many of Gandhi's Hindu Brahman supporters never understood why he strongly embraced those radical Muslim brothers in the first place. But Gandhi's earlier South African experience and success, so heavily dependent as it had been on Gujarati Muslim mercantile support and cooperation, made him mistakenly assume that India's Muslim majority would adhere to the same principles, accepting the very nonviolent vows he himself took. Shaukat and Mohamed Ali were soon to repudiate Gandhi for what they later call his "Hindu treachery" and "hypocrisy."

But young men like Jawaharlal Nehru, recently returned to his home in

Allahabad after seven years of aristocratic education in England, only to feel dreadfully disillusioned by the timidity of pre-Gandhian Indian politics and bored by provincial British Indian society and his father's legal practice, eagerly followed Gandhi to the dirt and poverty of India's village heartland and to prison. Nehru lived throughout 1921 "in a kind of intoxication," as he put it in his autobiography. "We sensed the happiness of a person crusading for a cause . . . the thrill of mass-feeling, the power of influencing the mass."[57] As many more ardent young radicals joined his growing army, however, Mahatma Gandhi became deeply aware and fearful of the pitfalls of power. "We are in sight of the promised land, but the danger is the greatest when victory seems the nearest," he warned in midyear. "God's last test is ever the most difficult. Satan's last temptation is ever the most seductive. . . . Non-violence is the most vital and integral part of non-co-operation. We may fail in everything else and still continue our battle if we remain non-violent."[58]

Despite the clarity of such warnings, however, as the movement gathered momentum, the masses joined with passionate enthusiasm, rallying behind their Mahatma-General, filling every cell in every prison of every province in the crown jewel of the world's mightiest Empire, on which the sun of British rule almost seemed in 1922 about to set forever. The darkness of mad violence descended instead. It happened at Chauri Chaura on February 4, 1922. Gandhi was poised to launch his most powerful no-tax-paying final step in the Satyagraha campaign in Bardoli district, whose disciplined Gujarati population of 87,000 awaited their Mahatma's call to action.

He had written a letter of final warning to Lord Reading, urging him to free noncooperation prisoners, revise his policy of harsh repression, and liberate India's press from administrative shackles to avert mass civil disobedience. He gave the viceroy ten days, until February 11, to respond positively, but two days before that he received wired confirmation from son Devdas of horrible violence in Chauri Chaura. A parade of so-called satyagrahis had marched past a police station in that village of the United Provinces' crowded Gorakhpur District. Some of the marching peasants were reported to have been goaded by laughing policemen until they broke ranks and set fire to the station, burning it to the ground and hacking to pieces the terrified police, who tried in vain to escape the conflagration. The fire consumed twenty-one innocents, including the young son of a sub-inspector. Gandhi convened a meeting of the Working Committee of Congress in Bardoli on February 11 and 12, which suspended all further civil disobedience, deploring the "inhuman conduct" of Chauri Chaura's murderous mob.

"We were angry when we learnt of this stoppage of our struggle at a time when we seemed to be consolidating our position and advancing on all fronts," jailed Jawaharlal Nehru wrote. "But our disappointment and anger in prison could do little good. . . . [C]ivil resistance stopped and non-cooperation wilted away."⁵⁹ That was young Nehru's first bitter disillusionment with Gandhi's leadership, but many more such frustrations would follow, each of them widening the gulf that was to divide India's two greatest nationalists. Mahatma Gandhi's disappointments with his Congress "heir" were to be at least as grave and disconcerting.

In calling a halt to his campaign, Gandhi assumed full "responsibility for the crime" committed at Chauri Chaura. "All of us should be in mourning for it," he added, praying, "May God save the honour of India."⁶⁰ He then resolved to perform the expiatory penance he would so often turn to when all else had failed, beginning a fast on February 12, 1922. "I could not have done less," he wrote Devdas, explaining: "To start civil disobedience in an atmosphere of incivility is like putting one's hand in a snake pit. Please do not take that as an example. It is [more like] the woman giving birth to a child who suffers the pains, others only help. I, too, wish to give birth to the ideals of non-violence and truth, so that I alone need bear the pains of fasting."⁶¹ From childhood, of course, he had always feared snakes, yet this is his first remarkable reference to himself as a "woman giving birth." It would not be his last.

Gandhi fasted only five days, suffering no ill effects in the aftermath. But the viceroy and his subordinate officials now recognized how much politically weaker Gandhi had become in the hearts and eyes of many of his followers, especially those ardent young men who had welcomed prison in response to his early passionate call for noncooperation. It was hardly surprising, therefore, that a month after he had called off the war, General Gandhi himself was arrested and sentenced to six years in jail. Among others, he wrote that day to his "Dear Child" Esther: "I hope you were . . . happy over the news of my arrest. It has given me great joy—I would like you to see the truth of the spinning-wheel. It and it alone is the visible outward expression of the inner feeling for humanity. If we feel for the starving masses of India, we must introduce the spinning-wheel into their homes. . . . [W]e must spin daily as a sacrament. If you have understood the secret of the spinning-wheel, if you realize that it is a symbol of love of mankind, you will engage in no other outward activity."⁶²

So in the aftermath of the wretched pain and horror of Chauri Chaura, instead of fighting on in Bombay's cities and the villages of Bardoli for political freedom and all the glories of Swaraj from foreign rule, Mahatma Gandhi did a complete about-face, turning inward again, back to the Truth in his heart, listening only to his inner voice and to the music of his spinning wheel of universal Love, which he passionately turned day after day in the sacrificial solitude of his otherwise empty cell.

11

Cotton Spinning

A T MIDNIGHT on March 20, 1922, Gandhi was transported in a special train from Sabarmati Jail south to Poona's massive Yeravda Prison, a giant fortress of gray stone. He would have ample time there in the next two years of his incarceration to reflect on the errors he had made, exciting so many ill-prepared, violent, and uncontrollable people to expect to win freedom overnight. Now he resolved to spin cotton thread without speaking, considering his *charkha* (spinning wheel) the "only device" capable of making all Indians who used it feel that "we are the children of the same land."[1] Gandhi took vows of silence while he spun for a week at a stretch, desiring no visitors, writing few letters, and seeking through spinning and silence to heal deep wounds in his heart and mind. "I am as happy as a bird," he soon wrote. "And if my prayers are true and from a humble heart, they, I know, are infinitely more efficacious than any amount of meddlesome activity."[2]

Soon, however, he weakened, growing frail from eating no more than minimal portions twice a day, often fasting, and undermining his physique until his weight dropped from 114 to barely 99 pounds. He trembled uncontrollably. Carefully examined by prison doctor Colonel C. Maddock, he was found to be suffering from appendicitis. After six months of pain and suffering, Gandhi finally agreed to permit Colonel Maddock to perform the necessary lifesaving operation in Poona's Sassoon Hospital on January 12, 1924.

Following the operation Gandhi became more abstemious, reducing even further his minimal diet. Shortly thereafter, Viceroy Lord Reading unconditionally released Gandhi from prison, on "considerations of his health." "I am sorry that the Government have prematurely released me on account of my illness," Gandhi wrote to Mohamed Ali, who had been elected to preside over the Congress that year. "Such a release can bring me no joy . . . no relief. . . . I am now overwhelmed with a sense of responsibility I am ill-fitted to discharge. . . . my utter incapacity to cope with the work before me humbles my pride."[3]

Lord Reading's decision was based as much on political as on medical grounds. Elections were held under the new Government of India Act of 1919 in the winter of 1920, and though Gandhi and his followers boycotted them, many moderate Congress leaders ran for the newly expanded Legislative Assembly. Nationalist heroes, like Motilal Nehru, M. A. Jinnah, and C. R. Das, all took seats in that inchoate Indian Parliament, launched with fanfare and solemnity by the Duke of Connaught, on behalf of King-Emperor George, on February 9, 1921. Later that year of mounting non-cooperation and black flag boycotts (during which black flags are flown over buildings and carried in parades), moreover, Edward, the young Prince of Wales, toured India, accompanied by his favorite cousin, young Lord Louis ("Dickie") Mountbatten. Mountbatten not only caught his first glimpse of the empire over which he would preside a quarter century later, but at twenty-one proposed marriage to flamboyant heiress Edwina Ashley, then a house guest of Rufus Isaacs, Lord Reading. The British imperial process of gradual devolution of power thus moved at its stately, though "glacial" might be more apt, pace toward the avowed goal of preparing India for dominion status.

Chauri Chaura and its aftermath proved less cataclysmic and disruptive of daily life for most nationalist leaders than it did for Gandhi, who had raced too far ahead of his ragtag army, the younger generation blaming him for calling a halt to the battle, the older for irresponsibility. But as a "Mahatma," his popularity among the Hindu peasantry remained undiminished, and though many sophisticated Congress leaders were disillusioned by his idealistic strategy, everyone recognized his unique powers and the yogic force of his great soul. As soon as Gandhi felt strong enough to see visitors, political pilgrimages began moving toward Poona, Akali Sikhs came in deputations to seek his sage advice and support in their struggle, and others came alone or in couples to wait in patient hope for a brief audience.

In early March he was driven to Juhu beach, a suburb of Bombay, where he stayed in his wealthy friend Narottam Morarji's sumptuous bungalow, named "Palm Bun." Soon he gathered several disciple-patients to nurse there, Vallabhbhai Patel's frail daughter Maniben, Maganlal Gandhi's ailing daughter Radha, and his asthmatic friend Charlie Andrews, defrocked soon after joining Gandhi, who acted as his channel to London's establishment, the British-Indian hierarchy, and English press. He tried to discourage visitors, explaining how "slowly" his wounds were healing, but people came just in hopes of catching a glimpse of him as he and Charlie walked along the beach before sunset. Great visitors also came: Motilal Nehru and C. R. Das, leaders of the Swarajist Party in the Legislative Assembly, the old Congress, and their respective provinces, Uttar Pradesh and Bengal. They all sought to lure him back to political life, but he was still depressed at how badly he had misjudged his followers and the strength of the British Raj. So he quietly spun cotton, committing to no great work or party, waiting for advice from his inner voice.

What troubled him most at this time was the breakdown in Hindu-Muslim relations that had intensified during his years in prison, collapsing first in Turkey, then in India. Mustafa Kemal Ataturk led his ardent Young Turk followers after World War I first to abolish the Ottoman Sultanate in 1922, finally to discard the Khilafat itself in March of 1924. India's Muslim leaders refused at first to believe the news, later thinking that Mustafa Kemal was a British "agent," a Western imperialist stooge in Turkish dress. Gandhi was also shocked at the news; the Khilafat bridge of Hindu-Muslim cooperation he had so carefully built with his "Brothers" Ali broke down, leaving India's hopes and any prospects of Hindu-Muslim unity in ashes.

"For me the attainment of swaraj depends not upon what the English Cabinet thinks or says but entirely upon a proper . . . solution of the Hindu-Muslim questions," Gandhi wrote in *Young India* on learning of the Khilafat's demise. "Without it all before us is dark. With it swaraj is within immediate reach."[4] Gandhi's pacifist solution was to urge all those who followed him to spend their time hand spinning, weaving, and laboring as he did, in "quiet, honest undemonstrative work."

But as Hindu-Muslim rioting grew more violent, many believers in both faiths called Gandhi the worst culprit for having raised the hopes of so many only to watch them now shatter so miserably. Shaukat and Mohamed Ali, the latter currently presiding over the Congress, appealed to Gandhi to take up the presidency himself at the next Congress. He resisted the invitation at first, but then Motilal promised him full backing and Swarajist Party support. Sarojini Naidu pleaded as did Birla and virtually all of the great leaders of nationalist India, for each of them knew that he alone could bring millions into the struggle, magnetizing peasant masses by his mere presence. In late August he penned his "surrender" to "Dear Motilalji." He promised to preside on the condition that every member of Congress agree to wear homespun clothing and to spin at least two thousand yards of yarn every month. "I see no other way of making the Congress organization a real and living thing," Gandhi explained to Jawaharlal Nehru's elegant father, who had by now totally abandoned his Saville Row wardrobe, "nor can I see any hope for the poor of India without the spinning-wheel and we shall never fire their imagination unless we spin our-selves."[5]

The spinning wheel was at the heart of his program for Congress and for India. He also stressed the elimination of untouchability and service to the poor, urging everyone to teach them to spin and grow more food so as to keep themselves warm and strong. Gandhi's passionate sincerity and the depth of his humility won converts wherever he spoke, even the most af-fluent audiences in Bombay rising to applaud his message, his courage, his passion and wisdom.

But communal killing, looting, and burning of mosques and temples continued. "Surely there are sane Hindus and sane Mussalmans enough," Gandhi cried out, appealing to both sides "to adjust their differences and forget past wrongs."[6] Yet that hope proved an illusion, as premeditated murder continued to break each bridge of Hindu-Muslim unity Gandhi sought in vain to rebuild. In mid-September of 1924, he left his ashram and went by train to Delhi to live with outgoing Congress president Mohamed Ali in preparation for assuming the reins of Congress power.

Two days after he moved into Mohamed Ali's home, however, news of a terrible communal riot and massacre reached them from Kohat in the North-West Frontier Province. Sarojini Naidu reported that more than a hundred Hindus and Muslims were dead or dying in that frontier town, where every tribal slept with his rifle. "I passed two nights in restlessness and pain," Gandhi wrote. "On Wednesday I knew the remedy. I must do penance."[7] He decided to fast for twenty-one days. He had not consulted his Muslim host, however, and Mohamed Ali feared that if his guest was not strong enough to survive three weeks without food, Hindu-Muslim unity, which Gandhi hoped to restore by this fast, might break down en-tirely. Gandhi survived, but unity was not restored. An exodus of thou-sands of terrified Hindus from Kohat to Rawalpindi began that dark day and continued for the remainder of the year.

At the Belgaum Congress, president-elect Gandhi addressed his "Brothers and Sisters" first in Hindi, then in English. He had accepted the "burden of the honour" of presiding over Congress for the next year only after "much misgiving." The "passive non-violence of helplessness" was at the heart of the failed movement of the last few years. The result was an eruption of intolerance rather than the "boycott of violence."[8] Now he ap-pealed for "enlightened non-violence of resourcefulness," continued na-tional boycott of foreign cloth, and the universal use throughout India of the spinning wheel. "Hindu-Muslim unity is not less important than the spinning-wheel. It is the breath of our life." Finally, he spoke of the need to eliminate untouchability, as "a penance that caste Hindus owe to Hinduism and to themselves."[9] He would soon turn the full intensity of his passionate yogic focus upon that ancient Hindu prejudice.

Cotton Spinning

As president of the Congress, Gandhi toured India in 1925, speaking everywhere about the importance of spinning, urging every member of his party to contribute 2,000 yards per month of his own hand-spun cotton or to pay someone to spin that amount for him. Annie Besant tried, but complained that she could never spin so much. Nehru did for a while, but preferred to read and write, especially when in jail. Gandhi knew that many of his colleagues considered his insistence on so much hand-spun cotton quite "mad," but he argued that if every Indian spun, no matter how little each day, the spinning wheel would unite the nation as nothing else could. He also noted its real economic value as well as its therapeutic utility. He was less sanguine, however, about its efficacy in restoring Hindu-Muslim unity, as communal breakdowns continued along the frontier and throughout the land.

"Of Hindu-Muslim unity," he reported at a public meeting in Madras," the more you try to undo the tangle the more knotty it becomes, and a wise spinner leaves his tangle aside for the moment when he has lost his temper." For Gandhi the Hindu-Muslim question had become a "hopeless tangle," but he urged Indians not to lose faith and "to be loving to one another, remembering that the same Divine Spirit inhabits whether it is the Hindu body or Muslim body."[10] But the days of Khilafat cooperation were over, and his "Brothers" Shaukat and Mohamed Ali no longer viewed the causes of communal riots, whether in Kohat or Lucknow, from the Mahatma's perspective, nor did they really trust him any more.

So Gandhi turned back to Hinduism, not merely for the comfort he naturally found among his own soulmates, but to help reform its darkest practices. "So long as we have not rid Hinduism of the stain of untouchability, it is impossible to achieve real Hindu-Muslim unity," he argued.[11] "Very thoughtful" Muslim friends had frankly told him that they could have very little "regard" for a faith that so demeaned millions of its members. At Vykom in Travancore State on the Malabar coast of South India, a Satyagraha struggle had been launched more than a year before to open to untouchables a public road that passed close to a Hindu temple. Gandhi had been too weak soon after his operation to join that struggle but had kept in touch with its imprisoned leaders, and he now resolved to visit them.

"In my opinion, untouchability is a blot upon humanity and therefore upon Hinduism. It cannot stand the test of reason. It is in conflict with the fundamental precepts of Hinduism," he told a cheering public meeting at Vykom on March 10, 1925.[12] The next day Gandhi addressed some fifty satyagrahis in their Vykom ashram, advising them of what to expect on the long road ahead. "We are endeavouring to rid Hinduism of its greatest blot. The prejudice we have to fight against is age-long prejudice."[13] He urged them to be sanitary, frugal, and punctual and to spin every day. "We

[119]

have become lazy as a nation, we have lost the time sense. Selfishness dominates our action. There is mutual jealousy amongst the tallest of us. We are uncharitable to one another." He was thus teaching them much more than how to open a road; he was sharing the wisdom he had acquired so painfully in many an arduous struggle. Before year's end the roads had been fully opened round Vykom, but the blight of untouchability had still to be removed from Hinduism.

His strength and spirits restored in the aftermath of that Vykom victory, Gandhi embarked on a nationwide tour, starting in Bengal. At the end of May he met with India's Nobel laureate poet Gurudev Rabindranath Tagore at his rural college, Santiniketan. They spent three days together in talks, which proved so disheartening to Gandhi that none of them is reported in his *Collected Works*, which contain virtually every other speech, interview, verbatim discussion, and letter written by or to him that year. Tagore's earlier rejection of Gandhi's insistence on hand spinning, as well as Gandhi's negative judgments on Western civilization and modern science, remained unchanged. Gandhi tried his best to win over India's greatest literary figure but failed to do so. Gandhi's faith in God was matched by Tagore's faith in art, but Bengal's Divine-Teacher Poet and Gujarat's Great-Souled-Saint never could agree about how best to cure the grave ills of their beloved motherland.

From Santiniketan, Gandhi went to Darjeeling to visit C. R. Das, Bengal's greatest political leader at this time. "I do want you to learn spinning," Gandhi urged reluctant Das. "You can do it if you will but put your mind to it. . . . Do learn the thing and spin religiously for half an hour for the sake of the millions and in the name of God. It will give you peace and happiness."[14] But Das died on June 16, 1925, before learning to spin.

Gandhi decided not to convene an All-Parties Conference in the wake of Das's death, though many urged him to do so. He argued that Hindus and Muslims "are not more ready today for coming together than we were in Delhi [last year]."[15] Motilal Nehru was now left alone to lead the Swarajist Party that Das had helped him to organize and run. Motilal himself was quite ill and his barrister son, Jawaharlal, was unwilling to help him run either his law firm or the Swaraj Party, though he accepted Gandhi's invitation to serve as Congress's general secretary. Young Nehru's wife was suffering from tuberculosis, and he soon decided to take her to Switzerland for treatment, eager to return to Europe and London.

Gandhi had a more permanently alienated son of his own, Harilal. A Muslim shareholder in a "Stores" company of which Harilal became a director hired a lawyer to try (to no avail) to locate him and reclaim money invested in shares. The lawyer appealed to Gandhi for help. "I do indeed happen to be the father of Harilal M. Gandhi," Gandhi replied, disclaiming, however, "all responsibility, moral or otherwise, for the doings of even those who are nearest and dearest to me except those wherein they act with me or, I permit them to act in my name. . . . I alone know my sorrows and my troubles in the course of the eternal duel going on within me and which admits of no truce. . . . [E]ven my swaraj activity has a bearing on that duel. It is for the supreme satisfaction of my soul that I engage in it. 'This is self-ishness double distilled,' said a friend once to me. I quickly agreed with him."[16] Rarely did Gandhi more frankly or poignantly reveal his innermost passionate pain, the "eternal duel" in his heart, triggered by Harilal's tragic fall. "I do not know Harilal's affairs," the wounded father wrote on being told of his son's bankrupt business ventures. "He meets me occasionally, but I never pry. . . . I do not know how his affairs stand at present, except that they are in a bad way. . . . There is much in Harilal's life that I dislike. He knows that. But I love him in spite of his faults. The bosom of a father will take him in as soon as he seeks entrance."

Britain's Tory party was returned to power before the end of 1925, bringing Stanley Baldwin to 10 Downing Street and devout Christian Vice-roy Lord Irwin to Calcutta, on the eve of that city's most bloody communal rioting in decades. Baldwin's arch-conservative secretary of state for India, Lord Birkenhead, appointed seven Englishmen to a Statutory Commission early in 1927 to devise the "next stage" of constitutional reforms for India. Without a single Indian member, that commission, chaired by Sir John Si-mon, roused universal opposition, with every Indian party, Congress, and Muslim League vowing to boycott all of its hearings. Birkenhead's arro-gance almost sufficed to untangle Hindu-Muslim differences, briefly bring-ing Congress and the League to the brink of what had been their heyday of cooperation at Lucknow in 1916.

Gandhi's reaction to Britain's electoral shift to the right and to Birken-head's racist intransigence was, however, to withdraw again from the polit-ical front-line position he had taken up only after grave hesitation. After turning over his Congress presidency to Sarojini Naidu in December 1925, Gandhi announced his decision to retire for a full year to his ashram to de-vote himself to spinning, writing, and the needs of his ashram family. He no longer believed in the efficacy of parliamentary commissions, whether Eng-lish or Indian, to resolve India's deep-rooted conflicts and painful prob-lems. He needed no Simon Commission to tell him what to do, no narrow-minded racist British "trustees" like Birkenhead, who held India in "bondage for their own benefit."[17] He knew the way out, but he was also acutely conscious of just how painful a road it would be for his army of barefoot pilgrims to follow. Instead of steaming off to London as he had two decades earlier from South Africa, to plead with prideful, overfed lords on behalf of his starving naked children, Gandhi turned back to his ashram, passionately spinning, weaving, reconstructing, planting seeds for a better future, and working to mend every heart and soul there in the hopes of tapping into the eternal faith of Indian civilization.

Not every English aristocrat agreed, of course, with Birkenhead's myopic views of India and its leaders. Many of Britain's best and brightest sons and daughters now looked to Gandhi as much more than the former president of a distant nationalist party. Madeleine Slade, the brilliant daughter of British Admiral Slade, learned from her friend Romain Rolland, when she visited his Swiss chateau in 1924, that Gandhi "is another Christ."[18] Rolland's brief but compelling appreciation *Mahatma Gandhi*, first published in French, won many new Gandhian admirers throughout Western Europe at this time. None was more devoted than Miss Slade, however. Gandhi's "sister" (*behn*) disciple soon joined his ashram, reborn and renamed by him Mirabehn. She learned to spin cotton and weave, remaining one of his most beloved followers and serving her "Dear Master" Mahatma faithfully, tirelessly, as a "bridge between West and East."[19] Though Mira became his most famous and politically helpful Western follower, she was not, of course, the only European woman lured by his saintly reputation and growing international fame to join the ashram. Helene Haussding, a German singer whom Gandhi named his "Sparrow," also came to join his busy ashram in 1926. Poor Sparrow fell ill, however, and thus felt obliged to fly home in less than a year. Gandhi reprimanded her for so swiftly losing "mental equanimity" and "hugging" her disease, rather than warding it off, as Mira so resolutely did every time she fell victim to malaria, dysentery, or ennui. Gandhi regarded every "disease" as "a result of some conscious or unconscious sin or breaches of Nature's laws."[20] He was keenly conscious at this time of what he confessed to be an "eternal duel" within his passionate nature, "a curious mixture of Jekyll and Hyde."[21]

Prayer remained Gandhi's first line of defense, though he continued to experiment with dietary means of warding off evil attacks, mental as well as physical. "If you give up salt and ghee," he advised wealthy friend and patron G. D. Birla, "it will certainly help you in cooling down your passions. It is essential to give up spices as well as pan and the like. One cannot subdue one's sex and allied passions merely with a restricted diet. . . . Absolute cessation of desire comes only after revelation of the Supreme."[22] Gandhi often spoke of the virtues of austerity, urging all of his children and friends to abstain from sex, arguing that it was easier to practice *Brahmacharya* (sexual abstinence) than strict restraint of the palate. His most devout disciples, like Vinoba Bhave and Mirabehn, never married, but most ashramites did. Austere marriage ceremonies, with no gifts, jewels, or flowers, were performed at the ashram, with Gandhi invariably urging sexual "self-restraint" upon each of the couples.

By focusing his energy on his ashram family and hand-spinning labors,

Gandhi hoped to create an ideal community that would serve as an example to all of India and to the rest of the world, of the virtues of a harmonious society built on principles of truth and love. The *Sarvodaya* ("uplift of all") socialist revolution thus started would, he believed, do more to bring India true freedom than all of Britain's costly commissions and ponderous constitutions.

Several American friends invited Gandhi to visit the United States, offering to arrange a lucrative speaking tour for him. His rejection of that offer contains one of Gandhi's clearest articulations of his passionate hopes and priorities. "I do want to think in terms of . . . the good of mankind in general. Therefore, my service of India includes the service of humanity. But I feel that I should be going out of my orbit if I left it for help from the West. . . . If I go to America . . . I must go in my strength, not in my weakness, which I feel today—the weakness I mean, of my country. For the whole scheme for the liberation of India is based upon the development of internal strength. It is a plan of self-purification. . . . I believe in thought-power more than in the power of the word, whether written or spoken. And if the movement that I seek to represent has vitality in it and has divine blessing upon it, it will permeate the whole world. . . . I must patiently plod in India until I see my way clear for going outside the Indian border."[23]

He subsequently told an American visitor to his ashram: "My message to America is simply the hum of this spinning-wheel. It is to me substitute for gun-power. For, it brings the message of self-reliance and hope to the millions of India. . . . A century ago every cottage was able to replenish its resources by means of the spinning-wheel. . . . But now it has all but died away."[24] He no longer focused on rapid revolutionary changes through political pressure or even by victorious Satyagraha, but on the slow, daily incremental socioeconomic changes every peasant could bring to his and her life, each contributing to India's eventual Swaraj, by hourly hand spinning. "The mother is groaning under poverty," Gandhi continued, explaining why he felt compelled so passionately to shift his focus from the world and national scene to the poorest peasant's household. "She has no milk. . . . What am I to ask these millions to do? To kill off their babies? . . . I take to them the gospel of hope—the spinning-wheel."[25]

Asked by an Indian correspondent living in London what India could contribute toward world peace, Gandhi replied from his ashram that "if India succeeds in regaining her liberty through non-violent means, she would have made the largest contribution yet known to world peace."[26] He was thus well aware of the universal significance and potential power for the salvation of humanity of the revolutionary movement he led, but now concentrated more on each revolution of his small wheel and on not breaking the single fragile strand of cotton thread he drew from it, than on remote world peace.

In response to an American skeptic, who challenged the viability of his message, arguing that "the average person is not a Mahatma," Gandhi insisted: "I am as frail a mortal as any of us and . . . I never had anything extraordinary about me. . . . I claim to be a simple individual liable to err like any other fellow mortal. I own, however, that I have humility enough in me to confess my errors and to retrace my steps. I own that I have an immovable faith in God and His goodness and unconsumable passion for truth and love. But is that not what every person has latent in him?"[27]

He equated cotton spinning with his own religious quest "to see God face to face," as he explained to a young correspondent from Kerala. "I do not think that there ever will be one religion in India. . . . But there will be and should be sincere respect and toleration for one another's religion. . . . If everybody spins regularly there need be no surplus self-spun yarn but there will be enough for all."[28] So on he spun, working long hours, at times more than ten daily at his wheel, whose soft hum sounded like heavenly music to his protruding ears. He rejected many invitations to travel, one from China, another from Austria, and several more from America, firmly resolved to focus on the task he had taken in hand. His preoccupation with spinning, like his passionate devotion to God, whose "presence" he felt "within me" as he spun, saved Gandhi, he now confessed, from becoming "a raving maniac," since "I see so much of misery."[29] He tried to teach sensitive, tortured Mirabehn to "love humanity in spite of itself," opening his yogic mind as well as his heart to her whenever she despaired in the face of India's ocean of misery. "The Ashram is finally not at Sabarmati but in yourself," Gandhi explained. "The vilest beings must enter there purified . . . in this universe of opposites remaining unaffected even as the lotus remains unaffected by water though immersed in it. . . . With love, Bapu."[30]

Hindu-Muslim conflicts claimed more lives in British India in 1926–7 than during the previous decade. "It has passed out of human hands, and has been transferred to God's hands alone," Gandhi cried. "We are disgracing His earth, His name and this sacred land by distrusting and fearing one another. Although we are sons and daughters of the same motherland, . . . we have no room for one another."[31] On December 23, 1926, Swami Shraddhanand was assassinated in his Calcutta home by a Muslim fanatic, who fired two bullets point blank into the ailing old Hindu Brahman's chest. Gandhi prayed that Indians of every faith might learn as their "lesson" from that treacherous crime that "we cannot live together in perpetual conflict."[32]

In the wake of Swami Shraddhanand's assassination, Gandhi was lured away from his ashram to memorialize his old friend. The Swami's Hindu devotees, many belonging to the Arya Samaj and studying Vedic scripture that promised a return for India to its mythical "golden age" when divine Raja Rama supposedly ruled over Ayodhya, now hailed Gandhi as their

Mahatma, believing him to be, like Rama, an "earthly emanation" (*avatara*) of Lord Vishnu.

Gandhi's blood pressure rose alarmingly. Doctor Wanless prescribed complete rest for Gandhi, including no spinning, as well as daily doses of patent medicine, both "remedies" rejected by the Mahatma who always considered himself the best doctor. He may have suffered a mild heart attack, which Mahadev Desai called "apoplexy," but other than rest, it went virtually untreated. "I had my own illusions and I over-worked myself, for which God has laid me low," Gandhi wrote, seeking to comfort another sick friend. To his patron and disciple, Jamnalal Bajaj, he said: "The light is bound to go out one day; now it has only dimmed."[33] By April 1, 1927, he was "tied down to the bed." Dr. Jivraj Mehta persuaded his stubborn friend to accept his invitation to recuperate in a cooler, calmer climate in the Nandi Hills near Bangalore, where he could indulge in "light reading" and finish writing his autobiography.[34]

Mira was so despondent without him that she wrote daily of her depression and weakness, eliciting his response in late April: "If the separation becomes unbearable, you must come without waiting for an answer or any prompting from me. . . . On no account should there be a breakdown. . . . [T]he Devil is ever after us and catches us at our weakest. He found me weak and wanting and trapped me. Your fast therefore does not worry me. . . . You must develop iron nerves. It is necessary for our work. God be with you."[35]

Gandhi left his sickbed to open the national *Khadi* (hand-spun and handwoven cloth) Exhibition in Bangalore on July 3, 1927. "I stand before you as a self-chosen representative of the dumb, semi-starved . . . millions of India," he told the wealthy thousands gathered outside the beautiful exhibit stalls displaying a rich variety of handmade goods. "Every pice you contribute to the support of khadi, every yard of khadi you buy, means so much concrete sympathy . . . for these millions. . . . Fifty-thousand spinners worked during the year. . . . These spinners, before they took to hand-spinning had not other earnings or occupation. . . . The very fact that fifty thousand women were eager to do this work for what may appear to us to be a miserable wage should be sufficient workable demonstration that hand-spinning is not an uneconomic, profitless . . . proposition. . . . God willing, at no distant time we shall find our villages, which at the present moment seem to be crumbling to ruins, becoming hives of honest and patient industry. . . . In the work of God, as I venture to suggest it is, the harvest is indeed rich."[36] He never tired of spinning or recruiting spinners, rich and poor, peasants and kings.

"The opening ceremony went off . . . well," Bapu wrote devoted Mira the next day. She had come to spend a week with him before leaving to join Vinoba Bhave in Wardha at the ashram he started building there on Jamnalal Bajaj's land, which he had given to Gandhi for his disciples. "The doctors came afterwards and they were satisfied to find no alteration in the pulse."[37] Thus he focused mostly on spinning, his own health, and the movements of his ashram family in the half decade after the tragic trauma that forced him to call off his first nationwide Satyagraha. But he had not lost hope of regrouping his army of the unarmed, marshaling his own strength again for the next big push, waiting for the voice of God to rouse him to action.

12

Rising of the Poison

"THINGS ARE GOING from bad to worse," Gandhi wrote Jawaharlal Nehru in mid-1927, "and it is quite plain that we have not yet drunk the last dregs. But I regard all this rising of the poison to the surface as a necessary process in national up-building."[1] Britain's Tory government ended all attempts at liberal cooperation, begun by ministers like Morley and Montagu, trusting instead to racist reactionaries like Birkenhead. Young Nehru, expecting nothing better from London, turned to Moscow for his ideological inspiration. Gandhi looked within, waiting for a whispered message.

Devastating floods washed away entire subdistricts of Gujarat that August, turning once fecund fields into a "howling wilderness."[2] Shocked though he was by the flood, Gandhi never lost his equanimity, recalling Lord Krishna's admonition to Arjuna that "what is unavoidable thou shouldst not regret."[3] To Gandhi this flood was, moreover, but a prelude to "the final deluge. None need doubt it. . . . [A]ll of us are condemned to death the moment we are born."[4] Vallabhbhai Patel led the relief work in flooded Nadiad and wired to reassure Gandhi that he need not personally risk a relapse by coming to join the massive depressing effort to salvage ruined villages. Others, however, wired to rebuke him for not rushing "home" to help save his province in its hour of greatest need. But he felt himself "fully occupied in grappling with the fatal disease which is eating into the vitals not only of Gujarat but of India as a whole."[5]

Gandhi was finishing his tour of South India and preparing to begin a sea voyage from Bombay to Colombo when he received a wired invitation from Viceroy Lord Irwin, who was "anxious" to discuss "important and rather urgent matters"[6] with him. The viceroy asked Gandhi to call upon him in Delhi on November 2, and the Mahatma agreed. He was still frail, recuperating from his illness, but took the crowded train ride some 1,200 miles from Mangalore to Delhi just to see what the new austere Christian viceroy, a friend of Charlie Andrews, wanted. Their first meeting lasted less than an hour, the viceroy handing Gandhi Whitehall's memo on the Simon Commission. The Mahatma warned that it would accomplish nothing without Indian members and wondered why Irwin could not have sent him that piece of paper through the mail. "He is a good man with no power," Gandhi concluded.[7] Irwin's view of Gandhi, who had tried to convert him to hand spinning, was "rather like talking to someone who had stepped off another planet." Each, in fact, underestimated the other's political perspicuity and power.

In September 1927, Jinnah chaired a conference of Hindu and Muslim leaders in Simla, hoping, in vain, to restore Hindu-Muslim unity in the spirit of Lucknow, 1916. Congress also tried, in late October 1927 in Calcutta, to resurrect the postwar feeling of cooperation between India's two greatest religious communities. Gandhi was invited, but he had "no faith" in such meetings and so attended neither. "In an atmosphere which is surcharged with distrust, fear and hopelessness, in my opinion these devices rather hinder than help heart unity."[8]

Gandhi's health continued to preoccupy him, particularly given his belief that every disease was caused by some "sin," whose exact source might remain unknown. "When the mind is disturbed by impure thought," he wrote a friend seeking advice on how to restrain himself, "one should occupy it in some work. . . . Never let the eyes follow their inclination. If they fall on a woman, withdraw them immediately. . . . [D]esire for sex-pleasure is equally impure, whether its object is one's wife or some other woman."[9] The fifty-eight-year-old Mahatma had just returned from his visit with Ba to Sri Lanka and was touring Orissa alone, until Mira left the ashram to join him there. He did not bother to attend the annual Congress session in Madras, so alienated did he feel from the organization he had dramatically refashioned less than a decade earlier.

Jawaharlal Nehru went directly to the Madras Congress, however, on returning from Europe, where he had visited Moscow and the Kremlin for celebrations of the tenth anniversary of the Bolshevik revolution. "This Congress declares the goal of the Indian people to be independence with full control over the defence forces of the country," Nehru moved as the first Congress resolution carried in Madras.[10] Gandhi was shocked when he heard of that impractical demand and criticized the decision in his correspondence with Nehru. The rift between Congress's two greatest leaders, begun after Chauri Chaura, thus widened and would continue to grow. Not only twenty years younger than Gandhi but armed to the teeth with

Marxist dialectics, Jawaharlal pressed on: "What then can be done? You say nothing—you only criticize and no helpful lead comes from you."[11] Nehru had no faith in hand spinning and considered Gandhi's ancient Hindu ideals outdated and impractical, if not reactionary. Jawaharlal felt certain that old Bapu badly misjudged the civilization of the West and attached much too great importance to its weaknesses and failings, ignoring the potent strengths of industrialism.

Gandhi tried to explain why he found Nehru's "independence" resolution so obnoxious. "Personally, I crave not for 'independence,' which I do not understand, but I long for freedom from the English yoke. I would pay any price for it. I would accept chaos in exchange for it. For the English peace is the peace of the grave."[12] Britain's "Satanic rule" had ruined India, Gandhi argued, not only materially, but also morally and spiritually. Three hundred million Indian souls were crushed under the heels of a hundred thousand Englishmen. Nehru had argued that class conflict made armed revolution inevitable to liberate India. Gandhi insisted on nonviolent conversion rather than coercion, reiterating his passionate yogic faith in self-suffering. His ambition was "higher than independence. Through the deliverance of India, I seek to deliver the so-called weaker races of the earth from the crushing heels of Western exploitation." Finally, he wanted to convert enough Englishmen to his faith so that Britain and India would join one day as peaceful partners in a world commonwealth. Nehru's harsh critique had forced Gandhi to explain his true long-range plan, to convert the world to his religious philosophy of love and truth through the might of his great soul's self-suffering. He had, after all, converted Mirabehn from the admiral's daughter to his loving sister, and the Reverend Charlie Andrews to his dearest male disciple, and Muriel Lester, Henry Polak, and Dr. Joseph Doke.

In his remaining two decades he would gather millions more such good and selfless souls from Great Britain, America, and Europe to help India not only liberate its hundreds of millions from harsh imperial shackles but also to try to transform the starving poorer half of that continent's population into working spinners and weavers, capable of feeding their families. Nehru, like Marx and Lenin, favored a far different sort of revolution, though he was clever enough to remain this powerful Mahatma's chosen "successor," rather than bolting Congress to lead a youthful left-coalition on his own.

From his ashram in late January 1928 Gandhi wrote to urge Jawaharlal to break free of him. "If any freedom is required from me, I give you all the freedom you may need," the Mahatma suggested. "I see quite clearly that you must carry on open warfare against me and my views. For, if I am wrong I am evidently doing irreparable harm to the country and it is your duty . . . to rise in revolt against me. . . . Write to me a letter for publication showing your differences. I will print it in *Young India* and write a brief reply. . . . With love, Bapu."[13] That forthright offer sufficed to bring a halt to young Nehru's criticism, at least for the time being. After he presided over the Congress, thanks to Gandhi's support and his father's initiative, he would grow much more confident of his own judgment.

Gandhi's blood pressure rose so high in February 1928 that he was advised by doctors to stay at the ashram, preferably lying down as much as possible. "Except for spinning, therefore, I am on my back," he wrote his "Dear Child" Esther, in Denmark.[14] He did not participate in the massive boycotts of the Simon Commission, organized in Bombay with a black flag "welcome" by Jinnah, and in Delhi and Allahabad by both Nehrus, Ansari, and other Congress leaders, all of whom rallied India's youth to leave their college lecture halls and protest the racist arrogance of imperial paternalism. Gandhi alone remained away from that All-Parties Conference in Delhi, which was chaired by Ansari. Young Nehru attended for more than a week, but the endless arguments over how precisely to draft a formula agreeable to all the deeply divided Hindu and Muslim parties represented there drove Jawaharlal away "to avoid riot and insurrection!"[15] So at least he reported to Gandhi, reaffirming the latter's wisdom in remaining aloof from that futile conference. Jinnah blamed that Delhi conference's final breakdown on extremist Hindu Mahasabha ("Great Society") pressures that convinced Congress leaders to back off. It was one of the last major opportunities and rational attempts to reconcile Hindu and Muslim political demands, hopes, and aspirations, another tragic failure to resolve South Asia's most explosive internal problem.

Motilal Nehru now sent Jawaharlal to Sabarmati to seek Gandhi's advice on how best to respond to Great Britain's challenge that India's political leaders draft their own new constitution if they persisted in boycotting the Simon Commission. "Personally I am of opinion that we are not ready for drawing up a constitution," Gandhi wrote. "I would . . . prefer instead of a constitution, a working arrangement between all parties . . . the Hindu-Muslim arrangement, the franchise, the policy as to the Native States. . . . I should bring in total prohibition and exclusion of foreign cloth."[16] Father Nehru and his brilliant son thus lured the Mahatma back from his ashram retreat to the center of the political struggle that engulfed all of South Asia in its titanic battle with Britain's imperial raj. "Unless we have created some force ourselves, we shall not advance beyond the position of beggars, and I have given all my time to thinking over this one question," Gandhi added. "I can think of nothing else but boycott of foreign cloth." Boycotting British cottons raised the value of India's hand-spun cloth, which still preoccupied Gandhi's mind. Soon, however, he would think of another "force," turning his laser-like yogic passion from cotton to salt.

Many friends now urged him to return to the political arena to lead them on the long road to freedom. "I am biding my time and you will find me leading the country in the field of politics when the country is ready," he responded to one such appeal.[17] Then in May he wrote to Motilal Nehru, who also pressed him to return to active political duty: "I have no faith in a legislative solution of the communal question. And who will listen to my drastic views on almost every matter?"[18] Nonetheless, he answered the elder Nehru's call to go to Bombay to be "available" to those who planned to attend the Congress Working Committee's meetings there.

Motilal hoped at this time to win the working committee's support for his son Jawaharlal to become next president of Congress. Some Congress leaders preferred Sardar Vallabhbhai Patel to young Nehru, however, especially in light of the heroic satyagraha Vallabhbhai led in Bardoli District. Bengal's members were not willing to host the Congress in Calcutta if Jawaharlal presided. So Gandhi decided to urge Motilal to take the burden one last time rather than handing it down to his as yet untested son. Ailing Motilal, though long since dead by the time India won its independence, was thus the founding father of India's Nehru dynasty.

It was Vallabhbhai Patel's victory in the Bardoli Satyagraha campaign, won that August of 1928, that restored much of Gandhi's lost faith in his ability to rally again the nonviolent army he had mobilized in 1921. "The noble band of volunteers who had the privilege of serving under Vallabhbhai deserve the highest praise for their devotion and splendid discipline," Gandhi wrote.[19] A week later he reminded his faithful *Young India* readers: "The bigger battle is still before us—the battle for freedom of which the campaign was planned in 1921 and which has yet to be fought."[20] Motilal Nehru now also completed his report on India's constitutional "All-Parties" demand for immediate self-governing dominion status, which unfortunately satisfied none of the major Muslim parties or their leaders, since it eliminated separate election seats reserved for Muslims on all councils. Shaukat Ali and Jinnah both believed that Motilal's mind had been "captured" by orthodox Hindu Mahasabha leaders, thus irreparably widening the communal ravine.

That November of 1928, Gandhi noted "deep darkness all round," especially in the growing number of Hindu-Muslim riots. Mounting frustrations caused by the Simon Commission triggered popular boycott of its hearing and black flag protests wherever it went. In Punjab's capital of Lahore, one such march, led by Lala Lajpat Rai, ended in a violent charge by police, whose iron-tipped lathi blows on Lala's chest and back mortally wounded him. Gandhi eulogized Lala Lajpat as a martyr to India, urging all patriotic Muslims to join Hindu mourners in their prayers for Punjab's fearless fallen leader. Shaukat Ali replied, however, with an angry, anti-Hindu speech, and though Gandhi pleaded with his former "brother" to retract what he'd said, Shaukat refused Gandhi's invitation to talk about ways of avoiding future communal strife.

Jawaharlal Nehru led a Lucknow rally against the Simon Commission that December and was also severely beaten by police lathis. "My love to you," Gandhi wrote when he learned of the struggle. "May God spare you for many a long year to come and make you His chosen instrument for freeing India."[21] Motilal, outraged by that police attack against his son, prepared himself for the second and last session of Congress over which he would preside. Gandhi traveled with a party of twenty-five ashramites to Calcutta to attend that Congress session in late December.

Hindu Mahasabha leader Dr. B. S. Moonje of Nagpur invited Gandhi to become leader of all "Hindus" on the eve of the Congress, which the Mahatma declined, humorously asking "How can a Mahatma living up in the clouds give any lead?" He also asked the arch-reactionary Hindu zealot, whose violent feelings about Indian Muslims were hardly disguised, "Why do you expect Mussalmans to be Hindus in Hindustan?"[22] All Indians, Hindus, Muslims, Jews, and Christians alike should be allowed freely to follow their own religions, Gandhi argued. For advocating so enlightened a policy of multicultural coexistence, Gandhi's own life would be taken two decades later by one of Dr. Moonje's equally fanatical disciples.

Gandhi spoke at the Congress Subjects Committee meeting in support of Motilal Nehru's report on December 26, 1928, calling for full dominion status as the next constitutional step for India. Jawaharlal Nehru and his youthful cadre of Congress followers insisted on total independence as the only honorable goal for India, arguing that dominion status left India "enslaved" to British imperial rule. "The fire of independence is burning within me as much as in the most fiery breast of anyone in the country but the ways and methods may differ," Gandhi passionately responded. "Freedom has never come by stealing. It has come by bleeding and you will have to bleed even for getting what is attempted in that Report."[23] More blood had just been spilled in Punjab, when the assistant superintendent of Lahore, Mr. Saunders, was assassinated by Bhagat Singh and Sukhdev in "retaliation" for Lala Lajpat Rai's death. Gandhi denounced that "dastardly act" and expressed his unchanging wish that it was possible to convince "hot youth of the utter futility of such revenge."[24] The assassins were later hanged and hailed as martyrs to the nation's fight for freedom.

Only two days after introducing his resolution in support of Motilal Nehru's report, Gandhi felt obliged to withdraw it and offer another resolution. His action was spurred by the angry opposition to the ideas of the elder Nehru spearheaded primarily by his son's insistence on complete independence. "National life is a perpetual struggle," a weary Gandhi commented in moving his new compromise motion. "Often the struggle between our own ranks is more prolonged, more exacting and even more bitter than the struggle against the environment which is outside our-selves."[25] Jawaharlal absented himself from the Congress Subjects Com-mittee meeting Gandhi now addressed, sulking in his tent, after having re-versed his position following several sleepless nights. Gandhi sympathized with young Nehru's idealistic impatience but knew that Britain's Tory government would only scoff at any demand now for independence, prob-ably even ignore the more moderate call for dominion status.

Gandhi's empathetic insight into Jawaharlal's mercurial, Hamlet-like psyche and temperament made him resolve at this Calcutta Congress, where he met and argued with both Nehrus around the clock for two long days and heated nights, to return to Congress's political frontline. He per-ceived that brilliant barrister Jawaharlal was so thoroughly disillusioned by Motilal's pleas for patience and so contemptuous of the bourgeois values and ideas of his father's generation of liberal Anglicized Indians that he was chafing dangerously at the bit, ready to quit Congress to lead an Indo-Bol-shevik party in revolution. Gandhi alone had the passionate authority to hold Jawahar and his comrades within Congress's national harness, for Gandhi lived the penurious peasant life of hardship, whose virtues they ide-alized and romanticized. He lived it, of course, as his preferential penance of suffering and pain to share the privations of India's landless laboring outcaste starving children. But to hold such an idealist as young Nehru in check Gandhi knew that he would have to abandon his life of rural retreat, returning first to the hurly-burly of urban political chaos like that he had found so hateful in Calcutta, and then to the enforced solitude of long years behind British bars and barbed wire walls.

"Our life is a perpetual struggle against oppressive environments and . . . within our ranks," a bone-weary Gandhi sighed. He then read and moved the new resolution, which endorsed the Motilal Nehru Report's proposed Dominion Status Constitution for only one year, until December 31, 1929. If by that date Great Britain did not accept this offer by Congress to remain within its Commonwealth, Congress would then organize a na-tionwide, nonviolent campaign of noncooperation, including nonpayment of taxes as well as total boycott of all British imports and institutions. Then the cry of *Purna Swaraj* ("Complete Independence") was to be raised as the National Congress demand, and Mahatma Gandhi promised young Nehru and his comrades that he personally would lead them in a new Satyagraha revolution to the promised land they so desperately longed for and were so impatient to reach. But after his "all-night vigil" in the little tent where he'd been dragged by Motilal, anxious to keep his rebel son in harness, the fifty-nine-year-old Gandhi confessed as he moved the new resolution that "my brain is muddled."[26]

Gandhi wrote a lengthy account, published in his *Young India* on Jan-uary 10, 1929, of the Congress meeting, calling for its "complete overhauling. . . . We shall gain nothing by a policy of 'hush hush.' The disease must be made known all over the Congress world. . . . The volunteers dressed in European fashion presented, in my opinion, a sorry spectacle at Calcutta and the expense incurred was out of keeping with the pauperism of the nation. . . . Congress must not be used for making money. . . . We are a nation passing through the valley of humiliation. So long as we have not secured our freedom we have not the least excuse at the annual stock-taking season for amusements, riotous or subdued."[27] Now that he was called back into political harness he resolved to try at least to whip Congress's laggard army of shoddy recruits into shape for the struggle ahead.

13

The Road Back to Satyagraha

F OR GANDHI the call to action proved a tonic. By mid-January of 1929 he resolved to cancel a tentatively planned tour of Europe that would potentially have included a visit to America. Though he had barely had time for sleep in Calcutta, he had lost only one pound there. His health was suddenly better than it had been for seven years, since last he led a national struggle. Work had always agreed with him; work with the prospect of national liberation, Swaraj, proved to be his best medicine.

He drew up a scheme for reactivating the Congress and mobilizing its local committees to serve as volunteers going "from door to door in every town and village" to collect foreign cloth that was to be "publicly burnt" and to take orders for handwoven cloth from every householder. "Picketing foreign cloth shops may be undertaken wherever possible. . . . All units should from day to day report to the Central Office details of work done. . . . Help of patriotic ladies should be enlisted. . . . A small Foreign Cloth Boycott Committee should be formed and entrusted with an initial fund with power to collect more funds."[1] He was in his element, organizing, ordering, and auditing, all his inherited Vania (merchant caste) virtues brilliantly sparking his Mahatmaic spirit to practical action.

Gandhi toured Sind, collecting money and gathering new disciples for the struggle he would soon lead, which all believed would be the final push to achieve national independence. Even when he learned that his grandson, seventeen-year-old Rasik, Harilal's boy, lay dying in Delhi, he continued to work. Ba and the boy's mother and his uncle Devdas were at Rasik's bedside for the last painful days and nights, but not Gandhi, who was in Larkana when he received news of his grandson's death. Gandhi recalled, after reading Devdas's wire, that "I took my meal as usual and kept on working."[2] His karma yogic indifference to pleasure and pain alike helped sustain him, as did his faith that Rasik's soul (*atman*) was liberated to a "better state," closer to Lord Rama, whose devotee he, like Gandhi, had been. True Hindu that he was, Gandhi never shed any tears over the death of a loved one, for such grief would only inhibit the soul's release from karmic snares of mortal name and form and the delusions of earthly existence. "The cage had become old, was decaying and the swan flew away," he wrote of Rasik's death, "no cause in this for mourning."[3]

While in Delhi in mid-February, Gandhi had tea with the viceroy at Legislative Assembly Speaker Viththalbhai Patel's house. Of the meeting, Gandhi wrote, "nothing" happened. "Our salvation lies in our own hands. A fruitful meeting can only take place when we have gathered strength and become conscious of it."[4] He also met with the Congress Working Committee, including Motilal and Jawaharlal, who were planning the next move, not optimistic enough to expect the British to surrender India without a fight to a Congress Raj at year's end.

In early March he left by train for Calcutta en route to Burma, his party given a third-class carriage all to themselves, making him feel so pampered by authorities that he confessed to fearing he was "becoming a fraud."[5] In Calcutta he addressed a large crowd, urging them to burn all foreign cloth. "I want you to pledge yourselves," he told his receptive audience, "that you will burn them even as you burn rags . . . even as a drunkard suddenly become teetotaller empties his cupboard and destroys every bottle of brandy and whiskey. . . . You will count no cost too great against the . . . liberty and honour of your country."[6] He was almost back in his stride, broken seven years ago, when standing on the platform in Shraddhanand Park, staring down at the ocean of adoring eyes. The Calcutta police, however, served notice against any public bonfires, which made him hesitate to call for the burning of British cloth, for since his first jail term he was no longer permitted to practice law and was anxious not to provoke any violence. But the police moved in around the distant fringes of the crowd, using their loaded lathis, claiming that hoodlum-tossed brickbats had provoked them. Gandhi was charged with provoking an illegal demonstration, but the commissioner agreed to postpone his trial until Gandhi returned from Burma. He now urged his followers immediately to boycott all foreign cloth "charged as it is with such poisonous germs," removing all of it from Bengal, to be consigned to "flames."

That April, after several Hindu terrorists had thrown bombs into the Delhi Assembly and a Muslim assassin had knifed a Sikh to death in Punjab, Gandhi wrote forcefully against such "mad deeds." He urged Congressmen not to give "secret approval" to the bombers and Muslims to abstain from supporting the dagger-assassin. But then he wisely noted that bombs and knives really derived "their lease of life from the world's belief in violence as a remedy for securing supposed justice. . . . The insensate speed with which the nations of the West are hourly forging new weapons of destruction for purposes of war is suffocating the world with the spirit of violence. . . . The bomb-thrower and the assassin will live on so long as public opinion of the world tolerates war."[7] Whenever questioned about his earlier assistance during World War I and the wars in South Africa, Gandhi explained that he no longer felt as he had when he was so much younger and had viewed war in a less negative light. He would never revert to his previous position.

War resister, the Reverend. B. de Ligt, asked Gandhi to write more about his attitude toward war. Gandhi responded, "I know that if India comes to her own . . . through non-violent means, India will never want to carry a vast army, an equally grand navy, and a grander air force. . . . Such an India may be a mere day-dream, a childish folly. But such in my opinion is undoubtedly the implication of an India becoming free through non-violence. . . . [I]f India attains freedom by violent means she will cease to be a country of my pride; that time would be a time for me of civil death. There can therefore never be any question of my participation direct or indirect in any war of exploitation by India."[8]

During his visit to the Nehrus in Almora, Gandhi and Motilal agreed that Jawaharlal should be the next president of the Congress. Most Congress leaders wanted Gandhi himself, and young Nehru was reluctant to accept the "crown of thorns," but Gandhi launched his campaign with a strong article in *Young India* that August. "I am not keeping pace with the march of events. . . . I must take a back seat and allow the surging wave to pass over me," Gandhi wrote. "In my opinion the crown must be worn by Pandit Jawaharlal Nehru. . . . Older men have had their innings. The battle of the future has to be fought by younger men and women."[9] Most senior members of the Working Committee were unhappy at Gandhi's decision not to run, though Gandhi himself had no regrets about yielding to Motilal's insistence that his brilliant son sit on the throne he would vacate before year's end. Gandhi worked just as hard with or without the crown, still virtually worshipped by millions of Indians as their Mahatma, and he continued to enjoy the support of most of the Working Committee of Congress.

That August of 1929 Gandhi journeyed to Bombay to meet with Jinnah, the first of several summits between these two founding fathers of India and Pakistan, seeking a magic formula to resolve communal conflicts that soon tore apart British India. "No speculation need take place regarding my meeting Mr. Jinnah," Gandhi reported after they met in Jinnah's grand house atop Malabar Hill. "Our conversation was as between friends. . . . I have no representative capacity. . . . But naturally I want to explore all possible avenues to peace. . . . Meanwhile let those who believe in prayer pray with me that there may soon be peace between Hindus, Mussalmans and all the other communities."[10]

Britain's Tory government had fallen in May, and Labour's Prime Minister Ramsay MacDonald, Jinnah's old friend, moved into 10 Downing Street. Eager to untangle India's constitutional knots, MacDonald called Viceroy Lord Irwin home for consultations with his new Labour Secretary of State for India William Wedgwood Benn (later Viscount Stansgate). Prospects for dominion status within the year, as resolved by the last Congress, never seemed brighter. Jinnah's first recommendation to the new prime minister was for Great Britain to declare "without delay" its unequivocal pledge to a "policy of granting to India full responsible Government with Dominion status."[11] To implement so important a declaration he urged his liberal friend in power to invite those representatives of India, who could "deliver the goods" to a conference in London as quickly as possible. That brilliant advice would have short-circuited the unpopular Simon Commission's glacial labors and, had it been taken swiftly, might have saved India the endless agony of partition and Great Britain the loss of India's national support throughout World War II. Had Ramsay MacDonald courage enough to accept brilliant barrister Jinnah's astute advice, he would have aborted the Tory Simon Commission and offered India dominion status, with separate electorate reservations for Muslims, as Jinnah also suggested by way of modifying Motilal Nehru's Report, before the new year. With the dawn of 1930, then, India's Dominion, united and grateful to its British friends and allies, might well have embarked on an era of economic growth and political independence.

But Simon's conservative old guard proved too powerful to be scuttled by a fledgling prime minister, who felt he needed their foreign policy support to survive. The compromise reached in London, therefore, was for the new Home Government to convene a series of Round Table Conferences, to consider the "next step" for India's Constitution, based on the report of the Simon Commission. Since 1917, when Secretary of State Montagu first mentioned it, dominion status had been the ultimate goal of British policy for India. It remained so in 1929, but the question of just how long it would take before Westminister's Parliament felt her Indian offspring and ward ready for so "burdensome" a responsibility as freedom remained unanswered. So the golden opportunity was lost. Even as Gandhi's meeting with Jinnah proved little more than tea conversation, resolving nothing, so too did Irwin's meetings with Benn and MacDonald melt none of the ice that kept India locked in Britain's frozen imperial embrace.

A few days after his futile meeting with Jinnah, Gandhi's health broke down, his most recent dietary experiment of eating only uncooked vegetables and raw grains exposing him to so persistent a case of dysentery that he felt weaker than he had all year. By mid-August, he was forced to take to his ashram bed in Sabarmati. He gave up on raw food, returning to goat's milk, diluted curds, and fresh fruit juice. The Congress reception committee now met in Lahore, and by an "overwhelming majority" chose Gandhi to preside over the Punjab annual session in December. He wired his reply: "WHILST THANKING YOU UNABLE ACCEPT HONOUR. CONSIDER SELF UNFIT. APART FROM WANT OF ENERGY . . . AM OUT OF TUNE WITH MANY THINGS DONE CONGRESSMEN . . . PRAY ELECT PANDIT JAWAHARLAL NEHRU."[12] A month later he elaborated upon what he called "my limitations" for presiding over the Congress. "I have no faith in the council programme. I have no faith in Government schools and colleges. I have still less in the so-called courts of justice. . . . I have no faith in spectacular demonstrations. Whilst I want power for labour and its progressive welfare, I do not believe in its exploitation for a mere political end. I believe in unadulterated non-violence. . . . I believe that unity between Hindus, Mussalmans, Sikhs, Parsis, Jews, Christians and others is essential for the attainment of Swaraj. I believe the removal of untouchability to be equally essential. . . . I feel that among Congressmen there can only be a microscopic minority going with me in this long recital of credos. . . . I feel that as president of the Congress I should be a round man in a square hole."[13] Gandhi reiterated all these arguments at the All-India Congress Committee meeting in Lucknow in late September, after which the delegates elected Jawaharlal Nehru their next president.

"I have seldom felt quite so annoyed and humiliated," Jawaharlal recalled of that moment of his annointment. "It was not that I was not sensible of the honour. . . . But I did not come to it by the main entrance or even a side entrance; I appeared suddenly by a trap-door and bewildered the audience into acceptance."[14] His two patrons, father Motilal and adopted Bapu Gandhi, had conspired to elevate their son and heir to the Congress throne, but instead of feeling exalted at having achieved the summit on the eve of turning forty, moody Jawaharlal's "pride was hurt" and he "stole away with a heavy heart." A month after winning the presidency he tried to resign, crying to dear Bapuji, "I feel an interloper and am ill at ease. . . . I must resign. . . . I was a wrong choice."[15] Gandhi's response was brief but firm. "About the crown, no one else can wear it. It never was to be a crown of roses. Let it be all thorns. . . . [M]ay God give you peace."[16] Jawaharlal did as his Bapu told him about the crown, but, like Hamlet, never found peace.

Vallabhbhai Patel and his brother Viththalbhai tried their best to reach agreement with Jinnah in order to present a united front of India's political leadership to the viceroy and accept his invitation to a Round Table Conference to be convened by the Labour prime minister the following year in London. Sardar Vallabhbhai, destined to become India's first deputy prime minister, was as cool-headed as Jawaharlal was mercurial. "I sent you a wire after having had a long talk with Mr. Jinnah," he wrote Gandhi. "Before it is finally decided to close the door upon all future negotiations . . . yourself, Jinnah, Motilalji, Vithalbhai and Sapru should confer . . . or Jinnah and Vithalbhai should be given an opportunity to discuss the matter with you."[17] Vallabhbhai never mentioned Jawaharlal, knowing how dead set he then felt against reaching any agreement with any English leaders that resulted in dominion status. Jinnah had been assured by the viceroy that the conference could be "summoned" next July, a "general amnesty" declared, and an announcement made in London that the purpose of the conference was to "frame a scheme for Dominion Status."

It was everything they had so long hoped to achieve, most of them, both Patels, Motilal Nehru, and all the liberal and moderate leaders of the older generation. "Jinnah . . . is quite convinced of the good faith of the Labour Government as well as the Viceroy, and thinks that this opportunity should on no account be missed," Vallabhbhai wrote in his "personal" confidential letter to his beloved Bapuji. Gandhi, of course, agreed to the proposed meeting, but knew how unhappy and disgruntled Jawaharlal would be if instead of raising his cry of "Complete Independence" (*Purna Swaraj*) in two months, as promised at last year's Congress, he would be obliged to restrain his revolutionary frustrations and fury and return to long, arduous sessions of negotiation with Jinnah, the viceroy, and his own father. Had Motilal not insisted on crowning his son, Vallabhbhai instead could have been chosen and, despite his well-known Hindu-first reputation and orthodox prejudices, would clearly have been more prone to reach a realpolitik agreement with Jinnah than Marxist-Leninist-Shavian-Hamlet Jawaharlal ever was or would be.

Gandhi responded positively to cables from many English friends urging him to "reciprocate" to the new Labour government's overture. He was eager to cooperate and willing to wait for the Dominion Status Constitution, if the British people expressed "a real desire" to see India a "free and self-respecting nation." By that he meant replacing steel bayonets with "goodwill." If India was to remain in the Empire, it would only be to make Anglo-India's partnership one for promoting peace and goodwill in the world. Imperialistic "greed" must end, he insisted.[18] Sarojini Naidu, who adored Jinnah even more than Nehru or Gandhi, wired to Motilal to urge Gandhi to meet him, Jinnah, and the viceroy for a "private interview" in Bombay, but Gandhi found it "impossible" to alter his tour of the United Provinces at this time, unwilling to "disappoint tens of thousands" of villagers waiting to catch but a glimpse of their Mahatma.[19] One more golden window of opportunity lost.

No one at this time imagined, of course, that after this brief interval of sympathetic Labour rule in London, Britain's imperial raj would revert for over a decade and a half to the steel grip of Tory reactionaries. Having absented himself from England so long, Gandhi misjudged the importance of Labour's first government, downgrading the strong appeals and advice of English friends, and failed to negotiate in one week (or one month) what would never again be resolved short of war. Nehru, on the other hand, had more recent firsthand knowledge of England, yet unwisely lumped all Liberal-Labour leaders of London in the same "bourgeois" bag of antiquities that his Marxist comrades used for history's "dying class."

The viceroy once again suggested meeting with Motilal, Jinnah, and Gandhi, who stopped overnight in December's frosty Delhi. No political ice melted in that last-ditch meeting with Lord Irwin, who told them that they still had a chance "of doing something big," if only they would accept the "great opportunity" offered by the Round Table Conference.[20] Jawaharlal, however, had not been invited to the meeting and felt bitter at his exclusion, happy to note that the viceregal summit "came to nothing." The Calcutta Congress's year of grace was over.

In the early light of a freezing morning in Lahore, Jawaharlal Nehru unfurled India's tricolor, the "national flag of Hindustan," and told his Congress comrades, "it must not be lowered so long as a single Indian . . . lives in India." Congress opted to send no representatives to the forthcoming London Conference, and in keeping with their new demand of nothing less than complete independence, they also resolved in Lahore to boycott all legislative assemblies and local bodies. They thus prepared for the resumption of nationwide noncooperation, with Gandhi empowered to launch a new Satyagraha campaign in the new year. On New Year's Eve a bomb exploded after the train carrying Lord and Lady Irwin passed over the track, leaving them unscarred. Gandhi moved a resolution deploring that "bomb outrage," insisting that so long as Congress's creed remained to attain Swaraj "by peaceful and legitimate means," it was imperative for Congress to condemn such violent acts.[21]

When asked by a reporter to explain how the present noncooperation movement differed from the one launched in 1921, Gandhi said that this time the goal was "complete independence," whereas before it was only to address Khilafat and Punjab "wrongs." Would another Chauri Chaura event mean calling off the movement again? No suspension need take place by reason of any outside disturbance, he replied.

"We had burned our boats and could not go back," Jawaharlal recalled of that freezing dawn in 1930 when he grasped the banner of Congress, raising its battle cry of *Purna Swaraj*. "We believe that it is the inalienable right of the Indian people, as of any other people, to have freedom and to enjoy the fruits of their toil and have the necessities of life."[22] The pledge was taken publicly on January 26, 1930, thereafter celebrated annually as *Purna Swaraj* Day. Gandhi drafted it, and Nehru revised it and led the nation in stating, "The British Government in India has not only deprived the Indian people of their freedom but has based itself on the exploitation of the masses, and has ruined India economically, politically, culturally and spiritually. . . . We hold it to be a crime against men and God to submit any longer to a rule that has caused this fourfold disaster to our country."[23]

The dangers inherent in so bold a declaration were uppermost in Gandhi's mind, but he had decided that "[t]o sit still at this juncture is stupid if not cowardly. I have made up my mind to run the boldest risks," he confided in Charlie Andrews. "Lahore revealed it all to me. The nature of the action is not yet clear to me. It has to be civil disobedience. How it is to be undertaken and by whom besides me, I have not yet seen quite clearly. But the shining cover that overlays the truth is thinning day by day and will presently break."[24] The brilliant plan that would soon emerge from that shining cover was still incubating in his mind: the great march to "rob" salt from Dandi's beach.

Gandhi was encouraged by the peaceful mass turnout of January 26. Throughout India, millions affirmed their faith in the Purna Swaraj pledge, which they hailed. A few days later he published a list of specific reforms, which were required if Britain would avert civil disobedience. Among those proposals were total prohibition, the reduction of land revenue demands as well as military expenditure by at least 50 percent, and abolition of the salt tax. "Well might the points suggested by me as for immediate attention raise a storm of indignation in the British Press," he wrote a week later. "Englishmen . . . must part with some of the ill-gotten gains."[25] Millions had been looted from India by British rule, which he called the personification of violence, comparing the British to paralyzing snakes. Their violence hid behind camouflage and hypocrisy, declarations of good intentions, and dishonest conferences, designed to mask British greed and deceit. Imperial violence concealed itself under a "golden lid," provoking frustrated Indians to violence of the weak. Gandhi warned his followers that they must be on guard to work nonviolently in the midst of such double violence. He also alerted them to the ubiquitous presence of indigenous monied men, speculators, landholders, and factory owners, all of whom had emerged from and were sustained by British imperial rule. They must be taught to give up their "blood-stained gains." As soon as they became enlightened enough to see that holding onto millions was a crime, when millions of their own people were starving, freedom would be achieved. But as it drew near, the British would spread their "red paws" and seek to provoke violence. "The non-violent party must then prove its creed by being ground to powder between the two millstones."[26] Not a very cheerful prospect, but worthy of so passionate a leader, wed to suffering.

"Next to air and water, salt is perhaps the greatest necessity of life," Gandhi wrote now in *Young India*. "It is the only condiment of the poor.

Cattle cannot live without salt. . . . It is also a rich manure. There is no article like salt outside water by taxing which the State can reach even the starving millions, the sick, the maimed and the utterly helpless. The tax constitutes therefore the most inhuman poll tax that ingenuity of man can devise . . . 2,400 per cent on sale price! What this means to the poor can hardly be imagined by us. . . . [I]f the people had freedom, they could pick up salt from the deposits made by the receding tides on the bountiful coast."[27] He had found the key he'd been searching for, the simple universal grievance to rouse the masses from apathy and to fire their hearts with righteous indignation against the usurping imperial power, whose greed and pompous pride in its cruel exploitation of the poorest of India's downtrodden peasantry was no longer tolerable.

"Many curses have been handed down to us from time immemorial," Gandhi taught his awakening readers of *Young India*. "Only the whole people were never in the grip of the salt tax curse in the pre-British days. It was reserved for the British Government to reduce the curse to a perfect formula covering every man, woman, child and beast."[28]

14

The Salt March and
Prison Aftermath

"**B**EFORE EMBARKING on civil disobedience and taking the risk I have dreaded to take all these years, I would fain approach you and find a way out," Gandhi wrote "Dear Friend" Viceroy Lord Irwin on March 2, 1930.[1] "If India is to live as a nation, if the slow death by starvation of her people is to stop, some remedy must be found for immediate relief. The proposed Conference is certainly not the remedy. . . . I know that in embarking on non-violence I shall be running what might fairly be termed a mad risk. But the victories of truth have never been won without risks. . . . I respectfully invite you then to pave the way for immediate removal of those evils [earlier noted], and thus open a way for a real conference between equals. . . . But if you cannot see your way to deal with these evils . . . on the 11th day of this month I shall proceed with such co-workers of the Ashram as I can take, to disregard the provisions of the salt laws." Lord Irwin replied that he "regretted" Gandhi's decision "contemplating a course of action . . . bound to involve violation of the law and danger to the public peace."

Thus was launched Gandhi's most famous and difficult struggle against the world's largest, wealthiest, and most powerful empire. He told his band of male ashram followers to be ready to leave Sabarmati on the morning of March 12, 1930, and resolve not to return there until India was free. A horse accompanied them, just in case he felt too weak to walk the 240 miles to Dandi's beach, the final destination of this historic trek. A week before the march started, Vallabhbhai Patel was arrested, which Gandhi hailed as "a good omen for us. . . . The fight has now commenced."[2] Gandhi, who called Vallabhbhai "my right hand," said that his arrest had "broken" it. Three ashram children died of smallpox that week, which Gandhi also viewed as a portent. "On the eve of what is to be the final test of our strength, God is warning me through the messenger of death. . . . I may have to see not three but hundreds and thousands being done to death during the campaign I am about to launch. Shall my heart quail . . . or will I persevere in my faith? No, I want you, everyone, to understand that this epidemic is not a scourge, but a trial and preparation, a tribulation sent to steel our hearts."[3] His thoughts were focused on salt and the struggle ahead, which he viewed as "the final test."

Fresh volunteers kept arriving at Sabarmati and shortly before they started he estimated their number to be almost a hundred men. He expected "to be arrested" before the historic march began. "Either we shall be effaced out of the earth or we shall spring up as an independent nation enjoying full freedom," he told reporters.[4] "This fight is . . . a life-and-death struggle," he told seventy-eight stalwarts ready to follow him that Wednesday before dawn, asking them to return to the ashram they were about to leave only "as dead men or as winners of swaraj."[5] They left at 6:30 A.M., stopping first at Chandola, seven miles south. Many observers and women had followed that far, but now he turned them all away. "Go back and resolve to do your share. . . . Your way at present . . . lies homeward; mine straight on to the sea-coast."

At his second stop, Bareja, he was "pained" to find none of those waiting to welcome him wearing khadi. "There is a khadi store here and you can certainly remove this blot," he urged them. "Foreign cloth will never bring us freedom . . . renounce luxuries and buy khadi."[6]

"My fatigue so far seems to be health-giving," he wrote Mira on the fifth day of his trek. "For it enables me to take milk twice instead of once and plenty of fruit. Today the fatigue . . . made me sleep five times during the day . . . so you will not worry about me. . . . The struggle has been a veritable godsend for all of us. It is, as it should be, a process of cleansing."[7] Next day at Borsad he told those gathered to listen: "At one time I was wholly loyal to the Empire and . . . sang 'God Save the King' with zest. . . . Finally, however, the scales fell from my eyes, and the spell broke. I realized that the Empire did not deserve loyalty. . . . it deserved sedition. Hence I have made sedition my dharma . . . to be loyal is a sin. . . . We get nothing in return for the crores of rupees that are squeezed out of the Country; if we get anything, it is the rags from Lancashire. . . . It is our duty as well as our right to secure swaraj. I regard this as a religious movement. . . . Today we are defying the salt law. Tomorrow we shall have to consign other laws to the waste-paper basket."[8] He expected each day to be arrested, reporting that government had just recently made salt problems the special job of all police officers above the rank of constable. But much to his disappointment, each day ended without his arrest, Irwin proving himself at least as clever as Smuts had been in dealing with this remarkable adversary.

Both Nehrus visited him midway, after they'd been to a Working Committee meeting of the Congress in Ahmedabad. "You are in for a whole night's vigil," Gandhi warned Jawaharlal. "The messenger will bring you . . . reaching me at the most trying stage in the march. You will have to cross a channel at about 2 A.M. on the shoulders of tired fishermen—I dare not interrupt the march even for the chief servant of the nation."[9] After they spent a few midnight hours with him, Bapu moved on, and Nehru recalled, his last glimpse was of Gandhi, staff in hand, "marching along at the head of his followers, with firm step."[10] Jawaharlal would be arrested the following month, before Gandhi, and cheerfully conveyed as his message, through Motilal, "I have stolen a march over you."

At Ras, in the taluka of Gujarat where Vallabhbhai had been arrested, Gandhi asked those villagers, who still served the British, "Have not your eyes been opened to the robbery that is being committed by the Government? . . . The money that you have given me today has no value for me. . . . I do not need money but your services. . . . Say that you are prepared, when your turn comes to violate the salt law."[11] He reiterated that the movement he initiated in 1920 was but preparation for this "final conflict," for the "mass civil disobedience" which his march was designed to awaken. Yet he was never positive of how many of his countrymen were ready to respond as passionately, as sacrificially as they must to make this Satyagraha a success. "If the salt loses its savour, wherewith shall it be salted? The students are expected to precipitate a crisis not by empty meaningless cries but by . . . action worthy of students. It may again be that the students have no faith in self-sacrifice, and less in non-violence. Then naturally they will not . . . come out. . . . The awakening of the past ten years has not left them unmoved. Let them take the final plunge."[12] But what if they chose to stay at home, or in their classrooms, ignoring his sacrificial march and call? What if their apathy matched the viceroy's cool in holding his fire and ordering his subordinates to leave this Little Father of the nation free to roam where he liked and rave as he wished, hoping his call to action would soon fizzle out and fall flat on deaf, selfish ears?

Fearing that the movement might perhaps die away, Gandhi now called on all students to leave their schools and colleges immediately. "Suspend your studies and join in the fight for freedom. When victory is won . . . you will resume your studies in schools of our own Government. For to my mind it is a fight to the finish."[13] Now he taunted the Government, challenging someone to arrest him. "Although I make strong speeches and have set out to violate the law, the Government dare not arrest me. Why are you afraid of such a Government? . . . I have only 80 volunteers with me. Even then the government cannot arrest me. What then could it do if there were

80,000 volunteers?"[14] He kept urging village headmen and other local officials to resign, winning eighty such resignations in the first two weeks. But some fifteen of his pilgrims were disabled by the difficulty of this march. Several had to drop out because of smallpox, others from physical pains. They were sent ahead by him to recuperate in Broach. Gandhi himself took the journey "very well indeed."

Then at Broach itself, almost two-thirds of his march behind him, Gandhi told a large audience that last December in Lahore "I saw nothing on the horizon to warrant civil resistance. But suddenly, as in a flash, I saw the light in the Ashram. Self-confidence returned. Englishmen and some Indian critics have been warning me against the hazard. But the voice within is clear. I must put forth all my effort or retire altogether and for all time from public life. I feel that now is the time . . . so I am out for battle and am seeking help on bended knees."[15] His health was "excellent," and he had put on two pounds, he reported to Mira.

Impatience as well as illness, however, started to take a toll on the nerves of many marchers. "Those who wish to leave before we reach Dandi may do so," he told them at his Sajod prayer meeting. "It is all right even if I alone stick on. I shall keep smiling. If the world criticizes me, I shall join in that criticism and conclude that I merit the charge of being stupid. However, despite this, I shall fight alone and continue to prepare salt."[16] He recognized more clearly now that the struggle for Swaraj would take much longer to win than he had anticipated, but his passionate resolve for nothing less than complete independence intensified. Two days later he concluded his prayer speech and "nearly broke down" as he said "I would rather die a dog's death and have my bones licked by dogs than that I should return to the Ashram a broken man."[17]

On April 5, Gandhi reached the end of his march in Dandi. At his meeting with both Nehrus they agreed that mass civil disobedience should be launched on the first day of National Week. "The workers will merely guide the masses in the beginning stages," Gandhi explained. "Whenever there is a violent eruption, volunteers are expected to die in the attempt to quell violence. Perfect discipline and perfect co-operation among the different units are indispensable for success. . . . those who are not engaged in civil disobedience are expected to . . . induce others to be engaged in some national service, such as khadi work, liquor and opium picketing, foreign-cloth exclusion, village sanitation. . . . Indeed . . . we should . . . secure boycott of foreign cloth . . . and total prohibition . . . a saving of 91 crores [910 millions of rupees] per year."[18]

"God be thanked for what may be termed the happy ending of the first stage . . . in the final struggle for freedom," Gandhi told the Associated Press. "God willing, I expect my companions to commence actual civil disobedience at 6.30 tomorrow morning."[19] He sent as his message to the world, "I want world sympathy in this battle of Right against Might." He confessed to those gathered in Dandi he had not expected the government to allow him to complete his march. He thought by now he would have been incarcerated. Many others had been arrested, and some had been beaten and wounded, unwilling to part with their salt, clutched tight in their fists. "But I remain unmoved," Gandhi reported. "My heart now is as hard as stone. I am . . . ready to sacrifice thousands and hundreds of thousands of men if necessary. . . . In this game of dice we are playing, the throw has been as we wanted. Should we then weep or smile?"[20]

The next morning, April 6, 1930, he marched early to the sea, followed by some 2,000 admirers, among them Sarojini Naidu, who had come to cheer him on in breaking the British salt law. He dipped his bare legs in the sea and then picked up a lump of sea salt that had dried on the sand. "Hail, Deliverer!" Sarojini shouted, and a chorus of deeper voices added *"Jai!"* ("Victory!") as their mantra.

Several marchers were arrested on April 7 at the village of Aat, four miles from Dandi. Police tried to remove the salt from the fingers of those civil resisters and one man's wrist was broken. The entire village then rushed to the scene, and women and children all began to dig for salt. "Salt in the hands of satyagrahis represent the honour of the nation. It cannot be yielded up except to force that will break the hand to pieces," Gandhi noted. He then wrote "To the Women of India," explaining how he felt they might best enter the struggle to save the nation.

"The impatience of some sisters to join the good fight is to me a healthy sign. . . . In this non-violent warfare, their contribution should be much greater than men's. To call woman the weaker sex is a libel. . . . is she not more self-sacrificing, has she not greater powers of endurance, has she not greater courage?"[21] Before the struggle was over, hundreds of thousands of women, who had never before emerged from the hidden quarters of their own homes or cast off the dark veils that hid their faces and bodies, would join the picketing for Swaraj. Gandhi thus launched as potent a social revolution in India as the political revolution he'd started a decade and a half earlier. He did more to bring India's second sex to a state approaching freedom and demanding equality with their male lords and masters than any other single Indian had in four thousand years of India's history. Hindu and Muslim women alike suffered ancient tyrannies from their fathers and male sons as well as their husbands and brothers, worse than the dreadful slavery of untouchability, since women had always been India's majority. "Highly educated women have in this appeal of mine an opportunity of actively identifying themselves with the masses."

Daily Gandhi kept expecting arrest. Jamnalal Bajaj and Gandhi's sons Ramdas and Devdas were arrested by April 10, and rumors of his own imminent arrest kept him awake nights writing what he thought would be his

London Barrister Mohandas K. Gandhi in 1906. *(Hulton Getty/ Liaison Agency)*

Mahatma Gandhi with his wife, Kasturba, in Gujarat, 1922. *(Hulton Getty/Liaison Agency)*

Mahatma Gandhi eating and reading a newspaper in his ashram, 1924.
(Hulton Getty/Liaison Agency)

Mahatma Gandhi demonstrating cotton-spinning on his own *charka* in Mirzapur, 1925. *(Hulton Getty/Liaison Agency)*

Mahatma Gandhi reaches Dandi at the end of his famous Salt March to the sea, poetess Sarojini Naidu and others waiting to welcome him, April 5, 1930. *(Hulton Getty/Liaison Agency)*

Mahatma Gandhi spinning cotton on the compact *charka* he developed, inside the cabin of reclining Pandit M. M. Malaviya, aboard the S.S. *Rajputana*, steaming toward London for the second Round Table Conference held there in September 1931.
(Hulton Getty/Liaison Agency)

Mahatma Gandhi standing outside No. 10 Downing Street, London, before his meeting with Prime Minister Ramsay MacDonald on November 3, 1931.
(Hulton Getty/Liaison Agency)

Mahatma Gandhi with the Aga Khan and Sarojini Naidu in the lobby of the Ritz Hotel, London, September 29, 1931. *(Hulton Getty/Liaison Agency)*

Mahatma Gandhi meets with Charlie Chaplin at the home of Dr. Kaitial in Canning Town, London, September 22, 1931. *(Hulton Getty/Liaison Agency)*

Mahatma Gandhi in London with Sarojini Naidu at his side, Mahadev Desai behind her, and Mirabehn (Admiral Slade's daughter) to the right.
(Hulton Getty/Liaison Agency)

Mahatma Gandhi, accompanied by Mira, visiting Cotton Mill workers in Darwen on September 26, 1931. *(Hulton Getty/Liaison Agency)*

Mahatma Gandhi with his old Vegetarian friend, Dr. Josiah Oldfield, in London, September 1931. *(Hulton Getty/Liaison Agency)*

Mahatma Gandhi in Rome, where he met with Mussolini on his way home from London's Conference, December 12, 1931. *(Hulton Getty/Liaison Agency)*

Kasturba Gandhi in 1934, age sixty-five. *(Hulton Getty/Liaison Agency)*

Mahatma Gandhi in rural Navsari, Gujarat, writing a letter in May 1932.
(Hulton Getty/Liaison Agency)

Mahatma Gandhi at the Indian National Congress annual meeting in Haripura in 1938. Congress President Subhas Chandra Bose is wearing the ribbon, seated behind him is Dr. Rajendra Prasad, and to the right of Bose is Sardar Vallabhbhai Patel. *(Hulton Getty/Liaison Agency)*

Mahatma Gandhi talking to Jawaharlal Nehru inside the car taking them away from Calcutta's Congress meeting on May 8, 1939. *(Hulton Getty/Liaison Agency)*

Mahatma Gandhi walking to meet Viceroy Lord Linlithgow in Simla, with Rajkumari Amrit Kaur behind him, September 12, 1939. *(Hulton Getty/ Liaison Agency)*

Mahatma Gandhi and Quaid-i-Azam Jinnah leaving Jinnah's home in Delhi to drive to the Viceroy's mansion, November 1, 1939. *(Hulton Getty/Liaison Agency)*

Mahatma Gandhi attends a Congress Working Committee meeting at *Anand Bhavan* in Allahabad, Vallabhbhai Patel to the left, Madame Vijaya Lakshmi Pandit to the right, January 1940. *(Hulton Getty/Liaison Agency)*

Mahatma Gandhi meets with China's Generalissmo Chiang Kai-shek and Madame Chiang, visiting India during the war, Calcutta, February 18, 1942.
(Hulton Getty/Liaison Agency)

Mahatma Gandhi writing in his ashram during his weekly "silent" day, while devoted disciple Abha prepares his meal, c. 1942. *(Hulton Getty/Liaison Agency)*

Mahatma Gandhi
inside Viceroy Lord
Wavell's car in Simla,
July 11, 1945.
*(Hulton Getty/ Liaison
Agency)*

Mahatma Gandhi, after meeting with Britain's Cabinet Mission in Delhi in 1946, leaning on "walking sticks," Dr. Sushila Nayar to the left, and son Manilal Gandhi's wife, Susilaben, on the right. *(Hulton Getty/Liaison Agency)*

Mahatma Gandhi with
his friend Secretary of
State for India Lord
Pethick-Lawrence, leader
of the Cabinet Mission in
Delhi, April 18, 1946.
*(Hulton Getty/ Liaison
Agency)*

Mahatma Gandhi talking with Congress President Jawaharlal Nehru on the first
day of the All-India Congress Committee meeting, July 6, 1946.
(Hulton Getty/Liaison Agency)

Mahatma Gandhi's corpse surrounded by flowers and his mourning closest ashram disciples, Manu, Abha, and Sushila, inside Birla House in Delhi, February 2, 1948. *(Hulton Getty/Liaison Agency)*

last uncensored letters. By April 11, women had started picketing foreign-cloth shops in Delhi, as they did in Dandi. Gandhi wrote to Dr. Jivraj Mehta's wife, Hansa, urging her to rouse the women of Bombay to picket liquor shops as well as foreign-cloth distributors. He was, of course, invited to visit many other cities far from Gujarat but insisted on remaining where he was, mustering strength for his anticipated prison ordeal. His son Devdas was beaten by police. "A bonfire should be made of foreign cloth," Gandhi cried. "Schools and colleges should become empty."[22] He wrote Mahadev Desai, "Tell Ba that she has been posted to do picketing of liquor booths at Jalalpur and that she should, therefore, come after making all necessary preparations."[23] He rarely wrote directly to his wife any more, almost never referring to her, except in such matters of urgent deployment or family crisis.

After learning of young Nehru's arrest, Gandhi wrote to his father. "So Jawahar is to have six months' rest. He has worked like a Trojan. He needed this rest. If things continue to move with the present velocity, he won't have even six months' rest. . . . whole villages have turned out. I never expected this phenomenal response."[24] Motilal Nehru's health, however, was rapidly deteriorating. His asthmatic lungs and enlarged heart were to give out in less than one year, though he struggled valiantly until the bitter end, taking back his jailed son's presidency of the Congress after Gandhi again refused it.

Violence erupted in mid-April in Calcutta and Karachi, and even in predominantly peaceful Gujarat there had been scuffles with police, who angrily grabbed at salt in satyagrahis' fists. Unlike eight years ago, all reports of such violence, even deaths, now left Gandhi "unmoved." This time there was to be no suspending of Satyagraha by its initiator. The port of Chittagong exploded a few days later. Two young men were shot dead and seven others wounded. Gandhi appealed for all violence to end, reiterating its negative impact on the movement. He honored the brave youths who had sacrificed their lives, however, and congratulated their parents "for the finished sacrifices of their sons. . . . A warrior's death is never a matter for sorrow."[25]

On April 24, Mahadev Desai was arrested in Ahmedabad, but still Gandhi remained free. He felt frustrated by the viceroy's persistent protection of him and decided to intensify the struggle by launching what he fore-shadowed in a brief letter to Mirabehn as "the last move that must compel decisive action."[26] The carefully guarded giant British Salt Depot was at Dharasana, quite close to Surat, where Gandhi and his followers now rested. "I do not let anyone approach . . . that," Gandhi wrote Mahadev the day after his secretary was arrested. "When it is ultimately decided to attempt to seize the stocks there, a pilgrim party will start for the purpose."[27]

"People have conferred on me the title of salt-thief as a substitute for Mahatma. I like it," Gandhi told his peasant audience at Chharwada. "When blood flows from heads not only will the salt tax go but many more things. . . . You may call me a salt-thief but only when we take possession of the salt-beds of Dharasana."[28] He urged them to come out and loot the salt-beds, inviting those who heard him speak to "join me in the fun" on the day the "real game" would begin. He told them that if they had a finger broken by police, they should offer their wrists and arms to be broken as well, passionately welcoming pain, inviting lathi blows to their heads. He reminded them to wear only khadi, needing no more of it than the loincloth he wore.

On the eve of his arrest on May 5, 1930, Gandhi drafted his second "Dear Friend" letter to Viceroy Irwin. "God willing, it is my intention . . . to set out for Dharasana and . . . demand possession of the Salt Works. . . . It is possible for you to prevent this raid, as it has been playfully and mischievously called . . . 1. By removing the salt tax; 2. By arresting me and my party unless the country can, as I hope it will, replace everyone taken away; 3. By sheer goondaism unless every head broken is replaced, as I hope it will."[29] Gandhi most passionately protested the savage and indecent assault by the viceroy's forces unleashed against his unarmed pilgrims. He informed Irwin that according to the "science" of Satyagraha greater wrath and more violent repression could only be diverted and effectively countered by greater "suffering courted by the victims." Therefore, unless the salt tax was removed he would be obliged immediately to launch a frontal march on the salt depot.

Shortly past midnight, just a few hours after drafting that letter but before it could be sent, Gandhi was arrested by a British magistrate, accompanied by his armed troop of constables. Charged with violating a regulation of the British Raj passed more than a century earlier, Gandhi was to be detained indefinitely without trial. He was taken from his bed, all telephone wires in his camp carefully cut beforehand. He washed himself, recited his prayers, and was taken to the train that transported him under cover of darkness more than a hundred miles south to Poona, then driven in a curtained car back to the cell in Yeravda fortress prison from which he had been released some six years ago. "So Bapu has been arrested!" Jawaharlal noted in his own prison cell, as soon as he heard the news that night. "It is full-blooded war to the bitter end. Good."[30]

As news of Gandhi's arrest spread, people poured out onto the streets of big cities, protesting, shouting, and being in turn assaulted by mounted police to be dragged off themselves. Soon every prison cell in India was filled. Before year's end some 60,000 satyagrahis would be jailed. "You seem to ignore the simple fact that disobedience ceases to be such immediately [when] masses of people resort to it," Gandhi wrote his Dear Friend

Viceroy on May 18. "They are no law-breakers; they are no haters of the English. . . . You protest your affection for India. I believe in your profession. But I deny the correctness of your diagnosis of India's disease."[31] Then he reiterated his demands: first the abolition of all salt taxes, then an end to all foreign-cloth imports. Buoyed by reports that hundreds of thousands of men and women had joined the Satyagraha, Gandhi taunted Irwin, asking that good Christian if he thought all of them "wicked-minded or misled or fools"? No Round Table Conference would do any good, he argued, until Great Britain stopped treating India as a "slave nation." He appealed instead to Britain's goodness and greatness, which had enabled India to do so much to help advance world progress.

From his prison cell, Mahatma Gandhi thus sought to win over Viceroy Irwin, much as he had worked at winning over Smuts and Morley and Charlie Andrews, and Muriel Lester and Mirabehn Slade. His undying, passionate faith in the powers of love and its other divine side, truth, gave him strength and hope enough to carry on his labors of spinning out the reasons that 300 million Indians could no longer be held hostage to the greed of a small, remote island, no matter how powerful or wealthy, sinister and brilliant all its leaders might be. Gandhi knew that the days of empire were numbered, and he knew that Irwin was clever enough to know it as well. Only Gandhi thought the residual number of days much lower than it actually was, while Irwin believed it much higher. At any rate, their negotiations had begun from inside his prison cell, and soon its venue would shift to a series of talks in the viceroy's palace in New Delhi, thence on to Round Tables in London. Before the golden dawn of any agreement appeared, however, rivers of Indian blood would flow.

The first of those rivers started at Dharasana on May 21, 1930, when Sarojini Naidu and Manilal Gandhi led a khadi-clad band of satyagrahis toward the barbed-wired gate of the giant salt depot protected by armed constables and helmeted British police officers. "Scores of native police rushed upon the advancing marchers, and rained blows on their heads with steel-shod lathis," United Press correspondent Webb Miller reported. "Not one of the marchers even raised an arm to fend off the blows. They went down like ninepins. . . . In two or three minutes the ground was quilted with bodies. Great patches of blood widened on their white clothes. The survivors without breaking the ranks silently and doggedly marched on until struck down. . . . I could detect no signs of wavering or fear."[32] Sarojini Naidu and Manilal Gandhi were arrested, not beaten, but former Speaker of the Assembly Viththalbhai Patel, watching that brutal massacre of innocents, softly remarked: "All hope of reconciling India with the British Empire is lost for ever."

15

From Prison to London
and Back

F OR ALMOST nine months Gandhi remained behind bars in Ye-ravda prison, while Britain's Labour government tried in vain to untangle India's constitutional knots. The Nehru Report had left most Muslims dissatisfied. The Simon Commission's report provoked universal discontent and repeated protest. Then, just as global economic depression threw millions of British factory laborers out of work, Gandhi's boycott of British goods and his Satyagraha movement added to Britain's market misery by shutting down India's once inexhaustible demand for British fine cottons, silks, and other manufactured products.

"Idealism sometimes causes pain, but a human being without idealism is like a brute," Gandhi wrote from prison. "Our highest duty is to see that our idealism takes the right direction."[1] In June, before he too was jailed, Motilal Nehru was interviewed by the London *Daily Herald*'s George Slocombe, who asked what terms he required to attend a Round Table Conference. "We must be masters in our own household," Motilal replied, insisting that India's Congress would only meet Britain now "nation to nation on an equal footing."[2] Slocombe had earlier interviewed Gandhi in prison and fearlessly reported British brutality against satyagrahis. His reports and interviews added to worldwide calls for Gandhi's release. So the viceroy tried reconciliation, using as his emissaries Tej Bahadur Sapru and M. R. Jayakar, both ex-Congress Brahmans, now leaders of the Liberal party. They went to Gandhi's prison cell seeking his approval of a note they had drafted before bringing it to both Nehrus, who shared a cell in Naini Prison. Gandhi told Sapru and Jayakar that he would be willing to attend the Round Table Conference in London if, on behalf of the Congress, he could raise the "question of independence."³ He would then call off civil disobedience, though not the picketing of liquor shops or foreign cloth merchants. He would promise to end raids on salt depots, but Indians must be allowed to obtain their own salt from near the sea, all satyagrahi prisoners must be released, and all fines paid under the recent repressive Press Act refunded. On July 28, 1930, Sapru and Jayakar brought Gandhi's note to the Nehrus in Naini, returning the next day.

The mediators went back again in August, arranging to bring both Nehrus as well as Sarojini Naidu, Vallabhbhai Patel, and two other Congress leaders to confer with Gandhi in Yeravda. On the next day, August 15, 1930, anticipating by seventeen years the birthday of independent India, they all signed a "Dear Friends" letter to Sapru and Jayakar to be taken to the viceroy. Drafted by Jawaharlal, their letter called upon the British government to cease its "age-long exploitation" of the Indian people, and "to get off our backs and do some reparation for the past wrongs, by helping us to grow out of the dwarfing process that has gone on for a century of British domination."⁴ The viceroy was not, however, ready to agree to any of those demands, so the first Round Table Conference convened in London before year's end without a single Indian National Congress representative in attendance.

Gandhi remained calm within his prison "Temple" (*Mandir*) as he called his cell. "The sky is the ceiling of my train," he wrote Vallabhbhai Patel's devoted daughter Maniben, a few days before he was released in January of 1931.⁵ To beloved Mira, now journeying through Sind, he wrote at greater length. "What you say about rebirth is sound. It is nature's kindness that we do not remember past births. . . . A wise man deliberately forgets many things."⁶ The next day, Purna Swaraj Day, Gandhi was informed of his release by viceregal amnesty. "My present feeling is that I shall be leaving peace and quiet and going into the midst of turmoil."⁷

The first Round Table Conference had ended a week earlier. Prime Minister MacDonald declared that India's new central government should be a federation embracing all Indian states and British India, with a bicameral legislature. The precise structure would have to be determined after further discussion among princes and elected representatives of British India. The central legislature and the executive would have features of dualism, dyarchy, first introduced into British India's constitution in 1920. Special powers were "reserved" by the executive, including those related to the military, police, and treasury, while some powers were "transferred" to departments run by elected representatives, notably education and public health. Hoping that Gandhi might help him to inaugurate power sharing at the center, the viceroy granted unconditional amnesty to his greatest prisoner.

"I have come out of jail with an absolutely open mind, unfettered by enmity, unbiased in argument and prepared to study the whole situation from every point of view," Gandhi informed the press as he emerged from prison and headed for Bombay.[8] The next day he learned of Motilal's rapidly failing health and took a train to Allahabad, reaching his old friend's bedside late that night. "I am going soon, Mahatmaji, and I shall not be here to see Swaraj," old Nehru told him. "But I know you have won it and will soon have it."[9] Congress leaders gathered in Motilal's great mansion, *Anand Bhavan* ("Abode of Peace"), which he'd bequeathed as a national trust to the Congress several years earlier. "Government's capacity for brutality is so great that we must gird up our loins to face more of it," Gandhi told his Congress comrades. "We have still to free the oppressed millions in the world, to free the entire world. It waits for a miracle from India."[10] He spoke to them softly in Gujarati, but the passionate intensity and power of his message rivaled that of any general. Congress resolved not to retract its resolutions on civil disobedience and to continue peaceful picketing of all foreign-cloth and liquor shops.

Motilal Nehru died on February 6, and Gandhi spoke at his funeral in Allahabad. "What we see before us is a national sacrifice," he told the vast crowd assembled to honor the dead lion of India. "We are here today to serve the cause of peace, and it behooves us to be peaceful. . . . May God inspire you."[11] Gandhi remained at Anand Bhavan, where the Congress Working Committee met a few days later to elect Vallabhbhai Patel as its next president and to plan its next move. Some moderates urged negotiations with the viceroy, but Gandhi was hesitant in view of reports of continued police brutality. "Under organized despotism lucklessness is luck, poverty a blessing, riches a curse, evil is enthroned, goodness nowhere," he explained to a follower, "all values are transposed. We have only felt from afar the heat of the fire we must pass through. Let us be ready for the plunge. That is my reading just now. And it fills me with joy. A halting peace will be dangerous and I can see no sign of real peace coming."[12]

But before taking the plunge, he wrote again to "Dear Friend" Irwin, asking if they might meet, hoping "to meet not so much the Viceroy of India as the man in you."[13] Irwin wired his reply that night, inviting Gandhi to New Delhi on Tuesday, February 17, 1931, for what would become a most remarkable summit, the tiny half-naked Mahatma meeting alone with Britain's tallest, most immaculately attired viceroy.

"There was no one present except Gandhi and myself," Irwin noted after their first meeting. "I dwelt upon the change in British opinion, which I hoped India would not make of no avail."[14] The viceroy urged Gandhi to accept the principles of federation as well as "reservations and safeguards" that had been hammered out at London's first conference. He asked whether Gandhi and his friends had in mind a "grudging truce" or a "permanent peace" and was pleased to be assured it was the latter.

That night Gandhi wrote his own version of their meeting: "very well" impressed by the viceroy, who talked "frankly" and "wants to make peace."[15] In response to Gandhi's insistence on release of all satyagrahis, the viceroy said that "would be difficult." Irwin had drawn a clear distinction between those prisoners guilty of "violence or inciters to violence" and others, rejecting the possibility of any early release for the former. He promised, however, that "justice should be done." When Gandhi pressed him to withdraw all repressive ordinances and punitive police, the viceroy promised to make "enquiries" into both matters. Irwin in turn urged immediate "lowering of the temperature" of Bombay's picketing of cloth and liquor shops and salt protests. Gandhi promised to look into that. They agreed to meet alone again the next day.

Before the second meeting, Gandhi wired his friend Perin Captain in Bombay, asking him to alert Congress to "SCRUPULOUSLY AVOID ALL VIOLENCE DIRECT INDIRECT PASSIVE OR ACTIVE" by any picketers. "Wire received," came the immediate reply. "Instructions will be carried out."[16] On Wednesday at 1:40 P.M. Gandhi emerged from Dr. Ansari's house in Delhi, where he stayed during the summit, to cheers of a waiting crowd. "Use khaddar," he told them, smiling, before he got into the car that drove him to the viceregal palace. His second meeting, however, was hardly as encouraging as the first. He found Irwin "more cautious," noting, "Today the salt tax, suspension of collection of land revenue and picketing alone were discussed."[17] Irwin feared the reactions of his own friends in London, like Winston Churchill, who was "nauseated" to see the "half-naked fakir" striding upstairs to the residence of the viceroy. "I explained to him that in everything I had said I was only speaking personally for myself, and on many matters it would be necessary to consult local Governments or the Secretary of State, and on all matters it would be necessary for me to consult my own Council."[18] The viceroy went on to insist that "everything" he'd said about reciprocal action by government was based on the "effective abandonment" by Gandhi of his civil disobedience campaign.

Gandhi refused to promise the abandonment of Satyagraha and explained that, if after attending the next London Conference he remained dissatisfied with "results," he would have to "resume the movement."[19] That really worried Irwin, who said it would put him in an "impossible position." His Majesty's government should never consider taking the steps they were discussing if at any moment in subsequent discussions they might be told that Congress planned to resurrect its campaign. Then Gandhi agreed not to do so as long as "talks" were in progress.

Irwin now wanted to open further talks to more voices and ears, suggesting that Sapru and Jayakar be invited to join them. Gandhi agreed, later referring to those two as "sub-viceroys," but said he would like to invite Jawaharlal and Vallabhbhai for his side. The viceroy then expanded his guests to include several officials, thus turning their personal summit into a mini-Round Table Conference. That night Irwin cabled Secretary of State Wedgwood Benn, requesting clear and "precise" instructions from the India Office as to just how far he might go in his negotiations with Gandhi. "I am sure it would be dangerous to permit Congress to say to the world that everything was open for discussion, and that they had made it clear as a condition of participation that if they were not satisfied they would resume civil disobedience."[20] He liked Gandhi and had learned "privately" that he too was "pleased" with their talks and "wants peace." Nonetheless Irwin remained "very apprehensive" of Gandhi's clever "manoeuvering" to re-open constitutional issues resolved by the first Round Table Conference.

On the next day Irwin told Gandhi he needed time to consult London and hoped they could resume their talks with a larger group in another week. Gandhi regretted the delay, but never lost patience. That week he addressed crowds in Delhi, urging pickets to abjure violence. He also spoke to the Muslim League Council, accepting their invitation as coming from "21 crores" (210 million) of his "brethren," continuing: "I am a Bania, and there is no limit to my greed. It has always been my heart's desire to speak, not only for 21 crores, but for 30 crores of Indians . . . to strive for Hindu-Muslim unity."[21] To achieve such unity was "the mission of my life" he told them, adding that "if I die striving for it, I shall achieve peace of mind."

On February 27, after receiving his instructions from London, Irwin invited Gandhi to meet him again. They talked for three hours, going over all earlier points, each digging deeper into his entrenched position. "He was in a very obstinate mood" Irwin wrote after Gandhi left him, concluding that "he was either bluffing or had made up his mind that he did not mean to settle."[22] Gandhi opted that evening to walk the five miles back to Ansari's house in Daryaganj, rather than allowing himself to be driven in a viceregal vehicle.

They next met on March 1, and were quickly deadlocked over questions of boycott and picketing. Gandhi insisted that he meant peaceful picketing, which was permissible under Britain's common law. Irwin maintained that "peaceful picketing" was impossible in the present overheated political climate of India. Next they tackled police violence, which Gandhi called "savagery." The viceroy nodded, but explained that were he to "admit" that "justifiable point" it would open floodgates of charges, inquiries, and bitterness against the police. "I therefore told him that, inasmuch as we really wanted peace, would not it be better to drop it altogether?"[23] Much to Irwin's surprise and delight, Gandhi agreed. Then they moved on to the salt tax, Irwin startled by how much importance Gandhi attributed to it. The viceroy insisted that he "could not condone publicly the breaches of law . . . nor could we in present financial circumstances sacrifice revenue by repealing it."

After prolonged arguing, Irwin suggested that Gandhi meet with Sir George Schuster, the finance minister. Gandhi agreed, and Irwin conceded in his minutes that "it may be necessary to do something to meet him on Salt." They broke for dinner, and Gandhi returned at 9:30 P.M. to continue negotiations with Irwin and his home secretary, Mr. Emerson. At that late hour Gandhi agreed to abandon the boycott, assuring "complete freedom for cloth merchants" to do as they liked, which so cheered the viceroy that he noted: "we shall succeed." On the difficult question of how to reduce sterling debts, Irwin explained he must telegraph the secretary of state. The thorny question of "secession" remained unresolved, but they both knew it was much less urgent than the other issues.

So Gandhi was driven home that March night, feeling rather proud of himself and more hopeful as to the prospects for peace in India's future than he had felt for many a year. Most of the older members of Congress's Working Committee, who waited up to welcome him back to Ansari's house, were equally enthusiastic, but Jawaharlal was deeply depressed by what he heard. To Nehru's revolutionary mind Gandhi had surrendered too much. "You seem to be feeling lonely and almost uninterested," Gandhi wrote him next morning. "That must not be, my strength depends upon you."[24] He passionately pressed Jawahar to criticize, amend, or reject any or all of the points he had discussed with Irwin. Gandhi was determined at whatever the cost to keep Nehru in the Congress, fearing otherwise that the heart of India's nationalist movement would break away, its vital youth brigade rushing off in rage and frustration.

The next day's meeting focused on confiscated land sold to third parties during Satyagraha campaigns. Gandhi insisted that such lands be returned to their original owners. Irwin argued that local governments were in charge of land revenue and he could not interfere. Gandhi said that Vallabhbhai Patel was doubtful whether he could carry the settlement in Gujarat unless they got "some accommodation" on this land question, but the viceroy simply repeated that it was not in his power.[25] Irwin then "pressed him very hard" to give up picketing. Now it was Gandhi's turn adamantly to refuse, though he promised all picketing would remain courteous and peaceful. After "much wrangling," Irwin agreed, when Gandhi pledged Congress would immediately suspend picketing if there was any abuse. They were still arguing about salt, however, when it looked as if Gandhi was going to have to leave for his evening meal, which as he previously told the viceroy he could not eat after the sun had set. Irwin asked Gandhi to invite Miss Slade, whose father he had known, to bring up his food to him in the viceregal palace. "I was greatly interested in meeting her. . . . She evidently venerates him very profoundly, and one felt one had suddenly been switched into a rather different world."[26] What a shock it must have been to Lord Irwin to watch that tall, khadi-clad, English-born Admiral's daughter bowing low, reverently to set the simple food she had prepared with her fair hands at the dark naked feet of the man she worshipped as Master-Mahatma. Did he realize then that the days of British rule here were numbered? Or did he simply think poor Mira quite mad?

It was almost midnight before they finally reached an agreement, the viceroy noted, "[w]ith the old man telling me that he was going to throw his whole heart and soul into trying to co-operate in constitution-building."[27] Gandhi returned to meet with Emerson the next day for two hours, Irwin seeing him only briefly to initial their agreement.

The Congress Working Committee met on March 5 to endorse the Gandhi-Irwin agreement, directing all Congress committees to discontinue civil disobedience. Gandhi graciously acknowledged the viceroy's inexhaustible patience, industry, and courtesy throughout the very delicate negotiations. He elaborated upon each of the provisions of the agreement, urging all Congressmen "honourably and fully" to implement every clause to "ensure peace."[28] A day later Irwin wrote to thank Gandhi. "It has been a great privilege to me to be given this opportunity of meeting and knowing you. . . . I do pray—as I believe—that history may say you and I were permitted to be instruments in doing something big for India and for humanity."[29]

The euphoria and mutual admiration felt by Gandhi and Irwin was hardly shared by their younger friends and lower echelons of the British services. Jawaharlal's depression only deepened when he read the final draft of the agreement. "Was it for this that our people had behaved so gallantly for a year? Were all our brave words and deeds to end in this?" he cried, quoting from T. S. Eliot's *The Waste Land*, "'This is the way the world ends, not with a bang, but a whimper.'"[30] Irwin's right-wing "steel-frame" of sunbaked ICS men and British police sullenly showed their contempt for the viceroy's "surrender" to the "seditious little fakir." They were not going to let any Indian assassins like Sikh Bhagat Singh escape the gallows merely because a "salt-thief" pled with the viceroy for his clemency. In London, Stanley Baldwin, leader of the Tory opposition, announced that his party would not join in any Round Table Conference attended by Gandhi.

On March 23, Gandhi tested the power and limits of his new friendship with Irwin, writing a "Dear Friend" letter to the viceroy in which he passionately appealed for commutation of the death sentences passed on Bhagat Singh and two other terrorists. "Popular opinion demands commutation,"[31] Gandhi wrote, warning that the executions, if carried out would endanger "peace." The "revolutionary party" had assured him that sparing Bhagat's life would halt terrorist activities. That very day Bhagat Singh and his companions were hanged. A general strike, protesting the deaths of those "martyrs" was called by Nehru and Subhas Bose, whose hatred for British rule blazed on the eve of the meeting of the Congress, held that year in Karachi.

From Prison to London and Back

On his arrival at the Congress, Gandhi was confronted with a protest demonstration by many young men wearing red shirts, carrying black flags, and shouting slogans of denunciation, "Down with Gandhism," and "Go back Gandhi."[32] He was unruffled by those insults, viewing them as but mild expressions of youthful grief. Communal riots racked Cawnpore (Kanpur) even as the Congress Working Committee began its deliberations in Karachi, which was destined to become the first capital of Muslim Pakistan. Gandhi passionately addressed the Congress on its first day, speaking under the open sky: "Having flung aside the sword, there is nothing except the cup of love which I can offer to those who oppose me. . . . I live in the hope that if not in this birth, in some other birth I shall be able to hug all humanity in friendly embrace."[33] He then turned to the carnage in Cawnpore, where deadly violence by Hindus and Muslims followed Bhagat's execution. They were all children of the same soil, of one Motherland, Gandhi reminded them.

Many young delegates at the Karachi Congress were apprehensive over Gandhi's settlement with Irwin and told him so. "My mind is full of misgivings," he agreed, disarming critics with his lack of vanity and readiness to admit he might be wrong. "But it is a sin not to do what circumstances have made it a duty to do. It is a principle of satyagraha that if there is an opportunity for talks . . . talks should be tried."[34]

The Karachi Congress ended in a record-breaking two days, Vallabhbhai delivering an even shorter speech than Gandhi had previously done when he'd presided. Nehru drafted an impressive list of fundamental rights and economic changes that were easily carried, but most of those goals, especially ones like "equal rights . . . without any bar on account of sex" and "a living wage for industrial workers . . . healthy conditions of work, protection against . . . old age, sickness and unemployment," would take longer than the century's remaining seven decades to enforce.[35]

Returning to Delhi, the Congress Working Committee agreed that Gandhi should serve as Congress's sole delegate to any future Round Table Conference, a strategic error that imposed an impossible burden on Gandhi, reflecting his own mistrust of Nehru's judgment and fear that if he took Vallabhbhai Patel, who could have helped him mightily, Jawaharlal would have quit Congress. Karachi and his summit with Irwin had worn Gandhi out, and though he rested in late April, by early May he wrote Charlie Andrews to report that "[i]mplementing the Settlement in the teeth of official sullenness, unwillingness and even opposition is a very difficult business. It tries even my patience."[36] He received many letters and wires from London and America, inviting him to visit, speak, and stay with friends, but he turned down virtually all of them.

On May 13, Gandhi went up to Simla to meet with the new viceroy, Lord Willingdon, former governor of Bombay, a more conservatively rigid imperialist than Irwin, whose viceregal term had ended in April. Willingdon was neither as gracious nor as generous as Irwin had been in dealing with Gandhi, who would soon become his prisoner.

From Simla he went to the United Provinces Nainital hill station to meet with Governor Malcolm Hailey, Motilal's old friend. They discussed the recent tragic communal riots and proliferating agrarian problems that plagued India's most populous province. Gandhi disclaimed any idea of a "no-rent" campaign, which Hailey told him the local Congress was trying to launch in order to establish a "parallel government" in the United Provinces.[37] Before year's end, Gandhi would hear much more about that from Nehru, who took a lead in organizing agrarian unrest in his province.

By late June of 1931, Gandhi prepared his entourage for the Round Table trip, his first visit to London since he'd gone there from South Africa seventeen years earlier. He decided his wife was too sick to travel "any place" outside of India, and he was eager to take only Mira with him to prepare his food in London.[38] "You are on the brain," Gandhi now wrote his beloved "Sister," who "managed to tear myself away" from him that June, returning alone to Sabarmati Ashram. "I look about me and miss you," he confessed to Mira. "I open the charkha [spinning-wheel] and miss you. So on and so forth. But what is the use?" he conceded, taking both sides of his dialogue with himself. "You have left your home, your people and all that people prize most, not to serve me personally but to serve the cause I stand for. All the time you were squandering your love on me personally, I felt guilty. . . . And I exploded on the slightest pretext. Now that you are not with me, my anger turns itself upon me for having given you all those terrible scoldings. But I was on a bed of hot ashes all the while." Then he reminded himself that soon they would travel to London together, and that elicited a happy forty-year-old memory of an English public school cheer, with which he ended his letter: "'Cheer boys cheer, no more idle sorrow.'"[39]

Charlie Andrews managed the mundane housing details of his visit from London, accepting Muriel Lester's offer to accommodate Gandhi's small entourage in her East End welfare settlement, Kingsley Hall. "I would rather stay at your settlement than anywhere else," Gandhi confirmed, "for there I will be living among the same sort of people as those for whom I have spent my life."[40] He decided to bring along Mahadev Desai and Pyarelal as well as son Devdas to serve as his London secretariat. Neither of his Congress heirs, Vallabhbhai or Jawaharlal, was invited, though both had been eager to join.

On August 29, 1931, Gandhi slowly climbed aboard the S.S. *Rajputana* with his intimate band of faithful followers. "I shall endeavour to represent every interest that does not conflict with the interests of the dumb millions for whom the Congress . . . exists," he told a Reuters correspondent on the ship.[41] He kept "excellent health" at sea. It was raining when he reached London on September 12, 1931. Asked if he planned to go to the theater, he said he wouldn't have time, but recalled that when he studied in London he used to visit the Lyceum, liked Shakespeare's plays, and "adored the incomparable Ellen Terry—I worshipped her."[42] He was driven to Friends House at Euston Road and informed the crowd awaiting him there that "the Congress wants freedom unadulterated for the dumb and starving millions."[43]

The second Round Table Conference had already begun, and Gandhi addressed the Federal Structure Committee soon after he arrived, on September 15, 1931. "I am but a poor humble agent acting on behalf of the Indian National Congress" he told that assembly of more than a hundred elegantly attired delegates, twenty-three representing bejeweled princes of Indian states, sixty-nine from British India, twenty representatives of Great Britain. He began with a history of the Congress, which represented, he told them, "all Indian interests and all classes."[44] He stressed, however, its commitment to the "dumb, semi-starved millions" living in India's 700,000 villages. "Time was when I prided myself on being, and being called, a British subject. I have ceased for many years to call myself a British subject; I would far rather be called a rebel than a subject."

Charlie Chaplin went to meet him at the home of a mutual friend. Gandhi had never heard of Chaplin, but Charlie was eager to shake his hand. The next day Gandhi met with the Aga Khan at his suite in the Ritz, but it did not result in any breakthrough agreement leading to Hindu-Muslim unity. Though cautioned to stay away from Britain's depressed Midlands, Gandhi journeyed to Lancashire, where he spoke to unemployed millworkers, many of whom blamed him and India's boycott for the hard times that had thrown them out of work. He was "pained" at the unemployment he saw there, but he told them that if they went to India's villages they would find starvation and living corpses. "Today India is a curse," he said, explaining that was why he had taught Indians to spin, "work with which they were familiar, which they could do in their cottages."[45] The unemployed British workers responded warmly to Gandhi's unadorned simplicity and the passion of his argument.

After returning from Lancashire, Gandhi met with Prime Minister Ramsay MacDonald, advising him that the conference was "futile because the other delegates were only the nominees of Government."[46] He insisted that he could represent the Muslims and the depressed classes much better than those who claimed to do so. He and the British alone could settle the entire question if he was treated as "representing everybody." The prime minister wryly remarked that the conference had been slightly successful, since it brought Gandhi back to London. MacDonald then told him that his civil disobedience movement was a "mistake and only hindered the British Government."

Fenner Brockway and his Independent Labour party hosted a lunch to celebrate Gandhi's sixty-second birthday, four hundred English guests packing the festive Westminister Palace rooms. Yet by early October he knew, as he told a meeting of Friends of India, that "I seem to be failing."[47] How could it possibly be otherwise? He hardly had time to meet with, read, or hear all the speeches of other members at the conference, and barely strength enough to survive London's autumnal chills. He was obliged to confess to the "Prime Minister and Friends" at a meeting of the Minorities Committee "with deep sorrow and deeper humiliation that I have to announce utter failure" to secure any "solution of the communal question."[48] None of the Muslim delegates with whom he spoke in London and few of the Sikhs would agree to follow his lead. He suggested, therefore, to adjourn the Minorities Committee and refused to agree to any separate electorate formula for untouchables. He announced that "the conscience of Hindus has been stirred, and untouchables will soon be a relic of our sinful past."[49]

In mid-October he received a cable from Jawaharlal informing him of the "critical" agrarian situation in the United Province. Tenants were being "ejected" from their property, then arrested for criminal trespass, Nehru reported. He was eager to launch a Congress-led action, clearly contrary to the Gandhi-Irwin truce; hence, he was requesting Gandhi's permission. "You should unhesitatingly take necessary steps," Gandhi wired back. "Expect nothing here."[50] He had talked himself hoarse in richly paneled rooms filled with princes and British officers, none of whom sympathized with his revolutionary arguments. And he had seen enough outside Westminister Palace to know how little depressed Englishmen worried about India's poverty. He knew before leaving Bombay, of course, how slight a chance he stood of turning the giant luxury liner of Britain's Empire around with his single voice and naked body. But he had resolved to leave no stone of possible reconciliation unturned, no barrier untested by the tap of his bare hands and the cry of his small voice.

"Independence has to be earned by sacrifice and self-suffering," he told a Nottingham College audience that October, reiterating the passionate lessons he'd learned long ago in South Africa. "Nations have come to freedom through rivers of blood."[51] India would have to go through the same fiery ordeal before England could be convinced that it was good for herself as well to grant India her freedom. He resolved a week later to return home, to "prove by suffering that the whole country wants what it asks for."[52] At Pembroke College, Cambridge, he admitted: "I know that every honest Englishman wants to see India free, but . . . feels that the moment

British arms are removed there would be invasions and internecine strife." But he argued, "my contention is that it is the British presence that is the cause of internal chaos, because you have ruled India according to the principle of divide and rule."[53]

By mid-November most of the Indian delegates wrote the prime minister and asked him to arbitrate a settlement to the communal question, apportioning what he considered to be a fair bloc of seats in every new council chamber to Hindus, Muslims, and Sikhs. Gandhi refused to join in that request. "Congress will never be reconciled to any further extension of the principle of separate electorate."[54]

Gandhi resolved to leave London on December 5, embarking with Mira directly to Paris, thence on to Villeneuve, Romain Rolland's home in Switzerland. "The little man, bespectacled and toothless, was wrapped in his white burnoose," Rolland reported, "but his legs, thin as a heron's stilts, were bare. His shaven head . . . was uncovered and wet with rain. He came to me with a dry laugh, his open mouth like a good dog panting."[55] They stopped in Italy before sailing on to India. In Rome, Gandhi was brought to Mussolini by Rolland's friend, General Moris, accompanied by Mira. Mussolini "addressed Bapu in quite good English," Mira recalled, "and asked a number of questions about India. . . . When about ten minutes had passed, he rose from his seat . . . and accompanied us . . . to the door . . . quite unusual behaviour for Mussolini, who did not rise from his chair as a rule."[56]

British repression had begun with a vengeance before Gandhi reached Bombay; Jawaharlal Nehru was arrested on December 26, 1931, and sentenced to two years of rigorous imprisonment. Agrarian unrest rocked the United Provinces. When Gandhi disembarked in Bombay on December 28, he learned from reporters of the arrests of Nehru and many Congress leaders. "Last year we faced lathis," Gandhi told a meeting in Bombay, "but this time we must be prepared to face bullets."[57] He was now prepared to sacrifice "a million lives for achieving freedom," passionately urging his followers to embrace death "as we embrace a friend." On January 1, 1932, he wired the viceroy for "guidance" and clarification as to the meaning of such harsh repression, but Lord Willingdon was not interested in meeting Gandhi again nor in explaining his tactics or strategy to the man he now viewed as Britain's archenemy.[58]

The Working Committee of Congress met in Bombay to hear Gandhi's negative assessment of the Round Table Conference, and now resolved to reaffirm its demand for complete independence and the boycott of liquor shops and all foreign cloth. They also called for the resumption of unlicensed manufacture of salt and for civil disobedience against every unjust ordinance. "It grieves me," Gandhi wired the viceroy again, disappointed by Willingdon's ignoring his advance. "I had approached as a seeker wanting light."[59] By now he learned that he too would be arrested, so instead of venturing north to Ahmedabad, he waited in Bombay's Mani Bhavan, sleeping on the roof of that sturdy three-story building, now a museum to his memory. "Bapu slept like a child committed to his Father's hands," Verrier Elwin recalled. "I thought of Christ . . . suddenly . . . a whisper: 'The police have come.' We started up and I saw . . . a fully uniformed Commissioner of Police at the foot of Bapu's bed. . . . 'Mr. Gandhi, it is my duty to arrest you.' A beautiful smile of welcome broke out on Bapu's face."[60] He never resisted arrest, but since it was silent Monday he did not say a word, taking out a pencil to write, "I will be ready to come with you in half an hour." Then he brushed his teeth and retired. Mirabehn, Devdas, and Ba all touched his feet before he left, following him down the three flights of stairs. A crowd had gathered around the car that drove him back, with Vallabhbhai, also arrested that day, to Yeravda jail.

Under Regulation XXV of 1827, Gandhi was jailed "during the pleasure of Government" to avoid greater public attention or the embarrassment of a minutely reported trial. Four harsh new ordinances had been passed, stripping India of all its residual civil rights. Arrests of all Congress leaders now followed swiftly. Thus India's brief political truce reverted to war. In four months, 60,000 passionate resisters filled every prison cell in the land.

16

Imprisoned Soul of India

G ANDHI NEVER despaired behind bars. Adversity only cheered his passionate nature and intensified his resolve. The 1932–33 prison interlude brought the purifying rays of his inner light to focus on Hinduism's gravest injustice, the crime of untouchability.

On March 11, 1932, Gandhi wrote to India's new secretary of state, Sir Samuel Hoare, to remind him of a warning he had issued in the closing days of the Round Table Conference "that I should resist with my life the grant of separate electorate to the Depressed Classes."[1] Now he explained at length why he opposed Britain's announced intention of awarding separate electoral status, which would grant a bloc of separate seats on all the new councils to candidates born only in untouchable communities. Gandhi insisted that untouchable castes remain integral parts of Hinduism's body politic. So strong was his opposition to any political vivisection of his faith that Gandhi informed Sir Samuel, "I must fast unto death" if Britain went ahead and created separately elected representation of untouchables.

When Nehru in his own distant prison cell later learned of Gandhi's decision, he felt "annoyed with him for choosing a side issue for his final sacrifice."[2] Jawaharlal was angry with Bapu for taking this religious, sentimental approach to a political question. "And his frequent references to God—God has made him do this—God even indicated the date of the fast. . . . What a terrible example to set!" the agnostic Nehru noted. Hoare, however, was neither annoyed nor angry. "The dogs bark," he said, "the caravan moves on." His reply to Gandhi was that realizing "fully the strength of your feeling upon the question we intend to give any decision that may be necessary solely and only upon the merits of the case."[3]

As soon as Charlie Andrews learned of Gandhi's resolve to fast unto death, he wrote to try to dissuade his friend. "I understand and even appreciate the moral repulsion against 'fasting unto death,'" Gandhi replied. "I will make myself as certain as it is humanly possible to be, that the will that appears to me to be God's is really His, and not the Devil's."[4]

To Mira, who was at this time also jailed far away, he wrote more intimate details: "Had I learnt to use the body merely as an instrument of service and His temple, old age would have been like a beautiful ripe fruit. . . . My only consolation in thinking over the past is that in all I did I was guided by nothing else than the deepest love for you."[5]

To son Devdas, also then in another prison, he wrote of the daily routine he and Mahadev and Vallabhbhai followed: "We are happy here. . . . All three of us get up at 3.45 A.M. After we have prayed together, Mahadev goes back to sleep and we two take honey and water and then have a walk. Afterwards I sleep for about a quarter of an hour. At 6.30 all the three have our breakfast."[6] Gandhi's only other daily meal was at 4 P.M. In between, however, he ate dates and almonds. He spun more cotton than either of his prison mates. Mahadev went through proofs of his book, being published by Oxford University Press, and took dictation from Gandhi daily for about two hours. Gandhi learned Urdu, read Ruskin [*Fors Clavigera*], and taught himself astronomy. Vallabhbhai "remains content with reading newspapers mostly," Gandhi reported, the Sardar sometimes reading aloud to them when he came across an interesting or amusing article.

From his prison "temple" Gandhi continued to offer sage medical advice to all who sought his help. To one supplicant he offered a remedy for constipation. "You may try it for two or three days and, if it does not work, give it up. Eat twice or thrice a day cooked *tandalja* [Amaranth] or *palak* [Spinach] leaves—eat nothing else."[7] To another he gave his "immediate, and unfailing, remedy for migraine": to bind a mud-pack around one's head before retiring.

On August 17, 1932, Ramsay MacDonald announced his Communal Award, reserving seats for "Depressed Classes" as well as Muslims and Sikhs. "In pursuance of my letter to Sir Samuel Hoare," Gandhi wrote "Dear Friend" MacDonald next day, "I have to resist your decision with my life."[8] He declared a fast unto death against the reservation of separate seats for untouchables, to begin in one month, on September 20, 1932.

"What do you think these people will do?" Vallabhbhai asked his cell mate on September 6, 1932. "I still feel that they will release me on or before the 19th," Gandhi replied. "It will be the limit of wickedness if they let me fast, let no one know about it and then say that I did what I as a prisoner ought not to have done, and that they could do nothing."[9]

Three days later MacDonald replied, arguing that his award, having doubled the number of Depressed Class votes, should have met with

Gandhi's approval, rather than eliciting his threat to fast. "What I am against is their statutory separation, even in a limited form, from [the] Hindu fold," Gandhi explained. "Do you not realize that if your decision stands and constitution comes into being, you arrest the marvellous growth of work of Hindu reformers who have dedicated themselves to the uplift of their suppressed brethren in every walk of life?"[10]

Gandhi considered his fast a "unique opportunity" for self-purification, urging all his ashram family and others close to him to shed "tears of joy," rather than sorrow on his behalf.[11] "It is both a privilege and a duty," he explained. "In non-violence it is the crowning act."[12] "If the Hindu mass mind is not yet prepared to banish untouchability root and branch, it must sacrifice me without the slightest hesitation,"[13] he told the press. Untouchables were an integral part of Hinduism's "indivisible family." Removal of the "infliction" of separate electorate privileges on Depressed Classes would end his fast, Gandhi added, though not the struggle against untouchability, which would then move into "high gear."

"I know you have not missed the woman in me," Gandhi responded to "Dear Mother, Singer and Guardian of My Soul," Sarojini Naidu, who begged him not to fast. He thus credited his "feminine" qualities of heart and soul with his resolve now to choose a "way of life through suffering unto death. I must therefore find my courage in my weakness."[14] Gandhi's astute consciousness of his own painfully passionate motivation on the eve of this momentous, potentially fatal, step was revealing. "She who sees life in death and death in life is the real Poetess and Seeress." He prayed that "God may give me strength enough to walk steadily through the vale. If Hinduism is to live, untouchability must die."

At 3 A.M. on September 20, 1932, Gandhi awoke and prepared himself to "enter the fiery gate at noon."[15] To his beloved Mira he wrote that "the voice within said, 'If you will enter in, you must give up thought of all attachment!' . . . No anguish will be too terrible to wash out the sin of untouchability. . . . [T]he spirit which you love is always with you. The body through which you learnt to love the spirit is no longer necessary for sustaining that love."[16]

"My ambition is to represent and identify myself with, as far as possible, the lowest strata of untouchables," Gandhi told the press, explaining his reasons: "for they have indeed drunk deep of the poisoned cup . . . if they are ever to rise, it will not be by reservation of seats but will be by the strenuous work of Hindu reformers."[17] Reporters were allowed inside Poona's prison, to the open sky compound where Gandhi lay on his fasting bed. "What I want," he passionately confessed as he started to fast "and what I should delight in dying for, is the eradication of untouchability root and branch."[18]

A conference of Hindu leaders was convened in swift response to the fast in Bombay, including Dr. B. R. Ambedkar, brilliant lawyer and political leader of India's untouchables, who later became India's first minister of law and chair of its Constitution-drafting Committee. Ambedkar was furious that Gandhi "singled out" special representational advantages for his community as his "excuse" for fasting unto death. Nonetheless, he agreed to go to Poona to discuss the issue with Gandhi, and on September 22 they met for their prison summit.

"I want political power for my community," Ambedkar told Gandhi. "That is indispensable for our survival."[19] He demanded his just "compensation" and "due," having himself insisted in London on the seventy-one specially reserved seats that MacDonald granted.

"I want to serve the *Harijans*," Gandhi replied, using the name which means "children of God." First coined by Narasinh Mehta, the "father of Gujarati poetry," the term was made popular by Gandhi, whose adoption of it for the remaining years of his life gave fresh nominal dignity at least to India's millions of outcastes. Gandhi assured Ambedkar that as a "new convert" to his community he was most zealous and wanted a Harijan to be the viceroy of India and a Bhangi "untouchable" sweeper to serve as president of the Congress. Ambedkar had brought an outline of his demands, which Gandhi asked Devdas to have redrafted and which they soon accepted as their agreement. It promised Harijans many more seats in Parliament than MacDonald's award had, but they would not run or be elected separately from the great body of Hinduism. All enfranchised Indians would vote only for competing Harijan candidates for those affirmative action "general" seats.

Congress Brahmans from north and south India, including such eminent leaders as Sapru, Jayakar, Malaviya, Rajendra Prasad, and Rajagopalachari, met with Devdas and others the next day to hammer out the scheme that satisfied Ambedkar, guaranteeing almost double the number of legislative assembly seats to his community than MacDonald had offered the "Depressed Classes." Meanwhile cables poured in from around the world, wishing India's Great Soul and "Magician" success and long life. Thousands of Indians had started to fast in sympathy, including Mira.[20]

The Hindu Leaders' Conference met in Bombay again on September 25 and unanimously resolved "henceforth" that no Hindu should be regarded as "untouchable by reason of his birth." Those so regarded hitherto should all have the same rights as other Hindus "to the use of public wells, public roads and other public institutions."[21] The agreement was wired to London, and MacDonald accepted it on behalf of the British government. On September 26 Gandhi broke his fast, drinking a glass of orange juice handed to him by Kasturba. Surrounded by about two hundred people, Gandhi lay on his cot as Bengali Nobel laureate Gurudev Tagore sang a poem from his *Gitanjali*. Gandhi prayed and expressed his hope that all caste Hindus would carry out to the letter and spirit every clause of the settlement. He warned, however, that he would fast again if they were too slow in carrying out the reforms. "I would like to assure my Harijan friends, as I would like henceforth to name them, that . . . I am wedded to the whole . . . Agreement, and that they may hold my life as hostage for its due fulfilment."[22] His weight had fallen to ninety-three and one-half pounds, but his passionate faith was never greater.

"Bapu is an extraordinary man and it is very difficult to understand him," Nehru wrote to his daughter, Indira. "But then great men are always difficult to understand. . . . [H]e conquers his opponents by his love and sacrifice. By his fast he has changed the face of India and killed untouchability at a blow."[23] Not "killed," but weakened.

That November, Gandhi wrote a series of essays on "untouchability" that helped to popularize the problem that had almost cost him his life. "Socially they are lepers," he reminded his readers. "Economically they are worse than slaves. Religiously they are denied entrance to places we miscall 'houses of God.' They are denied the use . . . of public roads, public schools, public hospitals, public wells, public taps. . . . Caste Hindu lawyers and doctors will not serve them. . . . They are too downtrodden to rise in revolt. . . . Every Hindu should have in his home a Harijan who would be for all practical purposes a member of the family."[24]

Gandhi now focused his heart and mind on how best to remove the blight of untouchability from Hinduism. He initially hoped that winning unhindered entry for Harijans to a Hindu temple in Malabar might prove the most effective lever. Mr. K. Kelappan, a singularly courageous self-sacrificing Kerala worker, had launched his own fast in September to open that Guruvayur temple to untouchables, and Gandhi persuaded him to suspend his fast by promising to help him achieve his goal or to join him later in fasting as well. Gandhi sent C. R. Das's widowed sister, Urmila Devi, to Kelappan in November 1932 as his messenger. American Margaret Cousins accompanied Urmila, but no sooner did Gandhi publicly announce his intention to join Kelappan in his fast than several orthodox Hindu Brahmans said they too would fast unto death *against* admitting any untouchable to their sacred temple. Gandhi was never intimidated by such threats. He resolved, therefore, to begin his fast on January 2, 1933, unless the temple opened all its gates wide to Harijans.

Charlie Andrews was "troubled," fearing that fasting "will certainly be used by fanatics to force an issue which may be reactionary instead of progressive."[25] That December a referendum was taken of all those Hindus eligible to enter the Guruvayur Temple, and some 55 percent favored temple entry for Harijans. Gandhi argued that this poll confirmed the validity of his intention to fast, but then a viceregal decision to permit the introduction of special Temple-entry legislation in Madras Province on January 15, 1933, convinced him to postpone his fast "indefinitely."[26]

Orthodox Hindus attacked Gandhi with "hard swearing at me and libellous charges," making him "feel like the wife whom her many husbands profess to reject because the poor woman cannot give equal satisfaction to all."[27] This polyandrous gender role reversal clearly underscores Gandhi's earlier admission to Sarojini Naidu of his passionate preference for feminine sacrificial pain. He was, he insisted, a "faithful wife, staunch in her loyalty" to all those angry "husbands" now maligning her. To pacifist friend Horace Alexander, he regretfully confessed, "I knew that that little fast was not enough penance for moving to right action the great mass of Hindu humanity. Many lives might have to be given before the last remnant of untouchability is gone."[28]

Congressmen who were not devout Hindus questioned Gandhi's intense preoccupation with this religious issue to the "detriment" of political activity and viewed it as dangerous, focusing India's masses on "magic" fasting, and seeking "divine guidance" in down-to-earth matters of state and social conflict. Nor were all Harijan leaders by any means satisfied with their caste Hindu "Saviour." Many wondered at his choices of venue for launching his attack against Hinduism's orthodox establishment, while others, including Ambedkar, were bewildered by the speed with which he chose first to fast, then not to fast.

After his September euphoria, even Gandhi now started to doubt himself. In late January of 1933, three weeks after he postponed his fast, he was chagrined to learn of the viceroy's decision to veto Madras's temple-entry bill. The prison superintendent asked Gandhi what he proposed to do. "There is no Inner Voice urging me to go on a fast," he softly replied, "perturbed" though not enough to risk his life again.[29]

In municipal elections in Cawnpore (Kanpur) at month's end, every Harijan candidate was defeated, making Gandhi appreciate for the first time Ambedkar's insistence on separate electorate reservations. "This defeat makes me sad," Gandhi confessed to an old friend. "I cannot help owning to you my utter stupidity." He had "fondly believed" that the excellent Harijan candidates would easily win most of the elections. "I see, however, that without reservation they would have a poor chance . . . unless caste Hindus develop a high sense of honour."[30] Those elections opened Gandhi's eyes wider to the deep roots of caste Hindu prejudice, nourished by several millennia of arrogant repression and inhuman behavior. Now he conceded that perhaps "statutory reservation" was the "fit punishment for our selfishness." What a confession so soon after having nearly fasted to death to stop Harijan affirmative action. Some leaders, who once believed Gandhi infallible, started to doubt his mental stability.

That February Gandhi announced the first edition of his new weekly, *Harijan*, for which he asked Ambedkar to write something. "The outcaste is a bye-product of the caste system," Dr. Ambedkar wrote. "There will be outcastes as long as there are castes. Nothing can emancipate the outcaste except the destruction of the caste system."[31] Gandhi commented that Ambedkar had every right to be "bitter," but insisted that Hinduism's caste system was not "odious" or "vicious," merely misguided in its treatment of outcastes. Gandhi never lost faith in the caste system itself, only in the "ugly growth" of malignant untouchability on its otherwise healthy "body."

In late April of 1933 Gandhi resolved to fast for three weeks, this time as penance "against myself." "A tempest has been raging within me for some days," he wrote. "I have been struggling against it. . . . But the resistance was vain. . . . The fast is against nobody . . . But . . . myself. It is a heart-prayer for the purification of self and associates, for greater vigilance and watchfulness."[32] He had just learned that several young ashramites had broken their vows of celibacy. Again, many friends tried to persuade him to abandon the fast. But having heard his inner voice, Gandhi refused to disobey what he believed to be God's will. He cabled Mira to reassure Ba, who was "greatly shocked" by what Mira reported. "Tell Ba Father imposed on her a companion whose weight would have killed any other woman . . . Love."[33]

To "My Dear Jawaharlal," he wrote: "The Harijan movement is too big for mere intellectual effort. There is nothing so bad in all the world. . . . My life would be a burden to me, if Hinduism failed me."[34] Nehru replied: "What can I say about matters I do not understand?" He had developed "a horror of nostrums and the like," what he called Bapu's "strange methods" and "magic" ways, which to his rational mind only "leads people inevitably to give up troubling their minds for solutions of problems and await for miracles."[35]

On the day he started fasting, Gandhi was released from prison, British authorities fearing that his death in jail would ignite revolt. He was driven to his friend Lady Premlila Thackersey's bungalow near Yeravda in Poona's cantonment. "I cannot regard this release with any degree of pleasure," Gandhi told reporters. He promised the government not to "abuse" his release and appealed for the unconditional discharge of all civil resisters, indicating his hope for a general amnesty and peaceful cooperation.

After five days of fasting, Gandhi took the advice of Dr. Deshmukh and began drinking bottled Vichy water to reduce the acidity in his stomach. After completing twenty days of fasting he told Devdas, "It is due to God's mercy that I am living."[36] On the twenty-first day Lady Thackersey brought him the fast-breaking orange juice. Sarojini Naidu and Dr. Ansari were there to celebrate with a group that included many Harijans, young and old. Ansari read from the Quran he had brought, Christian brothers sang "When I Survey the Wondrous Cross," Professor Wadia sang a Parsi prayer, and then came Gurudev Tagore's prayer from *Gitanjali*, followed by the final prayer hymn of "the true Vaishnava," Gandhi's favorite.[37]

Leaders of the Congress came to Poona to confer with Gandhi, most of them urging him to end the civil disobedience campaign. Gandhi sought an interview with the viceroy before committing himself. However, Willingdon was not Irwin. The reply was negative, and Willingdon warned him against resuming Satyagraha of any kind. Gandhi remained defiant, insisting to his Congress comrades that their workers were "not tired. The country was not tired."[38] Government saw that by pursuing his Harijan cause as vigorously as he had, Gandhi lost the support of many powerful Hindus. Nor had he won any Muslim League support, Jinnah having always insisted on the need for separate electoral seats for Muslims and for untouchables as well. The viceroy, therefore, felt quite confident that he could treat Gandhi's offer to talk "peace" with imperious contempt. Gandhi now announced his decision to disband his Sabarmati ashram. Most of his devoted inmates moved to Wardha, soon to become the major new ashram of *Sevagram* ("Village of Service"). Gandhi informed the government of Bombay that his former ashram's property was held in a registered trust, valued at well over half a million rupees. But since the ashram had refused to pay revenue for the last two years, the government seized and sold much of the movable property. Gandhi turned over the land and its empty buildings to the Servants of Untouchables Society for Harijan work.

At the end of July 1933, Gandhi wired Bombay's home secretary to notify him of his intention to lead a Satyagraha march from Ahmedabad to Ras to urge all villagers there to boycott liquor and foreign cloth. He was not, however, permitted to take a single step. He and Mahadev were arrested at midnight on August 1, 1933, first taken to Sabarmati Jail and then transferred the next day to Poona's Yeravda. There he was tried by Magistrate Hyam Israel. When asked his occupation, Gandhi replied: "I am by occupation a spinner, a weaver and a farmer."[39] Asked his residence, he said "Yeravda jail now." He did not dispute any charge brought against him, but made a brief statement. "I am a lover of peace, and I regard myself a good citizen voluntarily tendering obedience to the laws of the State to which I may belong. But there are occasions in the lifetime of a citizen when it becomes his painful duty to disobey laws. . . . I have had recently a spell of freedom and was in the midst of people . . . living in a perpetual fear of loss of liberty and their possessions. . . . I sought shelter in self-suffering."[40] After that reaffirmation of his passionate credo of civil resistance, Gandhi requested to be treated as a grade "C" prisoner. Magistrate Israel sentenced him, however, to one year as a grade "A" prisoner, "considering your age and the present state of your health." He was almost sixty-four and weighed less than one hundred pounds.

Eager to resume the Harijan work he had done earlier from his prison cell, Gandhi requested secretarial assistance for preparing his weekly *Harijan*, but now the prison authorities were totally unsupportive. On August 14, 1933, he therefore wrote to Bombay's home secretary and informed him of his decision to resume fasting in two days. The strain of his not being allowed to work had become "unbearable." Life "ceases to interest me if I may not do Harijan service," Gandhi explained.[41] He began his fast August 16, ending it eight days later when he was unconditionally released. "How I shall use this life out of prison, I do not know," he wrote,[42] though Harijan service would remain from now on, he added, "the breath of life for me, more precious than the daily bread." He was returned to Lady Thackersey's bungalow on August 23, 1933, free at last and to remain so for nine unbroken years.

17

Return to Rural Uplift Work

"I HAVE NO ready-made plan," Gandhi told reporters soon after his release from jail. "It is nothing less than a new life for me."[1] He had been so severely nauseated on the last day of his fast that he gave away all his worldly possessions, thinking he would die. He now planned to retire from Congress completely and to devote himself only to Harijan work and other constructive programs of social uplift: spinning, weaving, and prohibition.

Jawaharlal, also just released from prison, went to Poona to meet with Gandhi in mid-September of 1933. They conferred alone long enough to agree on how much they disagreed and how best to advance common goals they still shared for the good of the nation and its masses. "Vested interests in India will have to give up their special . . . privileges," Jawaharlal insisted soon after leaving Bapu, agreeing with him, however, that "divesting should be done as gently as possible and with every effort to avoid injury."[2] Nehru wanted such change to be accomplished as swiftly as possible. Gandhi was more concerned with the morality of the means rather than the swiftness of achieving the end. Both agreed the Round Table Conferences were "useless," Nehru calling them "a fascist grouping of vested and possessing interests." Having participated in one such conference himself, Gandhi was less harsh, unwilling to label its members "fascist."

While Gandhi stressed the importance of "uttermost truthfulness and non-violence," Jawaharlal also favored "secret methods," his faith in the class struggle and most Marxist-Leninist doctrine convincing him of the utility of secrecy in fighting British imperialism to the death.[3] They parted company as well over Gandhi's insistence on communal unity, hand spinning, weaving, and the abolition of untouchability as prerequisites to independence. Nehru focused his dynamic mind and youthful energy on the primacy of winning political freedom, strongly supporting other international socialist forces in Europe and Asia. Nevertheless, Gandhi agreed to help Nehru and Congress with his sage advice, whenever they called on him for assistance.

Gandhi devoted the last quarter of 1933 and much of 1934 to Harijan relief, appealing to caste Hindus and Harijans alike from Bombay to the remote villages of Gujarat, Maharashtra, and Bengal to touch, marry, and serve every Indian of one's own faith as a blood brother and sister. To many Congress leaders, Gandhi knew, "I stand thoroughly discredited as a religious maniac and predominantly a social worker."[4] He felt certain, however, that political reform prior to social reform would only replace insensitive British rule with insensitive Indian rule. In a village in Ahmedabad District, Gandhi disgustedly reported that high-caste Hindu men had "horsewhipped some Harijans . . . because one of them had the temerity to bathe in a public tank."[5]

During his tour Gandhi encountered fierce Hindu protesters led by saffron-clad Swamis, who were furious at his calling himself a Harijan and serving "outcastes." They waved black flags of protest against him, the way the Simon Commission and the Prince of Wales had been greeted by angry nationalists. His effigy was burned by frenzied hoodlums, who shouted "Death to Gandhi!" He felt "pained" by such wretched protests, but was undeterred by them. "I have got to follow my dharma even if everybody deserts me. . . . One must do one's duty to the best of one's ability."[6] His karma yogic philosophy remained pure in the face of every dark challenge and criminal insult. Passionate devotee of Krishna that he was, Gandhi insisted that unless the "blot of untouchability" was removed, "Hinduism and Hindu society will perish."[7]

Gandhi was in south India in mid-January of 1934 when a devastating earthquake struck Bihar, reducing many cities to rubble, claiming over 10,000 lives, and leaving hundreds of thousands homeless. On learning of the catastrophe, he commented, "We who have faith in God must cherish the belief that behind even this indescribable calamity there is a divine purpose that works for the good of humanity. You may call me superstitious . . . but a man like me cannot but believe that this earthquake is a divine chastisement sent by God for our sins."[8] He blamed the sin of untouchability, insisting that everything happened by "divine will."[9] Nehru and Tagore were shocked and dismayed by Gandhi's reaction to the quake.

"It has caused me painful surprise to find Mahatma Gandhi accusing those who blindly follow their own social custom of untouchability of having brought down God's vengeance upon certain parts of Bihar . . . because this kind of unscientific view of things is too readily accepted by a large section of our countrymen," Gurudev Tagore announced.[10]

Bihar's Dr. Rajendra Prasad, who had just been released from prison, worked round the clock to help save those most severely burned and wounded. Prasad's selfless quake relief work first brought the name of India's first president to national prominence. Though many urged him to rush to Bihar, Gandhi refused to cancel his Harijan tour. "I am tied to Bihar by sacred ties," Gandhi replied. "Perhaps I am serving her best by remaining at my post."[11] He then repeated his belief that the calamity was God's "chastisement" for the "grave sin" of untouchability. "Visitations like droughts, floods, earthquakes and the like, though they seem to have only physical origins, are, for me, somehow connected with man's morals."[12]

Pacifist Muriel Lester now came to India, and visited her friend the governor of Bengal, after meeting with Gandhi. She was invited to dine with the governor but failed to get him to commit resources to Bihar. She then went to see the viceroy. By late February, Gandhi decided to alter his Harijan tour itinerary so as to visit Bihar before going to Bengal. Muriel joined Gandhi on his tour of Bihar in mid-March 1934. Agatha Harrison, who was also a leader of London's Quakers, reached Bombay two days later, and journeyed directly to Bihar to tour with them. Gandhi addressed Bihar's Central Relief Committee in Patna, after visiting several centers of disaster. "Let us, in the face of this calamity, forget the distinction between Hindus and Mussalmans as well as between Indians and Englishmen," he told them. "We are going to work not as Congressmen but as humanitarians . . . in a humane task."[13]

Gandhi now found it more difficult to sleep as this tour continued, rising at one in the morning instead of three. "Please do not get alarmed," he wrote Brother Vallabh. A gang of angry, high-caste Hindu thugs had just recently attacked him as he was getting into his car, badly denting the car with stones. He narrowly escaped that assault, after which he decided to leave the temple town of Puri and its vehicular travel, venturing off on a walking tour of rural Orissa, alone with Mira and just a few others. He enjoyed this pilgrimage on foot, along village paths and tribal jungle trails. "We are camping in the open air on the outskirts of the village. A hut-like structure has been put up for me."[14] He knew, of course, that as soon as the "rains set in" this method of touring would prove more difficult, if not impossible. He was ready then to "camp" in the hinterland, finding it much more congenial to his passionate, aging temperament than the hustle and bustle of urban life.

In mid-June, Gandhi and his followers all returned by train to Bombay, where Muriel and Agatha awaited him to say good-bye before sailing home. Mira then impulsively decided to join the other English ladies. Gandhi's first letter to his departed beloved began: "It was a chilly parting.

But I know that I shall never have deeper or richer yet unselfish affection bestowed upon me."[15] He returned to Lady Thackersey's bungalow in Poona, where now Ba joined him. The next evening a bomb was thrown by an assassin at a car mistaken for the one transporting Gandhi to speak in Poona's Municipal Building. "I have had so many narrow escapes in my life that this newest one does not surprise me," he calmly remarked. "I am glad it happened on account of my Harijan work," he wrote Vallabhbhai.[16] No one in the car hit by the bomb was fatally injured, nor was the culprit caught, though Gandhi knew he must have been a hate-crazed high-caste Hindu. "The sorrowful incident has undoubtedly advanced the Harijan cause. . . . causes prosper by the martyrdom of those who stand for them."[17] Many angry Brahmans of Poona, long a bastion of Hindu orthodoxy, had demanded Gandhi's death since he started his Harijan campaign. In less than fourteen years another mad Poona Brahman would succeed in murdering him.

By mid-July, Gandhi felt "intense mental and physical" exhaustion, sleeping "whenever I get the opportunity."[18] He missed Mira and wrote to tell her "you are constantly with me. Love."[19] He decided on a week's "penance and self-purification" fast, confessing to his departed love that "many changes are taking place in my mind just now." Congress "corruption" was also "preying on me." To Agatha Harrison he wrote: "What occupies my mind at present is how to achieve purity of the Congress and to rid the Ashram here [Wardha] of subtle untruth and breaches of *brahmacharya*."[20] The fast weakened him but did no permanent damage to his health. Its purifying "torture" relieved his passionate mind of otherwise unbearable pain. The scramble among Congressmen for power sickened him, as did his own frustrations, and fasting helped Gandhi to concentrate "on the great necessity of achieving internal purity."[21]

He urged Brother Vallabh to join him in Wardha before the end of August, when Charlie was coming. Nehru had written angrily to him, after Gandhi denounced him for pursuing his "private studies" (reading and writing) in prison, rather than spinning his Congress quota of cotton. He knew that Jawaharlal and his young radical supporters considered him too conservative, if not reactionary, to lead them to freedom. "I seem to be obstructing the growth of the Congress," Gandhi confessed to Vallabhbhai, the one Congress leader to whom he could unburden himself. "But what can I do?"[22] Most Congressmen made no distinction between "truth and falsehood, violence and non-violence." Nehru missed the barricades, Gandhi knew, and considered virtually all current members of the Congress Working Committee too old or weak-minded ever to lead India's revolution. "You are hard on the members of the Working Committee," Gandhi wrote Jawaharlal. "They are our colleagues. . . . After all we are a free institution."[23] But he remembered what Motilal had once told him and was ready now to step aside, to leave politics and all the vanities of power to a younger generation of eager leaders.

That September of 1934 Gandhi decided to quit the Congress he had revolutionized and led since 1920. "It is not with a light heart that I leave this great organization," he wrote to Vallabhbhai. "My presence more and more estranges the intelligentsia from the Congress. I feel that my policies fail to convince their reason. . . . [T]here is the growing group of Socialists. Jawaharlal is their undisputed leader. . . . The Socialist group represents his views more or less. . . . I have fundamental differences with them."[24] Thirteen years before the Congress took control of independent India, Gandhi thus quietly removed himself from its organization and petty power plays as well as the growing corruption and violence of its leaders.

Gandhi turned back to central India after quitting Congress, devoting all his time and energy to rural uplift work. Since the birth of his first ashram in South Africa he had viewed rural self-sufficiency and self-help, as well as communal harmony, as his ideal goals for society. Sabarmati's Satyagraha Ashram in its last years proved most disillusioning, however, leading him to abandon it. Proximity to fast-growing, industrial Ahmedabad was much less congenial to his aging temperament than the more isolated rural *Sevagram*, just a few miles from Wardha.

Much as he hoped for peace in this retreat so remote from urban chaos and Congress conflicts, Gandhi no sooner settled in Sevagram than his prodigal son, Harilal, wrote to ask his Bapu if he might join the ashram. He invited Harilal, only after satisfying himself that his son had not touched liquor in many months and was striving valiantly to give up "smoke" as well as "sexual pleasure." Widower Harilal hoped, however, to "remarry," an idea Gandhi was initially amenable to, if an appropriate mature Hindu widow could be found. In welcoming Harilal, Gandhi warned him never to "deceive me" or misbehave. "I am an old man now, and you are not a child," sixty-five-year-old Gandhi wrote to his forty-six-year-old son.[25]

Harilal very much enjoyed ashram life, making many friends there and attracting most inmates merely by virtue of being their Mahatma's son. He became attracted to and hoped to marry Gandhi's "mad," blonde, beautiful German disciple, Margarete Spiegel, whom Bapu had renamed *Amala* ("Spotless"). When Harilal informed Bapu of his desire and Amala's agreement, Gandhi was so shocked that he insisted "you will have to drop the idea."[26] Gandhi ordered Harilal to write and tell her that it was a bad idea. If her response was that "she cannot live without you," Gandhi advised "patience." Harilal tried to remain patient and thought he was doing a perfectly natural thing, wishing to marry a beautiful woman who could speak twelve languages and had left the comforts of her Central European parental home to serve India's Harijans and follow her adored Mahatma. Margarete-Amala loved Harilal with all the unrequited passion for Gandhian progeny she could never dream of having with Bapu. Yet the prospect of their marriage drove Gandhi to distraction. "How can I, who have always advocated renunciation of sex, encourage you to gratify it?" Gandhi wrote his son. Even worse to Gandhi's deeply troubled mind was that "you carry on your search for a wife while staying with me."[27] Few things depressed Gandhi as much as the thought of his own children wishing to marry and to have children of their own. So his son, Harilal soon fled from that remote ashram, which Gandhi wanted to turn into a model community, not only for India, but for the world. Harilal returned to Rajkot where Gandhi's cousin Narandas allowed him to live in a small room in his home there. Gandhi told Narandas to give him Rs.100, but nothing more. "He is still addicted to smoking."[28] A month later Gandhi reported that Harilal was "off the rails" and "may be considered as lost to us."[29]

Gandhi now immersed himself in the struggle to save India's starving millions from hunger and unemployed despair, starting his All-India Village Industry's Association in November 1934. He recruited wealthy backers like industrialists G. D. Birla and Jamnalal Bajaj, and Vinoba Bhave helped him organize the movement to "rejuvenate" India's villages. He taught peasants that it was healthier for them to eat unpolished grains than vitamin-poor polished flour and rice. He also taught that uncooked cabbage and cauliflower were particularly healthful.

At a kitchen meeting in Wardha, Gandhi noted that he had been "a cook all my life," since London student days and running his South African kitchen for two decades. "Now we have embarked on a mission the like of which we had not undertaken before. We have got to be ideal villagers . . . to show them that they can grow their vegetables, their greens, without much expense, and keep good health. We have also to show them that most of the vitamins are lost when they cook the leaves."[30] Gandhi was passionately devoted to dietary reform and ancient India's Ayurvedic naturopathy to prolong life. Among other remedies, he taught his agents the value of tamarind for constipation. "Medical men of the West are slowly but surely finding out that the less drugs they prescribe the better it is for their patients," he wisely noted, reaching back thousands of years to the scientific roots of India's precocious medical traditions and believing decades before most Westerners in the value of alternative, holistic paths to healing.[31] He also stressed the vital values of proper village sanitation and good hygiene.

Another devastating earthquake struck South Asia on May 31, 1935, in Quetta, reducing that Baluchistan city to rubble and claiming tens of thousands of lives. "The appalling disaster in Quetta paralyses one," Gandhi wrote. "It baffles all attempt at reconstruction."[32] He then repeated what he had said of the Bihar disaster, insisting that there was "a divine purpose" behind every calamity. He prescribed "inward purification" through prayer as the only cure for such natural tragedies.

Six months later, when his blood pressure jumped to over 200, Gandhi broke down and was confined to bed under doctors' orders for almost two months. "The strings of your life, mine and everybody else's, are held by Mira's Lord,"[33] he wrote Vallabhbhai, disobeying his doctors' orders by doing so. Though he, Mira, Vinoba, and many other worthy members of his ashram labored every day round the clock, their village uplift work proved so daunting a task that few tangible results could be seen, leaving him as tired and depressed as he had ever been. "The people's indifference persists," one village volunteer reported wearily. "There is no end to the difficulties."[34] Mira volunteered to live in village Sindi, where she labored every day, picking up all the excrement of its villagers, dropped as "night-soil" along the road. She tried her best to teach them the sanitary utility of latrines, until she too fell ill, and high fever forced her to leave for the hills. Many educated Indians viewed Gandhi's passionate preoccupation with rural uplift with skepticism, one writing to ask him if it would not be wiser to focus first on winning political power. "One must forget the political goal in order to realize it," Gandhi replied. "I am afraid the correspondent's question betrays his laziness and despair. . . . [T]he activities that absorb my energies . . . are calculated to achieve the nation's freedom."[35] The revolution on which he focused all his passionate strength was in the heartland of rural India, more remote from viceregal palaces than was London from New Delhi. He knew India's heartland, mired deep in mud or dusty soil, better than any politician, Indian or English.

On May 29, 1936, Harilal embraced Islam. He changed his name to Abdulla. The announcement was made to a large congregation in Bombay's Jumma Masjid. The assembled Muslims hailed his conversion, many rushing up to shake his hand. Gandhi was "hurt" by the news but expressed "gravest doubt about his [Harilal's] acceptance [of Islam] being from the heart or free from selfish considerations."[36] He knew that Harilal was indebted to "some Pathans from whom he had borrowed on heavy interest" and suggested that his conversion was mercenary opportunism. "Harilal's apostasy is no loss to Hinduism and his admission to Islam is a source of weakness to it if, as I apprehend, he remains the same wreck that he was before."

Despite his withdrawal from Congress and retreat to a life of remote rural service, Gandhi was forced to return to the maelstrom of politics to resolve a bitter conflict that erupted soon after Jawaharlal Nehru reclaimed Congress's presidential crown but lost the confidence of most members of his own Working Committee. Nehru wanted to reject Britain's offer of responsible provincial governments under completely elected ministries as a step toward full dominion status under the Government of India Act of 1935. Rajendra Prasad, who had presided over the Congress a year earlier, Vallabhbhai Patel, C. Rajagopalachari (C. R.), and a majority of the Working Committee favored the British offer as half the loaf of freedom. Gandhi tried to talk Nehru out of his resolve to resign, whereas Nehru's comrades pressured him to quit the Congress and lead India's youth and impoverished workers in a "real" revolution to "topple" the British Empire. Gandhi understood the weakness of India's masses and knew that men like Vallabhbhai Patel, Rajendra Prasad, and C. R. more accurately reflected the feelings and desires of most Indians than did the Western revolutionary ideals of Nehru and his cohort.

"You are exaggerating," Bapu wired Jawaharlal, urging him to "consider the situation calmly and not succumb to it in a moment of depression so unworthy of you."[37] Gandhi knew how mercurial and temperamental Nehru's heart and mind were. "You feel to be the most injured party," Gandhi wrote a week later, knowing Nehru's sensitivities. "Your colleagues have lacked your courage and frankness. . . . They have chafed under your rebukes and magisterial manner and. . . . [t]hey feel that you have treated them with scant courtesy and never defended them from socialists' ridicule."[38] So Bapu healed wounds on both sides, averting Congress's proclivity to fission, patching up divisions destined to tear the party apart many times in the aftermath of independence.

A month later Gandhi talked with Nehru at length, but then wrote to ask him, "Why is it that with all the will in the world I cannot understand what is so obvious to you? I am not, so far as I know, suffering from intellectual decay. Should you not then set your heart on at least making me understand what you are after?"[39] Though Gandhi continued to speak of Jawaharlal as his "heir" to national leadership, thereby keeping him in the Congress, they never again really saw eye-to-eye on how to tackle India's intractable problems. Nehru ridiculed Gandhi's focus on rural uplift and his attempt to nurse India's village populace, comparing it to King Canute's attempt to turn back the tide. "Who else is to do it?" Gandhi replied. "If you go to the village nearby, you will find . . . out of 600 people there 300 are ill. Are they all to go to the hospital? We have to learn to treat ourselves. We are suffering for our own sins. . . . How are we to teach these poor villagers except by personal example?"[40] Gandhi, just turned sixty-seven, thus labored passionately and strenuously to cure by personal example all of India's 300 million of their countless ills.

18

Prelude to War and Partition

T HOUGH GANDHI reported in March of 1937, "I am concentrating my attention on village work . . . and cannot think of anything else," less than a month later, he was lured from his rural retreat, back into the political fray.[1]

The 1935 Government of India Act that had emerged from London's three Round Table Conferences enfranchised some thirty-five million Indians, more than half of whom trekked to polling places throughout British India in February of 1937. Congress candidates won 716 seats, capturing majorities in six of British India's eleven provincial legislative assemblies. Nehru, whose electrifying air-borne campaign, had led the euphoric Congress party to its stunning victory, ordered all minority parties to "line up!" saying there were only two parties left in India, Congress and the British. Jinnah rejected that argument, insisting that the Muslims represented by his Muslim League, were a "third party."[2] Then Lord Zetland, the new Tory secretary of state for India, insisted that British provincial governors would all be "obliged," under the new Constitution, to "safeguard the legitimate interests of the minorities."[3] And the new viceroy, Lord Linlithgow, firmly reiterated his secretary of state's message, which Congress viewed as nothing but the old British policy of divide and rule with a vengeance. "The latest gesture is one of the sword not of goodwill," Gandhi told the Associated Press, "certainly not of democratic obedience to the will of a democratic majority."[4]

Zetland refused to back down, however, so the much-hailed, eagerly anticipated experiment in provincial "self-rule" under the 1935 Constitution was suspended, replaced by appointed official ministries. Nehru's fury flared to white intensity; Gandhi urged moderation. "Jawaharlal reads one meaning and I another," he told his *Seva Sangh* ("Service Society") conference in April. Instead of launching a violent civil war, Gandhi told Nehru that "we can wreck the Constitution through non-violence," advising use of Motilal's old Swarajist technique of joining the government to obstruct its operations from within.[5] Gandhi knew that Jawaharlal was ready to fight, and that "if for the sake of the freedom of India he feels compelled to cut the throats of Englishmen; he will not hesitate."[6] Most of the elected Congress members agreed with Gandhi so Nehru was obliged to "surrender" to Zetland's insistence on safeguards.

That July the Working Committee of Congress met in Wardha and resolved to form ministries in all six of the provinces of British India in which they had won majorities. Jinnah tried to meet with Gandhi to discuss some formula by which his Muslim League, having taken only 109 seats out of the total of 1,585, winning none of the provinces, might share in the running of the United Provinces, Punjab, and Bengal, where enormous Muslim minorities represented powerful interests. "I wish I could do something, but I am utterly helpless," Gandhi replied. "My faith in unity is as bright as ever; only I see no daylight out of the impenetrable darkness."[7] It was to be the last time Jinnah would appeal politely for Gandhi's help in winning the support of his more radical young Congress friends for any multiparty provincial cooperation. Nehru's plan for governing all pluralistic provinces was to appoint Congress "National" Muslim ministers to every province with a substantial Muslim populace. Congress Maulana Abul Kalam Azad helped Nehru to select the "best" Congress Muslims for each of those powerful cabinets, thereby leaving "reactionary" Jinnah and his Muslim League out in the cold.

That October, sherwani-coated Jinnah, wearing a black Persian lamb hat soon identified the world over as the "Jinnah cap," addressed 5,000 members of the Muslim League over which he now permanently presided in Lucknow. "The present leadership of the Congress," Jinnah thundered, "has been responsible for alienating the Mussalmans of India more and more, by pursuing a policy which is exclusively Hindu; and since they have formed Governments in the six provinces . . . they have . . . shown, more and more, that the Mussalmans cannot expect any justice or fair play at their hands. . . . [T]hey refused to co-operate with the Muslim League . . . and demanded unconditional surrender."[8] Jinnah spoke with such power and authority that he was hailed thereafter by millions of Muslim followers as their *Quaid-i-Azam* ("Great Leader"). Bracing his party for the struggle ahead, he reminded them, "No individual or people can achieve anything without industry, suffering and sacrifice. Eighty millions of Mussalmans in

India have nothing to fear. They have their destiny in their hands, and as a well-knit, solid, organized, united force can face any danger, and withstand any opposition."

Vallabhbhai, always the supreme realist, understood how potent a political force Jinnah was destined to become, and urged Gandhi to meet with him in October 1937. But Bapu replied that "Jawaharlal doesn't desire it."[9] Nehru's personal and ideological antipathy to Jinnah thus prevented a meeting that might have brought Congress and the League together to govern India's most populous provinces. Gandhi also appreciated Jinnah's power but feared losing his hold over Nehru more than risking greater alienation of the League's Quaid.

Gandhi journeyed to Calcutta, at the urgent request of Nehru, Subhas Bose, and other members of the Congress Working Committee, who were all eager to consult him on many troubling matters. He also met with the governor of Bengal. By mid-November, when he headed back to Wardha, he felt weaker than he'd been since his long fast. "I need prolonged rest from all mental toil," he informed Jawaharlal, reporting on his efforts to resolve the conflicts in Bengal. "If we cannot control the situation . . . our holding of offices is bound to prove detrimental to the Congress cause."[10] A few days later he wrote in *Harijan* of those "Storm Signals" indicating that Congress provincial ministries were losing "control over forces of disorder."[11] The pains and problems of power daily loomed larger. To Gandhi's mind at least, it seemed "certain" that the Congress organization needed "strengthening and purging." But "extreme exhaustion" caused his blood pressure to shoot up again and doctors urged rest on Juhu Beach, where he went in December.

In mid-January he returned to his ashram to meet there with Whitehall's Under Secretary of State Lord Lothian. "My ambition is to see the Congress recognized as the one and only party that can . . . deliver the goods," Gandhi told Lothian.[12] The British Indian Federation, a union of princely states and provinces, was to have been inaugurated as the final fruition of the 1935 act, but Gandhi and Congress urged the British to wait, eager for the election of an Indian "Constituent Assembly" to draft a Constitution to replace the present act.

Though a Congress ministry now ruled in the United Provinces, Hindu-Muslim riots continued in many parts of that most populous multicultural province of British India. Allahabad itself, Nehru's birthplace and now headquarters of Congress, was the venue of deadly riots in March 1938. "The communal riots in Allahabad," Gandhi wrote, "and the necessity of summoning the assistance of the police and even the military show that the Congress has not yet become fit to substitute the British authority. It is best to face this naked truth, however unpleasant it may be."[13] Congress ministries were not only corrupt and ineffectual but riddled with nepotism, leaving most Muslims feeling neglected in employment as well as education. "I do not want swaraj without Hindu-Muslim unity," Gandhi told a large meeting of his Seva Sangh. "I want that in independent India Hindus should not suppress Muslims, nor Muslims Hindus. I want to see that all are equal."[14]

Late in April of 1938, Gandhi agreed to meet with Jinnah alone in his home atop Bombay's Malabar Hill. That Congress-League summit attracted press notice in London as in India, rousing popular hopes that a Hindu-Muslim settlement might at last be imminent. Gandhi cautioned against undue optimism, telling reporters on the eve of that "interview" with Jinnah that he felt himself "in a Slough of Despond."[15] Nehru strongly opposed the meeting but had just been obliged to relinquish his Congress crown to Subhas Bose and was preparing to leave India for Europe and London. "It hurts me that, at this very critical juncture in our history, we do not . . . see eye to eye in important matters," Gandhi wrote Nehru. "I can't tell you how positively lonely I feel to know that nowadays I can't carry you with me."[16]

Gandhi reached Jinnah's home late on the morning of April 28, 1938. "We had three hours' friendly conversation over the Hindu-Muslim question and the matter will be pursued further. The public will be informed in due course of its developments," was the only statement they agreed to issue to the press.[17] Immediately after what he later termed that "galling" meeting, sixty-nine-year-old, exhausted Gandhi left by train for the North-West Frontier, to meet with his Muslim disciple, "Frontier Gandhi" Khan Abdul Ghaffar Khan. Jinnah was seven years Gandhi's junior, and thanks to his impeccable attire and elegant grooming looked much stronger as well as younger. But he too was exhausted, his smoke-riddled lungs afflicted by pleurisy as well as the incipient tuberculosis that would claim his life a decade later.

"The Allah of Islam is the same as the god of Christians and the Ishwara of Hindus," Gandhi told his large Pathan Muslim audience assembled in Peshawar's Islamia College. "Living faith in this God means acceptance of the brotherhood of mankind. It also means equal respect for all religions."[18] Gandhi hoped to win back the support of most Muslims, which he had enjoyed during the Khilafat struggle in the aftermath of World War I. He tried his best to develop his powerful Frontier Khan into a reincarnated image of the Brothers Ali, but though thousands of loyal Pathans cheered Gandhi's speech and giant Abdul Ghaffar Khan embraced his tiny mentor as well as his ideas of Ahimsa, Gandhi sadly confessed: "There is as yet no sign of the end of the crisis."[19] Not only did Hindu-Muslim conflicts and communal killings continue in Bengal, Bihar, and the United Provinces, but in his own heart and mind Gandhi found that "Darkness is still there . . . an unaccountable dissatisfaction with myself. Moodiness . . . wholly unnatural to me."

Gandhi reported his unnatural moody despair to one of his newest disciples, "Princess" *Rajkumari* Amrit Kaur of Kapurthala State, whom he playfully addressed as "Idiot," signing off most of his letters to her either as "Tyrant" or "Robber." Christian Amrit was strongly attracted by Gandhi's rural uplift movement and by his self-sacrificing spirit, becoming one of his most generous followers. On the eve of Gandhi's seventies, she was to take Mira's place as his favorite "sister" and most trusted confidante. "The sexual sense is the hardest to overcome in my case," he confessed to her. "It has been an incessant struggle . . . Love."[20] Gandhi had decided to try an ancient "magic" method to help revitalize his waning yogic powers. To test and "strengthen" his Brahmacharya he started sleeping naked with several of his young female ashram inmates. Mira was so upset when she learned of his latest test that she felt compelled to remove herself from his presence, rushing off to England, prolonging her absence by extending her trip abroad to the United States. "I must change my manners," he now promised Mira. "About Lilavati [a young ashramite virgin] I can't recall anything of what you say. But once I felt that I had put my arm around her neck. I asked her in the morning. She said she had no knowledge of any touch. Nevertheless from that day I asked her to sleep at a proper distance."[21] Gandhi sent Mira's critical letters to "Idiot" Amrit, telling her to "destroy them" as soon as she finished reading, adding that "Robbed of Mira's hysteria, they are sound. I am contemplating some changes."[22]

"Where am I, where is my place, and how can a person subject to passion represent non-violence and truth?" Gandhi now asked himself, adding in his letter to another ashram woman: "Am I worthy of you all who follow me, am I fit to lead you all?"[23] The magic powers of restraint he sought to develop so intensely would allow him to control his feelings completely. Even intimate proximity to naked, nubile bodies should arouse no feelings in him other than a "Mother's love." He believed that this most difficult and challenging test of his celibacy was somehow mystically connected to the purity and perfection of his Ahimsa, and to his power to stop Hindu-Muslim violence and reach an enduring agreement with Jinnah. "The two hang together," he argued. "I may neither tempt God nor the Devil."[24] Dr. Sushila Nayar, another young disciple, the sister of his secretary, helped ease his pain at times by lying on top of him, or massaging his legs and feet. Lilavati also massaged him, and both of them helped daily to rub his body clean in his bathtub. When questioned about his intimacy with Dr. Sushila Nayyar, Gandhi replied: "I have regarded Sushilabehn [Sister Sushila] in the same way as Ba . . . my heart feels no sin in the contact of these two. . . . Sushila has observed *brahmacharya* since childhood but her observance does not include the exclusion of innocent contact with men. . . . Once I intended to give up all personal services from Sushila but within twelve hours my soft-heartedness had put an end to the intention. I could not bear the tears of Sushila and the fainting away of Prabhavati."[25] Prabhavati Narayan was Jaya Prakash Narayan's young wife, who had for years after her marriage suffered from migraines, sleeplessness, and constipation. Gandhi recommended mud-packs, dietary cures, and enemas, but the remedy Prabhavati found most effective was daily darshan of her Mahatma and his tender touch. Like Sushila and Mira, Prabhavati adored his loving care. Each time she was driven away by his slightest reprimand she broke down, falling into such deep depression that he feared for her life. "Sushila has been present in the bathroom while I have bathed in the nude and in her absence Ba or Prabhavati or Lilavati have attended on me," Gandhi explained. "But I see nothing wrong in it. . . . I have never felt any embarrassment in being seen naked by a woman."[26]

Congress provincial ministries now lost control of their own cadres as growing violence plagued India's polity. Picketers of clothing mills and liquor shops linked arms to make a wall blocking every entrance. When Gandhi was informed of such violence he denied encouraging it. "In Dharasana the objective was the salt works of which possession had to be taken," he argued in self-defense. "The action could hardly be called picketing. But to prevent workers from going to their work by standing in front of them is pure violence."[27] He also denounced Congress hoodlums who took violent "possession" of Congress committee offices. Meetings in many provinces were, moreover, broken up by noisy young men, who clearly enjoyed "creating disturbances." Mill owner capitalists as a class were now "reviled" and thugs were incited to "loot them. . . . If violence is not checked in time, the Congress will go to pieces," Gandhi warned. Reports of discrimination against Muslims were by now compounded with those of violence against Muslim butchers leading cows to slaughter and of dead pigs tossed provocatively into mosques during prayers.

"The Congress has now . . . killed every hope to Hindu-Muslim settlement in the right royal fashion of Fascism," announced Quaid-i-Azam Jinnah to his Muslim League, meeting in Patna on the night of December 26, 1938. "The Congress . . . makes the preposterous claim that they are entitled to speak on behalf of the whole of India, that they alone are capable of delivering the goods. . . . The Congress is nothing but a Hindu body."[28] Jinnah now called upon India's 90 million Muslims to join him under the green and white crescent moon and star flag of the Muslim League, mobilizing one-fourth of South Asia's population to prepare to demand separate nationhood.

Crediting Gandhi as the evil "genius" behind Congress's religious ideal, namely to establish a "Hindu Raj" over India, Jinnah was trying more effectively to unite British India's deeply divided Muslim forces under his own leadership. But Gandhi was faced with more powerful opposition within the Congress itself than he had confronted since Nagpur in 1920. Bengal's brilliant young *Netaji* ("Leader") Subhas Chandra Bose, who had presided over the last Congress session at Haripura, insisted on a second term, which he won over Gandhi's outspoken criticism in 1939, the first contested election ever held for Congress president.

Like Nehru, Bose was much more militant than Gandhi, and also socialist, though closer to Mussolini's variety of national socialism than either to Marxism or Fabianism. Bose had earlier cooperated with Nehru in organizing peasants and workers as well as young intellectuals to fight against exploitative Indian landlords, mill owners, and the British Raj. Gurudev Tagore warmly supported Bose's candidacy and aspirations, as did virtually all Bengalis. Gandhi never trusted Bose, however, fearing his faith in violence, and Nehru viewed him more as rival than comrade. Bose not only defied the Mahatma, who had urged him to step down after completing his year as president but narrowly won reelection. Bose felt most treacherously betrayed by Nehru, moreover, as by the rest of his Working Committee, all of whom resigned shortly after his reelection. He knew then that though he had beaten Gandhi at the polls, the Working Committee's Satyagraha against him would paralyze him from attempting more radical reforms.

"Shri Subhas Bose has achieved . . . victory over his opponent," Gandhi wrote in January 1939. "I must confess that . . . I was decidedly against his re-election . . . .[T]he defeat is . . . mine."[29] Hardly the sort of admission to expect from Congress's supreme dictator, as Jinnah had accused him of being less than a month before. Yet if Gandhi was not, in fact, the all-powerful leader of India's largest political organization, to which he no longer even belonged, neither was he devoid of unique influence over its Working Committee and policies. Vallabhbhai Patel, Rajendra Prasad, Maulana Azad, Sarojini Naidu, and most other Working Committee leaders not only listened to him with unique admiration but almost always did exactly what he advised. Nehru neither worshipped him nor always listened any more, but he was wise and ambitious enough to realize that without Bapu's support he could never win premier power.

"It grieves me to find that Mahatma Gandhi has taken it as a personal defeat," reelected President Bose replied. "I have on some occasions felt constrained to differ from Mahatma Gandhi on public questions, but I yield to none in my respect for . . . India's greatest man."[30] Bose could not, however, win back Gandhi's support. Subhas suffered a physical breakdown in the next month, his weakened lungs succumbing to tuberculosis and obliging him to travel to Tripuri's Congress in March in an iron lung. He wore his khaki uniform, nonetheless, the martial costume that would remain his most famous attire throughout World War II, when he led India's National Army, with Japanese backing and support, from Singapore to the eastern borders of Bengal.

Hitler's virulent anti-Semitism had, since 1933, helped fuel his rise to dictatorial power over Nazi Germany, whose aggressive expansion into defenseless Czechoslovakia in 1938 was sanctioned by Britain's Prime Minister Neville Chamberlain at Munich. On the eve of World War II, Chamberlain spoke of his pathetic betrayal as "peace with honour," claiming it would bring "peace in our time." Gandhi, when asked what he thought of Hitler's persecution of Jews, replied: "My sympathies are all with the Jews. ... The tyrants of old never went so mad as Hitler."[31] But when asked what he would do to help move the world toward peace, Gandhi expressed his support of Chamberlain's policy of appeasement and called for simultaneous world disarmament: "I am as certain of it as I am sitting here, that this heroic act would open Herr Hitler's eyes and disarm him."[32] To Agatha Harrison he wrote in May: "My position in the event of war would be personally no participation."[33] He could not forget India's tragic aftermath of World War I and would never again raise an ambulance corps to serve any British army.

Gandhi tried in vain to bring peace at this time to Rajkot, the Gujarati princely state in which his own father had served as chief minister and where he had spent so much of his youth. Despite Congress's victory in elections and the substantial power Congress ministries enjoyed in most of the provinces of British India, some 570 princely states still remained autocratic enclaves, ruled mostly by petty tyrants. Gandhi wanted to help his Brother Vallabhbhai, who had negotiated what he thought was an agreement for Congress with Rajkot's prince, only to find it sabotaged by that puppet monarch's own chief minister. Surely, Gandhi thought, these Gujarati brethren of his would be sensible enough to allow him to resolve their "family" squabble. So he returned to his home state to straighten everything out, or so he imagined. But neither the prince nor his minister cared for this Mahatma's advice or would follow it, and soon their intransigence proved so galling that Gandhi announced his resolve to launch individual Satyagraha against them by fasting. That precipitous decision was abandoned just a few days after his fast began, however, with Gandhi appealing for help to the viceroy, whose paramount power ruled over all the princes. He obviously should have known better than to expect any English officials to protect him or his people from the violent incompetence, stupidity, and venality of his fellow Gujaratis. At the same time, Subhas Bose's rebellion paralyzed the Congress, leaving all its leaders tied up in personal vendettas, with no resolution after six months of backbiting conflict. "It is growing upon me every day that we shall have to lower . . . our demand for full responsible government," he confessed in mid-1939. "We have not the will for it, we are not ready to pay the price."[34] It was a painfully sobering confession, its truth made clear to him by the frustration he suffered in his old home state.

"What is to be done with the Princes?" Gandhi asked "My Dear Idiot" Amrit Kaur in June. "Gods confound those whom they want to destroy. It may be that their days are numbered. Only as believers in ahimsa we have to so act that we do not become . . . instruments of their destruction."[35] At seventy, Gandhi considered total retirement from public life. "Jawaharlal is quite convinced that I have put back the clock of progress by a century," Gandhi told his new confidante. "I can voluntarily retire from all activity."[36] Nehru had his own frustrations on the eve of turning fifty, for not only had he lost his Congress leadership to Bose, who reviled his "treachery," but he had also recently parted from his daughter Indira, who was eager to return to Europe to her brash young lover, Feroze Gandhi, of whom Nehru disapproved.

To compound Gandhi's frustrations and feelings of impotence, the early agreement he had struggled so hard to reach in South Africa suddenly dissolved in the acid of resurgent white racism there. "Why is Agreement 1914 being Violated with You as witness?" Gandhi wired his erstwhile "Friend," Prime Minister Smuts. "Is there no Help for Indians except to pass through Fire?"[37] But the whole world stood poised now on the brink of a tragic conflagration.

On July 23, 1939, Gandhi wrote his "Dear Friend" letter to Adolf Hitler. "It is quite clear that you are today the one person in the world who can prevent a war which may reduce humanity to the savage state. . . . Will you listen to the appeal of one who has deliberately shunned the method of war not without considerable success?"[38] He wrote that ignored appeal shortly before war was declared by Britain on September 3, 1939, in response to Germany's invasion of Poland. Viceroy Linlithgow immediately proclaimed India at war, his announcement broadcast twelve hours before Gandhi, whom the viceroy had invited there, reached Simla. They met on September 4. "I told His excellency that my sympathies were with England and France from the purely humanitarian standpoint," Gandhi reported.[39] He wished England well, and, though he came to the conclusion that Hitler was "responsible for the war," could not in good conscience support either global combatant.

19

War and Peaceful Resistance

THE OUTBREAK of World War II served to galvanize and reunite the Congress in opposition to British imperial rule. The viceroy's autocratic declaration of war, without consulting any Congress leader, infuriated Nehru and led to Subhas Bose's resignation. The Working Committee met in Wardha from September 10 to 14, electing Rajendra Prasad as its new president. Nehru took the lead in drafting the Congress resolution on the war, inviting Great Britain first to declare unequivocally that its "war aims" included freedom and democracy for India, after which India would cooperate fully in the global struggle against fascism and Nazism.[1] Gandhi personally had argued for a wholly nonviolent response, but he had won little support, silently bowing to Nehru's militant majority position. Bose started his own Forward Bloc party, which openly favored the Axis powers, leading to Subhas's arrest and his subsequent daring escape through Afghanistan to Berlin, and from there to Japan.

"Will Great Britain have an unwilling India dragged into the war or a willing ally co-operating with her in the prosecution of a defence of true democracy?" Gandhi asked the press, after the Working Committee agreed upon its resolution. "Congress support will mean the greatest moral asset in favour of England and France."[2] Jinnah, on the other hand, met with the viceroy immediately after his declaration that India was at war, assuring Lord Linlithgow of loyal Muslim support, urging him to "Turn out" the Congress provincial ministries "at once. Nothing else will bring them to their senses. . . . They will never stand by you."[3]

Gandhi was invited back to Simla by the viceroy in late September. Immediately after their meeting, when he realized in what high regard Linlithgow held Jinnah and his advice, Gandhi wrote an unusual piece on "Hindu-Muslim Unity." "The Muslim League is a great organization," the Mahatma told his *Harijan* readers. "Its President was at one time an ardent Congressman. He was the rising hope of the Congress."[4] He appealed equally to Congress and League members, urging them all to stop attacking one another and to reconcile differences. If enough of them worked and prayed to achieve Hindu-Muslim unity, Gandhi insisted, God would make it "possible tomorrow."

On October 3, 1939, a day after his seventieth birthday, Gandhi sent a message to the British people, through the *Manchester Guardian's* correspondent: "It will be a . . . tragedy in this tragic war if Britain is found to fail in the very first test of sincerity of her professions about democracy."[5] But on October 17, the viceroy issued his declaration of His Majesty's government's wartime objectives, none of which satisfied the Congress. For India the Act of 1935 remained its wartime Constitution, and Great Britain would only be prepared to open that Act to modification in the light of "Indian views" after the war ended. "The Congress asked for bread and it has got a stone," Gandhi commented.[6] Nehru was even more angry at Lord Zetland's negative remarks about the Congress in the House of Lords, charging that he had learned nothing "from events during the past twenty years."[7] Thus the stage was set for the resignation of Congress provincial ministries, ending the two-year experiment in Anglo-Congress cooperation.

"The Working Committee are of opinion that the Viceregal statement . . . is wholly unsatisfactory and calculated to rouse resentment among all those who are anxious to gain . . . India's independence," Congress's leaders resolved on October 22, 1939. "In the circumstances, the Committee cannot possibly give any support to Great Britain. . . . The Committee call upon the Congress Ministries to tender their resignations."[8] Jinnah breathed a deep sigh of relief, but not as yet too loud a sigh. He was reluctant to reveal how delighted he was until every Congress ministry agreed with its impulsive Working Committee and removed all of its members from office. Gandhi disliked Nehru's impulsive and angry reactions and knew that the resignation of all Congress provincial governments would strengthen the League and give the British full freedom in militarizing India throughout the war. But he felt too tired to argue with Nehru so he simply told him to "take full charge and lead the country."[9] Nehru was hardly ready, however, to break with Gandhi, so their façade of Congress harmony remained to mask the deepening ideological gulf that divided them.

"Jinnah Saheb looks to the British power to safeguard the Muslim rights," Gandhi rightly noted on October 30, 1939. "Nothing that the Congress can do or concede will satisfy him."[10] The next day he left his ashram for Delhi, where he and Rajendra Prasad drove to Jinnah's new house, No. 10 Aurangzeb Road. All three were then driven in Jinnah's new green Packard to the viceroy's palace, barely a mile away for another brief, futile, communal summit. Nehru was now preparing his militant army of ardent followers in the United Provinces for civil revolt, circulating "anonymous placards" calling upon eager patriots "to cut wires and tear up rails."[11] Gandhi urged restraint, warning him to desist; otherwise "I must give up command." So Nehru agreed to meet Jinnah once more to try to bridge the unbridgeable gap.

On December 2, 1939, Jinnah proclaimed Friday, December 22, a "Day of Deliverance and thanksgiving as a mark of relief that the Congress regime has at last ceased to function."[12] The Muslim League's Quaid-i-Azam charged Congress ministries with anti-Muslim policies whenever they held power. He accused them of undermining "Muslim opinion" and of seeking to "destroy Muslim culture."

Gandhi appealed through the press from Wardha to Jinnah to call off that Day of Deliverance, fearing it would only intensify Hindu-Muslim conflicts, but Jinnah refused. Nehru now canceled their scheduled meeting, saying, "I would have to repudiate all . . . nationalism and my self-respect if I were to resume the talk with Mr. Jinnah in the face of his appeal to the Muslims."[13] Nehru repudiated all of Jinnah's discriminatory allegations against Congress ministries, insisting that they were baseless. Gandhi was more prudent, imploring Jinnah and his colleagues to await review by the viceroy and the governors of those "serious allegations" before calling upon millions of Muslims to endorse them and condemn the Congress. But Jinnah was unwilling to wait any longer, determined not only to celebrate the demise of Congress ministries but to demand a separate nation for South Asia's Muslims, which he now resolved to carve out of north India.

Before the end of January 1940, Gandhi had received word of Jinnah's idea of calling for separate nationhood for India's Muslims. "I hope that Quaid-i-Azam Jinnah's opinion is a temporary phase in the history of the Muslim League," Gandhi wrote in alarm. "Muslims of the different provinces can never cut themselves away from their Hindu or Christian brethren. Both Muslims and Christians are converts from Hinduism or are descendants of converts. They do not cease to belong to their provinces because of change of faith. Englishmen who become converts to Islam do not change their nationality."[14] It was his first tentative attempt to avert the disaster of partition, the horror he would call the "Vivisection of the Mother."

Still trying to win Congress support for the war, Viceroy Linlithgow invited Gandhi to meet with him in New Delhi on February 5, 1940, and saw Jinnah the next day. The viceroy tried to convince Gandhi that dominion status was the British goal for India after the war was won. Gandhi insisted that wasn't enough to satisfy the Congress, though he could not officially speak for its Working Committee, only for India's "dumb millions." Asked by reporters what the failure of this latest summit meant, Gandhi replied,

"I can only say Heaven help India, Britain and the world. . . . If Britain cannot recognize India's legitimate claim, what will it mean but Britain's moral bankruptcy?"[15] When asked about prospects for reconciliation between the Congress and the League, he replied that he saw none. Nehru viewed all these meetings called by the viceroy as nothing other than the "Old Game" of British imperial duplicity.

By March of 1940, Gandhi felt certain that "there can be no manly peace in the land unless the British bayonet is withdrawn. The risk of riots has to be run. Non-violence will be born out of such risks."[16] But few of his own Congress comrades were convinced any more of their Mahatma's peaceful prescription for freedom and communal harmony. Nor were the British, in the midst of the fiercest war the world had ever experienced, listening to his advice that it was time to sheath every bayonet. Nor did Quaid-i-Azam Jinnah or his leading lieutenants of the Muslim League pay much attention now to what they had come to regard as the futile rantings of a mostly-naked, old Hindu Vania.

The Congress Working Committee met at Ramgarh March 15–19, 1940, with Maulana Azad presiding. Gandhi attended by "special invitation," and Nehru and Patel were there, of course, as well as Khan Abdul Khan and Rajendra Prasad. Most of them favored launching civil disobedience, but Gandhi was against it. "What has been done in United Provinces is good but I cannot evolve non-violence from the awakening created there by Jawaharlalji," Gandhi warned them. "I don't want people to be crushed. If a fight is launched without proper preparations, it is the poor who will suffer."[17] He then offered to withdraw entirely, to remove the "incubus" of his fear of violence from the committee's deliberations, future decisions, and actions. But the Congress Working Committee would not release him. "If after twenty years of practice," Gandhi argued, "I have not been able to win the affection and trust of the Mussalmans, my ahimsa must be of a very poor quality indeed. . . . I am sure that, if you release me, I may be able to give civil disobedience a purer and a nobler shape." Azad would not hear of it, however, reminding Gandhi that he had only agreed to wear the Congress crown because Gandhi had pressed him to accept.

A week later the Muslim League met in Lahore. It was the League's largest and most important session. "It has always been taken for granted mistakenly that the Mussalmans are a minority," Quaid-i-Azam Jinnah told his attentive audience of some 100,000 Muslims from every state and province of South Asia. "The Mussalmans are not a minority. The Mussalmans are a nation. . . . The problem in India is not of an inter-communal but manifestly of an international character, and it must be treated as such."[18] He therefore urged the British to transfer their power after the war to the "autonomous national states" of South Asia's subcontinent. Next day the League's Subjects Committee met to hammer out the "Pakistan" resolution that translated their Quaid's desire into constitutional language: "That . . . no constitutional plan would be workable in this country or acceptable to the Muslims unless . . . areas in which the Muslims are . . . a majority, as in the North-Western and Eastern zones of India, should be grouped to constitute Independent States . . . autonomous and sovereign."[19] When Jinnah was asked by the press if that meant one or more than one Muslim "Land of the Pure"—*Pakistan*—his answer was one.

Nehru called it a "mad scheme."[20] C. R. considered it "a sign of a diseased mentality that Mr. Jinnah has brought himself to look upon the idea of one India as a misconception and the cause of most of our trouble."[21] Gandhi was more cautious: "I am proud of being a Hindu, but I have never gone . . . as a Hindu to secure Hindu-Muslim unity. . . . Can a Hindu organization have a Muslim divine as President . . . ? I still maintain that there is no swaraj without Hindu-Muslim unity. . . . The Constituent Assembly as conceived by me is not intended to coerce anybody."[22] But Jinnah would never agree to join that assembly, nor would any member of his League, destined in seven years to take power over Pakistan.

Gandhi refused at first to take the League's partition demand seriously. Most members of the Congress, like most British officials, considered "Pakistan" a mere bargaining chip, which the League would use to raise its political demands and muscle within a united dominion of India. Gandhi called the partition scheme "an untruth," insisting there could be "no compromise with it. . . . Does Islam bind Muslim only to Muslim and antagonize the Hindu? Was the message of the Prophet peace only for and between Muslims and war against Hindus or non-Muslims? . . . Those who are instilling this poison into the Muslim mind are rendering the greatest disservice to Islam. I know that it is not Islam."[23]

The advance of Nazi tanks in Norway and Denmark and the daily escalation of deaths made many Indians lose all faith in the power of nonviolence, writing to ask Gandhi what was the good of his life's message and all his prayers? But Gandhi retained firm faith in Ahimsa. He blamed its failure on the weakness and distrust of most of his followers in its divine power and on the religious disunity within India's multicultural society.

Charlie Andrews died in Calcutta in April 1940, three days after he was "successfully" operated on. Gandhi never mourned death, not even Charlie's, and he was becoming more deeply, impenetrably withdrawn as the war, the League, and Congress squabbles took their inexorable toll of his feelings, his strength, his hopes, and fast fading dreams. "I cannot say I miss you," he wrote Amrit in May, no longer playfully saluting her as Idiot, Rebel, or even "Stupid." "I am daily getting more and more detached. I seem to miss nobody and nothing. I have no time to think of these things . . . Love. Bapu."[24] No longer did he sign himself "Tyrant" or "Warrior."

The war's "mad slaughter" so depressed him by late May that he wrote the viceroy to offer his personal services to help end the fighting. "I am prepared to go to Germany or anywhere required to plead for peace . . . for the good of mankind. This may be a visionary's idea. . . . Perchance it may be wisdom more than a vision."[25] Linlithgow replied that there was "nothing for it" now but to fight on until "victory is won." Gandhi imposed total silence on himself, feeling too impotent to speak and finding all that he said useless to stop the "frightful" violence now tearing the world apart.

Amrit wrote to ask why he had taken a vow of silence. "It is to avoid irritation and save my energy," he replied. "The output of my work has certainly doubled. Irritation is almost nil. It would be a strain now to speak."[26] To another old follower he wrote, "Everything is in a mess." Refusing her request for guidance in trying to organize a women's wing of the Congress, he answered: "We are in God's hands. . . . As regards the organization do as your heart bids you."[27] So he sank ever deeper into solitude and inaction, just a week before the Congress Working Committee descended upon him to seek his wise counsel. The Working Committee rejected his appeal to reaffirm Congress faith in nonviolence. "The attempt made by me to form peace brigades to deal with communal riots and the like had wholly failed."[28] He then asked to be released from the committee, feeling it was no longer appropriate to remain when so many fundamental differences were discovered. He now felt himself "Wandering alone on the cremation ground," he told a dear friend.[29]

The viceroy invited him to Delhi for a private meeting at the end of June, though Gandhi was at pains to explain to Linlithgow that after his most recent meeting with the Working Committee he could only speak as an individual. The viceroy indicated that he was ready to advise London to announce that self-governing dominion status for India would be "granted within one year of the termination of the war."[30] Many commercial, defense, and external affairs details would have to be hammered out, of course, as would the "rights of minorities and the position of Princes." If Congress agreed, the viceroy would increase the number of its leaders on his executive council, which would also include representatives of other parties. Gandhi replied that without a prior "declaration of independence" Congress was not likely to agree to serve on the council.

At the meeting, Gandhi gave the viceroy his open letter "To Every Briton." Linlithgow did not pass it along to the British press or His Majesty's government, since Gandhi's appeal to every Briton was that they should all accept nonviolence and stop fighting. He argued that this war was "a curse and a warning" to mankind. He feared that no one and nothing would be spared and that all humans would be reduced to "beasts" unless hostilities swiftly ended. Though he did not want Britain defeated, he claimed to see no difference between the destruction caused by the Nazis in England and that caused by the Allies in Germany. He seriously suggested that Hitler and Mussolini should be invited to "take what they want" of Great Britain, and "If these gentlemen choose to occupy your homes, you will vacate them. . . . you will allow yourself man, woman and child, to be slaughtered."[31] The viceroy was dumbstruck by Gandhi's letter, unable to utter a word in response, refusing even to call for his car to take the now more deeply despondent Gandhi home.

When Gandhi next met Nehru and other members of the Working Committee, he told them of his depressing meeting with the viceroy and expounded on his ideal hopes for the world and for India. "The terrible things that are going on in Europe fill me with anguish," he said, explaining that armies had never appealed to him. The masses were always exploited and forced to give their last penny to support armies that were supposed to defend their hearths and homes. Gandhi wanted instead for Congress now to proclaim that India would defend itself nonviolently. C. R. and Nehru disagreed, insisting, "Ours is a political organization . . . [or] else we cannot function on the political plane."[32] Political realists, Indian and English alike, now viewed Gandhi as hardly more than a visionary in matters of statecraft. The viceroy and Britain's home government felt, therefore, that it might be best to carry on the war without further wooing or waiting for Congress to join the Allied forces in the monumental global struggle.

In mid-September of 1940 Congress met in Bombay, this time resolved to ask Gandhi to take responsibility for leading it in Satyagraha against British repression and indifference to India's passionate longing for freedom. For Gandhi, the invitation from his old comrades on the Working Committee once again to lead them into the wilderness of civil disobedience was too flattering to reject. "I have made repeated statements that I would not be guilty of embarrassing the British . . . when their very existence hung in the balance," he admitted. He added, however, "There comes a time when a man in his weakness mistakes vice for virtue. . . . I felt that, if I did not go to the assistance of the Congress and take the helm even if it be in fear and trembling, I would be untrue to myself."[33] Overcoming all uncertainty and reticence, he thus agreed to lead his sorely divided party into battle against the world's mightiest raj.

Gandhi met with Linlithgow in Simla on September 28 and 30, 1940, but neither moved from his position of entrenched antipathy. "It is a matter of deep regret to me [that] the Government have not been able to appreciate the Congress position," Gandhi informed the viceroy before departing. "Since you and the Secretary of State for India have declared that the whole of India is voluntarily helping the war effort, it becomes necessary to make clear that the vast majority of the people of India are not interested in it. They make no distinction between Nazism and the double autocracy that rules India."[34]

Gandhi now decided to launch an individual, rather than mass, Satyagraha. He chose as his first satyagrahi, not Nehru, who was most eager to be selected, but quiet, unassuming Vinoba Bhave.

To explain why he chose an unknown rather than flamboyant Pandit Nehru to serve as his surrogate, Gandhi wrote about him at length in *Harijan*, answering the widely asked question: "Who is Vinoba Bhave and why has he been selected?" He elaborated first upon the Sanskritic scholarly and cotton-spinning virtues of the painfully thin, obscure man, soon to be revered as "India's Walking Saint."[35] Vinoba would devote the last decades of his life, after Gandhi's murder, to walking the length and breadth of India's village hinterland, seeking land for the landless and dedicating his frail body to the task of translating his Mahatma's dream of *Sarvodaya*—"The Uplift of All"—into socioeconomic reality. "He believes in communal unity with the same passion that I have," Gandhi continued. "He has never been in the limelight on the political platform . . . he believes that silent constructive work . . . is far more effective. . . . Vinoba is an out-and-out war resister."[36]

In direct violation of the British gag order against antiwar speech, Vinoba addressed over three hundred persons in central India on October 17, asking why Britain claimed to fight for "democracy" when she continued to deny it to India. Gandhi wrote to inform the viceroy of that breach of the British ban. Each day, prior to his arrest, Vinoba continued to speak out in the same firm, but nonviolent, voice in opposition to the war. At 3 A.M. on October 21, 1940, Vinoba was arrested.

By now Gandhi had a long list of volunteers. His second choice was Jawaharlal, who was, of course, "ready." But Gandhi remained unsure of Nehru's true feelings, hence wrote to probe his mind: "I would still like to ask you whether you can see anything to commend itself to you in all I am writing and doing. . . . My present conception requires those who believe in the plan—not in every detail but in the main."[37] Nehru cabled at once: "Agree generally."[38] Two days later, Gandhi summoned him to Wardha and gave him his marching instructions. On October 31, 1940, Nehru was arrested in the United Provinces and found guilty of sedition for three speeches he had made to villagers earlier in the month. At fifty-one, the man destined in little more than half a decade to become India's first prime minister, was sentenced in Gorakhpur to four years of rigorous imprisonment.

Gandhi, however, still remained free. He had expected and hoped since early November to be taken off "at any moment," but the government was in no rush, recalling the troublesome popular reactions to his previous arrests and reluctant to cause so much of a stir in the midst of a war. Gandhi knew that the British had "no faith" in his nonviolence. He now suspected that the viceroy and other officials believed him "a fool," the unwitting tool of Congress colleagues who used his idealism as "a cloak for hiding their violence."[39]

Throughout the war, Hindu-Muslim tensions and conflict mounted, taking a growing toll of lives. On May 1, 1941, Hindu-Muslim riots in Dhaka claimed so many that Gandhi was deeply saddened to see that Congress influence was "practically unfelt during the dark days." He passionately cried out: "We have proved ourselves barbarians and cowards. . . . Arson, loot and killing of innocent people including children, have been common."[40] Thousands fled from their homes, while other villagers, who tried to defend themselves against Muslim or Hindu fanatics, were cut down in cold blood. The British abdicated all responsibility for protecting the innocent, and the Congress did nothing to fill the utter void in civil defense. The new British Secretary of State for India Leo Amery insisted, however, that Indian political parties had only to agree among themselves for Great Britain to "register the will of a united India."[41] Gandhi angrily responded: "I am amazed at Mr. Amery's effrontery in saying that the Congress wants 'all or nothing' and 'refused even to discuss the matter.'"[42] Before the end of May, Hindu-Muslim riots had ravaged Ahmedabad, Bombay, and Bihar as well as Bengal.

"The riots this time have no resemblance to the former ones," Gandhi wrote Agatha Harrison. "This time it is a rehearsal for a civil war."[43] His once-robust faith in British fairness and justice was so rudely shaken as to make him wonder if Britain had ever been truthful with India. Each time the secretary of state spoke, Gandhi felt the "breach" widening or sensed himself lost in a land of "make-believe." Still, he refused to surrender all hope in despair, passionately insisting that his Ahimsa was working, though silently and "tortuously slow." He decided then to fast for twenty-four hours "for the sake of Hindu-Muslim unity." Seven ashramites joined in that day's abstention from food. But still the riots continued.

Many of Gandhi's followers questioned the wisdom of his strategy of sending just a few individuals out to court prison, while others claiming to be satyagrahis roamed India's streets and preached against the war, yet were ignored by police and officials. "How can such a struggle be effective?" they asked him. "In ahimsa there is no scope for . . . sudden miracles," Gandhi explained.[44] He preached patience, urging them to pray as passionately as he did. "'Defeat' has no place in the dictionary of ahimsa."

To celebrate Gandhi's seventy-second birthday, villagers all around his ashram brought millions of yards of hand-spun cotton and 12,000 rupees they had collected for him to distribute among the poorest of the poor. To thank them, he spoke from his heart of his dreams, insisting that there could be no true Swaraj as long as exploitation impoverished most of them. Mere change from British to Indian exploiters did not mean Swaraj, he argued: "As long as the poor remain poor or become poorer, there will be no swaraj. In my swaraj the millions will live happily. They will get food, decent houses and enough clothing."[45]

His passionate life's message, however, went far beyond achieving self-sufficiency in food, housing, and hand-spun cottons. The greatest power of Ahimsa's deep roots applied to the polity of his dream as well. "There are only two courses open—either Hitler's, that is, the way of violence, or mine, that is, the way of non-violence. Hitlerism and Churchillism are in fact the same thing. . . . It is my belief that a time will come when everyone in India will realize that the only correct course is to follow ahimsa."[46]

It seems that Gandhi was completely unaware of the Japanese attack on Pearl Harbor. He did not, at any rate, remark about the United States joining the war until December 20, 1941, when he responded to questions from the press. "I cannot welcome this entry of America . . . the one country which could have saved the world from the unthinkable butchery that is going on."[47] He then reasserted his commitment to nonviolence. In his address to a meeting of the Congress Working Committee in Wardha, Gandhi said that if he were "Viceroy of India today" he would not ask India to "take up the sword" to keep the Empire alive. "I for one should feel that I was committing moral suicide . . . abandoning the faith of a lifetime."[48]

"I have been taunted as a Bania," Gandhi told his dear friends of the Working Committee. "How can I help it? I was born a Bania. I shall stay a Bania and shall die a Bania. Trade is my profession. I am trading with you and with the world. The article in my possession is an invaluable pearl. . . . I am a trader in ahimsa. Those who can pay the price for it may have it. . . . You have taken a pledge that you would win swaraj only through ahimsa. . . . Today you are ready to depart from it. . . . [T]his bargain will not bring you complete independence."[49]

Gandhi's personal feelings of goodwill to all and his sweetness even to the viceroy at this time of severe stress, hardship, and bitter conflict shone through in an exchange of letters with Linlithgow in February 1942. Bania that he was, Gandhi wrote to request the viceroy's help, of course, in waiving taxes imposed by Bombay on his All-India Spinners' Association. "You will forgive me for inflicting this on you when every moment of yours is pre-mortgaged for winning the war," Gandhi concluded, adding his "love" to Linlithgow's daughter, son-in-law, and grandchild.[50] The request for tax exemption was not granted by His Lordship, but Bapu's sweetness elicited an equally charming postscript: "I will give your message to Southby and my daughter, and I know they will value it. . . . 'Richard' is the most wonderful baby . . . the very flower of the flock!"[51] That postscript, Gandhi wrote in his reply, "breaks the pervading gloom. I wish the general public had the privilege of knowing that your cheerfulness never forsakes you."[52] So shone the light of his faith in Ahimsa, piercing the wartime darkness and helping to overcome the war's all but fatal blitz to bonds of friendship forged over the past century in London, Bombay, Calcutta, and New Delhi.

The lightning Japanese conquest of Singapore in February 1942 and the humiliating surrender of its garrison of 60,000 Indian troops, soon to be reincarnated as the Indian National Army of Subhas Bose, shook Britain enough to launch a diplomatic initiative to win India's support for the war a month later. Sir Stafford Cripps, leader of the House of Commons and one of Labour's prime ministers-in-waiting, was selected by Churchill and his Cabinet's Labour Deputy Prime Minister Clement Attlee to fly to India with an offer of dominion status immediately after victory if India would agree to help win the war. Cripps landed in Karachi on March 22 and touched down in Delhi the next day, "Pakistan Day," where a mile-long procession of Muslims marched to hear their Quaid-i-Azam speak to an overflow crowd in Urdu Park. "We are asking for justice and fairplay," Jinnah said. "We have no designs upon our sister communities. . . . We are not a minority but a nation."[53]

Cripps wired Gandhi to request a meeting. "You know my anti-all-war views," Gandhi replied. "If despite that you would like to see me I shall be glad to see you."[54] Cripps met first with Congress President Azad and next with Muslim League President Jinnah, seeing Gandhi as soon as the Mahatma reached Delhi two days later. Sir Stafford showed Gandhi the "War Cabinet's Proposals," which Bapu referred to as "a post-dated cheque on a bank that was failing."[55] He informed Cripps that he did not for a moment believe that Congress would accept the offer of dominion status with its proviso that any province wishing not to belong to the dominion could "opt out." That clause was viewed as Britain's escape hatch for Pakistan. "He acknowledged the great influence of Jinnah and that the movement for Pakistan had grown tremendously," Cripps recorded after his first meeting with Gandhi. "I . . . asked him how, supposing Jinnah were to accept the scheme and Congress were not to, he would himself advise me to proceed. He said . . . for me to throw the responsibility upon Jinnah . . . to get Congress in either by negotiating direct with them or . . . with myself. He thought that if it was pointed out to Jinnah what a very great position this would give him in India if he succeeded, that he might take on the job and . . . succeed."[56] It was Gandhi's first inspired attempt to resolve the Congress-League deadlock by giving Jinnah primary responsibility for its resolution. But Cripps was no better prepared to accept the Mahatma's brilliant advice now than Mountbatten would be in five years. Cripps also liked and trusted Nehru's judgment and negative advice about Jinnah more than he did Gandhi's unexpectedly outlandish suggestion, which none of his staff members had armed him seriously to consider.

When Cripps flew home, his scheme rejected by the Congress, his high hopes of becoming Labour's next prime minister had gone up in flames of Hindu-Muslim mistrust. Nehru felt much angrier and more frustrated than Gandhi by Cripps's failure to agree with him, having had far more faith in the Labour leader of the House of Commons, whose intellect was much like his own. In the aftermath of that fruitless mission, "Jawaharlal now seems to have completely abandoned ahimsa," Gandhi confided to Brother Vallabh.[57] Nehru now advocated guerrilla warfare and the scorched-earth policy used by Russia against Hitler's invasion of the Soviet Union, should the Japanese invade India. In Orissa, Indian communists were arming themselves and training in guerrilla tactics, while in Bengal cadres of Subhas Bose's Forward Bloc were preparing to help Japan.

Nehru called on Colonel Louis Johnson, President Franklin Roosevelt's personal representative to India, on April 5, 1942, offering guerrilla support to the U.S. troops and informing him that the Congress was "ready to hitch 'India's wagon to America's Star.'"[58] "Whereas we have always had differences of opinion it appears to me that now we also differ in practice," Gandhi wrote Jawaharlal when he learned this. "I feel that you are making a mistake. I see no good in American troops entering India and in our resorting to guerrilla warfare. It is my duty to caution you."[59] But the United States was not going to abandon Great Britain, though Roosevelt personally favored granting India independence and urged Churchill to do so.

Gandhi never approved of either American or Chinese troops in India. "We know what American aid means. . . . I see no Indian freedom peeping through all this preparation for the so-called defence of India. It is a preparation pure and simple for the defence of the British Empire."[60] His firm belief now was that the British should leave India in an orderly manner "to her fate."[61]

Asked by reporters what his call for British withdrawal would mean in terms of India's internal security, Gandhi replied: "Under my proposal, they have to leave India in God's hands, but in modern parlance to anarchy, and that anarchy may lead to internecine warfare for a time or to unrestrained dacoities. From these a true India will rise."[62] Asked next what he intended to do if the British ignored his advice to leave, Gandhi explained, "I shall have to force them to go, by non-co-operation or by civil disobedience. Or it may be by both."[63] Gandhi had gone to Bombay to raise money for a memorial to Charlie Andrews and in eight days collected half a million rupees with the help of Vallabhbhai and Birla, who arranged his talks to appropriate groups of businessmen. Now riots and lawlessness spread throughout mostly Muslim Sind. Gandhi advised Congress members of Karachi's assembly to resign and form a "peace brigade" to settle in the most troubled regions of the faction-riven province and risk their lives trying to persuade criminal elements to desist from murder. A day later more violent deaths occurred, no Congress members proving brave enough, some would say foolish enough, to heed his advice.

On July 1, 1942, Gandhi wrote a "Dear Friend" letter to Franklin Roosevelt. Seeking to "enlist" FDR's "sympathy," he noted how much he had profited from works by Thoreau and Emerson, and how many American friends he had. "I hate all war," Gandhi explained. "I venture to think that the Allied declaration that the Allies are fighting to make the world safe for freedom of the individual and for democracy sounds hollow so long as India and . . . Africa are exploited by Great Britain and America has the Negro problem in her own home. . . . So far as India is concerned, we must become free even as America."[64] He assured Roosevelt that Allied troops might be permitted to remain in India until the war ended, under a treaty with independent India's own government. Louis Fischer, who had come to India to interview and write about Gandhi, living at his ashram for several weeks, carried that letter to Washington, at Gandhi's behest. Roosevelt answered the letter politely, ending his reply with "hope that our common interest in democracy and righteousness will enable your countrymen and mine to make common cause against a common enemy."[65]

One of Gandhi's wisest old friends and greatest Congress comrades, C. R., disagreed with him on two most important points, believing it would be best to acknowledge the Muslim League's demand for Pakistan now and negotiate early agreement with Jinnah as to how least painfully to divide the subcontinent. He also urged Gandhi to assist the viceroy in running a national government during the war, rightly recognizing that such cooperation would prove at least as valuable to India as to Great Britain. But he found it impossible to convince his old friend on either vital point. "I am built that way," Gandhi stubbornly replied. "Once an idea possesses me I can't easily get rid of the possession."[66] Had C. R. prevailed, of course, the war years might have been spent in productive preparation for freedom, as well as in careful planning of partition, instead of leaving Congress's leaders all to rust behind bars. In frustration, C. R. now quit the Congress.

Gandhi urged Nehru also to resign, but Jawaharlal, who had so often threatened resignation, was unwilling to risk losing his power. "I have thought over the matter a great deal and still feel that your capacity for service will increase if you withdraw," Gandhi wrote. "You may attend the Committee [W.C.] occasionally as I do."[67] He hoped perhaps by removing Nehru from the Working Committee that it might be possible for Vallabhbhai Patel to come into his rightful inheritance as Gandhi's true heir to leadership over the Congress and the nation. He also tried in vain to get rid of Congress President Maulana Azad, Nehru's closest comrade on the Working Committee. "This is my plea about Maulana Saheb [Azad]," Gandhi's letter to Jawaharlal continued. "I do not understand him nor does he understand me. We are drifting apart on the Hindu-Muslim question as well as on other questions. . . . We have to face facts. Therefore I suggest that the Maulana should relinquish Presidentship but remain in the Committee, the Committee should elect an interim President."[68] That "interim" president, of course, would have been Vallabhbhai Patel, the strongest and most respected Congress leader. This was Gandhi's most courageous attempt to strip Nehru of political power. But age and physical frailty left Gandhi too weak to insist upon his proposals or to put them before the committee, of which he was no longer even a member. "You may reject them," he told Nehru, who did just that.

Gandhi took the train to Bombay for the meeting of the Congress Committee on August 3, 1942, carrying with him a "confidential" draft of instructions for civil resisters. "The object of our Satyagraha is to secure the withdrawal of British rule and the attainment of independence for the whole of India. . . . Every satyagrahi should understand before joining the struggle that he is to ceaselessly carry on the struggle till independence is achieved. He should vow that he will be free or die."[69] The mantra Gandhi coined was "*Karega ya marega!*" meaning "Do or die!" This last of his Satyagraha movements, however, came to be known as his "Quit India" movement, the catchy phrase soon shouted by Indians to every British soldier and civilian.

"The Congress will be satisfied with a plebiscite or any other reasonable manner of testing public opinion . . . that is real democracy," Gandhi wrote on August 6. "The cry of 'Quit India' . . . comes not from the lips but from the aching hearts of millions."[70] He was asked by the Associated Press that day if the Congress resolution meant "peace or war?" He replied: "The emphasis in any non-violent struggle . . . is always on peace."[71] On August 7, Gandhi addressed the All-India Congress Committee and assured them that "Britishers will have to give us freedom when we have made sufficient sacrifices and proved our strength. . . . Sardar Patel . . . said that the campaign may be over in a week. . . . If it ends in a week it will be a miracle and if this happens it would mean melting the British heart."[72] He also called upon Jinnah and the Muslim League to join the Congress's movement to win democratic freedom for every Indian, indeed, for all mankind. "We are aiming at a world federation in which India would be a leading unit. It can come only through non-violence."[73]

On August 8, 1942, the day Congress was to vote on his Satyagraha proposal, Gandhi told the *News Chronicle*: "I have equal love for all mankind without exception."[74] That night his resolution was unanimously passed by Congress. Gandhi's last words to the Congress demanded "freedom immediately, this very night, before dawn."[75] But before dawn he was arrested, together with every member of the Congress Working Committee in Bombay and fifty additional leaders. "Everyone is free to go the fullest length under ahimsa," Gandhi passionately shouted before he was driven off with Ba, Mira, Sarojini, and Mahadev to the Aga Khan's palace in Poona, where they were all incarcerated. "Satyagrahis must go out to die not to live. . . . It is only when individuals go out to die that the nation will survive."[76]

20

War behind Bars

G ANDHI'S PRISON TERM in the Aga Khan's Poona palace lasted for almost two years, in many ways his most bitter, painful incarceration. Though the old palace was hardly jail, the malarial swamp on which it stood made its venue more deadly than many of British India's darkest prisons. Mahadev Desai was the first of his tiny band of faithful ashram inmates to expire there. Though Mahadev had been frail for years, fainting at times and complaining of severe headaches, he was only in his early fifties. His death on the morning of August 15, 1942, deeply depressed Gandhi.

"Mahadev, Mahadev," Gandhi cried, imploring his faithful secretary's corpse to awake. "Mahadev has lived up to the 'Do or Die' mantra," Gandhi eulogized, as the corpse he had prepared was burned. "This sacrifice cannot but hasten the day of India's deliverance."[1]

He had written Linlithgow the day before, urging the viceroy to change policy and accept the support of Congress once India was proclaimed a free nation. "Do not disregard the pleading of one who claims to be a sincere friend of the British people," Gandhi argued. "Heaven guide you!"[2] Linlithgow refused to reconsider, however, agreeing with Churchill's harsh assessment of Gandhi's "treacherous" nature.

In the aftermath of Congress arrests, 250 railway stations were attacked by satyagrahis, telegraph wires cut all across Bihar and in the Eastern United Provinces, and more than a hundred police stations were burned down, with thirty policemen killed inside them. Before the end of 1942, over 60,000 Indians would be jailed, 600 flogged, and 900 officially reported as killed. Military aircraft would be used to machine-gun unarmed protesters in Bihar, as had hitherto been done only against armed tribals along the frontier. Many Congressmen went underground, doing as much damage as they could to rail and truck transport, British military establishments, and Allied troops stationed in India. The Quit India Satyagraha thus soon turned into a violent civil conflict, a miniwar fought mostly within north India during the remaining years of World War II.

"I had thought we were friends and should still love to think so," Gandhi wrote Linlithgow on New Year's Eve 1942. "However what has happened since the 9th of August last makes me wonder."[3] He then listed a series of complaints that had sorely tried his patience over the last six months. He was, of course, considering the last "remedy" available to a satyagrahi when all else had failed—fast unto death.

The viceroy cabled Gandhi's letter to London, and Linlithgow replied to Gandhi on January 13. "I have been profoundly depressed . . . by the policy that was adopted by the Congress in August. . . . [T]hat policy gave rise . . . to violence and crime . . . the burning alive of police officials, the wrecking of trains, the destruction of property."[4] The viceroy asked Gandhi why he had not publicly condemned such crimes.

Gandhi responded immediately: "Your letter gladdens me to find that I have not lost caste with you."[5] He then countered each of Linlithgow's points with stronger charges against officialdom's repressive actions, insisting that he was constrained to be "a helpless witness" to all that was happening outside, including the starvation of millions owing to scarcity of food supplies throughout the land. Bengal's worst famine of the century, exacerbated by a lack of vehicular transport, had already taken countless lives, a number that would rise into millions by year's end. After a week of silent reflection and prayer, Gandhi set his fast to begin on February 9, 1943. He would take no solid food, only citrus juices added to water. He proposed to end the fast in less than three weeks if the government gave him "needed relief," but the viceroy's position was unchanged. He expressed "regret" in view of Gandhi's health and age at the decision to fast, adding, however, "I regard the use of a fast for political purposes as a form of political blackmail (*himsa*) for which there can be no moral justification."[6]

"You quote my previous writings on the subject against me," Gandhi responded. "You have left me no loophole for escaping the ordeal I have set before myself."[7] Posterity would judge, he insisted, which of them had best served his nation and humanity. The Home Department offered to release him before he started to fast, but Gandhi refused, writing "I must not hustle the Government into a decision on this."[8] Linlithgow allowed his government's best Indian heart specialist, Dr. Gilder, to be transferred to Gandhi's side, and three days into the fast permitted naturopath Dr. Dinshaw Mehta to check Gandhi's condition. Dr. B. C. Roy, Bengali leader of the Congress, was permitted to join his medical team and stayed in attendance throughout the fast. Gandhi was so weak after ten days that Government prepared for his possible funeral, gathering sandalwood "for the cremation."[9] But he survived.

Soon after his fast ended, on May 4, Gandhi felt strong enough to write to Jinnah, after reading in Jinnah's newspaper, *Dawn*, that he would "welcome" speaking to Gandhi if he were really willing to come to a "settlement." "Dear Qaid-e-Azam," he wrote. "I welcome your invitation. I suggest our meeting face to face."[10] Though Linlithgow favored their meeting, Gandhi's letter was never sent, for Churchill himself vetoed that summit, determined to keep Gandhi isolated. Britain's prime minister wanted no Gandhi-Jinnah talks to upstage his own forthcoming summit with Franklin Roosevelt.

By surviving his fast, Gandhi felt a new sense of divine mission. He wrote at great length to many British officials, desperately trying to win back their trust, reaffirming his faith in nonviolence and his trust in truth and his hopes for world peace. But nothing he wrote elicited any positive response, not from the viceroy, nor his Home Minister Sir Reginald Maxwell, nor from any of the powerful civil service secretaries in the government of India. He failed to understand how betrayed those British officers felt by his not supporting the Allies in their war against Axis powers. Since his launching of the Quit India movement, they all viewed him as their enemy.

Gandhi completely failed in his incarcerated isolation to recognize the difference between all his earlier Satyagrahas and this last one, when Japanese troops were at India's eastern gateway. While he advised Britain to retreat and remove all its troops and allied forces from India, Tojo's forces, among them Subhas Bose's Indian National Army, marched up the Malay Peninsula into Burma. Gandhi blamed the government, of course, for not earlier welcoming Congress's offer of support if Swaraj were first granted. However, Churchill's Cabinet never dreamed of negotiating any agreement with India during the London blitz, and thus viewed every act by the Congress throughout the war as mad or treasonous.

Even Agatha Harrison wondered if he was a "different man" since the traumas of war had wreaked so much havoc in India, as in Europe and Asia. She wrote, nonetheless, before year's end to send her season's greetings. "It was a perfect pleasure to receive your unexpected letter," Gandhi replied. "I am the same man you have known me. The spirit of Andrews is ever with me. But the suspicion about my motives and utter distrust of my word in high places has hitherto rendered every move made by me nugatory."[11]

At this time, imprisoned Ba was "oscillating between life and death."[12] Doctors prescribed many medicines, including the new miracle sulfa drugs and penicillin, but Gandhi rejected them all. He prescribed nature cures and prayers and chanted around the clock at her deathbed. Devdas came to visit his parents, suggesting to his Bapu that an Ayurvedic doctor be brought to treat his mother. So Gandhi requested permission for Dr. Mehta to be called back, as well as Vaidyaraj Shiv Sharma of Lahore. Ramdas also came and tried to get his mother released from detention, but Gandhi objected. Harilal tried to visit, but Gandhi never wished to see him again. Manilal was still living in South Africa and cabled in February to know if he should come, but Gandhi replied that he should continue working where he was. Vaidya Sharma tried every Ayurvedic remedy to no avail. Ba died on the evening of February 22, 1944. She was cremated in the same corner of the Poona palace grounds as Mahadev had been. Devdas lit the fire after Gandhi spoke briefly and prayed for his wife of sixty-three years.

Gandhi was comforted at this time primarily by Manu, the young daughter of his nephew, Jaisukhlal, who had first come to live with him at the Sevagram ashram after her mother's death in 1942. She became one of his favorite "walking sticks" before his arrest and would later return to stay at his side for the last lonely years of his life. Manu had been permitted to join him shortly before Ba died, and now she remained with him. He later called her his "grand daughter." The "war" he now fought behind bars was waged in his own mind as to whether he should keep young Manu with him in detention or liberate her to pursue her education outside. "I kept thinking over the matter the whole of last night and could get no sleep," he reported, finally deciding that "we must endure our separation. You are a sensible girl. Forget your sorrow. . . . Stop crying and live cheerfully. Learn what you can after leaving the jail."[13] He wrote of himself hereafter as her "mother," taking Ba's place as her closest, dearest protector. Manu was eleven at this time. He sent her off to Rajkot, where she lived with cousin Narandas Gandhi, learning accounting as well as music and studying Gujarati literature. She would never marry and would later return to Gandhi as his constant closest companion until his assassination.

While Congress leaders languished behind bars, Subhas Bose's Japanese-supported Indian National Army (INA) advanced to the outskirts of Imphal. Anglo-American forces stopped Bose's INA in early May 1944, before they could cross Bengal's eastern border, where Netaji Bose would have been hailed by millions as the "liberator" of his nation. A year later, he died after his plane crashed on Formosa. On May 6, 1944, with the INA bogged down, India's new martial viceroy, Lord Wavell, felt secure enough to release his most famous prisoner and his disciples. Gandhi weighed less than one hundred pounds and was almost seventy-five years old. He and his depleted band of faithful followers were driven directly to Lady Thackersey's Poona mansion, where he was warmly welcomed with marigold garlands, nourishing juices, and the chanting of melodic mantras. He soon regained his strength, thanks to the nurturing care of his "Sister" Premlila Thackersey.

On May 11 he entrained for Bombay, where he stayed again in "Palm Bun" bungalow on Juhu Beach. He confessed "about this release . . . I feel . . . ashamed . . . if they do not arrest me, what can I do? . . . I am silent."[14] He now often retreated into his silent shell, withdrawing as had India's ancient yogis and sages, called *Munis* ("Silent Ones") in the *Rig Veda*. Silence helped him listen for his inner voice. He was free to walk alone along the beach, watching the sun set as he had done so often a decade ago with Charlie Andrews. To Mahadev Desai's widow he indulged in a rare note of self-pity: "I may be regarded as crippled for the present. God does not allow even a Mahatma's pride to last."[15]

In July he returned to his Wardha ashram but felt so weak he had "hardly enough energy" to cope with his daily mail. Still, he was strong enough to prescribe cures for friends. "So the fat on your body has proved completely deceptive, hasn't it?" he wrote one old friend who'd just sustained a heart attack. "If you had given up salt, etc., from the beginning. . . . But never mind. Rest for four months now and make your body quite strong. Maybe, this ordeal will improve your hearing too. Show this to the doctor. He is no doctor who treats a patient only for one symptom. The root cause of all diseases is generally one."[16]

Before leaving Bombay, Gandhi was interviewed for three hours by English journalist Stuart Gelder, who then cabled an unauthorized report to *The Times of India* claiming: "Mr. Gandhi is prepared to accept and to advise the Congress to participate in a war-time national government in full control of the civil administration."[17] The viceroy would retain control of the armed forces alone and Gandhi would promise not to resume civil disobedience. According to Gelder, Gandhi was also willing to seek agreement with Jinnah and the Muslim League on the basis of C. R.'s proposals to recognize the Pakistan demand if a "plebiscite" held in Muslim majority districts of Punjab and Bengal approved it. Gandhi expressed shock at Gelder's unauthorized release and distortions of his interview. Many old Congress colleagues were outraged at what sounded like the repudiation of his entire Quit India movement. He would never accept Pakistan, though his regard for Jinnah remained high, and he continued to hope that they might reach an amicable settlement. "Mr. Jinnah does not block the way," Gandhi said that July, "but the British Government do not want a just settlement of the Indian claim for independence which is long overdue, and they are using Mr. Jinnah as a cloak for denying freedom to India."[18]

In mid-July 1944, Gandhi wrote to Churchill himself, who never replied. "You are reported to have a desire to crush the simple 'naked fakir,'" Gandhi wrote. "I . . . ask you to trust and use me for the sake of your people and mine and through them those of the world."[19] Gandhi wrote to Jinnah as well, saluting him as *Bhai* ("Brother") Jinnah. "Let us meet when you wish to. Please do not regard me as an enemy of Islam and the Muslims here. I have always been a friend and servant of yours and of the whole world. Do not dismiss me."[20]

Jinnah replied in August, inviting Gandhi to his house for talks in early September. So Gandhi journeyed back to Bombay for the longest, most arduous summit meeting of his life, passionately seeking to forestall the vivisection of Mother India. But suffering from a tubercular lung infection, Jinnah was obliged to postpone their meeting. "May Allah grant your early and complete recovery," Gandhi replied after learning of Jinnah's fever. "I don't want you to hurry for my sake."[21]

Their summit began a few days later, on September 9, 1944. They conferred for over three hours. "It was a test of my patience," Gandhi reported to C. R. "However, it was a friendly talk. His contempt for your Formula and his contempt for you is staggering."[22] Jinnah argued that his demand and that of his League was nothing less than Pakistan, as described in the 1940 Lahore Resolution. Gandhi had "not studied it," but promised to do so before their next meeting. Jinnah insisted that Gandhi "represented" the "Hindu Congress." But Gandhi replied that he had come only "as an individual." Jinnah was annoyed by that; he spoke as the president of the Muslim League, and if Gandhi did not represent Congress, what was the "basis" for their talk? Who was to deliver the goods? "I told him, 'Is it not worth your while to convert an individual?' . . . He said I should concede Pakistan and he would go the whole length with me. He would go to jail, he would even face bullets."[23]

Despite the ever-growing gulf that divided their ideologies, Gandhi and Jinnah deeply respected each other's virtues and remarkable strengths. In 1945, Jinnah told barrister Yahya Bakhtiar that "What I am afraid of is . . . Gandhi. He has brains and always tried to put me in the wrong. I have to be on guard and alert all the time."[24] Both of these great leaders tried the other's powers and patience to their limits. Each man was frail, ill, and the target of fanatics and assassins in his own party; both were destined to die in 1948.

Jinnah urged Gandhi to accept Pakistan "now," before the war ended. "We should come to an agreement and then go to the Government and ask them . . . force them to accept our solution," Jinnah told Gandhi on the first day of their summit. "I said I could never be a party to that. . . . I agree the League is the most powerful Muslim organization. I might even concede that you as its President represent the Muslims of India, but that does not mean that all Muslims want Pakistan. Put it to the vote of all the inhabitants of the area and see."[25] That was C. R.'s proposed "formula," for which Jinnah had contempt. He demanded of Gandhi "Why should you ask non-Muslims?" to which Gandhi replied: "You cannot possibly deprive a section of the population of its vote. You must carry them with you, and if you are in the majority why should you be afraid?"[26] Jinnah then cross-examined him on the clauses of C. R.'s formula. Gandhi suggested he invite C. R. to explain its details, but Jinnah didn't want to negotiate with any Hindu but Gandhi in his sitting room. Gandhi finally asked him to reduce his objections to C. R.'s formula to writing. Jinnah was reluctant, but agreed. "I would like to come to an agreement with you," Jinnah told him before Gandhi left, and Bapu warmly responded that they should "not separate" until they reached "an agreement." Jinnah nodded, but when Gandhi suggested they also reduce that to writing, Jinnah said, "No, better not." They agreed to resume their "frank and friendly talks" on September 11 at 5.30 P.M., following the Muslim holiday of Ramadan.

In a letter on September 10, Jinnah meticulously challenged every clause of C. R.'s formula.[27] Gandhi wrote his reply and sent it the following day to Jinnah's house before they resumed their talks that evening. "My life mission has been Hindu-Muslim unity," Gandhi wrote.[28] He insisted that so long as the British remained in India to stir up trouble, they would never cease fighting among themselves. "Hence the first condition of the exercise of the right of self-determination is achieving independence by the joint action of all the parties and groups composing India."[29]

Nehru, then still in prison, was "very much put out" when he learned that Gandhi was meeting Jinnah. Jawaharlal considered C. R.'s proposal that Congress accept Pakistan even more contemptible than did Jinnah, calling it a "devil dance." "The very frequent utterances of Rajagopalachari [C. R.] have overwhelmed me," Jawaharlal noted in his prison diary. "I feel stifled and unable to breathe."[30] Nor would Nehru listen any longer to the little father, who had adopted him politically long years ago and called him his "heir." Gandhi's reminder to Jinnah that he spoke only as an "individual" may more accurately have reflected the reality of most younger Congressmen's disenchantment with him rather than his own Mahatmaic modesty.

Gandhi and Jinnah met again on September 12 from 10.30 A.M. to 1 P.M. and from 5.30 to 7 P.M. "Jinnah Saheb and I have only God between us as witness," Gandhi told his prayer meeting. "My constant prayer these days is that He may so guide my speech that not a word might escape my lips so as to hurt the feelings of Jinnah Saheb or damage the cause that is dear to us both. He told me today, 'If we part without coming to an agreement, we shall proclaim bankruptcy of wisdom on our part.' What is more, the hopes of millions of our countrymen will be dashed to pieces."[31]

That bankruptcy was declared a week later. Those dashed hopes would in a few more years turn into rivers of blood. Each titan tried his best to convince the other of the wisdom and validity of his own view of South Asia's destiny. "Can we not agree to differ on the question of 'two nations' and yet solve the problem on the basis of self-determination?" Gandhi wrote to ask "Dear Quaid-e-Azam" on September 19. "If the regions hold-

[211]

ing Muslim majorities have to be separated according to the Lahore Resolution, the grave step of separation should be specifically placed before and approved by the people in that area."[32] Jinnah replied, "It seems to me that you are labouring under some misconception of the real meaning of the word 'self-determination.' . . . [C]an you not appreciate our point of view that we claim the right of self-determination as a nation and not as a territorial unit, and that we are entitled to exercise our inherent right as a Muslim nation, which is our birth-right?"[33] Gandhi's answer was, "I am unable to accept the proposition that the Muslims of India are a nation, distinct from the rest of the inhabitants of India. Mere assertion is no proof. The consequences of accepting such a proposition are dangerous in the extreme. Once the principle is admitted there would be no limit to claims for cutting up India . . . which would spell India's ruin."[34]

Announcing the final breakdown of their talks, Gandhi told the press he was "convinced that Mr. Jinnah is a good man," but "he is suffering from hallucination when he imagines that an unnatural division of India could bring either happiness or prosperity to the people concerned."[35]

21

No Peace

"WHAT IS A WAR CRIMINAL?" Gandhi responded to a Western reporter on the eve of the war's end. "Was not war itself a crime against God and humanity and, therefore, were not all those who . . . conducted wars, war criminals? . . . Roosevelt and Churchill are no less war criminals than Hitler and Mussolini."[1] He saw little hope for peace through the United Nations, born in San Francisco that April of 1945, and was unwilling to journey west to teach the "art of peace" to America. He felt challenged to the limits of his waning strength in his quest to bring peace to India.

Viceroy Wavell tried to lure Congress and Muslim League leaders into his administration, thereby launching the last phase of Britain's devolution of power prior to granting independence. His broadcast in mid-June 1945, unveiling the plan he'd been hatching since his appointment, revealed his political naivete. He proposed a new Executive Council with an equal number of "caste Hindus and Muslims," functioning under the 1935 Constitution. Under his plan only the viceroy and commander in chief would remain Englishmen.

Wavell wired his first invitation to Gandhi, who responded with the disclaimer that he represented "no institution." Nonetheless, Wavell urged him to join his Simla Conference, and Gandhi agreed. His acceptance wire, however, informed the viceroy that there were "no caste and casteless Hindus" who were "politically minded" and insisted that Congress alone represented "all Indians." Gandhi urged Wavell to invite Maulana Azad, president of the Congress, and told Azad to convene a Working Committee meeting in Bombay. So, by the eve of the Simla Conference, Gandhi was back in harness as the force behind Congress, despite his repeated disclaimers of power or influence. Viceregal wires energized Gandhi. He felt much stronger since meeting with Jinnah and started talking again about his much earlier expressed desire to live for 125 years. "That should be everybody's life-span."[2] He met Vallabhbhai Patel in Panchgani, a hill station near Poona, where they rested for a few days before journeying on together to Bombay to meet with the Congress Working Committee there on June 22.

In Britain, general elections that July brought an end to Churchill's power. Labour's Clement Attlee moved into 10 Downing Street, and Gandhi's old vegetarian friend, Lord Pethick-Lawrence, took control of Whitehall as secretary of state for India. Bengal-born British communist R. Palme Dutt ditched former Tory secretary Leo Amery for the House of Commons seat in Birmingham, and Nehru's close friend Krishna Menon and L. S. E. professor Harold Laski became deputy chairs of the Labour party. Labour's victory brought Congress aspirations and demands for Swaraj from the remote realm of dreams to imminent realization. Wavell's conference was thus overtaken on the eve of its start by the swiftness of political change in London.

Nonetheless, the Simla show went on as planned. Gandhi was greeted en route there by "crowds at every station, delirious and deaf with love or joy."[3] He immediately met the viceroy and remained in the salubrious summer capital of the British Raj until mid-July 1945. Nehru arrived a week after Gandhi did and tried without success to reach agreement with Jinnah on a power-sharing formula. Jinnah refused to negotiate with Azad, whom he called a "show-boy" Muslim. Wavell soon viewed Jinnah's intransigence as "the main stumbling-block" to agreement.[4] By remaining aloof at Simla, Gandhi conserved his strength and permitted Nehru to return to Congress's center stage a year before he reclaimed its presidency from Azad. Wavell liked Nehru better than either Gandhi or Jinnah, viewing him initially at least as "an idealist . . . straight and honest."[5] Gandhi, Nehru, and every member of the Congress deputation in Simla blamed Jinnah's refusal to allow any Congress Muslim to join the viceroy's council for the conference failure. But Gandhi also believed "that the deeper cause is perhaps the reluctance of the official world to part with power."[6]

A special train transported him back to Wardha, stopping briefly at Agra Cantonment station to allow him to address a student crowd gathered to await him there. "Study and work for the country's freedom" was his brief message. From there he went to Poona with Vallabhbhai Patel, where they were both treated for various digestive tract ills by Dr. Dinshaw Mehta. Gandhi long suffered from amoebic dysentery and hookworm, Patel from constant intestinal blockage and prostate problems. The Congress Working Committee set its meeting in Bombay in September of 1945 to allow both patients to attend. Nehru joined them at Mehta's clinic before the meeting started in mid-September.

Gandhi proceeded to Bombay but was too weak from an attack of influenza to attend the Congress meeting. After talking for hours with Nehru, both in Poona and Bombay, Gandhi wrote to him about "the sharp difference of opinion that has arisen between us." Gandhi reaffirmed his own faith in everything he had written thirty-five years ago in *Hind Swaraj*, and wrote of how troubled he was by Jawaharlal's rejection of virtually all he believed. "I believe that if India, and through India the world, is to achieve real freedom," Gandhi informed Nehru, "we shall have to go and live in the villages—in huts, not in palaces. Millions of people can never live in cities and palaces . . . in peace. Nor can they do so by killing one another, that is, by resorting to violence and untruth."[7] His "ideal village" still only existed "in my imagination," Gandhi conceded. Nonetheless he outlined its noble virtues and characteristics: "In this village of my dreams the villager will not be dull. . . . He will not live like an animal in filth and darkness. Men and women will live in freedom. . . . There will be no plague, no cholera and no smallpox. Everyone will have to do body labour." He passionately confessed his dream to Nehru, knowing that Jawaharlal was young enough and strong enough to carry it to fruition in freedom after the British left. They disagreed on many things, but "we both live only for India's freedom," Gandhi told the man destined to be prime minister. "Though I aspire to live up to 125 years rendering service, I am nevertheless an old man, while you are comparatively young. That is why I have said that you are my heir. . . . I should at least understand my heir and my heir in turn should understand me."[8]

Nehru was eager to oust the British by force, if they lacked sense enough to leave quickly. That October in Bombay, Nehru called upon a cheering crowd to "prepare" for the last "battle for freedom."[9] Amrit told Cripps that Gandhi alone could keep India's masses nonviolent, but he had less control over Congress youth ready to fight at the behest of Nehru. The British now made the political mistake of bringing captured officers of Bose's Indian National Army to trial for treason in Delhi's Red Fort. Nehru led their defense in a flamboyant trial, rousing popular revolutionary fervor among Delhi's Hindus, Muslims, and Sikhs, since all three religions were represented by the INA defendants. Wavell feared that Nehru might try to use Netaji Bose's popular militant mantra, *Jai Hind!* ("Victory to India") to rouse his former troops in support of Congress's demands for the more rapid transfer of power. Hindu-Muslim rioting rocked the slums of North India's most crowded cities, from Bombay to Calcutta, as preparations began for national assembly elections scheduled to start in December.

Gandhi journeyed to Calcutta in December of 1945 to meet with Bengal's governor Richard Casey, one of the brightest British administrators. As governor, Casey had encouraged schemes for river water conservation throughout Bengal, employing millions of idle workers, raising rice enough to feed that recently famine-stricken province. Gandhi now advised Casey to focus on hand spinning rather than longer-range schemes, advocating the immediate employment of peasants who had nothing to do for at least half the year. Gandhi also urged the release of all political prisoners now that the war was over and independence was near at hand. Casey had the good sense to act upon much of Gandhi's advice. On Christmas Eve, Gandhi wrote "Dear Friend" Casey to urge him for "humanitarian" reasons to cancel the salt tax, but the governor wasn't quite ready to go so far.[10]

Gandhi no longer delivered long speeches "[n]ow that I am old," but softly prayed at his evening meetings, which in Bengal were often attended by more than 100,000 people. "I experience supreme peace here," Gandhi confessed to his worshipful admirers. "Is it not enough that we should cheerfully shoulder the burden of the small tasks that fall to our lot?"[11]

But in 1946 Gandhi's tasks became much larger. Britain's Labour government geared up to transfer its power over India. In January, a British parliamentary delegation led by Robert Richards arrived in India. Elections held throughout British India in December of 1945 proved how powerful a force Jinnah's Muslim League had become, sweeping all thirty separate Muslim seats in the Central Assembly, while the Congress only won fifty-five of the general seats, four less than it had held before. In Delhi the parliamentary delegation heard as many loud shouts of "*Pakistan Zindabad!*" ("Victory to Pakistan!") as of Bose's battle cry "*Jai Hind!*" Jinnah assured his joyous followers that "Pakistan" would soon "be at your feet."[12] Communal conflicts continued to escalate in Bengal, yet Gandhi optimistically advised Hindu friends: "We can achieve everything by love. Love can never be impatient nor can it ever be angry. If you behave with Muslim brethren in this spirit their anger will go."[13] He scheduled a meeting with the Aga Khan to discuss Hindu-Muslim problems in Bombay or Poona in February.

In late January of 1946, Gandhi left by train for Madras where Agatha and C. R. were waiting to join him in celebrating the silver jubilee of South India's Hindi Language Society. There he urged every Tamil Indian to learn Hindi, soon to be India's national language. He also appealed for money for his Harijan Fund and called for total abolition of untouchability. In Madras, he met Richards and the other members of his British parliamentary delegation, urging them to lobby in London for India's freedom and for immediate release of all political prisoners. In Madras he told students and teachers that "truth and non-violence were really more powerful than the atom bomb." Gandhi spoke and wrote passionately of the dreadful destruction caused by that bomb, hoping India would never be "so foolish" as to rely upon such weapons of mass destruction. "Do I still adhere to my faith in truth and non-violence? Has not the atom bomb exploded that faith?" he asked in his revived *Harijan*. "Not only has it not done so but it has clearly demonstrated to me that the twins constitute the mightiest force in the world. Before it the atom bomb is of no effect."[14] His faith in twins Satya and Ahimsa had never been stronger.

By February 1946, famine threatened much of India, at a time when the entire world's stock of food grains was severely depleted. Wavell invited Gandhi to New Delhi, hoping to persuade him to meet with Jinnah and himself so that all three of them could sign a national appeal against hoarding or wasting food. Gandhi was, however, unwilling to join what he considered Britain's "same old game of parity between Hindus and Muslims."[15] So the viceroy sent his secretary George Abell to Sevagram to try to change Gandhi's mind. Abell was pleased to find Gandhi "more friendly" than he'd anticipated and to learn that he'd already written an article for *Harijan* that mostly met Wavell's requirements. Abell urged a stronger statement and persuaded Gandhi to agree to a number of things he wrote down against wasteful use of food grains and "criminally wicked" hoarding.[16] Gandhi advised that the viceroy immediately install a national government ready to cope with the anticipated disaster, which Abell admitted wouldn't be easy since they must first try to get the Muslim League to join, as well as the Congress.[17]

Before month's end, Gandhi urged Abell to put the Indian army to "constructive" antifamine work, digging wells where most urgently needed. He also pointed out the potential for growing more food by turning all public gardens into vegetable plots and distributing such food through cooperative societies. Foodstuffs in military warehouses should be "released forthwith" to starving people, and bribery as well as hoarding must be repressed with impartial vigor.[18]

Gandhi promised Vallabhbhai to join him in Bardoli in late February, but shortly before, on February 18, 1946, India's first naval mutiny—"strike"—erupted in Bombay harbor, aboard the Indian Navy's cruiser *Talwar*. Young nationalist mutineers, excited by reports of Bose's rebel army "heroes," and Nehru's ardent defense of those charged with "treason" in the Red Fort trial, took control of India's largest naval vessel, hauling down its Union Jack and raising India's tricolor in its place, pointing their ship's big guns at the city. Congress quickly sent its strongest troubleshooter, Vallabhbhai Patel, to deal with that crisis. Patel firmly called on the mutineers to surrender, before a British naval cruiser, *Glasgow*, reached Bombay. "To what a pass have things come!" Gandhi commiserated with Brother Vallabh. "I hope you are well."[19] He was very much relieved a few days later when the mutineers all listened to Sardar Patel and peacefully surrendered. "They were badly advised," wrote Gandhi. "They were thoughtless and ignorant, if they believed that by their might they would deliver India from foreign domination."[20]

Gearing up to transfer its imperial power to India, Prime Minister Clement Attlee's Labour Cabinet appointed a troika of its ministers, Pethick-Lawrence, Stafford Cripps and A. V. Alexander, to undertake Britain's final Cabinet Mission to India. "My colleagues are going to India with the intention of using their utmost endeavours to help her attain . . . freedom as speedily and fully as possible," the prime minister announced in mid-March.[21] India herself would have to choose her future situation and position in the world, Attlee explained to Britain's House of Commons. He hoped India would decide to remain within the British Commonwealth.

The Cabinet Mission reached India on March 23, 1946, the sixth anniversary of the Muslim League's Lahore resolution, celebrated by Muslims as "Pakistan Day." Cripps met with Jinnah on March 30, finding him "reasonable but completely firm on Pakistan."[22]

The troika all met Gandhi three days later. He began by urging them to abolish the salt tax. Briefing them on his recent talks with Jinnah, he told them that "Jinnah is sincere but his logic is utterly at fault," but then advised them to invite Jinnah to "form the first Government and choose its personnel."[23] The Cabinet Mission was not willing to take his advice any more than Mountbatten would be a year later. They later opted instead to ask Nehru, considered by Attlee as well as Cripps to be India's best potential prime minister due to his Harrow-Cambridge sophistication, brilliance, and charm. Pethick-Lawrence thanked Gandhi for coming to help them in their mission and expressed "penitence" for Britain's many "misdeeds in the past."[24]

Though Gandhi met with the Cabinet Mission as often as they wished and did his best to assist them to reach their painfully delayed decision and devise their final formula, his primary passion and interest at this time was to teach nature cure therapy to India's impoverished villagers. His recent prolonged stay with Vallabhbhai at Dr. Mehta's clinic had reignited his old interest in naturopath cures. He now purchased the clinic from Dr. Mehta, holding it in trust for "poor" patients, but impoverished villagers could hardly afford to leave their fields unattended to come for treatment to Poona. So Gandhi decided to go to them, choosing first the neighboring Maharashtrian village of Uruli for this experiment. "Why have I got involved in nature cure in the evening of my life?" he wrote about his decision in *Harijan*. "Was I not too old to take up new things? . . . The still small voice within me whispers: 'Why bother about what others say? . . . You have confidence in your capacity. . . . If you hide this talent and do not make use of it, you will be as a thief.'"[25] As long as he pursued his reborn passion for nature cures with "perfect detachment," he believed that his work would help him to live 125 years, since the primary goal of ancient India's Ayurvedic medicine was to prolong life.

Gandhi's universal cure for every sickness was prayer, primarily repetition of Lord Rama's name, which he always found salubrious. His inner voice told him that by helping to cure others he would ensure greater longevity to himself. His remedies in addition to constant prayer varied, as reflected in the careful records he kept of individual illnesses. He kept records of the remedies: For Vithabai he prescribed "sun-bath in the nude, followed by a hip-bath and a friction-bath in cold water."[26] For Hira: "She should chew fruit and. . . . mud-poultice on the abdomen." For Arjun, "Urine will pass regularly, if he is seated in hot and cold water by turns." Salu: "She should be given sun-bath even in this heat." Hirunana: "Fruit-juices for two days: then . . . [s]un-bath, hip-bath and friction-bath." For himself, Gandhi kept his second young "walking-stick" Abha with him throughout his village work. Abha's young husband, Kanu, was Gandhi's great-nephew, who remained too busy in Sevagram to join his wife as their Mahatma's helper. "I like my new occupation," Gandhi wrote Kanu. "Abha has been a good girl these days; she remains cheerful."[27]

For most of April, Gandhi stayed in Valmiki *Mandir* ("Temple") on the outskirts of Delhi's Harijan Bhangi-sweeper's quarter, keeping himself available to Pethick-Lawrence and Cripps whenever they called for him. He also met with Congress comrades, spun, and practiced his nature cures on Harijans. Thanks to his friend and patron Birla he had a telephone and electricity wired into the temple, as well as clean drinking water and a bathtub. He never missed his full massage, which Abha usually gave him, or his evening bath, part of his own nature cure therapy.

Congress's Working Committee met in Delhi that month and elected Nehru its next president. Attlee's three "Wise Men" worked around the clock through mid-May, finally agreeing upon a three-tiered scheme of confederation that would allow Britain to transfer its powers to a single, weak central government of India, under whose loose authority were to be powerful "groups" of provinces, essentially the Muslim majority provinces later to comprise "Pakistan," the rest being most of British India's Hindu-majority provinces. Those "groups" would enjoy virtual autonomy over most matters of government influencing the lives of their predominantly Muslim and Hindu populations. Within each of the group clusters the individual old British Indian provinces would remain with provincial assemblies, free to vote to change their "group" allegiance after five or ten years, should they opt to do so, based on provincial plebiscites. It was a brilliant confederal scheme, primarily drafted by Cripps, which would potentially have saved South Asia most of the slaughter and hatred that accompanied partition.

The Cabinet Mission moved up to Simla in May. Gandhi was invited to join them but initially refused. When Cripps pressed him, however, he finally requested government quarters for his entourage of fifteen, and noted his special food requirements, which included a goat, for his daily quota of milk. The official Simla residence, "Chadwick," was properly prepared by government for Gandhi's entourage, provisioned as he required. But soon after moving into that spacious mansion, Gandhi spent "half a day" searching anxiously for a small pencil he used to write notes and letters, which were not dictated to one of his secretaries. "I am very conservative in my feelings," he confessed to Agatha Harrison, trying to explain why he desperately needed that "small bit of pencil which had been with me for a long time. I could not reconcile myself to its loss."[28] Gandhi had become a villager in more ways than the spare simplicity of his attire. His life so fully integrated with nature's daily routine and seasons was unsettled by the speed with which he'd been "lifted" from central India's scorching May heat to Himalayan heights and cool breezes. He felt "grieved" by the "immorality prevalent among the people of Simla," Anglo-India's official playground-on-high for all who sought escape from India's crowded misery. Gandhi's old pencil was a familiar reminder of his true identity, a tiny anchor he needed now to help steady his fingers, to center his soul, suddenly swept away from its village moorings, flying too high too swiftly to this wasteland of luxury. Gandhi soon sent most of his entourage back to Delhi, resolving to carry on in Simla virtually alone, keeping only young Sudhir Ghosh, his liaison to the viceroy, and Rajkumari Amrit Kaur, who stayed with him in Chadwick.

By mid-May, the Simla talks stalled, halted by the familiar deadlock between Congress and the League and, restless and lonely, Gandhi decided to return to Delhi. From Delhi he wrote Amrit, "Of course I miss you and do not."[29] Sushila Nayar joined him in Delhi as did Abha. No agreement could be reached between Congress and the League, so the Cabinet Mission issued its own plan on May 16, of which Gandhi warmly approved. The three-tiered confederal constitution would give Muslims most of their Pakistan demand, while saving South Asia from the tragedy of partition. "It contained the seed to convert this land of sorrow into one without sorrow and suffering,"[30] Gandhi told his prayer meeting that evening in Delhi. The "alternative" as the mission's report rightly warned would be "a grave danger of violence, chaos, and even civil war."[31] The strong second-tier "groups of Provinces" were the creative key in the Cabinet Mission's plan, which as its authors cautiously explained would have to be accepted in its *entirety* in order to work properly.

Gandhi's enthusiastic positive response to the mission's proposal was not seconded by Nehru, who only read its strong "Pakistan" grouping as further proof of British divide and rule duplicity. Nehru, moreover, was now not only the president-elect of Congress, but also prime minister-in-waiting of India. On the eve of the Cabinet Mission's arrival in Delhi, fifty-eight-year-old widower Nehru had flown off to Singapore, where he met with royal Lord Louis Mountbatten and his flamboyant forty-four-year-old wife, Lady Edwina Ashley Mountbatten. For Jawaharlal and Edwina, whom Nehru helped to lift from the floor of Singapore's St. John Ambulance Welfare Center onto which she had fallen, it was love at first sight.[32] She had read and adored his autobiography, sharing his socialist ideas and his compassionate concerns for India's impoverished masses. Lord Mountbatten, soon to replace Wavell as India's next (and last) viceroy, also immediately admired Nehru, whose formal education, charm, and English accent matched his own. Nehru viewed the Cabinet Mission's plan as too generous to Jinnah's demands and rushed in frustration from sweltering Delhi to the cooler air of Kashmir after it was announced.

Gandhi left Delhi for the hills of Mussoorie on May 28 and returned on June 9 to attend a Working Committee meeting to decide on Congress's list of potential ministers for the viceroy's new interim cabinet. Jinnah insisted that the Cabinet be composed of five Muslim League ministers, five "Hindus" from the Congress, an additional Sikh, and a Christian or Anglo-Indian. Congress refused to surrender its right to select a Muslim, like Azad, which Gandhi informed Wavell "was a point of honour with Congressmen."[33] So India's unity shattered on the adamantine rock of a single "Muslim member," insisted on by Nehru and Congress, unacceptable to Jinnah and his League. Gandhi, for all his wisdom, was impotent to break the deadlock. To "Dear Friend" Pethick-Lawrence, sick and very tired by now of India, Gandhi wrote "that it will be wrong on my part if I advise the Congress to wait indefinitely until the Viceroy has formed the Interim Government or throws up the sponge in despair. Despair he must, if he expects to bring into being a coalition Government between two incompatibles."[34] When Agatha, Horace Alexander, and Sudhir Ghosh all read that letter, Gandhi's honest assessment of the impossibility of reconciling Congress and the League to joining an interim united government on the eve of independence, they urged him not to send it, fearing the negative impact it could have on Attlee's Cabinet. Though he pocketed that letter, Gandhi wrote Cripps in mid-June, advising him not to "choose" between "the Muslim League and the Congress, both your creations."[35] Cripps's health had also broken down, and Gandhi advised him to return to England. But Sir Stafford was not quite ready to pack up, determined "to leave nothing undone which may help a solution of the difficult problems here."[36] He could not yet bring himself to see he had failed a second time in less than half a decade to break the Hindu-Muslim deadlock. "The Mission . . . have done their best. But the best falls far short of India's needs," Gandhi told Norman Cliff on the eve of the troika's departure. "India is being robbed of millions of pounds by Britain."[37] He feared that Britain's entrenched Indian civil service was working "to torpedo" every decent proposal to expedite the transfer of power, as soon as the Cabinet Mission flew home on June 29.

At his first press conference after resuming his presidency of the Congress in early July 1946, Nehru insisted that Congress would enter the forthcoming Constituent Assembly "completely unfettered by agreements and free to meet all situations as they arise." This was a blatant repudiation of the Cabinet Mission's plan, especially the virtual autonomy promised to the groups of provinces, without which Jinnah's League would have rejected, instead of having accepted, the plan. When Jinnah read the press reports of Nehru's statement, he was outraged, calling on the Muslim League to prepare for "direct action," bidding "good-bye to constitutions and constitutional methods."[38] Gandhi was almost equally surprised at his "heir's" impulsive behavior. "If it is correctly reported, some explanation is needed," Bapu wrote to Jawaharlal. "It must be admitted that we have to work within the limits of the State Paper. . . . If we do not admit even this much . . . Jinnah Saheb's accusation will prove true."[39] But Nehru refused to retract a single word he said, not fearing Jinnah's threats and not caring for Bapu's anxiety.

"A great many things seem to be slipping out of the hands of the Congress," Gandhi sadly reported to Brother Vallabh in late July.[40] Violence had been rampant for the past week in Ahmedabad, a post strike had spread through Bombay, and Harijans as well as Muslims ignored the pleas of Congress for peace. Gandhi called for "senseless disorder" to end, pleading with Dr. Ambedkar to call off the Satyagraha he'd launched against all business in Bombay. Disorder was not conducive to independence, Gandhi insisted, and made many British officials shake their heads in amazement.

On August 16, 1946, Calcutta turned into a killing field, starting in Maniktolla, where mobs of Muslims, responding to the League's proclamation of direct action, butchered neighboring Hindus, who retaliated on the next day. For four days and nights, the city was a scene of continuous communal slaughter that claimed the lives of four hundred, left thousands wounded, and made tens of thousands homeless. The underworld of India's most populous city took unfettered control, as all of Calcutta's police and soldiers stayed home on officially proclaimed holiday or slept in their barracks. Congress blamed Muslim League Chief Minister H. S. Suhrawardy for having proclaimed August 16 a holiday and the viceroy for having failed to call out the troops. Eleven days after the Calcutta killing started, Wavell met with Nehru and Gandhi and told them that what he had seen could only be avoided elsewhere "by some lessening of communal tension" through coalition governments.[41] He urged them to reopen negotiations with Jinnah. Gandhi and Nehru believed, however, that Wavell himself was to blame and had to be replaced. Gandhi wired Sudhir Ghosh in London, asking him so to inform Pethick-Lawrence and Attlee of Congress's lack of confidence in the viceroy. Sudhir met at once with the old secretary of state, whose response was "rather sticky," but two days later Sudhir spoke to Attlee, who showed "more understanding."[42] The prime minister brought the matter before his entire Cabinet and appointed a new viceroy, Lord Mountbatten, within the year.

Gandhi felt obliged to remain in Delhi, but was so sick over the murderous Calcutta riots that he chose to remain silent, words failing him. A few days later he wrote in *Harijan*: "If through deliberate courage the Hindus had died to a man, that would have been deliverance of Hinduism and India and purification of Islam in this land. As it was, a third party had to intervene . . . to still mutual savagery."[43] He urged all the new ministers of the interim government, led by Nehru, sworn in by Wavell on September 1, 1946, to "ever seek to attain communal harmony."[44] Vallabhbhai Patel was put in charge of Home Affairs, which gave him control over India's police. Nehru kept External and Commonwealth Affairs portfolios himself. "The way to Purna Swaraj has at last been opened," Gandhi announced, but his optimism was overtaken by the chaos and violence spreading its poison throughout India.

Rioting rocked Bihar and deadly stabbings became daily occurrences in Delhi. Most passengers considered it unnecessary to buy train tickets and simply jumped aboard for long journeys. Looting, arson, and murder were rampant in the central provinces as well as in Bihar. In Jubbulpore, Hindu fanatics, shouting "Death to Christians," attacked actors, whose play ended with a prayerful hymn to Jesus. "We have gone completely mad," Gandhi wrote to a sadly depressed disciple.[45] Still, he strongly objected to Congress ministers calling upon the army and police to break up striking workers or stop protestors, arguing that would only "admit" Congress's "impotence." But every evening Gandhi prayed that Nehru and Jinnah would agree to cooperate in running the interim government and work together to stop the slaughter, hunger, corruption, and black marketing.

Deadly floods now ravaged Assam, and in Eastern Bengal there was greater violence caused by human intolerance. While in Delhi, Gandhi learned that the small Hindu community of Noakhali District had come under assault from Muslim neighbors and women were being abducted and converted to Islam. So, on the eve of what was to have been his return to Sevagram, Gandhi resolved that God wanted him to go to Bengal. Some of those who heard his protests, denouncing that "tarnishing" of Bengal's "fair name," asked Gandhi why he did not fast to stop such communal madness. "There is no inner call," he replied. "Let people call me a coward if they please. I have faith that when the hour arrives God will give me the strength."[46] Two weeks after he turned seventy-seven, Gandhi resolved to undertake his first pilgrimage to Noakhali in Eastern Bengal, determined to walk alone through that district's sea of blood, seeking by his act of passionate self-sacrifice to stop its deadly flow.

22

Walking Alone

"I HAVE COME to stay here with you as one of you," Gandhi told Bengali refugees gathered at Laksham Junction. "I have vowed to myself that I will stay on here and die here if necessary, but I will not leave Bengal till the hatchet is finally buried and even a solitary Hindu girl is not afraid to move freely about in the midst of Mussalmans."[1]

On the eve of his Noakhali pilgrimage, Gandhi was told of murderous riots by Bihar's Hindu majority against Muslims in "retaliation" for the attacks against Hindu women in Eastern Bengal. "Bihar of my dreams seems to have falsified them," he wrote just before leaving Calcutta for his rural pilgrimage. "A bad act of one party is no justification for a similar act by the opposing party."[2] Bengal's Chief Minister Suhrawardy had intended to accompany Gandhi to Noakhali but was detained by urgent business in Calcutta; he sent his Labour minister to facilitate Gandhi's journey. They traveled East initially by rail and boat, stopping to allow Gandhi to talk with refugees and villagers along the way. "Let us turn our wrath against ourselves," he told Hindus gathered to hear him at every stop.[3] His mantra for this pilgrimage was "Do or Die." He anticipated months of walking from village to wounded village to impart hope and courage to all who saw and heard him and witnessed his unarmed, intrepid bravery. "The work here may perhaps be my last," he confessed to Brother Vallabh. "If I survive this, it will be a new life for me. My non-violence is being tested here in a way it has never been tested before."[4]

Gandhi resolved to live in Muslim villages, attended only by his Bengali-speaking interpreter N. K. Bose and his secretary, Parasuram. Abha had come with him to Bengal, but not to the villages, and young Manu fell ill shortly before he left Delhi obliging her temporarily to remain at home. In each village Gandhi tried to establish a Peace Committee, comprised of at least one Hindu and one Muslim. He taught them Satyagraha and the values of Ahimsa. He prayed with them and told them of his early experiences in rural Bihar and of his struggles in South Africa, where most of his followers were Muslims. "War results when peace fails. Our effort must always be directed towards peace, but it must be peace with honour and fair security for life and property."[5]

Back in Delhi, Nehru urged Wavell to convene India's Constituent Assembly in December. Jinnah refused, however, to join it, and Gandhi rejected Nehru's appeal to him to return to the capital, determined to do or die in Bengal. Nehru, sick of arguing with Wavell, after having thought no less than "fifty times" of resigning from the viceroy's council, accepted Attlee's invitation to London in early December 1946.[6] Jinnah was also invited, going with Liaquat Ali Khan who became Pakistan's first prime minister. Nehru took his soon-to-be Sikh Minister of Defense Baldev Singh to London, rather than Vallabhbhai Patel, with whom he never felt at ease. The brief summit in London did not bring Nehru and Jinnah any closer, however. So Nehru flew home to convene India's Constituent Assembly on December 9, 1946, in the circular central hall of New Delhi's new Parliament House, all the Muslim League seats on the floor of which remained ominously empty.

Gandhi felt that in view of the Muslim League's "boycott," the Constituent Assembly should not have met.[7] He rightly anticipated that the Delhi meeting without the League was an admission of Pakistan's anticipated reality and only underscored the demise of India's unity. Nor was his pilgrimage through Noakhali successful. "In spite of all my efforts exodus continues and very few persons have returned to their villages," he informed Suhrawardy.[8] With most Muslim murderers still free, fearful peasants did not dare to return to their despoiled huts. Gandhi recommended an impartial official inquiry. To Agatha, he wrote, "I have never been in such darkness as I am in today. . . . It is due to my limitations. My faith in ahimsa has never burned brighter and yet I feel that there is something wanting in my technique."[9] He believed that there was a mysterious key and searched for the method of perfect self-purification and suffering to stop all killing, to turn hatred into love.

Manu was now quite well and most eager to join him. "I consider you silly," Bapu responded playfully. "You have received education but learnt no wisdom. I do not, however, wish to point out your faults. I will do so and pull your ears when you come here."[10] He agreed to allow Manu to be brought to him by her father, insisting that Jaisukhlal could "leave Manu with me on condition that she would stay with me till the end."[11] Manu felt nervous about what the "others" might say if they learned that she was sleeping alone with her "Mother"-Bapu. But Gandhi reassured her, promising that he would see to it nobody "harassed" her, and that she would be "perfectly safe."

Nirmal Bose, who stayed with him, noted how strangely Gandhi behaved shortly before Manu came. Sushila Nayar had joined him in mid-December, insisting she alone knew how to take care of him, and Bose was awakened after three in the morning by loud voices, Gandhi's shouting and Sushila's "anguished cry." Then Bose heard "two slaps" followed by "a heavy sob."[12] "At night while reading Bapu's diary," Sushila recalled, "I read 'I had a curious dream.' I casually asked him what it was. He did not say . . . At three o'clock the next morning, I woke up with the noise of Bapu jumping in bed. He said he was very cold and was taking exercise to warm up. After that, he asked me if I was awake and started telling me of his curious dream. . . . I could see that he was getting worked up. So . . . I walked away. Suddenly I heard him slap his forehead. I rushed back and stopped him."[13] Gandhi tried to convince Bose that he had "slapped himself," not Sushila. "I am not a Mahatma," Gandhi told a prayer gathering in Srirampur village the next day. "I am an ordinary mortal like you all and I am strenuously trying to practice ahimsa. Today I lost my temper."[14]

"Don't hide even a single thought from me," Gandhi told Manu three days later. "Have it engraved in your heart that whatever I ask or say will be solely for your good. . . . You will play your full role in this great sacrifice even though you are foolish."[15] That night he awoke at 12.30 A.M. "Woke up Manu at 12.45 A.M. Made her understand about her dharma," he reported in his diary. "She could still change her mind, but once having taken the plunge she would have to run the risks. She remained steadfast."[16] Next morning he walked "double the usual distance," but felt no fatigue. The following night he woke up at 1.30 A.M. and worked by candlelight until prayer time. A day later, his Monday of silence, Gandhi wrote to Bose: "I do not know what God is doing to me or through me."[17] He asked Bose to walk over to Sushila's village to report what he had written in his diary, thus remained entirely alone with Manu, whom he affectionately called by her diminutive Manudi. "Manudi is very well," he wrote her father. "She is giving me satisfaction."[18] On Christmas Day he dictated a letter to Brother Vallabh at 3 A.M., thanks to Manu: "I allowed her to come and stay with me. . . . And now I am dictating this to her, lying with my eyes closed so as to avoid strain."[19] He reported how difficult and problematic the "situation" remained. "Truth is nowhere to be found. . . . [H]einous crimes are committed in the name of religion." He was, nonetheless, "very happy" and considered his health "excellent."[20] Manudi's presence and support proved salubrious to her Bapu. She "alone" was now with him, "and does all work for me."

Nehru and Acharya Kripalani, newly elected president of the Congress came to visit Gandhi on December 28 and remained with him until December 30. They arrived at midnight, two hours after Gandhi had fallen asleep. Manu had transferred Gandhi's commode and hand basin to Nehru's hut for Jawaharlal's convenience. When Nehru later learned of it, he reprimanded her. "Bapu gave orders," she explained. "You could tell him that Jawaharlal forbade you,"[21] Nehru replied. Nehru told Gandhi about the growing rift between Congress and the League and of the latest Cabinet stalemate resulting from Finance Member Liaquat Ali Khan's refusal to approve any expenditure or accept any budget. Gandhi wrote a memo to the Working Committee expressing his belief that it was still best to leave the Constituent Assembly until Jinnah's League was persuaded to join it. "I feel that my judgment about the communal problems and the political situation is true," Gandhi wrote to warn Nehru the morning Jawaharlal left, rightly fearing that Congress's course was headed for partition and its disasters.[22]

"If the Hindus and Muslims cannot live side by side in brotherly love in Noakhali, they will not be able to do so over the whole of India, and Pakistan will be the inevitable result," Gandhi told his prayer meeting on New Year's Eve. "India will be divided, and if India is divided she will be lost for ever."[23] He well knew from all Nehru had told him that "today mine is a cry in the wilderness. But I repeat that there is no salvation for India except through the way of truth, non-violence, courage and love." His passionate faith in Ahimsa thus continued to grow, as he delved deeper into his *brahmacharya* yogic experiments.

Gandhi's typist and shorthand secretary, Parasuram, resigned on New Year's day 1947. He was shocked to find Gandhi sleeping naked with Manu. She also bathed and massaged his naked body, finding nothing wrong in doing anything Bapu asked of her. Gandhi insisted that he was never aroused when he slept beside her, or next to Sushila or Abha. He felt only as a "Mother" to these most intimate disciple-helpers. "I am sorry," Gandhi replied to Parasuram. "You are at liberty to leave me today."[24] He woke that morning at 2 A.M. "God's grace alone is sustaining me," he confided to his diary. "I can see there is some grave defect in me somewhere which is the cause of all this. All around me is utter darkness."[25] He woke Manu, telling her "to remain alert and wide awake." Pyarelal reported that he muttered to himself: "There must be some serious flaw deep down in me which I am unable to discover . . . could I have missed my way?"[26]

He walked four miles from Srirampur to Chandipur barefoot, reaching his destination before 9 A.M. Twenty gun-bearing military police traveled just ahead of him to be sure that no robbers lurked beside the overgrown paths. He spoke in each village to men, women, and children unafraid to come forward and offered them reassurance, urging them to pray and to be brave enough to be ready to die rather than to run away. Wherever he went, many houses had been looted, burned down, and left in rubble, testimony to the savagery of last year's riots. Leaning heavily on Manu's shoulder with his left hand, holding his walking stick in his right, Gandhi was wearied more by the violent scars he witnessed than the one to five miles he walked daily. By January 4 in Kazirbazar, he feared that attendance at his prayer meetings was so swiftly dwindling that one day soon he would be left "without any audience."[27]

Mira, who ran her own ashram for sick cows in the north, heard from Parasuram of their break. She expressed alarm at what she heard. "Everything depends upon one's purity in thought, word and deed," Gandhi replied. "We often use the word 'purity' and excuse all sorts of lapses. Do not ever worry how I am faring or what I am doing here. If I succeed in emptying myself utterly, God will possess me. Then I know that everything will come true but it is a serious question when I shall have reduced myself to zero."[28] Rajendra Prasad also heard, tactfully suggesting that it would be better for Gandhi to ask his grandnephew Kanu to take Manu's place. "It is futile to worry," Bapu replied to his friend. "Manu has come of her own accord. She was keen to come only to work under me and I agreed to it and she is working with zest. She is not as capable as Kanu, but where faith and purity exist talent and strength must follow."[29] Ramdas also heard, and was worried about his father. "Don't at all worry," Bapu replied. "Manu has taken up a lot of work and . . . I have asked her to write about her sharing the bed with me."[30] He still felt himself surrounded by "darkness," fearing that might indicate "a flaw" in his "method." He was scrupulously truthful enough, and passionately introspective enough to ask of his son, "Could it be that I am nurturing only weakness in the name of nonviolence!"[31] Gandhi was testing the "truth" of his faith in the fire of "experience." His had always been a practical philosophy, an activist faith. He appears to have hoped that sleeping naked with Manu, without arousing in himself the slightest sexual desire, might help him to douse raging fires of communal hatred in the ocean of India, and so strengthen his body as to allow him to live to 125 in continued service to the world. By January 19, however, less than a month since she had joined him, Manu showed signs of growing alienation. "I shall be happy if I know whether you will accompany me on the walk in the morning or in the evening or at both times."[32] She did not reply. Her withdrawal upset him. So he wrote, "I don't know how I can help if you are scared all the time."[33]

To celebrate Purna Swaraj day on January 26, 1947, a journalist brought the Indian flag to Gandhi in the village of Bansa, asking him to raise it. "But for the poisoned atmosphere prevalent here, I would have unfurled the tri-colour flag myself," he told his prayer meeting. The journalist did it, however, as those gathered there sang India's anthem, *Jana-gana-mana*. "There can be only one call at present that we shall not rest till freedom is won," Gandhi said. "Today brother is fighting brother. How can there be a Pakistan before we win our freedom?"[34]

He felt so troubled about Manu's anxiety and listlessness that he wrote to his old Calcutta comrade Satis Chandra Mukerji, seeking his opinion. "A young girl (19) who is in the place of a granddaughter to me by relation shares the same bed with me, not for any animal satisfaction but for (to me) valid moral reasons. She claims to be free from the passion that a girl of her age generally has and I claim to be a practised *brahmachari*. Do you see anything bad or unjustifiable in this juxtaposition?"[35] Mukerji chose not to answer that question. Manilal Gandhi, however, was shocked when he heard the news. "Do not let the fact of Manu sleeping with me perturb you. I believe that it is God who has prompted me to take that step," his Bapu replied. "Do not get [Father-in-law] upset and bear with me. I write this because Kishorelal and others have got upset. I see no reason for that."[36] Gandhi asked a Bengali doctor he met to "suggest any recipe" for helping him live to 125. The doctor only advised him to return to Calcutta "to recoup his health."[37]

He now spoke of his new technique for prolonging life and reducing conflict at his prayer meeting in Amishapara. "He had his granddaughter with him. She shared the same bed with him. The Prophet had discounted eunuchs who became such by an operation. But he [Gandhi] welcomed eunuchs made such through prayer by God. His was that aspiration. It was in the spirit of God's eunuch that he had approached what he considered was his duty . . . and he invited them to bless the effort."[38] Vallabhbhai was now worried about him from reports he received. Bapu wrote his "Brother": "I want you not to be unhappy. Please leave me in the hands of God."[39] District Muslim League Secretary Mujibur Rahman urged Gandhi to leave Noakhali, informing him that local Hindu and Muslim leaders could take responsible care of their own people. Some men asked him now if they too should sleep with young girls? "What he did was for all to do if they conformed to conditions observed by him," Gandhi replied. "If that was not done, those who pretended to imitate his practice were doomed to perdition."[40]

Gandhi believed, as he told Nirmal Bose, that "there is an indissoluble connection between private, personal life and public. . . . [Y]ou cannot overlook private deflections from the right conduct. If you are convinced . . . you should pursue my connection with Manu and if you find a flaw, try to show it to me."[41] Nirmal argued against the practice but failed to convince Gandhi that he did anything inappropriate, since he firmly believed God directed his actions, and approved of his loving (nonsexual) intimacy with Manu. Gandhi then wrote to Vinoba to explain that he slept with Manu in order to test what had been "my belief for a long time that that alone is true *brahmacharya* which requires no hedges. . . . I am not conscious of myself having fallen. . . . My mind daily sleeps in an innocent manner with millions of women, and Manu also, who is a blood relation to me, sleeps with me as one of these millions. . . . If I do not appear to people exactly as I am within, wouldn't that be a blot on my non-violence?"[42] Vinoba "did not agree," but he "did not wish to argue."[43] Gandhi's self-effacing passionate insistence on truth, much like his need to test the purity of this pilgrimage sacrifice, could to his mind, best be proved by his fearless confession that he daily contemplated sleeping with "millions of women," as he slept with Manu, innocently, unagressively, emptying himself of all masculine force and sexual violence, stripping himself naked of ego. Only when the painful pleasure of his passion left him fortified as a karma yogi-sadhu, his mind and heart perfectly indifferent to pleasure and pain, would he truly be ready to defeat the forces of evil hatred unleashed in his sacred Motherland and prove himself worthy of living to 125.

Manu now seems to have sought escape from her experiment in sickness. "You must discover a remedy for this cold of yours," he ordered. "*Ramanama* is an unfailing remedy."[44] But Manu's repetition of Lord Rama's name does not appear to have helped cure her. So he suggested that "you should wrap something round your chest and throat. . . . Nature's laws must not be violated. Learn to bear this in mind."[45] That same day he almost "collapsed," finding his one-and-a-half mile trek to Gopinathpur nearly more than he could manage. It was the first time since coming to Noakhali that he "retraced his steps." Gandhi's faith in himself also weakened now as Vallabhbhai Patel told him very forcefully, as Gandhi wrote to their mutual friend and generous patron, G. D. Birla, "that what I look upon as my dharma is really *adharma* [evil behaviour]. . . . The link between you and me is your faith that my life is pure, spotless and wholly dedicated to the performance of dharma. . . . I would therefore, like you to take full part in this discussion. . . . [I]f I am conducting myself sinfully, it becomes the duty of all friends to oppose me vehemently."[46] Gandhi's deep respect and love for Birla as well as Patel made him scrutinize his motives and his actions in light of their doubts, admitting: "I am not God. I can commit mistakes; I have committed mistakes; this may prove to be my biggest at the fag end of my life."

Gandhi's Noakhali frustrations were compounded by Muslim threats to boycott Hindus throughout that district as long as he remained there. Bengali Muslim League leaders like former Premier Fazlul Huq insisted that he stop "preaching Islam." To try to cheer him, Congress local leaders held a "grand reception" in Devipur, decorating the entire village with Congress flags, streamers, and floral garlands. But that "vain display" only angered Gandhi, who berated its Congress organizer, "knowing my strong views on khadi, that ribbons and buntings made of mill cloth would only hurt me."[46] After seeing so much costly décor hung in his "honor," Gandhi wondered to himself "whether I am not living in a fool's paradise. It seems that God has woken me up with a rude shock to enable me to see where I stand." Now accepting the futility of his mission, he resolved to leave Noakhali, "disgusted by myself," as he told Manu. "I even wonder whether I am really going to pass the test of my ahimsa."[47] A few days later Manu suggested that they stop sleeping together. Gandhi "readily agreed."[48]

On March 2, 1947, Gandhi left for Bihar, though Nehru and Kripalani urged him to come directly to Delhi for a Congress meeting and most Bihari Congress leaders wished he would leave their province alone. But he was determined, if possible, to find out how many Muslims had been murdered in the recent riots there. Reports were so widely conflicting that he found it hard to ascertain the exact number killed. Bihar's Congress government refused to appoint an impartial commission of inquiry, and Chief Minister Shrikrishna Sinha and Rajendra Prasad offered little help in answering his probing questions. "It was Bihar that made me known to the whole of India," Gandhi berated, reminding them of his Champaran inquiry so long ago. "This Bihar of ours has today committed a heinous crime. The atrocities perpetrated on a handful of Muslims have no parallel, so say the Muslims, in the annals of History. . . . We ought to overcome violence by love. . . . Are we going to compete in atom bomb? Are we going to match barbarism with even more barbarous acts?" Rather than do so, he argued, "India has placed before the world a new weapon."[49] That at least was his nonviolent hope, his fondest dream, to vanquish barbarism with Ahimsa.

Riots rocked Punjab following the resignation in March of its Hindu-Sikh-Muslim coalition ministry. The British governor proclaimed autocratic rule as the crowded bazaars of Lahore burned and mayhem spread across what was the richest wheat-producing province of India. Communal hatred and terrified cries of fear and pain rumbled louder all across north India, drowning out Gandhi's noble whispers of trust in love.

Gandhi wrote to Nehru to ask why the Working Committee of the Congress had passed a resolution on the "possible partition of the Punjab," which Kripalani was quoted as having said in Madras might also be "possible" in Bengal. Gandhi again informed Nehru of how adamantly he opposed any partition based on communal grounds and the two-nation theory. But as Gandhi had absented himself from the Working Committee meeting in Delhi, Nehru and Kripalani felt freed to ignore the old man, whose passions neither of those younger socialist modernists even pretended to understand. And the political situation kept deteriorating in every part of India. "Everyone is preparing openly for a fight and is busy collecting arms," Gandhi told his Patna prayer meeting on Pakistan Day. "If these preparations continued the peace established through the army or the police will . . . be the peace of the grave."[50]

Viceroy Lord Mountbatten invited Gandhi to meet with him in New Delhi at the end of March, and Gandhi agreed. Mountbatten asked Gandhi how to stop the rampant killing. Gandhi's answer was to "invite Jinnah to form a government of his choice at the centre and to present his Pakistan plan for acceptance even before the transfer of power. The Congress could give its whole-hearted support to the Jinnah Government."[51] Mountbatten was "staggered" by that suggestion, but when he later asked Nehru about it, Jawaharlal's response was totally negative. Old Bapu, Nehru insisted, had been away from New Delhi "too long" and was "out of touch."[52] "Whatever the Congress decides will be done; nothing will be according to what I say," Gandhi now realized, his depression deepening. "My writ runs no more. If it did the tragedies in the Punjab, Bihar and Noakhali would not have happened. No one listens to me any more. I am a small man."[53]

That evening, Gandhi tried to hold a prayer meeting in the garden of Valmiki Mandir, where he stayed, but when Manu began to recite the Muslim credo, an angry young Hindu rushed up to her, shouting "You go away from here. This is a Hindu temple!"[54] Gandhi told the intruder he was free to leave, but others wanted to pray. The young fanatic refused to be silenced, but he was not arrested. He belonged to the Hindu Mahasabha or *Rashtriya Swayamsevak Sangh* (R.S.S.) extremist Hindu group, one of whose followers would soon assassinate Gandhi. At another prayer meeting that week two well-dressed sturdy young Hindus rose to tell Gandhi to leave their temple. "This temple belongs to Bhangis [Harijan sweepers]," Gandhi replied. "I too am a Bhangi."[55] The arrogant toughs remained standing, however, shouting at him. Now others shouted that he should continue to pray. Gandhi tried to pray softly. "Go to the Punjab," someone shouted. Those standing near the angry man tried to force him out, but Gandhi urged patience, his Ahimsa now tried to its passionate limits. Then, wisely, he opted to leave the platform, sensing perhaps that his life was in danger. Still, Delhi's police took no notice, arresting none of the disrupters.

On April 3, 1947, Gandhi noted many more angry protestors and announced how "disturbed" he was to have learned "today" that those "persons obstructing prayers" belonged to a "big" organization, the R.S.S.[56] Gandhi still thought, however, that those zealous Hindu fanatics "love me," refusing to recognize the fact that many former Brahman admirers had lost respect for him. Some thirty young goondas now told him to go to "your room" if he wished to pray there. Then police hustled the thugs out of the temple, but Gandhi was not ready to resume prayers. His blood pressure had shot up again. "May God be kind to all and grant independence to India," he prayed, quickly leaving the platform.

Gandhi now talked with Punjab Hindu refugees, who urged him to visit the Punjab. "It is more valiant to get killed than to kill," Gandhi told them.[57] He counseled all refugees to return to their homes and nonviolently accept death if they could not convert their attackers with the silent power of their passionate suffering and Ahimsa.

Whenever he met with Mountbatten, Gandhi reiterated his "scheme" about inviting Jinnah to take Nehru's job as the "best solution" for India's problems. But Mountbatten liked and trusted Nehru more than Jinnah. The viceroy was too naïve about India to appreciate the wisdom of Gandhi's idea, and Nehru was too fond of power to surrender it so soon after grasping the golden ring of prime minister-in-waiting.

By April 1947, Gandhi understood that neither Nehru nor Mountbatten had the slightest intention of accepting his Jinnah plan to avoid partition. "He regretted his failure very much," Mountbatten noted in his top secret minutes of their final meeting. Gandhi also received many angry letters in Delhi, mostly accusing him of being "subservient" to Jinnah or a "fifth-columnist" or "communist."[58] One envelope addressed him as "Mahmud Gandhi," another as "Jinnah's slave." Nehru encouraged him to visit Punjab. He was also invited back to Noakhali by Hindu friends, who feared further violence there.

Disappointed not to be asked to stay in Delhi by Mountbatten, Gandhi headed back to Bihar on April 13. "I worship the *Gita*. The *Gita* ordains that one should perform one's own duty," he commented. Better "death in the discharge of one's own duty" the *Gita* taught; attempting to carry out "another's function" was "fraught with danger."[59] Hence, Gandhi concluded that staying in a place like Delhi, which was another's domain, would for him be both dangerous and frustrating. Unfortunately, later that year he would forget that wise scriptural warning.

Many Biharis asked why he did not go to Punjab, where countless fires raged and the riots had recently intensified, instead of returning to now peaceful Patna. His "inner voice," Gandhi told them, had ordered him to return to Bihar and to Noakhali. He received mostly "abusive letters" now, few admiring ones, and fewer seeking his advice. He kept calling for public exposure of Hindu criminals and an end to the conspiracy of official silence, urging Suhrawardy to tell everything that happened in the killings in Calcutta. He talked of another possible fast. "I cannot take poison nor hang or shoot myself. I can end my life only by fasting."[60] He no longer hoped to live to 125.

Gandhi was sensitive and wise enough to know that many of those around him had now stopped listening to his once universally respected advice. "Is my thinking out of tune with the times?"[61] he asked Saraladevi Sarabhai, whose sister-in-law had helped him in Ahmedabad's strike over thirty years before. To Muslim leaders in Bihar, he confessed: "I no longer command the same influence as I used to. . . . If I had been a minister, perhaps, I too would have acted similarly."[62] He knew how long it had taken before Nehru agreed to see him in Delhi, and how little of the prime minister's precious time could be spent on him. He had only one weapon left. But he wasn't ready to use it.

In New Delhi, Lord Mountbatten was daily briefed by Krishna Menon on Nehru's views as to remaining within the Commonwealth as well as accepting partition, and by the end of April Mountbatten and Nehru were in virtual agreement. Congress was to meet in Delhi in early May, and Gandhi agreed to return for that meeting from Patna. He reached Valmiki Mandir on May 1. "I am a prisoner of Jawaharlal and the Sardar [Patel]," Gandhi told Rajendra Prasad, who walked with him on May 2. "If they release me I would like to leave by the first available train."[63] That afternoon his prayer meeting was stopped by a Hindu thug shouting: "Victory to Hinduism."[64] Gandhi urged him to calm down, and then police dragged the antagonist away. Gandhi confessed that day that he wanted no "swaraj" if the British would only give it with partition.

Nehru told him that that was "Mountbatten's Plan," not daring to admit as yet that he and Krishna Menon had agreed. Gandhi warned: "Remember, if you divide India today, tomorrow. . . . [w]e might escape its consequences because we are on the brink of death but generations to come will curse us at every step for the kind of swaraj we shall have bequeathed to them."[65] He alone accurately anticipated the tragic aftermath of partition and its murderous legacy of more than half a century of Indo-Pakistani wars and hatred.

The more Gandhi saw of Delhi with its tide of war-weary hungry refugees, the more he heard of the fires raging all over Punjab, the more passionately depressed he became. On May 4 he told Rajendra Prasad that "what we regarded as non-violent fight was not really so. . . . Had we followed the path of truth and non-violence we would not have seen human hearts so devoid of humanity."[66]

Before leaving Delhi for Calcutta on May 8, Gandhi went to speak with Jinnah possibly to ask him if he would take the premiership of united India. "I cannot tell you everything that took place between us," Gandhi told his last prayer meeting in Delhi. "Let me tell you that everyone had tried to stop me from going to Jinnah Saheb. They asked me what I would gain by going to him. But did I go to him to gain anything? I went to him to know his mind. . . . I claim to have his friendship. After all he also belongs to India. Whatever happens, I have to spend my life with him. . . . We shall have to live in amity."[67] Whether or not he now told his old friend Jinnah of the brilliant "scheme" he had pressed in vain on Mountbatten, Gandhi had the courage to ignore Nehru's strong negative advice and met with Jinnah, in what proved to be their final meeting. Jinnah was almost as near the end of his life as was Gandhi. He too had one dream. Gandhi's was to save his Mother India from death by vivisection. Jinnah's was to bring his child, Pakistan, to birth by India's partition.

On the train to Calcutta, Gandhi wrote Mountbatten, continuing to warn him that "it would be a blunder of the first magnitude for the British to be a party in any way whatsoever to the division of India."[68] He felt particularly "sure the partition of the Punjab and Bengal" would prove to be "a needless irritant." He was quite prescient, almost clairvoyant in seeing the horror and tragedy bound to ensue from the partitioning of Punjab and Bengal. But Mountbatten's mind was made up. His marching orders in London had been to wrap up Britain's withdrawal from India by no later than June of 1948. Soon after landing in Delhi he had resolved to finish the job ten months earlier. With the help of Krishna Menon, Nehru, and his wife Edwina, Mountbatten managed to advance the deadline to mid-August 1947.

The Sikh minority of Punjab feared being under Muslim rule in Pakistan, yet could win no promise of their own *Sikhistan* from either Britain or India; however, the bloody implications of partitioning Punjab through the heart of this minority were recognized too late by Nehru to stop the British express. Jinnah was almost as shocked as Gandhi at the prospects of partitioning Muslim-majority Bengal as well as Punjab, but he too was powerless to halt Mountbatten's partition juggernaut that crushed a million lives under its wheels. In mid-May, Mountbatten flew to London to reassure Attlee, Cripps, and the new secretary of state for India, Lord Listowel, of the urgency of partition. He also visited the ailing Churchill, bringing back his last personal message to Jinnah: "[A]ccept this offer with both hands."[69] Mountbattan had tea in London with Krishna Menon, bearing Jawaharlal's surgical prescription for India's communal civil war. To "get rid of that headache," Nehru agreed to "cut off" India's head.[70] He accepted partition and Pakistan, urging Mountbatten to finish that surgery without delay, wanting no further discussions of it with Jinnah.

Gandhi reached Calcutta on May 10. The next day he met with Suhrawardy, who told Bapu of his dream of a united sovereign Bengal. Mountbatten had refused to consider Suhrawardy's plan, rejecting it without reference to London's Cabinet. Nor would Quaid-i-Azam Jinnah ever take the aspirations of Bangladeshi nationalists seriously. In Calcutta, Gandhi sought to reach an agreement with Suhrawardy that could save Bengal the terrors of partition. "If the Muslims believe that they can take things by force they will have nothing at all," Gandhi warned the chief minister, who came to call on May 12, 1947. "But, by peaceful means, they may have the entire country."[71] Suhrawardy confessed that his "chief obstacle" was that no Calcutta Hindus listened to him, though his proposals were "utterly sincere." Gandhi then offered to move into his house and serve as his "secretary." Suhrawardy was dumbstruck by the offer and left.

Nirmal Bose, who walked the chief minister to his car, heard Suhrawardy mutter, "What a mad offer! I have to think ten times before I can fathom its implications."[72] Then Gandhi wrote him: "If you would retain Bengal for the Bengalis-Hindus or Mussalmans—intact by non-violent means I am quite willing to act as your honorary private secretary and live under your roof till Hindus and Muslims begin to live as [the] brothers that they are."[73] He passionately resolved once again to "Do or die!" insisting: "I wish to die in harness, with the name of Rama on my lips. My faith in this *yajna* [sacrifice] is growing so strong that I feel God will grant me this wish. I am the lone adherent of my views today. But Gurudev's [Tagore's] *Ekla Chalore* ["Walk Alone"] sustains me. That is why I do not feel lonely and God gives me the courage to put up a determined fight with many of my friends."[74] So he walked on alone with God as his guide, the suffocating heat of Calcutta's summer a cool prelude to partition.

23

Freedom's Wooden Loaf

"WHY SHOULD a third party intervene in a dispute between us brothers?" Gandhi asked his Congress friends after returning at their behest to Delhi in late May of 1947. "This Viceroy is a very intelligent man. He will displease no party and still have his own way." Mountbatten, Gandhi warned, was "an unknown friend," much more "dangerous to us" than "known enemies" like his viceregal precursors, Lords Linlithgow and Wavell, "for we knew what their policy was."[1] He was asked by his followers in Delhi why Congress was ready to agree to partition, when he said it would be the worst possible thing. "Who listens to me today?" Gandhi replied. "I am being told to retire to the Himalayas. Everybody is eager to garland my photos and statues. Nobody really wants to follow my advice." Partition would destroy India, he passionately argued. "The prospect of power has demoralized us."[2]

Nehru and Patel told Gandhi "that my reading of the situation is wrong and peace is sure to return if partition is agreed upon."[3] He sensed they feared that he had "deteriorated with age." He remained certain, however, of the monstrous tragedy awaiting them all on that mine-strewn road of division. "Let not the coming generations curse Gandhi for being a party to India's vivisection." Independence with partition, Gandhi warned, would be "like eating wooden *laddoos*, if they eat they die of colic; if they don't they starve."[4]

"I have described Jawaharlal as the uncrowned king," Gandhi told his prayer meeting on June 3. Yet India remained "a poor nation," so poor, as he put it, that its elected leaders should walk rather than ride in cars. "One who lives in a palace cannot rule the Government."[5] He said it directly to

Nehru as well, every time they met, urging him and Patel to turn New Delhi's palatial homes and grand office buildings into hostels for homeless refugees, moving themselves into Harijan quarters, such as he occupied, or peasant huts. But none of Delhi's rulers listened any longer to the "ravings" of an old "fool," though not so long before most of them had considered him a "saint." "Corruption is rampant among the civil servants," Gandhi charged, and ministers of state were "surrounded by wicked persons whom they are not able to control," all of which left inadequate food supplies for the starving, no housing for naked refugees, and violence and "rot" throughout Delhi. Some old friends, seeing how disgusted and distressed Gandhi was, urged him to launch Satyagraha against Nehru's Raj, but he refused to lead any mass movement against the Congress he once resurrected and long led. "I would not carry on any agitation against that institution."6

He continued to be challenged at prayer meetings, urged to leave Delhi, to retreat as a true Sadhu (wise man) should to any cave in the Himalayas. He still hoped with the sublimated powers of his sexual restraint to prevail in his last valiant sacrificial effort to save Mother India from vivisection. "A perfect *brahmachari* never loses his vital fluid," Gandhi explained, reiterating ancient Hindu yogic philosophical faith in the magic powers of male seminal "golden" fluids, life-prolonging as well as life-generating, allowing him to "never become old in the accepted sense. . . . [I]ntellect will never be dimmed."7

Gandhi felt that nothing he told Nehru was now acceptable to his former political disciple. "The more I contemplate the differences in outlook and opinion between the members of the W. C. and me," he wrote Jawaharlal, "I feel that my presence is unnecessary even if it is not detrimental to the cause we all have at heart. May I not go back to Bihar in two or three days."8 As the death tolls mounted east and west of Delhi his sense of failure intensified. "There is no miracle except love and non-violence which can drive out the poison of hatred," Gandhi told all pilgrims who attended his evening prayer meetings. "I have faith that in time to come India will pit that against the threat of destruction which the world has invited upon itself by the invention of the atom bomb."9

To Mira, far away in her ashram in Uttarkashi, he regretfully wrote that "mine is a voice in the wilderness. Or could it be that I am growing too old and therefore losing my grip over things?"10 To beloved Manu, he admitted, "If I did not feel unhappy I would be a person with a heart of stone."11 Abha joined them in Delhi that July, though she, like Manu, had been quite sick. Gandhi loved to nurse his "daughters" back to health, administering mud-packs and enema nature cures himself, precisely monitoring their daily diets and hours of sleep. Despite his loving care, however, Manu ran so high a fever from appendicitis that he finally agreed to allow surgery, which saved her life, even as it had his own. Surrender to surgical aid, however, always left him feeling "defeated," impotent, and angry. He castigated himself for still getting so angry as to "scold" Manu. "He who has conquered anger has achieved a great victory in life."[12]

The Indian Independence Act passed through Britain's Parliament on July 17, 1947. It authorized the partition of British India along boundary lines to be drawn by a commission of Hindu and Muslim jurists, chaired by Sir Cyril Radcliffe, a London barrister. Radcliffe had never seen India before and would never dare to return there after carving out two new borders, one through the middle of Punjab, the other through the heart of Bengal. Mountbatten asked Gandhi to undertake a mission to Kashmir, which Nehru was so eager to do himself that the viceroy and Patel feared their impulsive prime minister would get arrested by yelling at the Maharaja of Kashmir before he officially took charge of India's dominion in New Delhi. Gandhi could not refuse a request to undertake a mission from the viceroy as well as from Princely States' Minister Sardar Patel. His doctors advised Gandhi not to take sick Manu along, but he felt certain that Kashmir's cool climate would "benefit her," as would close proximity to himself. "Even in her sleep she is often heard muttering, beseeching me not to leave her behind. . . . How then can I leave her here."[13] So they went up together in early August, Gandhi determined to head directly east again after completing his delicate mission in Srinagar to try to convince the Maharaja of Kashmir to accede to India, and first to release Sheikh Abdullah from prison. He failed on both points.

"I am not going to suggest to the Maharaja to accede to India and not to Pakistan," Gandhi wisely announced on the eve of leaving for Srinagar. Kashmir's procrastinating Hindu Maharaja Hari Singh could not make up his mind about whether to join India, whose radical leaders, though Hindu, he feared, or Pakistan in which most of his predominantly Muslim populace would have felt far more at home. "The real sovereign of the State are the people of the State. If the ruler is not a servant of the people then he is not the ruler."[14] Gandhi's conviction was that "now the power belongs to the people," and therefore, "The people of Kashmir should be asked whether they want to join Pakistan or India. Let them do as they want. The ruler is nothing. The people are everything."[15] How many lives would have been saved by India and Pakistan and most of all by the people of Kashmir, if only Nehru had been wise enough to listen to the man he once had considered his political guru. Had independent India the courage to endorse Gandhi's faith in self-determination for Jammu and Kashmir State, it should have agreed to hold a plebiscite there immediately, rather than fighting futile wars over the next half century without reaching any agreement with Pakistan as to the fate of Kashmir's long-suffering people.

From Kashmir, Gandhi and Manu left by train for Calcutta, via Lahore and Patna. At Lahore station he was greeted by Congress workers, who asked when he would come to stay there. "The rest of my life is going to be spent in Pakistan," Gandhi promised, "maybe in East Bengal or West Punjab, or perhaps, the North-West Frontier Province."[16] But he could not stop just yet, rushing on to keep promises to Noakhali to return before August 15. To him "the whole of India" remained his country, for, as he told Bihar's university students in Patna two days later, he could not reconcile himself "to the idea of partition. . . . He wanted to live both in Hindustan and Pakistan. . . . [B]oth were his homelands."[17] He urged everyone who heard him now to join him in a fast on August 15. "We do not have food grains, clothes, ghee or oil. So where is the need for celebrations? On that day we have to fast, ply the *charkha* [spinning wheel] and pray to God."

Gandhi reached Calcutta on Sunday, August 10. He had planned to move on to Noakhali the next morning, but "many Muslim friends" pleaded with him to stay, fearing renewed attacks by Hindu mobs as that premier city of Clive, Kipling, and Curzon was about to begin its much diminished incarnation as the mere capital of partitioned West Bengal. Calcutta's former Muslim majority had by then fallen precipitously to under a quarter of its multimillion population. That Monday evening, August 11, Suhrawardy came to add his voice to the moving appeals of West Bengal's other Muslim leaders. "I would remain if you and I are prepared to live together," Gandhi challenged his old friend. "We shall have to work till every Hindu and Mussalman in Calcutta safely returns to the place where he was before."[18] This time Suhrawardy agreed. Then they moved into abandoned old Hydari House, symbolizing by their courageous cohabitation the spirit of Hindu-Muslim unity that had so long eluded civil war-torn South Asia.

"I am stuck here and now I am going to take a big risk," Bapu wrote Brother Vallabh, alerting Sardar Patel to the dangerous move he had made on the eve of independence. "Keep a watch. I will keep on writing."[19] To add to their personal dangers from renewed communal conflict, drought now threatened the entire subcontinent. Monsoon rains, which should have started in June, were as yet nowhere to be seen in the Bay of Bengal's cloudless sky that hottest of all Indian summers. Terrified Hindu and Sikh refugees now marched over the dust-choked plains of Punjab toward Delhi in lines that soon were to stretch as long as a hundred miles.

"Suhrawardy and I are living together in a Muslim manzil in Beliaghata," Gandhi reported the day after Nehru delivered his famous midnight "Tryst with Destiny" speech in the packed central hall of New Delhi's Parliament, through which Bapu had slept. "We end today a period of ill fortune and India discovers herself again," Prime Minister Nehru told his national audience. "The future is not one of ease or resting but of incessant striving so that we might fulfill the pledges we have so often taken. . . . The service of India means the service of the millions who suffer. It means the ending of poverty and ignorance and disease and inequality of opportunity. The ambition of the greatest man of our generation has been to wipe every tear from every eye. That may be beyond us."[20] Then Nehru and Rajendra Prasad went over to the palace of Britain's last governor-general, Lord Mountbatten, to invite him to stay on as India's first governor-general. "At this historic moment, let us not forget all that India owes to Mahatma Gandhi—the architect of our freedom through non-violence," Mountbatten graciously told them, accepting the position he never offered to Gandhi himself, as first head of independent India's dominion, adding, "We miss his presence here today."[21]

That same day in Calcutta's old Hydari House, Gandhi noted, "Here in the compound numberless Hindus and Muslims continue to stream in shouting their favourite slogans."[22] Gandhi was encouraged by the loving enthusiasm of all those Bengalis, Hindu and Muslim, who came to cheer him and free India. "We have drunk the poison of mutual hatred and so this nectar of fraternization tastes all the sweeter and the sweetness should never wear out."[23]

A week later, Nehru wired, asking him to bring his "healing presence" to the Punjab, which was burning with communal hatred, the stench of rotting corpses left in bazaars overpowering the sweet smells of Lahore's long-fabled gardens. "Punjabis in Calcutta . . . tell me a terrible story," he replied to Jawaharlal. "Thousands have been killed. A few thousand girls have been kidnapped! Hindus cannot live in the Pakistan area, nor Muslims in the other. . . . Can any of this be true?"[24] Much worse was yet to come. The toxic fallout of partition had only begun to poison all of South Asia. "How can I choose where to go?" frail old Gandhi cried aloud, as he read so many desperate wires, all urgently appealing for his help.

Mountbatten tried to cheer him with royal flattery. "In the Punjab we have 55 thousand soldiers and large-scale rioting on our hands. In Bengal our forces consist of one man, and there is no rioting," Mountbatten wrote. "May I be allowed to pay my tribute to the One-man Boundary Force, not forgetting his Second in Command, Mr. Suhrawardy."[25] Gandhi rightly suspected that the "miracle" he'd wrought would not last long. Violence struck home on the night of August 31. Fortunately for Suhrawardy, he had returned to live in his own secure house that evening, feeling as proud as Gandhi did of their peace effort. Gandhi was asleep when the angry Hindu mob attacked Hydari House shortly before midnight. They shouted and tossed brickbats through its windows, broke open the compound gate, and battered on the front door. Manu and Abha could not silence them, nor could any of the Muslim servants or the police outside. The mob insisted on seeing Suhrawardy, claiming that Muslims stabbed their friends that night in Machhva Bazaar, bearing a bleeding body with them.

"I was in bed," Bapu wrote Brother Vallabh. "I . . . got up. . . . I went to face the crowd but the girls would not leave my side. . . . Glass windows were being broken and they started smashing the doors."[26] None of the angry mob would listen to him. Bricks were thrown, but when the police superintendent arrived, the "youngsters dispersed."

The next day, Gandhi decided to fast. He took water, however, without which he would have died in Calcutta's heat wave in just a few days. "What was regarded as a miracle has proved a short-lived nine-day wonder," he informed Patel. "Rajaji [C. R., now governor of Bengal] called at night. He admonished me a lot, tried hard to persuade me not to go on a fast."[27] Gandhi could not be dissuaded, however, from a course of action he considered divinely inspired. He always listened to his inner voice and promised to stop fasting only after the riots stopped. "If the riots continue what will I do by merely being alive? What is the use of my living? If I lack even the power to pacify the people, what else is left for me to do?"[28] Suhrawardy, Sarat Bose, Bengal's Hindu Mahasabha leader Debendra Nath Mukerjee, and many other Calcutta politicians came to his bedside, pleading with him to stay alive, promising to do nothing more violent, praying, cajoling, and trying to lure him back from the release he now so passionately sought.

On September 4 at 9.15 P.M. he drank a glass of diluted orange juice, after telling those crowded into his bedroom: "I am breaking this fast so that I might be able to do something for the Punjab. I am doing so at your assurance and . . . I expect that the Hindus and Muslims here will not force me to undertake a fast again."[29] To the apologetic young men, who bowed silently before him, Gandhi said: "Act as peace squads without arms."[30] To those who requested a message from him for their "Peace Army Party" (*Shanti Sena Dal*) he said: "My life is my message." On September 7, 1947, he entrained for Delhi, eager to move on to Punjab.

24

Great Soul's Death in Delhi

"I KNEW NOTHING about the sad state of things in Delhi when I left Calcutta," Gandhi confessed after returning to India's capital on September 9, 1947. He had heard so many stories of Delhi tragedies that day to resolve that "I must not leave Delhi for the Punjab until it had regained its former self."[1] Hindu and Sikh refugees from West Punjab brought with them tales of such horror and woe that Delhi itself turned into a killing field against Muslims, whose families had lived there in peace for centuries. "Retaliation is no remedy," Gandhi warned. "It makes the original disease much worse."

Sardar Patel and Rajkumari Amrit were waiting with several Cabinet ministers and thousands of others to greet him at old Delhi's jammed Shahadara Station. "After alighting from the train I found . . . others equally sad. Has the city of Delhi which always appeared gay turned into a city of the dead?"[2] Gandhi wondered, as he was driven from the station around the old city. He saw tens of thousands of squatters on the roads and in crowded dark alleys and heard horror stories in Delhi's Muslim university, the Jamia Millia. Its vice-chancellor, Dr. Zakir Hussain, who became India's first Muslim president a quarter century later, told of how he was almost murdered in Punjab. Gandhi lowered his head in "shame" as he listened to such reports. Then he went to where Hindu and Sikh refugees stayed and heard of the murders of their families by Muslims in Punjab. "They asked me how I could comfort them. . . . I would like to tell the refugees that they should live truthfully and without fear . . . not entertain any thoughts of revenge or hatred [nor] throw away the golden apple of freedom won at a great cost."[3] So Gandhi tried in Delhi what he had done in

Calcutta and before that in Bihar, appealing openly, equally to Hindus and Muslims and Sikhs, urging each to love the others and to abandon arms.

He had intended to move back to the old temple near Delhi's Harijan Bhangi quarters, but Nehru and Patel wouldn't hear of it, and Birla insisted he return to his own walled home in the safest part of New Delhi. Birla House had a large garden just behind Gandhi's bedroom and enclosed rear porch, where several hundreds could gather each evening to hear his prayers. The argument that finally convinced Gandhi to accept such elegant hospitality was that the Harijan temple was needed for Punjabi refugees. Bapu did not want to have them ordered out to make room for him.

On September 16, when Gandhi's prayer meeting opened with Abha reading from the Quran, an angry young man in the audience rose to shout: "To the recitation of these verses, our mothers and sisters were dishonoured, our dear ones killed. We will not let you recite these verses here." Someone else shouted: "Gandhi *murdabad* (death to Gandhi)."[4] The meeting had to be abandoned, and Gandhi returned with the help of his beloved walking-sticks to the enclosed rear porch of Birla House. He tried not to show his frustration at having once again failed to teach love and non-violence to the hate-crazed Hindu refugees from Punjab flooding daily into Delhi.

"Today we have all lost our senses, we have become stupid," Gandhi told those who gathered next evening to see him. "It is not only the Sikhs have gone mad, or only the Hindus or the Muslims. . . . India is today in the plight of the [sinking] elephant king. I want to rescue it if I can. What should I do?"[5] He wanted to go to Pakistan, prepared to die trying to save all Hindus and Sikhs there. He never spoke again of wanting to live 125 years. "When one's efforts do not bring forth results, one must dry up like a tree which does not bear fruits."[6]

Trains full of Hindu and Sikh corpses kept coming from Pakistan. In the opposite direction rolled other trains choked with the bodies of Muslims trying to flee retaliatory slaughter. Amritsar station was turned into a crematorium, the station of Lahore a cemetery. The death toll mounted so swiftly that no one could keep precise count of the butchery, but before year's end, hundreds of thousands of Hindu-Sikh corpses rolled east, almost the same number of murdered Muslims moving west. No Punjab train would be cleaned that year of its stench of rotting flesh. "Have they all been possessed by some madness now after freedom?" Gandhi cried. "Shall we throw away in our intoxication that freedom which has come after so many sacrifices? How shameful it is!"[7]

Yet even now, depressed, tired, disgusted, and frustrated as he was by everything he saw, read, and heard, Gandhi did not abandon his passionate hope that somehow this madness could be stopped. His answer was simple. "We must purify ourselves . . . [by] being courageous. A person who can be courageous would not indulge in such activities. You have the support of your Government," he told all who listened to him, reminding them that the British were gone. Now a Congress government ruled New Delhi, and they must have the courage to save India by feeding its hungry, protecting its minorities, and teaching its children to love one another. But few listened now to this frail old Mahatma. His words were either ignored in New Delhi's corridors of power or served to confirm growing feelings that he should make his final pilgrimage to the Himalayas to pray in silence there. "We must abandon the idea of taking revenge on the Muslims,"[8] he told them. Hindu fanatics now started to call him "Muhammad" Gandhi. "There is a fire raging in Delhi," he said the next day. "Every place is burning. It is our duty to extinguish that fire, pour water over it . . . the glorious land that was India has become a cremation-ground today."[9]

Gandhi found it impossible to pray in Birla's garden on most evenings, since in response to his initial question whether anybody objected to a recitation from the Quran, at least one or two hands were raised. So he spoke instead and told of the latest atrocities, which included abductions as well as arson and murder. He also read about Churchill's most recently reported speech on India's "fearful massacres," which, Churchill insisted, came as "no surprise to me." He smugly contrasted India's current "butcheries," perpetrated by "races" he called "cannibals" to the previous era of "general peace" credited to the "British Crown."[10] Gandhi reminded his audience that "the vivisection of India" was as much Britain's "gift" as was "freedom." He rightly advised Churchill to be more careful about apportioning blame and urged him to review and study "the situation" without prejudice.[11] In the very spirit of fairness, two days later, Gandhi told his own government to "look after its people or resign. . . . [O]ur Government is something which we can strengthen or bring down. That is democracy."[12] That could hardly have cheered Nehru or Patel. Bapu had turned into their most passionate, harshest critic.

Gandhi caught the flu but did not stop talking, praying, or seeking to make Delhi a safer, more civilized city. On October 2, 1947, to celebrate his seventy-eighth birthday, Gandhi fasted. "I am surprised and also ashamed that I am still alive," he said, adding that "today nobody listens to me." He told friends who came to celebrate his birth that "if there is any anger in your hearts you must remove it."[13]

But the violence all across South Asia continued to escalate. Sikhs in India's Patiala State now murdered most of the Muslims who had lived there. "What brutalities are going on! What a sequel to Pakistan! People are trying to see that there is no Hindu left in Pakistan and no Muslim in Hindustan," Gandhi groaned as he heard that shocking news.[14] He still hoped, with God's help, to contain the mad hatred he saw in Delhi and tried to hold one more summit with Jinnah.

Though he never sought conventional power or any job in India's government, Gandhi had waited within earshot of Nehru and Patel, hoping that they might invite him to replace Lord Mountbatten. It seemed gallingly inappropriate to Gandhi for this British royal naval person to remain the ceremonial head of independent India. Now that the cameras had stopped rolling at all the ceremonial speeches and changing of the flags, now that virtually all Britain's troops had sailed home, it was surely time for India to have its own Indian governor-general head of state, which Gandhi knew he deserved to be. He had playfully suggested several times that a "Harijan girl" would be India's "best" president, yet each time he said that he added how happy he would be to serve as her unpaid "advisor" or secretary. Those who understood Gandhi knew why he said that, and also why he now bemoaned the fact that no one *listened* to him any longer. What to Gandhi must have been doubly galling, moreover, was that Jinnah had taken over as Pakistan's governor-general from his nation's birth, refusing to acquiesce to Mountbatten's vain attempts to persuade him that *he* be permitted to serve both dominions jointly as supreme governor-general. Were Gandhi India's governor-general now he could easily have launched another summit with his old friend Jinnah. Together they might have been able to agree on a formula to stop the slaughter—Gandhi's most passionate aspiration.

"If we wish to bring about the rule of God or *Ramarajya* in India, I would suggest that our first task is to magnify our own faults and find no fault with the Muslims," Gandhi announced to his prayer meeting two weeks after his birthday and one week before the first Indo-Pak War over Kashmir started. "I do not say that the Muslims have done no wrong. They have caused a lot of harm. . . . But . . . If I start thinking about those wrongs, I shall go crazy and I shall not be able to serve India. What if I begin to think that I have no enemies and expose my own faults before the world and close my eyes to those of others?"[15] Gandhi had met with Mountbatten earlier that day and after asking him about the "situation" in Delhi, "I had to hang my head in shame. For, even now, the Hindus and the Muslims are not one at heart. . . . Today my wings are clipped. If I could grow my wings again, I would fly to Pakistan."[16]

Mountbatten had sense enough to realize that Gandhi truly deserved the job he retained as the historic hangover of his previous position as viceroy. And Mountbatten was keen to go back to command his fleet at sea. He had, after all, completed the mission Attlee had given him, withdrawing British forces from India without losing a man and transferring Britain's sovereignty to two dominions. Time for him to move on. Delhi was much too hot and dry. So Mountbatten was quite ready to let the old man, whom he never really understood but who had done rather well in keeping Calcutta more or less calm, take over as India's governor-general. Every Indian spoke of him as "Father" of the nation, after all, so why not let him end his life as its head of state? But Nehru, who had come to look up to Mountbatten for martial advice and strategic support as well as assistance in dealing with many delicate problems of state, rejected the idea of having Gandhi as his governor-general even more vehemently than he'd vetoed Gandhi's Jinnah "scheme" a year earlier.

Nehru never forgot that Gandhi believed Jinnah would have been a better prime minister of India than he was. With so many horrors of partition now grotesquely revealed, Nehru knew Bapu had been right, after all. So, less than a week after Mountbatten met with Gandhi and told him of his "desire to retire from the Governor-Generalship of India," Gandhi wrote him the most painful "Dear Friend" letter of his life: "I have spoken to Pandit Nehru. But he is adamant. He is firmly of [the] opinion that no change should be made until the weather has cleared. If it does, it may take two or three months."[17] The "weather" was the havoc wrought by partition's hurricane and the chaos left strewn across north India by tornadoes of intolerance. That would take more than "three months" to "clear," but three months was now all Gandhi had left. There would be no further summit with Jinnah, no flight to Pakistan, no governor-general Gandhi.

In late October, fighting started over the Muslim-majority state of Jammu and Kashmir, whose Hindu Maharaja, Hari Singh, refused to join either India or Pakistan. "I am aware of what is happening in Kashmir," Gandhi told his prayer meeting on October 26. "But I know only what has appeared in the newspapers." India's press reported that three days earlier several thousand Afridi Pathan tribals of the North-West Frontier had invaded Kashmir State and "indulged in large-scale loot, arson and murder."[18] It was also reported that Pakistan was trying to "coerce Kashmir" into joining the Dominion of Pakistan. "This should not be so," Gandhi insisted. "It is not possible to take anything from anyone by force." While no one should be forced into anything, however, he repeated what he had said before, that Kashmir's "real rulers" were its people, not its Maharaja. "If the people of Kashmir are in favour of opting for Pakistan, no power on earth can stop them from doing so. But they should be left free to decide for themselves."[19] True democrat that he was, Gandhi favored self-determination for Kashmir as much as he had for India, but he always remained opposed to violent coercion by any power. Nehru had clipped Gandhi's wings, however, and in all questions concerning India's Kashmir policy, Pandit Nehru listened to no one. Though his Brahman ancestors had left Jammu and Kashmir State more than a century before he was born, Jawaharlal Nehru romantically identified himself as "Kashmiri" and resolved never to surrender that state to Pakistan, no matter how high the price India might have to pay for its retention.

"It would be a tragedy, so far as I am concerned, if Kashmir went to

Pakistan," Nehru warned his colleagues. On October 25 he cabled Attlee that "a grave situation has developed" in the state, arguing that India might have to send aid, to help restore its "internal tranquility." He promised that such aid "in this emergency is not designed in any way to influence the State to accede to India." That question, Nehru declared, "must be decided in accordance with wishes of the people."[20] Less than a day later, Nehru and Mountbatten launched India's largest airlift. More than one hundred Indian planes took off from Delhi and neighboring airports, packed with Sikh soldiers carrying enough armor and ammunition to secure Srinagar and its airport from advancing Muslim tribals. Kashmir was to become the primary major preoccupation of India's central government for the next three months. Not only did it take up most of Nehru's and Mountbatten's time but it preempted all of India's air transport and virtually all of its fuel, arms, and martial supplies, flown round the clock, weather permitting, up to Srinagar, capital of India's only Muslim-majority state, with a total population less than 1 percent of India's. "The trouble in Kashmir has been thrust upon us and yet it may well be the saving of us in many ways," Nehru told his generals. "It may go a long way in settling our problem with Pakistan."[21] To anxious Attlee, who kept wiring Mountbatten asking what Dominion India was doing and why, Nehru cabled: "Our military intervention is purely defensive in aim and scope, in no way affecting any future decision about accession that might be taken by the people of Kashmir."

Jinnah angrily accused Nehru and India of trying to steal Kashmir from its rightful place in Pakistan by "fraud and violence."[22] Mountbatten had promised Jinnah to fly with Nehru to Lahore to negotiate a cease-fire and a settlement on Kashmir, but Nehru pretended to be sick on the eve of their flight, so Mountbatten had to go alone to confer with Pakistan's governor-general, who was in fact by then fatally ill.

"I hope that soon our troops will take the offensive," Nehru wrote aggressively to prod his officers in Kashmir. "This has been done at tremendous cost to us and holding up most of our other activities in India. All our air services have stopped and every available plane is going to Kashmir. . . . I see no reason why any of you should go to Lahore to confer with Mr. Jinnah. . . . There is very little to discuss. . . . It is obvious that a plebiscite cannot take place till complete law and order have been established. I see no chance of this happening."[23] Nehru had agreed to the plebiscite only at Mountbatten's insistence and to placate Attlee, since India was, after all, engaged in undeclared war with a fellow dominion of the British Commonwealth. But Nehru was determined to win his war in Kashmir at any price. He even turned now against his once dear "friend," Sheikh Abdullah, whom he had placed on Srinagar's throne as prime minister, when that Lion of Kashmir wanted to fly to Pakistan in order to negotiate with Jinnah. "All dealings with Pakistan, should be through the Indian Union," Nehru warned him. "Any direct contacts should be avoided." Nehru regularly flew to Kashmir to rally his troops in Srinagar: "I am proud of you. . . . You have not only saved Kashmir, you have also restored the prestige of India, your mother country."[24]

Gandhi knew how hollow Nehru's boasting was. When asked on November 5 why, though he always advised the British to "follow the path of non-violence," he did not now similarly advise India's government, Gandhi answered: "No one listens to me. . . . I have never abandoned my non-violence. . . . if I could have my way of non-violence and everybody listened to me, we would not send our army as we are doing now. And if we did send, it would be a non-violent army."[25] Gandhi was ready to lead such a peace army even now, as he told his prayer meeting: "I could myself go with a non-violent army to Kashmir or Pakistan or any place."[26] Militant Nehru feared that, of course, which was why he adamantly refused to allow this Mahatma to become India's head of state. "But when can I hope for such an occasion?" Bapu cried, bowing his bald head, closing his weary eyes as he continued softly, "Today I am helpless. . . . Today I have become bankrupt. I have no say with my people today. What I said in the past has no value."[27] Never had his feelings of impotent passionate despair been so palpable; nonetheless, he insisted: "I make bold to say that in this age of the atom bomb, unadulterated non-violence is the only force that can confound all the tricks put together of violence."[28]

Daily, Gandhi spoke out against the "way things are going" in India, especially bemoaning "the explosion of violence and the disappearance of human kindness," and at every Cabinet meeting Nehru and Patel clashed, often arguing angrily. Vallabhbhai felt so frustrated and depressed that he asked Gandhi's "permission" to resign, finding it more and more difficult to carry on as deputy of a prime minister who rarely listened to him and for whom he no longer had much respect. They had never been intimate friends, but now they barely spoke without snapping at each other. Gandhi advised them both to stop squabbling and to get on with more important national work, though if it were not possible for them to serve together in harmony then either Patel or Nehru should quit the Cabinet. He had no illusions, of course, about the efficacy of such sensible advice: "Not that what I say will be of any avail."[29]

The Congress Working Committee met in New Delhi that November, and after Gandhi attended several meetings, he told them "this organization should be wound up."[30] "I have seen enough to realize that though not all of us have gone mad, a sufficiently large number have lost their heads. What is responsible for this wave of insanity?" he asked at the mid-November meeting of the All-India Congress Committee, the last Congress session he would attend. "There are many places today where a Muslim cannot live in security. There are miscreants who will kill him or throw him out of a running train. . . . I have to fight against this insanity and find out a cure for it. . . . I am ashamed of what is happening today; such things should never happen in India."³¹ In his last speech to Congress in mid-November of 1947, Gandhi emphasized "that if you maintain the civilized way . . . whatever Pakistan may do now, sooner or later, she will be obliged by the pressure of world opinion to conform. Then war will not be necessary and you will not have to empty your exchequer."³²

· By the end of November, Gandhi felt that Delhi had turned into a "fire-pit," burning with communal riots, murders, and plunder, thousands of refugees continuing to pour in daily. Also, "Kashmir is in the cauldron," he wrote, while "those brothers and sisters who joined the Congress . . . are scrambling for power and fame."³³ He tried again now to convince militant Nehru to step down, saying at his prayer meeting, "Unfortunately, none of our Ministers is a peasant. The Sardar [Patel] is a peasant by birth and has some knowledge of agriculture, but . . . Jawaharlal is a scholar and a great writer, but what does he know about farming? More than 80 per cent of our population are peasants. In a true democracy, there should be the rule of peasants in our country. They need not become barristers. They should know how to be good farmers."³⁴ He suggested that Jawaharlal might at best be the "secretary" of a peasant prime minister. "Our peasant ministers would stay not in a palace but in a mud-house, and would toil on the land throughout the day. Then alone can there be a true peasant rule."³⁵

Nehru, however, was too busy fighting his war in Kashmir to think of stepping down. Instead he moved into New Delhi's Teen Murti Marg mansion, built by the British for their commander in chief, a grand residence with lovely spacious gardens and a high gate of spiked steel. Nehru's High Commissioner to Pakistan Sri Prakasha sensibly suggested that perhaps the wisest thing to do about Kashmir, since it was mostly Muslim, would be to let Pakistan have it. "I was amazed," Nehru thundered, "that you hinted at Kashmir being handed over to Pakistan. . . . The fact is that Kashmir is of the most vital significance to India. . . . Kashmir is going to be a drain on our resources, but it is going to be a greater drain on Pakistan."³⁶

Pakistan's ailing Prime Minister Liaquat Ali Khan flew to Delhi that November with his Finance Minister Ghulam Mohammed, at Mountbatten's invitation, to confer with Nehru and Patel about Pakistan's share of British imperial sterling assets. These were to have been released by India three months earlier but remained locked inside New Delhi's treasury vault. Mountbatten asked Gandhi to join him in his first meeting with Liaquat, knowing how negative Nehru felt, yet how dishonest it would be for India to rob Pakistan of its share of imperial assets. Gandhi, of course, insisted that India remain true to its word.

Gandhi worried more about how much money was being squandered in Kashmir to airlift everything to support the war. How long could such lavish expenditures continue? And what of the increasing and desperate needs of India's starving millions? Congress's government allotted virtually nothing to the constructive work of hand spinning and weaving he had devoted so many years of his life to fostering. "It is difficult to answer the question why constructive work is making so little headway, though the Congress has sworn adherence to it for years," Gandhi told a deputation of Constructive Workers, who came to him in early December. "It may be that we have no heart."37 He had lost faith in this government and advised his friends not to bother consulting it. "Your work is among the masses. The Constituent Assembly is today forging the Constitution. Do not bother. . . . We have to resuscitate the village, make it prosperous and give it more education and more power."38 He still passionately dreamed of establishing a totally nonviolent India under "Village Rule" (*Panchayat Raj*).

Before mid-December Gandhi launched the sort of attack on Nehru's Congress government that he'd long led against the British Raj. "We have to develop in us the power that non-violence alone can give," he urged all who listened to his Birla House speeches. "Today we have forgotten the charkha [spinning wheel]. . . . Today we have a larger army. We are trying to augment it further. Our expenditure on the army has increased enormously. . . . It is a tragedy and a shame. For so long we fought through the charkha and the moment we have power in our hands we forget it. Today we look up to the army."39

Not only did Gandhi urge the government to save money for constructive welfare by reducing martial expenditure, he also called for drastic reductions of all government salaries and urged employing more volunteers, rather than hiring high-priced Indian civil servants. It "pains me," he said, "when we throw money away so recklessly."40

"I am passing through a difficult time," Gandhi confessed to an old Gujarati friend. "I am convinced that this communal conflict is not of the common people's making. A handful of persons are behind it. Whose fault is it if I do not see amity even between these two [Nehru and Patel]? If the ocean itself catches fire, who can put it out? Falsehood has spread so much that one cannot say where it will end. . . . [P]eople deceive me."41

On Christmas Day, moved by its spirit of peace, Gandhi spoke to his meeting about Kashmir. "Can we not settle the issue between ourselves? . . . One should always admit one's mistakes. The Hindus and Sikhs of Jammu or those who had gone there from outside killed Muslims there. . . . I shall advise Pakistan and India to sit together and decide the matter. . . . The Maharaja can step aside and let India and Pakistan deliberate over the matter. . . . If they want an arbitrator they can appoint one."42 He advised Sheikh Abdullah to form an interim government and restore law and order. "The armies can be withdrawn. If the two countries arrive at a settlement on these lines it will be good for both." If India's Pandit Prime Minister had only listened to the man he was soon to hail as "the Light" of India's "life," India could have saved countless millions of pounds, two wars, and the lives of at least 50,000 men. But when Nehru heard what Gandhi had said, he angrily chastised him.

"I have been severely reprimanded for what I said concerning Kashmir," Bapu confided to the attendees at Birla House a few days later. "The advice I gave is the kind of advice the humblest man may give. Occasionally it becomes one's duty to offer such advice. . . . Kashmir is a Hindu State, the majority of its people being Muslims. The raiders . . . say that the Muslims of Kashmir are being ground down under the tyranny of Hindu raj and that they have come for their succour. . . . It seems obvious to me, as it should seem obvious to others . . . that if Sheikh Abdullah cannot carry with him the minority as well as the majority, Kashmir cannot be saved by military might alone."[43] Gandhi believed that "If the right thing is done and the right direction given to the process," the "present darkness in the country Kashmir may become . . . light." He passionately urged Pakistan and India to "come together and decide the issue with help of impartial" mediation. He all but openly offered himself as that mediator, asking aloud at his prayer meeting, "Is there no one in India who is impartial?"[44]

But Mahatma Gandhi's peaceful solution for the Kashmir conflict, formulating an honorable way for India to extricate itself from the costly, deadly war, was completely ignored by Nehru. Not only did Nehru silently reject Bapu's wise and kind offer, but he also resented Gandhi's daring to intrude into the one foreign policy area Nehru most coveted as his own personal domain.

"I hold that self-government is . . . only a means to good government," Gandhi wrote at year's end. "And true democracy is what promotes the welfare of the people. The test of good government lies in the largest good of the people with the minimum of control. . . . [I]n my view a system that admits of poverty and unemployment is not fit to survive even for a day."[45] He had tried his best to stop the bloodletting in Delhi, Punjab, and Kashmir. He had spoken out fearlessly and truthfully, hoping to elicit some compassionate deeds of wisdom from the powerful men who all loved to call themselves his disciples and him the nation's "Father." But as yet he heard no response from Delhi's power elite. He had but one weapon left, yet he hesitated to use it.

On January 2, 1948, Gandhi read an angry Hindu's letter, asking how he could still be "friendly with Muslims" when war with Pakistan might turn every Muslim in India into a traitor. "It is this attitude that was responsible for the partition of the country," Gandhi commented. "Only the good and the noble can be brave. Stupid people can never be brave. Today the poison around us is only increasing. Kashmir has added more poison."[46] He continued to call for an immediate negotiated settlement with Pakistan over Kashmir. "Whatever might have been the attitude of Pakistan, if I had my way I would have invited Pakistan's representatives to India and we could have met, discussed the matter and worked out a settlement."[47] A true fearless satyagrahi was always prepared to settle any conflict peacefully. "We should at least try to arrive at an agreement so that we could live as peaceful neighbors. . . . Mistakes were made on both sides. Of this I have no doubt. But this does not mean that we should persist in those mistakes, for then in the end we shall only destroy ourselves in a war."[48]

Still he was ignored. "Time was when what I said went home. . . . Today mine is a cry in the wilderness."[49] He was "helpless" to stop the war, he added softly, knowing just how little India's rulers now cared for his advice. His disciples asked why he didn't go to Pakistan and launch his Satyagraha there to stop the killing of Hindus, to which he replied, "I can only go to Pakistan after India has cleansed herself. I will do or die here."[50] Gandhi still passionately trusted to Ahimsa, which he called the "one thing" capable of saving "Delhi or the world."

On January 12 he told his friends: "I yearn for heart friendship between Hindus, Sikhs and Muslims. . . . Today it is non-existent. . . . Fasting is a satyagrahi's last resort."[51] He resolved to start his "indefinite" fast the next day. "It will end when and if I am satisfied that there is a reunion of hearts of all communities." He had met with Nehru and Patel just a few hours earlier. "This time my fast is not only against Hindus and Muslims but also against the Judases who put on false appearances and betray themselves, myself and society," Bapu told Manu that morning."[52] Since mid-August, Nehru and Patel had continued to resist releasing Pakistan's 550 million rupees owed from partitioned British imperial balances. Many Indians felt that Gandhi fasted only to encourage Delhi's Cabinet to pay Pakistan that money, but Gandhi's final fast, the penultimate passion of his life, was undertaken for more than one failure on the part of his two most powerful former disciples. He fasted to punish his impotent self for the general breakdown of Delhi, for the selfish corruption of the Congress, and for the criminal attacks against minorities in both dominions. If he could not stop so much poison with every word of sage advice he had repeated at least a thousand times, he passionately wanted to die, to release his Great Soul from his body's wretched shell full of aches and pains.

In mid-January, Patel offered to "resign" if that would end Gandhi's fast, but Bapu refused to allow it. He lost several pounds after three days, but felt strong enough to dictate his prayer speech on the fourth, though not to walk outside. His voice reached a large prayer crowd through a microphone brought to his bed inside Birla House. "Our Cabinet . . . deserve the warmest thanks," he said for having agreed that day to transfer to Pakistan the unpaid partition funds. "This is no policy of appeasement of the Muslims. . . . [T]he present gesture on the part of the Government of India . . . ought to lead to an honourable settlement not only of the Kashmir question, but of all the differences between the two Dominions. Friendship should replace the present enmity."[53]

Despite the swiftness of the Nehru Cabinet's action and dire warnings from his doctors that his kidneys were failing, Gandhi refused to break his fast until "complete friendship between the two Dominions, such that members of all communities should be able to go to either Dominion without the slightest fear of molestation" was realized.[54] Thousands, Sikhs and Muslims as well as Hindus, came to stand outside Birla House, all shouting slogans of peace and unity. The leaders of every community and party came to promise to love and trust one another as they loved him and to beg him to eat again. He asked them to put what they said in writing. On January 18, he stopped fasting when over one hundred leaders, from Nehru and Patel to Azad and Prasad, including all the heads of every party in Delhi, signed a seven-point declaration in Hindi and Urdu, promising to "live in Delhi like brothers and in perfect amity," taking "the pledge that we shall protect life, property and faith of Muslims."[55]

On January 20 Gandhi was carried out to a platform at the back of Birla's garden, but the microphone wasn't working. His feeble voice would only reach the ears of Manu and Sushila, who bent beside him and repeated aloud what he said. "I have no doubt that one who is an enemy of the Muslims is also an enemy of India," he said.[56] Then a hand grenade exploded behind him. The crowd ran in every direction. Gandhi alone stayed calm, unmoved by the terrifying sound. He thought some soldiers were practice firing. The explosion behind his back had been meant as a diversion by a terrorist Hindu gang who had come up by train from Poona and Nasik and were hiding in the Birla servants' quarters behind the platform. Terrorist Digambar Badge was then supposed to rush forward and toss a second grenade at Gandhi's head, but Badge's "courage failed." He and his five co-conspirators fled the garden instead, escaping in a taxi waiting for them just outside the gate. Only one terrorist, a Punjabi refugee named Madanlal Pahwa, who tossed the grenade, was caught and immediately taken into custody. Nathuram Vinayak Godse, his brother Gopal Godse, and their co-conspirator Narayan Apte, all escaped and remained free in Delhi until they attacked again ten days later. No policemen followed that taxi full of young, well-dressed Hindu fanatics. No one even reported the taxi's license or raced after it. Only trembling Pahwa was arrested, but he told his interrogators little more than that he was a Punjabi refugee, a "good Hindu," and an "Indian patriot."[57]

Daily looting of Muslim homes continued, moreover, as did the exodus from Delhi of terrified Muslim families. Gandhi was eager to leave as soon as possible for Pakistan. He received a wire from Sind's Chief Minister M. A. Khuhro inviting him to Karachi, but Nehru deterred him from going, not thinking "any useful purpose will be served thereby."[58] So Gandhi remained in Delhi. Birla House was put under military guard; Sardar Patel wanted every person who entered its garden searched, but "Bapu strongly disapproved."

"I believe that Rama is my only protector," Gandhi told his audience the next day. "If he wants to end my life, nobody can save me even if a million men were posted to guard me."[59] He planned to leave for Wardha on February 2 and hoped soon after that to go west to Pakistan. He was regaining strength slowly, and by January 25 was able to walk to his prayers.

Nehru and Patel continued their squabbling, and each wrote his own letter to Gandhi on Purna Swaraj Day, January 26, 1948, offering to resign and to let the other run the country "his own way." Both asked Gandhi to "decide" between them, but he refused to accept that burden, advising them to carry on as dutiful and dispassionate servants of India.

Gandhi woke, as usual, before dawn on Friday, January 30, 1948. He had finished his early prayers by 4 A.M. Manu chanted, at his request, "Whether tired or not, O man! Do not take rest!"[60] Then she covered him with a hand-spun "wrap." He drank hot water, honey, and lemon juice at a quarter of five, and a full glass of orange juice an hour later. Then he took a nap, while Manu massaged his feet. After waking again, they went out for the morning walk; when they returned, Manu helped him prepare for his bath. For lunch he ate goat's milk, boiled vegetables, tomato juice, and four oranges. He talked with Sushila's brother Pyarelal Nayar, who had recently returned from Noakhali. Then he lay down for another nap, before which Manu massaged his feet with ghee (clarified butter). "When he woke up," Manu saw him "coming from the wooden board to the bathroom. I said, 'Bapu, how well you look, walking by yourself!' . . . Bapu returned, 'Certainly! I look well, don't I? Foot it alone!'"[61] Then his afternoon visitors started to arrive. His most important visitor that day was Sardar Patel, who came at 4 P.M. to unburden himself, asking Bapu's permission once again to quit the Cabinet. Nehru was scheduled to come in the evening, to tell his side of their endless quarrel.

Gandhi and Patel were still talking at 4.30 when Abha brought Bapu his evening meal, which he always finished before the prayer meeting started at 5 P.M. Abha knew how punctual Bapu was, so precisely at 5 she returned to clear the tali (tray), coughing slightly to draw Patel's attention, hoping thus to end the intense tête-à-tête between the two brothers. But Gandhi focused on Vallabhbhai, whose pain was palpable in every deeply engraved line of his tortured face. Five minutes passed, and Abha held up Bapu's watch where he could see it. "I must now tear myself away," Gandhi told Patel, rising from the floor mat. Manu gathered up his pen, rosary, and glasses, keeping them with her notebook and his spittoon as she positioned herself on his right side. Abha was his left hand's walking stick, and she joked as she moved into place, "Bapu, your watch must be feeling very neglected. You would not look at it."[62] "Why should I, since you are my time-keepers?" They walked toward the garden. "But you do not look at the time-keepers," she responded gaily. He laughed.

As they headed down the crowded garden path, most of those waiting bowed to greet him, moving aside to allow them to pass without obstruction toward the platform. "I was walking on his right," Manu recalled. "From the same direction a stout young man in khaki dress, with his hands folded, pushed his way through the crowd and came near us. I thought he wanted to touch Bapu's feet."[63] But hate-crazed Nathuram Godse, whose small pistol was cradled in his chubby hands, was not interested in Gandhi's feet. He aimed his gun point blank at the Mahatma's bare chest and fired three bullets as fast as he could press the pistol's trigger. "The atmosphere was charged with smoke and the sky resounded with the boom. Bapu still seemed walking on. . . . 'Hei Ra . . . ma! Hei Ra . . . !' On his lips." Mahatma Gandhi's passionate heart poured its crimson blood out onto his white shawl. His gentle body collapsed and stopped breathing at 5.17 P.M.

25

His Indian Legacy

THE SHOCK OF GUILT and the remorse felt by most Indians as word of Mahatma Gandhi's assassination spread helped to subdue the fires of hatred that Bapu had failed to extinguish in his life. It was not a Pakistani Muslim but a self-proclaimed "devout" Hindu Brahman who murdered the Mahatma, a man who soon proudly insisted in court that he acted to "save" India as well as Hinduism.

"The light has gone out of our lives," Jawaharlal Nehru declaimed that night, fighting back tears as he delivered his beautifully poignant tribute to Gandhi over Radio India. "Our beloved leader, Bapu as we called him . . . is no more. . . . [W]e will not see him again as we have seen him for these many years. We will not run to him for advice and seek solace from him. . . . The light has gone out, I said, and yet I was wrong. For the light that shone in this country was no ordinary light. The light that has illumined this country . . . represented . . . the living, the eternal truths, reminding us of the right path, drawing us from error, taking this ancient country to freedom."[1] Nehru vowed to do everything in his power to stop the spread of communal hatred, insisting "We must . . . root out this poison. . . . We must hold together and all our petty . . . conflicts must be ended in the face of this great disaster."

All extremist Hindu parties were now banned, many of the better known Rashtriya Swayamsevak Sangh and Hindu Mahasabha leaders as well as terrorist gangs were arrested. In Poona, Bombay, and Nasik, angry mobs burned Brahman homes and beat many khaki-clad militants. India's police used their iron-tipped sticks vigorously, smashing the skulls of hitherto strutting young Hindu zealots. Tens were killed, hundreds wounded, thousands left homeless, and tens of thousands jailed for "disrupting" India's "peace."

Gandhi was dead by the time his bloodstained body was brought inside Birla House and laid on the hard board atop which he had slept. Manu continued to cry as she recited his favorite *Gita* stanzas. Vallabhbhai Patel and daughter Maniben were there as Dr. Bhargava bent over Bapu's corpse to confirm that it was devoid of breath. His Great Soul had flown to Lord Rama's heaven, or so every good Hindu believed, since his last passionate cry was "*Hei Rama.*" "Bapu is no more!" Bhargava solemnly announced. Devdas was the first of his sons to arrive. Nehru came with him, eyes swollen, hands shaking, distracted, tearful, and almost in shock, unlike Patel, who never trembled. Nehru embraced Home Minister Patel, and each of them vowed to stand beside the other, as Bapu had urged, and to discard the baggage of their petty disputes. Thus, Gandhi's death helped to unite India's government, as well as most of Delhi's now contrite Hindus, Muslims, and Sikhs. Millions of mourners gathered outside Birla House, and all along every road leading to it, promising to live up to Bapu's passionate teaching.

The crowd grew so restive, pushing, shouting, and pressing their faces against every steel bar at the gate that Patel wisely decided to have Bapu's corpse moved to the roof, where it was illuminated and elevated so it could be seen by many thousands. "*Mahatma Gandhi-ki-jai!*" they roared. He had finally won the martyr's "victory" and release he had so passionately desired. The army, which Gandhi might well have dissolved had he been governor-general, took charge of his state funeral. They placed his flower-covered body on a gun carriage made in America, and a seventy-nine-gun salute to the Apostle of Ahimsa incongruously shattered Delhi's mournful silence the next morning.

Ramdas reached Birla House at 11 A.M., and then the several-mile-long procession began. It was led by four armored cars, followed by the governor-general's horse guard of lancers and a specially selected force of two hundred of India's tallest army, navy, and air force guards who pulled the carriage with Gandhi's body at a slow march. The police followed, trying to keep the growing crowds at bay. Manilal remained in South Africa, but Harilal, though not invited, came from Madras to his father's cremation site, *Raj Ghat* ("Royal Steps"), along the river Yamuna (Jumna). He was seen lurking, bedraggled and bearded, around the pyre. As Gandhi's eldest son, Harilal should have been asked to ignite the fire, which Ramdas did. The heavily garlanded, wreathed, sandalwood pyre soaked with clarified butter and incense lit up Delhi's sky with its sparks at a quarter of five and burned all through the chilly night, as Gandhi's light of love and nonviolent passion for peace turned to ashes.

On February 12, 1948, Manu, Abha, Sushila, Devdas, and Ramdas

journeyed with Nehru and his cabinet to Allahabad, bearing Bapu's immo-
lated remains, part of which were scattered next morning in the muddy
confluence of Rivers Ganga and Yamuna, where according to ancient
Hindu lore, they were joined by their invisible sister River Saraswati.
Nehru and Patel took turns carrying the Mahatma's urn on their shoulders
as helicopters circled overhead, scattering rose petals. Four military jeeps
led the march from Allahabad's Queens Road to the rivers, followed by
cavalry guards and the Kumaun Regiment and supported by police and in-
fantry. "We followed the litter singing *Ramdhun*. Then followed the leaders
of the Country," Manu recalled. "Another military unit brought up the
rear. . . . All along the route masses of people had taken positions on roof-
tops, branches of trees, telegraph poles."[3]

"The last journey has ended," Nehru remarked, as Gandhi's ashes were
scattered in the churning yellow waters. "But why should we grieve? Do we
grieve for him or . . . for ourselves, for our own weaknesses, for the ill-will
in our hearts, for our conflicts with others? We have to remember that it
was to remove all these that Mahatma Gandhi sacrificed his life."[4]

Three months later, at his assassination trial, Nathuram Godse argued
defiantly before India's High Court, "My provocation was his constant and
consistent pandering to the Muslims. . . . I declare here before man and
God that in putting an end to Gandhi's life I have removed one who was a
curse to India, a force of evil, and who had, during thirty years of . . . hare-
brained policy, brought nothing but misery and unhappiness. . . . I do not
think that the Nehru government will understand me, but I have little
doubt that history will give me justice."[5] Godse's militant ultra-Hindu fa-
naticism was unfortunately shared by thousands of orthodox Hindus toward Mahatma Gandhi's repeated insistence that every human being deserved to be treated with loving kindness and equal respect. Nathuram
Godse was hanged, but his younger brother, Gopal, lives on in Poona (now
Pune), and like many disciples of the Hindu Mahasabha and R.S.S., has
continued to "celebrate" that most heinous assassination as an act of
Hindu "salvation."

Vinoba Bhave, Gandhi's most brilliantly dedicated disciple, carried on
the comprehensive *Sarvodaya* social reform work inspired by his guru at
Sevagram. He remained at that ashram, teaching, writing, spinning, weaving, and helping to wage the struggle against Harijan discriminatory practices nationwide. In 1951 Vinoba launched a series of new Gandhian agrarian reform movements, in response to growing revolutionary peasant
violence that flared up in the eastern half of the former Princely State of
Hyderabad. The miserly wealthy Muslim Nizam of Hyderabad with his
medieval coterie of Muslim landowners ruled an impoverished peasant
population. Communist party leaders in Hyderabad's Telengana preached
violent revolution, which Vinoba sought to counteract by appealing to

landlords for "gifts of land" (*Bhoodan*) to be distributed to their landless peasants. Looking even more frail than Gandhi, Vinoba walked from village to village with his disciples, young and old, mostly Indian, though some Europeans, Japanese, and Americans joined his entourage.[6] He asked the largest landowners of each village to "adopt" him as their "fifth son" and then to allocate one-fifth of their land to him for redistribution among the village's landless peasants. Vinoba's saintly appearance and his message of Ahimsa usually elicited a positive response, even from the most hard-hearted landlords. The land parcels given to him were often too steep or dry to cultivate and invariably took longer to transfer to hungry peasants than anticipated. In a few years, nonetheless, Vinoba collected millions of acres and had redistributed almost a tenth of those gifts, launching a non-violent agrarian revolution among many of India's most desperately depressed peasants.

In 1954, after years of struggling with *Bhoodan*, Vinoba embarked on his even more innovative *Gramdan* ("Gift of Village") movement. He asked every landholder to whose village he walked voluntarily to give him all their property deeds, so that he could equitably redistribute the land among all village tillers and workers. By 1957 he had walked through Bihar and most of Maharashtra and received over four million acres from 50,000 villages. Vinoba never lost heart or his temper, carrying on with perfect Ahimsa and infinite patience.

The last phase of his creative Sarvodaya movement was called *Jivandan* ("Gift of Life"), the sort of gift he and Gandhi gave of themselves to the service of India's poorest and neediest. Vinoba's call for Jivandani volunteers in 1958 was answered first by socialist Jaya Prakash (J. P.) Narayan. J. P. abandoned politics, at least its traditional Western form, in favor of selfless service and committed the remaining years of his life to peacefully trying to transform India's rural economy. J. P.'s goal, like Vinoba's, was to bring Gandhi's dream of *Ram Rajya* (the mythical "Golden Age" when Lord Rama ruled) to realization. Many others joined that idealistic movement. Considering the size of India's population, however, and its rapid growth, Jivandanis have remained a tiny minority, passionate in commitment and inspirational in their self-sacrifice, but hardly able to transform India's rural economy or remove the growing ills and inequities of urban magnets like booming Delhi, Bombay, Calcutta, Bangalore, and Madras. Urban industrial pollution and other barbarisms of civilization, especially violence, are the antithesis of everything Gandhi lived for and so passionately advocated.

In his birth centenary tribute to Mahatma Gandhi, G. Ramachandran, secretary of India's Gandhi Peace Foundation, sadly noted, "The world seems to have little to do with Gandhi and satyagraha. . . . [C]ivilization is now in the grip of escalating violence. . . . Non-violence is still only a trickle against the tidal waves of violence sweeping the world. But . . . [m]ilitarism and nuclear weapons are the blood-soaked sign posts of a vanishing era," he argued. "Gandhi and non-violence are the vibrant symbols of a slowly emerging epoch of justice and peace."[7] Yet, only five years later India exploded its first underground plutonium bomb, and just under a quarter century after that ignited five more powerful nuclear explosions at the same desert testing ground, proudly proclaiming it had joined the world's most deadly and dangerous arms race.

India's brilliant second president, philosopher Dr. S. Radhakrishnan, had wisely cautioned his countrymen and the world: "Man's greatest enemy is . . . nuclear weapons which in war may completely destroy civilization and in peace inflict grievous and lasting damage on the human race. Gandhi sought to prepare us for life in a disarmed world. We must pull out of the world of strife and hatred and get ready to work on the basis of cooperation and harmony . . . absolute adherence to truth, practice of love and self-suffering by the resister in cases of conflict."[8]

But it was Prime Minister Nehru, not pacifist President Radhakrishnan, who nurtured, controlled, and funded India's Ministry of Atomic Power. Nehru's equally militant daughter, Prime Minister Indira Gandhi, secretly ordered India's first plutonium bomb explosion in 1974, on the very day the birth of the Buddha was celebrated in India, and at the same desert site of Pokhran, where in 1998 India triggered its next five thermonuclear explosions. "India has nothing to hide," Nehru often insisted, claiming at every step in his escalation of the first war in Kashmir, that "we had consulted Gandhiji and secured the approval of the saint of truth and nonviolence."[9] In 1964, the year Nehru died, more than 100,000 regular Indian troops were stationed in Kashmir, and during his daughter Indira's decade and a half of premier power, that number more than doubled. By 1999, India was keeping almost half a million troops in Kashmir. Indira insisted, after exploding her bomb, that it had been done only for "peaceful" purposes, that India had no intention of becoming a "nuclear weapons power." In May 1998, however, Prime Minister A. B. Vajpayee, whose Bharatiya Janata Party (BJP) had defeated the corrupt and discredited Congress, proudly affirmed that India "has a very big bomb" and demanded entry into the small global club of nuclear weapons powers. Two weeks later Pakistan exploded an equal number of underground atomic bombs, ominously announcing its resolve never to give up its claim to Kashmir and proudly admitting that it too was now a nuclear weapons nation. Then, for two months in the summer of 1999, India and Pakistan fought a bitter and costly war along Kashmir's hotly contested line of control on the world's highest battleground—the ice-covered fields of Kargil.

India's "victory" in the Kargil war energized New Delhi's government and much of India's elite population, including virtually all increasingly affluent overseas Indians residing in the United States. They displayed a spirit of jingoism and militant confidence contrary to every facet of Mahatma Gandhi's philosophy. "What worries me is that security vis-à-vis Pakistan may become the top item on our policy agenda" was the correct prediction of one professor at Delhi's Center for the Study of Developing Societies. "That's very sad for a country like India. We have a lot of other things to handle—hunger, poverty, clean drinking water."[10] Secretary S. K. Bandopadhaya, of Delhi's Gandhi Memorial Trust, was equally explicit about the potential dangers to Indian development if India's leaders focused on martial defense, neglecting social and educational reforms, as well as Gandhian rural rehabilitation. "While our leaders are talking about nuclear bombs as a deliverance," Bandopadhaya warned, "350 million of our people remain below the poverty line, nearly 50 percent of our population is illiterate, and 100,000 of our villages don't even have safe drinking water."[11]

Half a century after Mahatma Gandhi's assassination, India has, nonetheless, continued to celebrate Gandhi's birth as a national holiday and has engraved his smiling face and message of peace on all of its newest treasury notes. India's leaders still reverentially place flowers on the hallowed ground where his corpse was cremated. But in its proliferation of arms and in its foreign policy, New Delhi has for the most part turned away from Bapu's ideal course and life's teaching. Sabarmati ashram survives as a museum and library dedicated to Mahatma Gandhi's memory, where his papers are lovingly preserved, carefully edited, and published under the auspices of the Navajivan Trust he established in Ahmedabad. Sevagram ashram remains a living legacy, where Gandhi's passionate band of spiritual heirs have dedicated their lives to Sarvodaya. In Porbandar and Bombay, Ahmedabad, Calcutta, and New Delhi, the buildings in which Mahatma Gandhi was born, lived, worked, and died have been preserved as national monuments and museums, where tourists and pilgrims with faith in truth and love come to pay their respects. In New Delhi, Birla House has been turned into a museum, repository of Bapu's last few precious possessions and the blood-drenched khadi he wore when assassinated. Outside that once elegant building, India's peasant poor and landless Harijans squat to mourn him every day. They arrive by bus, on bike, and on bare feet, praying as they move through the rear porch of the great house to circle the specially covered spot in the garden where a Mahatma was murdered. These mostly illiterate peasants seem to understand, as many better educated, wealthier Indians may never be able to, how great and wise a man their Bapu was. India's outcaste underprivileged millions and many of its minorities remember that he devoted his passionate life to them and died for them. Some gather each dawn to chant ancient Upanishadic prayers he loved best:

His Indian Legacy

Lead me from untruth to truth,
From the darkness to the light,
From death to immortality.

By pitting his Great *Maha-Atma* Soul against the vast armed force of the world's largest, strongest modern empire, Mahatma Gandhi proved the strength of invisible soul-force. By so passionately embracing suffering all his mature life and fearlessly following his inner voice wherever it led him, Gandhi lived the message of Love and Truth he believed to be twin faces of God. His greatest luxury was to serve those who needed him: the sick, the hungry, people without work or pride or hope. He never gave up his quest to liberate India from imperial bonds of exploitation and to liberate humankind from the shackles of prejudice, fear, and hatred, and from the terrors of brutal racial and religious, class and caste conflict. He courted pain as most men did pleasure, welcomed sorrow as others greeted joy, and was always ready to face any opponent or his own death with a disarming smile of love. He lived to the full his mantra, "Do or die!" Still, he failed to convert most of modern India to his faith in the ancient yogic powers of Tapas and Ahimsa as superior to the atom bomb. He was not, of course, the first or only prophet of peace murdered by a self-righteous killer, nor, most unfortunately, would he be the last. But he was the greatest Indian since the fifth-century B.C. "Enlightened One," the Buddha.

26

His Global Legacy

MARTIN LUTHER KING, JR., was "deeply fascinated" by the life and teachings of Mahatma Gandhi, reading about them first in his senior year at theological seminary. King found the power of Gandhi's passion "profoundly significant" and recalled: "As I delved deeper into the philosophy of Gandhi . . . I came to see . . . that the Christian doctrine of love, operating through the Gandhian method of non-violence, is one of the most potent weapons available to an oppressed people in their struggle for freedom."[1] As pastor of the Montgomery (Alabama) Dexter Avenue Baptist Church, King helped to liberate the United States from the poison of racial discrimination and nonviolently transformed America's civil rights movement, leading to his own assassination in 1968. King never met Gandhi, but he was so inspired by his life and work that he visited India in 1959, eager to meet Gandhi's disciples. "To other countries I may go as a tourist," the thirty-year-old King told Indian friends, "but to India I come as a pilgrim. This is because India means to me Mahatma Gandhi, a truly great man of the age."[2]

Martin Luther King was not the first nor the only great black leader in the United States to be inspired by Gandhi's life and its message of love, hope, faith, and courage. W. E. B. Du Bois had earlier invited Gandhi to visit America on behalf of the National Association for the Advancement of Colored People (NAACP). "It may well be," Du Bois prophetically predicted prior to King's assassination, "that real human equality and brotherhood in the United States will come only under the leadership of another Gandhi."[3]

In 1964, when King accepted his Nobel Peace Prize, he spoke, as he later would in every great city of America, in the language of nonviolent revolt made famous by Gandhi and Thoreau. "We will not obey unjust laws nor submit to unjust practices. We will do this peacefully, openly, cheerfully, because our aim is to persuade. We adopt the means of non-violence because our end is a community at peace with itself. . . . We are ready to suffer when necessary and even risk our lives to become witnesses to the truth. . . . This approach to the problem of racial justice . . . was used in a magnificent way by Mohandas K. Gandhi to challenge the might of the British Empire and free his people from the political domination and economic exploitation inflicted upon them for centuries."[4] King's generous tribute to his mentor in civil disobedience made some members of the Nobel committee feel ashamed at having never so honored Gandhi himself. The head of the Nobel committee after World War II, Gunnar Jahn, blocked Gandhi from getting the prize when two other members of the committee proposed his name. In his recently published diary, Jahn wrote that Gandhi "is obviously the greatest personality proposed. . . . But we must remember that he is not only an apostle of peace, he is also a nationalist."[5] Yes, his sacrificial genius at awakening India's masses and inspiring millions to follow his passionate march up the mountain to Swaraj did more than any of his contemporaries to integrate India's disparate castes and outcastes into a nation-state—no mean achievement, or negligible portion of his global legacy. But his life's message of the pervasive powers of truth and love transcends national boundaries and echoes across millennia.

Gandhi's "strategy of noncooperation . . . and his nonviolent resistance inspired anticolonial and antiracist movements internationally," wrote Nelson Mandela, South Africa's first black president, who was incarcerated in the same South African prison where Gandhi had first been locked in solitary confinement.[6] "Though separated in time, there remains a bond between us, in our shared prison experiences, our defiance of unjust laws," Mandela noted, paying his tribute to Gandhi's inspirational impact on his own passionate life.[7]

Soon after Gandhi was assassinated, Albert Einstein wrote: "The veneration in which Gandhi has been held throughout the world rests on the recognition that in our age of moral decay he was the only statesman who represented that higher conception of human relations in the political sphere to which we must aspire with all our power. . . . [T]he future of mankind will only be tolerable when our course, in world affairs as in all other matters, is based upon justice and law rather than the threat of naked power as has been true so far."[8]

UNESCO celebrated the one hundred twenty-fifth anniversary of Mahatma Gandhi's birth by proclaiming a year of "International Tolerance."

The director-general of UNESCO, Dr. Federico Mayor, wrote in his tribute that "Mahatma Gandhi gave us the example that throughout our lives we can be dissenters, even rebels, but never through violence, and this is what we must try to teach our children, . . . that 'All human beings are born free and equal in dignity and rights.'"[9] That first article of the International Declaration of Human Rights has thus been formally identified by the United Nations as one part of Gandhi's global legacy. A quarter century earlier, Burma's U Thant, the first Buddhist secretary-general of the United Nations, noted: "The Buddha taught his disciples never to show anger nor bear malice. . . . Gandhiji believed that non-violent methods . . . could achieve more enduring results than those obtained by the use of force."[10]

Religious genius and innovator that he was, Gandhi's emphasis on the primacy of moral principles and nonviolent means above any and all material ends, his faith in "God" as "Truth" and "Love," immortalize his global legacy. "Mahatma Gandhi cannot die!" wrote Kenneth Kaunda, first president of Zambia, who proudly considered himself and his nation's great Nobel Peace Prize winner Chief Luthuli, disciples of Gandhi. "His thoughts, words and deeds continue to influence and free millions of people in this our one world. Indeed they will continue to be a positive force for good . . . through non-violence."[11] Following King's assassination on April 4, 1968, cartoonist Bill Mauldin depicted Mahatma Gandhi waiting on his mat to welcome King into heaven with a loving greeting: "The odd thing about assassins, Dr. King, is that they think they've killed you."[12]

To millions unborn at the time of his death, Mahatma Gandhi's name continues to resound with inspirational powers unique to our century. In a world of plastic modernity and growing insensitivity to violence and pain, to the broadening chasm between the pleasure-loving wealthy and the hundreds of millions of people who never sleep a night without hunger, Gandhi's passionate life and his message of love, redolent more of Via Dolorosa than modern Delhi, inspires global admiration and emulation. "Sixties kids like me were his disciples when we went South in the Freedom Summer to sit in for civil rights and when we paraded . . . to stop the war in Vietnam," wrote Johanna McGeary for *Time*, which chose Gandhi as one of Einstein's millennial runner-ups. "Our passionate commitment, nonviolent activism, willingness to accept punishment for civil disobedience were lessons he taught. . . . His work and his spirit awakened the 20th century to ideas that serve as a moral beacon for all epochs."[13] In addition to America's Dr. King, Rosa Parks, and Cesar Chavez, among *Time*'s choices of Gandhi's global "children and spiritual heirs" were Tibet's Dalai Lama, Poland's Lech Walesa, Burma's Aung San Suu Kyi, South Africa's Desmond Tutu and Nelson Mandela, and assassinated Philippines' president Benigno Aquino, Jr. The list should have included Northern Ireland's Nobel Peace Laureate Mairead Maguire as well, who wrote on the fiftieth anniversary of Gandhi's murder: "Is it not insanity that India's government—currently the third or fourth most powerful military machine in the world—continues to waste so many resources on militarism, while so many of their people are in need of the basic necessities of life? . . . Yes, it is insanity. I believe with Gandhi that the insanity of violence can only be stopped by the sanity of non-violence."[14]

No populated portion of the world today is unaware of Mahatma Gandhi or immune to the global impact of his life. In Hiroshima, Beijing, Moscow, and Madrid his autobiography is read; his smiling face and naked torso are familiar to millions who have never visited India and know no other Indian leader's name or visage. Historian Rajmohan Gandhi's illuminating "portrait" of his grandfather, *The Good Boatman*, notes that most Indians were moved by Gandhi's "moral sense" as well as "his passion to identify with all."[15] His life thus became "a spark for consciences across the world." In his *Gandhi through Western Eyes*, Horace Alexander wrote of Gandhi not only as the "Moses" and "George Washington" of India, but also as "a world figure, a man who belongs to us all, and who has something to say that all the world should attend to."[16] Gandhi's most important universal message was embodied in "nonviolence." To Alexander he conveyed his last pacifist message just a few months before his death. "The world is sick of the application of the law of the jungle. It is thirsting for the brave law of love for hate, truth for untruth, tolerance for intolerance."

"Gandhi was no plaster saint," Professor Judith M. Brown concluded in her learned biography, *Gandhi: Prisoner of Hope*. "He was caught in compromises, inevitable in public life. But fundamentally he was a man of vision and action, who asked many of the profoundest questions that face humankind as it struggles to live in community. . . . As a man of his time who asked the deepest questions, even though he could not answer them, he became a man for all times and all places."[17] Our nation's greatest Indologist, Professor W. Norman Brown, believed that the "underlying basis" of Gandhi's lifelong quest was "simple." As Gandhi put it: "To see the universal and all-pervading Spirit of Truth face to face one must be able to love the meanest of creatures as oneself. And a man who aspires after that cannot afford to keep out of any field of life. That is why my devotion to truth has drawn me into the field of politics. . . . [T]hose who say that religion has nothing to do with politics do not know what religion means."[18]

Gandhi faced death without fear, thanks to his passionate faith in God's "Truth" as in the "law of Love"—*Ahimsa*—which he believed was as potent a remedy as prayer for all "our ills." His great soul's passionate courtship with suffering, which started in his twenties and grew ever more ardent over the last half century of his life, through his daily and nocturnal trials, tribulations, fasts, and failures ended in the "Liberation" (*Moksha*) he sought, with God's name on his lips. That he failed to avert partition or to convince his own "heirs" of the wisdom of his nonviolent faith neither nullifies the power of his passion to which he sacrificed his all nor the wisdom of his warnings against every war.

A hundred years from now, people the world over may still "scarcely" believe, as Albert Einstein once said of Gandhi, that "such a one as this ever in flesh and blood" did walk "upon this earth." As those who wait outside Birla House daily cry:

"Mahatma Gandhi amar rahe!"

"Mahatma Gandhi is immortal!"

NOTES

ABBREVIATIONS OF WORKS FREQUENTLY CITED

CWMG   M. K. Gandhi, *Collected Works of Mahatma Gandhi*, vols. 1–90 (Ahmedabad: Navajivan Trust, 1967–1984).

G's *A*   Mohandas K. Gandhi, *An Autobiography: The Story of My Experiments with Truth* (Boston: Beacon Press, 1957).

IO   *Indian Opinion.*

SSA   M. K. Gandhi, *Satyagraha in South Africa*, trans. V. G. Desai (Stanford: Academic Reprints, 1954).

YI   Mahatma Gandhi, *Young India*, 1919–1922, 2nd ed. (New York: B. W. Huebsch, 1924).

PREFACE

1. Stanley Wolpert, *A New History of India*, 6th ed. (New York and Oxford: Oxford University Press, 2000), p. 453.
2. Gandhi's Speech at Prayer Meeting, New Delhi, September 18, 1947, *The Collected Works of Mahatma Gandhi* (hereafter *CWMG*), vol. 89 (August 1, 1947–November 10, 1947) (Ahmedabad: Navajivan Trust, September 1983), p. 202.
3. M. K. Gandhi, "Atom Bomb and Ahimsa," *Harijan*, 7-7-1946, *CWMG*, 84 (April 14, 1946–July 15, 1946) (November 1981), p. 394.

INTRODUCTION

1. The translation of *Rig-Veda*: x, 129 is by W. Norman Brown, *Man in the Universe* (Berkeley and Los Angeles: University of California Press, 1966), pp. 29–30, quoted in Stanley Wolpert, *A New History of India*, 6th ed. (New York and Oxford: Oxford University Press, 2000), pp. 35–36.
2. M. K. Gandhi, "The Law of Suffering," *Young India,* June 16, 1920, in *Young India, 1919–1922* by Mahatma Gandhi (New York: V. W. Huebsch, 1924), pp. 230–31.
3. Linguistics professor Samuel R. Levin of the City University of New York and his wife, Classics scholar Dr. Flora R. Levin, kindly informed me of the Greek, Latin, and Gothic etymologies of and principal parts as well as complex meanings of the Latin verb *patior*, Greek *pascho* and *epaphon*, and Gothic *fijan*. Thanks also to Professor Henry Hoenigswald of the University of Pennsylvania, my authority for adding "hellish connotations" to the earliest Vedic Sanskrit meaning of *tapas*, "heat."

CHAPTER 1

1. Pyarelal, *Mahatma Gandhi: The Last Phase*, vol. 2 (Ahmedabad: Navajivan Publishing House, 1958), pp. 309–10.
2. D. G. Tendulkar, *Mahatma: Life of Mohandas Karamchand Gandhi*, vol. 8, 1947–48 (New Delhi: Publications Division, Government of India, 1963), p. 20.
3. Pyarelal, *Mahatma Gandhi*, p. 311.
4. *CWMG*, 81 (July 17–October 31, 1945), p. 319.

5. Nirmal Kumar Bose, *My Days with Gandhi* (Calcutta: Nishana, 1953), p. 72.
6. Pyarelal, *Mahatma Gandhi*, pp. 296–97.
7. Stanley Wolpert, *Jinnah of Pakistan* (New York: Oxford, 1984).
8. Rudyard Kipling's "City of Dreadful Night," quoted in Geoffrey Moorhouse, *Calcutta* (New York: Harcourt Brace, Jovanovich, 1971), p. 17.
9. Cardinal John Henry Newman's hymn begins "Lead, kindly Light, amid the encircling gloom, Lead Thou me on," and ends "I do not ask to see the distant scene; one step enough for me." Vincent Sheean's book on Gandhi was called *Lead, Kindly Light* (New York: Random House, 1949).
10. Sir Francis Tuker, *While Memory Serves* (London: Cassell, 1950), pp. 152ff.
11. Begum Shaista Suhrawardy Ikramullah, *Huseyn Shaheed Suhrawardy: A Biography* (Karachi: Oxford, 1991).
12. Tendulkar, *Mahatma*, p. 73.
13. Pyarelal, *Mahatma Gandhi*, pp. 365–67.
14. Ibid., pp. 368–70.

CHAPTER 2

1. Mohandas K. Gandhi, *An Autobiography: The Story of My Experiments with Truth* (Boston: Beacon Press, 1957), pp. 3–4. (Hereafter cited G's *A*.)
2. I am indebted to my friend and colleague Professor Stephen Hay of Santa Barbara for this information, based on his careful personal study of the records in Porbandar and Rajkot. Gandhi's report of his marriage at age "twelve" or "thirteen" is explained in part by the usual Hindu reckoning of one's age from conception rather than the actual date of birth, and perhaps because he also felt so ashamed of having married so very young that he slightly advanced the actual age in writing of his marriage in his autobiography; cf. G's *A*, pp. 8–14.
3. G's *A*, p. 9; next quote from G's *A*, pp. 10–11.
4. Ibid., p. 12.
5. Stephen N. Hay, "Jain Influences on Gandhi's Early Thought," in *Gandhi, India and the World: An International Symposium*, ed. Sibnarayan Ray (Philadelphia: Temple University Press, 1970), pp. 29–38; and Stephen Hay, "Jaina Goals and Disciplines in Gandhi's Pursuit of Swaraj," in *Rule, Protest, Identity: Aspects of Modern South Asia*, ed. Peter Robb and David Taylor (London: Curzon Press, 1978), pp. 120–32.
6. G's *A*, p. 19; and next quotes, ibid., pp. 20–24.
7. G's *A*, p. 24; and next quote, ibid., p. 25.
8. Erik H. Erikson, *Gandhi's Truth: On the Origins of Militant Nonviolence* (New York: W. W. Norton, 1969), p. 135.
9. Ibid., p. 140.
10. G's *A*, p. 27; and next quotes, ibid.
11. Ibid., p. 28.
12. Ibid., pp. 30–31.
13. Erikson, *Gandhi's Truth*, p. 128.
14. Bapu to Rajkumari Amrit Kaur, quoted in Tendulkar, *Mahatma*, vol. 7, p. 324.
15. G's *A*, p. 395.
16. Ibid., p. 36, and next quote, ibid.
17. From Gandhi's "London Diary," written by him in London, starting on November 12, 1888, reproduced in vol. 1 (1884–1896) of *CWMG* (1958), p. 3.
18. G's *A*, p. 38.
19. Ibid., p. 39.

CHAPTER 3

1. G's *A*, pp. 43–44.
2. Ibid., p. 46.
3. James D. Hunt, *Gandhi in London*, rev. ed. (New Delhi: Promilla, 1933), Appendix 2, is the best detailed "Guide to Gandhi's London," pp. 220–35.
4. G's *A*, p. 47.
5. Stanley Wolpert, *Morley and India, 1906–1910* (Berkeley and Los Angeles: University of California Press, 1967).
6. G's *A*, p. 48. For more information on Gandhi during this period of his first visit to London, see also Stephen Hay, "The Making of a Late-Victorian Hindu: M. K. Gandhi in London, 1888–1891," *Victorian Studies*, London, v. 33, no. 1, Autumn 1989, p. 86.
7. Gandhi's first (1891) articles, published in *The Vegetarian*, are reproduced in *CWMG*, 1 (1884–1896) (1958), pp. 24–52.
8. Wolpert, *Jinnah of Pakistan*, pp. 10–11.
9. G's *A*, p. 58.
10. Ibid., p. 59.
11. Ibid., pp. 67–68.
12. Annie Besant, *Speeches and Writings of Annie Besant*, 3rd ed. (Madras, n.d.); Arthur H. Nethercot, *The First Five Lives of Annie Besant* (London: Rupert Hart-Davis; 1961), and Arthur H. Nethercot, *The Last Four Lives of Annie Besant* (Chicago: University of Chicago Press, 1963).
13. Stanley Wolpert, *Nehru: A Tryst with Destiny* (New York and Oxford: Oxford, 1996), pp. 36ff.
14. G's *A*, p. 68.
15. Ibid., pp. 68–69. See Franklin Edgerton, trans. *The Bhagavad Gita* (Cambridge: Harvard University Press, 1972), 2 vols.
16. Ibid. For more about Tilak and his particular reading of the *Gita* and disagreements with Gandhi, see Stanley A. Wolpert, *Tilak and Gokhale: Revolution and Reform in the Making of Modern India* (Berkeley and Los Angeles: University of California Press, 1962), pp. 259–64.
17. G's *A*, p. 50.
18. Ibid., p. 79.
19. Ibid., p. 63.
20. G's *A*, pp. 64–65.
21. Ibid., p. 71.
22. Ibid., p. 75.
23. From Arnold Hills "Salvation," quoted in Hunt, *Gandhi in London*, p. 21.
24. Gandhi's interview, *CWMG*, 1, p. 53.
25. "On My Way Home Again to India," from *The Vegetarian* (9-4-1892), *CWMG*, 1, p. 64.
26. *CWMG*, 1, pp. 69–70.

CHAPTER 4

1. G's *A*, pp. 87–88.
2. Pyarelal, *Mahatma Gandhi: The Early Phase*, vol. 1 (Ahmedabad: Navajivan Press, 1965), p. 281.
3. G's *A*, p. 91.
4. Ibid.

5. Ibid., p. 93.
6. G's *A*, p. 94.
7. Pyarelal, *MG: The Early Phase*, 1, pp. 285–86.
8. Wolpert, *A New History of India*, pp. 233–38.
9. G's *A*, p. 98.
10. Ibid.
11. Ibid., pp. 98–99.
12. G's *A*, p. 99.
13. Ibid., pp. 100–101.
14. Ibid., p. 102.

CHAPTER 5

1. G's *A*, p. 102.
2. Ibid.
3. M. K. Gandhi, *Satyagraha in South Africa*, trans. V. G. Desai (Stanford: Academic Reprints, 1954), pp. 40ff. See also Maureen Swan, *Gandhi: The South African Experience* (Johannesburg: Raven Press, 1985) and Robert A. Huttenback, *Gandhi in South Africa* (Ithaca; Cornell University Press, 1971).
4. G's *A*, p. 111.
5. Ibid., p. 112.
6. Ibid., p. 113.
7. G's *A*, p. 114.
8. Ibid., p. 115.
9. Ibid., p. 117.
10. G's *A*, p. 188.
11. Chandran D. S. Devanesen, *The Making of the Mahatma* (Madras: Orient Longmans, 1969), p. 242.
12. G's *A*, p. 119.
13. Ibid., pp. 120–21.
14. Ibid., p. 126.
15. G's *A*, p. 127.
16. Ibid., p. 128.
17. Ibid., pp. 133–34.
18. G's *A*, p. 131.
19. Ibid., p. 139.
20. Ibid., p. 140.
21. "Petition to Natal Assembly," Durban, June 28, 1894, in *CWMG*, 1, p. 92, and next quote, ibid., pp. 93–94.
22. Ibid., p. 96.
23. G's *A*, p. 149.
24. "The Objects of the Natal Indian Congress," *CWMG*, 1, pp. 131–32.
25. "Deputation to Natal Premier," Durban, June 29, 1894, *CWMG*, 1, pp. 97–98.
26. "Deputation to Natal Governor," Durban, July 3, 1894, *CWMG*, 1, pp. 102–103.
27. G's *A*, p. 155.
28. Ibid., p. 162.
29. Ibid., p. 163.
30. G's *A*, p. 165.

CHAPTER 6

1. G's *A* pp. 169–70.
2. Ibid., p. 175.
3. Ibid., p. 178.
4. Tilak represented the Hindu "cultural nationalism" or "revolutionary" mainstream, Gokhale the moderate "Anglophile liberal" mainstream of "reform." Hence the subtitle of my *Tilak and Gokhale*, "Revolution and Reform in the Making of Modern India."
5. Published in a green cover, Gandhi's "green" pamphlet was called *The Grievances of the British Indians in South Africa: An Appeal to the Indian Public* (Ahmedabad, 1896).
6. G's *A*, pp. 188–89.
7. Ibid., p. 192.
8. Ibid., pp. 193–94.
9. G's *A*, p. 195.
10. Ibid., p. 199.
11. Ibid., p. 200.
12. Gandhi, *SSA*, p. 71.
13. Ibid., p. 72.
14. Ibid., p. 73.
15. Gandhi, *SSA*, p. 79.
16. G's *A*, p. 219.
17. Ibid., p. 222.
18. Ibid., pp. 223–24.
19. G's *A*, pp. 224–25.
20. Ibid., p. 226.
21. Ibid., pp. 228–29.
22. G's *A*, p. 230.
23. Ibid., pp. 232–33.
24. Ibid., p. 238.
25. G's *A*, p. 240.
26. Ibid., p. 248.
27. Ibid., p. 250.
28. G's *A*, p. 205.
29. Ibid., p. 250.

CHAPTER 7

1. G's *A*, p. 255.
2. Ibid., p. 259.
3. Gandhi, *SSA*, p. 83.
4. Ibid., pp. 84–85.
5. M. K. Gandhi, Johannesburg, February 23, 1903, in *CWMG*, vol. 3 (1898–1903) (1960), pp. 280–82.
6. "Ourselves," *Indian Opinion*, 4-6-1903, *CWMG*, 3, p. 313. (Hereafter *IO*.)
7. "Lord Milner on the Asiatic Question," *IO*, 11-6-1903, *CWMG*, 3, p. 337.
8. Ibid., p. 338.
9. M. K. Gandhi to Haridas V. Vora, Johannesburg, June 30, 1903, *CWMG*, 3, pp. 352–53.

10. Mohandas to "My Dear Chhaganlal" [Gandhi], June 30, 1903, *CWMG*, 3, pp. 353–54.
11. Henry Polak wrote on Gandhi's "Early Years, 1869–1914" in *Mahatma Gandhi*, by H. S. L. Polak, H. N. Brailsford, as Lord Pethick-Lawrence (London: Odhams Press, 1949), pp. 9–94. I am indebted to my good friend, English National Opera Director David Ritch, and to his dear departed mother, Beryl Ritch, for sharing with me their precious memoirs and memorabilia of Beryl's father, Louis W. Ritch, David's grandfather.
12. G's *A*, pp. 282–83.
13. Ibid., p. 284.
14. "Self-Sacrifice" from *IO*, 21-1-1904, *CWMG*, 4 (1903–1905) (1960), pp. 112–13.
15. G's *A*, p. 296.
16. Ibid., pp. 298–99.
17. "Ourselves," from *IO*, 24-12-1904, *CWMG*, 4, p. 320.
18. G's *A*, pp. 137–38.
19. Wolpert, *A New History of India*, pp. 273ff.
20. "Brave Bengal" from *IO*, 28-10-1905, *CWMG*, 5 (1905–1906) (1961), p. 114.
21. "Divide and Rule," *IO*, 4-11-1905, *CWMG*, 5, p. 121.
22. "Russia and India," *IO*, 11-11-1905, *CWMG*, 5, p. 132.
23. "Deputation to Lord Selbourne," Johannesburg, November 29, 1905, *CWMG*, 5, p. 144.
24. Ibid., p. 150.
25. "The Outlook," *IO*, 6-1-1906, *CWMG*, 5, p. 175.
26. *IO*, 10-3-1906, *CWMG*, 5, pp. 228–29.
27. *IO*, 14-4-1906, *CWMG*, 5, p. 282.
28. Gandhi to "Respected Brother" (original in Gujarati, trans. V. G. Desai), Johannesburg, May 27, 1906, *CWMG*, 5, pp. 334–35.
29. *IO*, 16-6-1906, *CWMG*, 5, p. 357; and next quote, ibid.
30. G's *A*, p. 206.
31. Ibid., p. 207.
32. *IO*, 28-7-1906, *CWMG*, 5, pp. 373–34.
33. *IO*, 25-8-1906, *CWMG*, 5, p. 399.
34. *IO*, 1-9-1906, *CWMG*, 5, p. 404.
35. *IO*, 9-9-1906, *CWMG*, 5, p. 418.
36. "The Mass Meeting," September 11, 1906, *CWMG*, 5, pp. 420–21; and next quote, ibid.
37. *IO*, 6-10-1906, *CWMG*, 5, p. 454.
38. *IO*, 29-9-1906, *CWMG*, 5, p. 457.
39. "Tyler, Hampden and Bunyan," *IO*, 20-10-1906, *CWMG*, 5, pp. 476–77.
40. "Memorial to Lord Elgin," London, November 8, 1906, *CWMG*, 6 (1906–1907) (1961), p. 111.
41. "Deputation Notes-1," Hotel Cecil, November 9, 1906, *CWMG*, 6, p. 139.
42. Gandhi to Sir Lepel Griffin, November 12, 1906, *CWMG*, 6, p. 159.
43. Gandhi to "The Editor, *The Times*" (London), November 13, 1906, *CWMG*, 6, p. 159.
44. Footnote 2 to Gandhi's November 24, 1906 letter, *CWMG*, 6, p. 225.
45. "Deputation Notes-3," November 23, 1906, *CWMG*, 6, p. 222.
46. "Reply to Welcome at Natal Indian Congress," Durban, January 1, 1907, *CWMG*, 6, p. 264.
47. January 3, 1907, *CWMG*, 6, p. 265.

48. "When Women Are Manly, Will Men Be Effeminate?" *IO*, 23-2-1907, *CWMG*, 6, p. 335.
49. Ibid., p. 336.
50. "Cable to South Africa British Indian Committee," March 23, 1907, *CWMG*, 6, p. 379.
51. *IO*, 11-5-1907, *CWMG*, 6, p. 458.
52. *IO*, 11-5-1907, *CWMG*, 6, p. 470.
53. "Mass Meeting at Pretoria," June 30, 1907, IO, 6-7-1907, *CWMG*, 7 (June–December 1907) (1962), p. 81.
54. "Johannesburg Letter," July 15, 1907, *IO*, 20-7-1907, *CWMG*, 7, p. 104.
55. "Poster," Pretoria, *IO*, 27-7-1907, *CWMG*, 7, p. 117.
56. "Staggering Humanity," *IO*, 27-7-1907, *CWMG*, 7, p. 119.
57. "Duty of Volunteers," *IO*, 28-9-1907, *CWMG*, 7, p. 258.
58. "Trial of Ram Sundar Pundit," Geriston, November 11, 1907, *CWMG*, 7, p. 352.
59. "Punditji's Patriotic Service," *IO*, 23-11-1907, *CWMG*, 7, p. 378.
60. Gandhi's "Trial at Johannesburg," December 28, 1907, *IO*, 4-1-1908, *CWMG*, 7, pp. 463–64.
61. *Rex v. Gandhi*, *IO*, 18-1-1908, *CWMG*, 8, (January–August 1908) (1962), p. 38.
62. Gandhi, *SSA*, 149.
63. Gandhi's "Johannesburg Letter" (before January 10, 1908), *CWMG*, 8, p. 23.

CHAPTER 8

1. Gandhi to "Colonial Secretary of the Transvaal," Johannesburg Gaol, January 28, 1908, *CWMG*, 8, pp. 40–42.
2. Gandhi, *SSA*, pp. 155–56.
3. Ibid., p. 162.
4. Ibid., p. 159.
5. Gandhi's "Speech at Meeting of British Indian Association," Johannesburg, January 31, 1908, *CWMG*, 8, pp. 45–46.
6. Gandhi, *SSA*, p. 167.
7. Ibid., p. 170.
8. Gandhi to "My Dear Friends," February 10, 1908, *CWMG*, 8, pp. 75–76.
9. "Secret of Satyagraha," *IO*, 22-2-1908, *CWMG*, 8, p. 91.
10. Ibid., pp. 91–92.
11. "A Brief Explanation," *IO*, 22-2-1908, *CWMG*, 8, pp. 99–100.
12. Gandhi, *SSA*, pp. 184–85, and last quote, p. 187.
13. Gandhi to "The Editor, *Indian Opinion*," *CWMG*, 8, p. 272.
14. "Satyagraha Again," *IO*, 27-6-1908, *CWMG*, 8, p. 323.
15. "Trial of Harilal Gandhi and Others," Johannesburg, July 28, 1908, *CWMG*, 8, pp. 405–406.
16. Gandhi to "The Editor, *Indian Opinion*," 8-8-1908, *CWMG*, 8, pp. 432–33.
17. "Satyagraha Again," *IO*, 27-6-1908, *CWMG*, 8, p. 324.
18. "Sarvodaya: What Is Just?" *CWMG*, 8, pp. 373–34.
19. Gandhi's "Speech at Mass Meeting," August 16, 1908, *CWMG*, 8, p. 458.
20. Gandhi's "Speech," August 23, 1908, *CWMG*, 8, p. 475.
21. Gandhi's "Message to Indians," Volksrust, October 14, 1908, *IO*, 24-10-1908, *CWMG*, 9 (September 1908–November 1909) (April 1963), p. 104.
22. Mohandas to "Beloved Kastur," Volksrust, November 9, 1908, *CWMG*, 9, p. 106.

23. Speech at Hamidia Islamic Society, Johannesburg, December 13, 1908, *CWMG*, 9, pp. 109–11.
24. "What Does the Struggle Mean?" *IO*, 23-1-1909, *CWMG*, 9, p. 159.
25. "English Influences in the Air," *IO* (from Gujarati), 30-1-1909, *CWMG*, 9, pp. 177–78.
26. The Reverend J. J. Doke's "protest" is noted in the "Chronology" appendix of *CWMG*, 9, p. 614.
27. Speech At Pretoria Meeting, May 24, 1909, Ibid., p. 215.
28. Speech at Johannesburg Meeting, May 24, 1909, *CWMG*, 9, p. 218; next quote, ibid., p. 219.
29. "Who Can Offer Satyagraha?" *IO*, 29-5-1909, *CWMG*, 9, p. 225.
30. Ibid., p. 227.
31. Wolpert, *Morley and India, 1906–1910*, p. 124.
32. Gandhi to "My Dear Henry" (H. S. L. Polak), Westminster Palace Hotel, London, July 14, 1909, *CWMG*, 9, p. 284.
33. Gandhi's "Deputation Notes [IV]," July 24, 1909, *CWMG*, 9, p. 313.
34. Gandhi's "Deputation Notes [V]," After July 26, 1909, *CWMG*, 9, p. 318.
35. "London"—"Suffragettes"—July 30, 1909, *IO*, 28-8-1909, *CWMG*, 9, p. 326.
36. Ibid.
37. Bapu to son Manilal, London, August 10, 1909, *CWMG*, 9, p. 352; next quote, ibid., pp. 352–53.
38. Mohandas to "Dear Kashi" (Gandhi), London, August 28, 1909, *CWMG*, 9, p. 374.
39. Gandhi's "This Crazy Civilization," before September 4, 1909, *IO*, 2-10-1909, *CWMG*, 9, pp. 388–89.
40. Speech at Farewell Meeting, London, November 12, 1909, *CWMG*, 9, pp. 539–43; quote from p. 542.
41. Gandhi's "Preface" to the English Edition of M. K. Gandhi, *Hind Swaraj and Other Writings*, ed. A. J. Parel (Cambridge: Cambridge University Press, 1997), p. 7.
42. Gandhi's *Hind Swaraj*, Ch. 6: "Civilization," *CWMG*, 10 (November 1909–March 1911) (September 1963), p. 20; next quote, ibid., pp. 21–22.
43. Ibid., p. 28; next quote, ibid., pp. 29–30.
44. "More Crusaders," *IO*, 19-3-1910, *CWMG*, 10, p. 186.
45. Mohandas to Maganlal (Gandhi), March 9, 1911, *CWMG*, 10, p. 446.
46. Gandhi's "What Has Satyagraha Achieved?" *IO*, 3-6-1911, *CWMG*, 11 (April 1911–March 1913) (March 1964), p. 104.
47. "The Great March," Volksrust, November 8, 1913, *IO*, 19-11-1913, in *CWMG*, 12 (April 1913–December 1914) (August 1964), Appendix 11, p. 592.
48. Gandhi's "Letter to Indians," before November 11, 1913, *CWMG*, 12, p. 262.
49. Trial at Dundee, November 11, 1913, *IO*, 19-11-1913, *CWMG*, 12, pp. 264–65.
50. Gandhi's Speech at Mass Meeting, Durban, December 21, 1913, reported by *The Natal Mercury*, 22-12-1913, reprinted in *CWMG*, 12, pp. 274–75.
51. Benarsidas Chaturvedi and Marjorie Sykes, *Charles Freer Andrews: A Narrative* (London: George Allen & Unwin, 1949), pp. 95–96; and next quote, ibid.
52. Interview with General Smuts, Pretoria, January 16, 1914, *CWMG*, 12, p. 324, f.1; next quote, ibid.
53. M. K. Gandhi to G. K. Gokhale, Cape Town, February 27, 1914, *CWMG*, 12, p. 360.
54. Ibid., pp. 360–61.

CHAPTER 9

1. Mohandas to "Dear Chhaganlal" (Gandhi), London, September 19, 1914, *CWMG*, 12, p. 533.
2. M. K. Gandhi to Col. R. J. Baker, London, October 13, 1914, *CWMG*, 12, pp. 536–37.
3. M. K. Gandhi to "Dear Colonel Baker," London, October 14, 1914, *CWMG*, 12, p. 539.
4. M. K. Gandhi to C. Roberts, London, October 25, 1914, *CWMG*, 12, pp. 543–45 quote from p. 545.
5. Mohandas to "Dear Maganlal" (Gandhi), London, December 10, 1914, *CWMG*, 12, p. 560.
6. Gandhi's speech at London Farewell, December 18, 1914, *CWMG*, 12, pp. 564–65.
7. Mohandas to "Dear Chhaganlal," S.S. *Arabia*, December 23, 1914, *CWMG*, 12, pp. 566–67.
8. M. R. Jayakar reported this story to me when I interviewed him for my dissertation on Tilak and Gokhale in his living room in his spacious Poona bungalow, in November 1957.
9. Gandhi's speech at Santiniketan on Gokhale's death, February 20, 1915, *CWMG*, 13 (January 1915–October 1917) (November 1964), p. 27.
10. Mohandas to "Bhaishri" (D. B. Shukla), March 2, 1915, *CWMG*, 13, p. 31.
11. Mohandas to "Dear Narandas" (Gandhi), On Way to Rangoon, March 14, 1915, *CWMG*, 13, p. 36.
12. Speech at Gurukul, Hardwar, April 8, 1915, from *The Hindu*, 12-4-1915, in *CWMG*, 13, pp. 46–47.
13. Speech on Arrival at Madras, April 17, 1915, *CWMG*, 13, p. 47.
14. Speech at Public Reception, Madras, April 21, 1915, *CWMG*, 13, p. 51.
15. "The Ashram," May 11, 1915, *CWMG*, 13, p. 85.
16. Draft Constitution for the Ashram, before May 20, 1915, *CWMG*, 13, pp. 91–94.
17. Gandhi to V. S. Srinivasa Sastri, Ahmedabad, September 23, 1915, *CWMG*, 13, pp. 127–28.
18. Fragment of Letter, before November 26, 1915, *CWMG*, 13, p. 144.
19. Gandhi's Speech at Benares Hindu University, February 6, 1916, *CWMG*, 13, pp. 210–16, quote from p. 210.
20. Ibid., pp. 214–15; and next quote, ibid., p. 216.
21. Letter to Darbhanga, February 17, 1916, *The Pioneer*, 9-12-1916, *CWMG*, 13, p. 217.
22. Reply to Mrs. Besant, before February 17, 1916, *CWMG*, 13, p. 240.
23. Speech at Conference for Elevation of Untouchables, March 18, 1916, *CWMG*, 13, p. 259.
24. Speech at Bombay Provincial Conference, Ahmedabad, October 21, 1916, *CWMG*, 13, pp. 303–304.
25. Speech at Common Language Conference, Lucknow, December 29, 1916, *CWMG*, 13, p. 321.
26. Interview at Lucknow, December 31, 1916, *CWMG*, 13, p. 324.
27. Speech at Muslim League Conference, Lucknow, December 31, 1916, *CWMG*, 13, p. 326.
28. Bapu to Manilal, Ahmedabad, before March 7, 1917, *CWMG*, 13, p. 355; next quote, ibid., p. 356.
29. G's *A*, p. 410.

30. Bapu to Maganlal (Gandhi), April 16, 1917, *CWMG*, 13, p. 365. Next quote, ibid., p. 366.
31. M. K. Gandhi to Mr. Maffey, Motihari, April 16, 1917, *CWMG*, 13, p. 368.
32. Gandhi to Mahatma Munshiram, Bettiah, April 26, 1917, *CWMG*, 13, p. 378.
33. Gandhi's Notes on the Position in Champaran, Bettiah, May 14, 1917, pp. 391–93; quote from p. 393.
34. Bapu to Maganlal (Gandhi), Bettiah, May 1917, *CWMG*, 13, p. 430.
35. M. K. Gandhi to Mr. Maffey, Bankipore, July 7, 1917, *CWMG*, 13, pp. 464–65.
36. Bapu to "My Dear Esther" (Faering), Nadiad, August 3, 1917, *CWMG*, 13, p. 485.
37. Talk with Mahadev Desai, August 31, 1917, *CWMG*, 13, pp. 510–11.
38. Gandhi's Speech at Godhra, November 3, 1917, *CWMG*, 14 (October 1917–July 1918) (March 1965), p. 49; next quote, ibid., p. 53.
39. "A Stain on India's Forehead," Godhra, after November 5, 1917, *CWMG*, 14, p. 74.
40. Bapu to Maganlal (Gandhi), Motihari, January 20, 1918, *CWMG*, 14, pp. 160–61.
41. Hallam Tennyson's title, *India's Walking Saint*, chosen for his fine "*Story of Vinoba Bhave*," a brief life of Gandhi's greatest follower, published in Garden City, New York, in 1955.
42. Mahadev H. Desai, *Day-to-Day with Gandhi*, vol. 1 (November 1917–March 1919), ed. N. D. Parikh (Varanasi: Sarva Seva Sangh Prakashan, January 1968), p. 26.
43. Bapu to Vinoba Bhave, Sabarmati, after February 10, 1918, *CWMG*, 14, p. 188.
44. M. Gandhi to "Dear Bhai Ambalalji" (Sarabhai), Motihari, December 21, 1917, *CWMG*, 14, p. 115.
45. Gandhi's Speech to Ahmedabad Mill-Hands, February 8, 1918, *CWMG*, 14, pp. 185–86.
46. Gandhi to Mill-Hands, February 26, 1918, *CWMG*, 14, p. 217.
47. Gandhi to "Dear Friend" Ambalal, March 1, 1918, *CWMG*, 14, pp. 229–30.
48. March 15, 1918, *CWMG*, 14, p. 256, fn. 2; and pp. 256–57.
49. Gandhi's Speech, March 18, 1918, *CWMG*, 14, pp. 268–69.
50. Gandhi to Commissioner, Northern Division, February 15, 1918, *CWMG*, 14, p. 195.
51. Speech at Nadiad, March 22, 1918, *CWMG*, 14, pp. 275–77.
52. Speech on Indian Civilization, Indore, March 30, 1918, *CWMG*, 14, pp. 299–300.
53. Speech at Uttarsanda, April 6, 1918, *CWMG*, 14, p. 313.
54. Gandhi to "My Dear Henry," April 10, 1918, *CWMG*, 14, p. 322.
55. Speech to Satyagrahis of Vadod, April 11, 1918, *CWMG*, 14, pp. 328–29.
56. Message to Satyagrahis of Nadiad, April 17, 1918, *CWMG*, 14, p. 346.
57. M. K. Gandhi to "Dear Mr. Maffey," Delhi, April 27, 1918, *CWMG*, 14, p. 374, and fn. 3.
58. Gandhi's Speech at War Conference, Delhi, April 28, 1918, *CWMG*, 14, p. 375.
59. M. K. Gandhi to "Sir" (Viceroy Chelmsford), Delhi, April 29, 1918, *CWMG*, 14, p. 380.
60. Letter to People of Kheda, Nadiad, June 6, 1948, *CWMG*, 14, p. 417.
61. G's *A*, p. 440.
62. Speech at Nadiad, June 17, 1918, *CWMG*, 14, p. 434.
63. G's *A*, pp. 445–46.
64. Gandhi's "Appeal for Enlistment," Nadiad, June 22, 1918, G's *A*, p. 440.
65. G's *A*, pp. 450–52; next quote, ibid., p. 452.
66. Wolpert, *A New History of India*, p. 298.
67. Gandhi to Srinivasa Sastri, Bombay, February 9, 1919, *CWMG*, 15 (August 1918–July 1919) (March 1965), pp. 87–88; next quote to Pragiji Desai, ibid., p. 88.

CHAPTER 10

1. Gandhi's Telegram to Viceroy, Ahmedabad, February 24, 1919, *CWMG*, 15, p. 102.
2. Letter to the Press, February 26, 1919, *CWMG*, 15, pp. 120–22.
3. Bapu to son Devdas, Delhi, March 5, 1919, *CWMG*, 15, p. 126.
4. Gandhi's Chowpatty Speech, April 6, 1919, *CWMG*, 15, p. 186; and next quote, ibid.
5. Gandhi's Speech on Hindu-Muslim Friendship, Bombay, April 6, 1919, *CWMG*, 15, pp. 188–89.
6. Wolpert, *Jinnah of Pakistan*, p. 70.
7. "Satyagrahi"-I, Bombay, April, 7, 1919, *CWMG*, 15, p. 190.
8. "The Swadeshi Vow"-I, April 8, 1919, *CWMG*, 15, pp. 195–97.
9. "Vow of Hindu-Muslim Unity," April 8, 1919, *CWMG*, 15, pp. 202–203.
10. Satyagraha Leaflet, No. 3, April 11, 1919, *CWMG*, 15, p. 211.
11. Stanley Wolpert, *Massacre at Jallianwala Bagh* (New Delhi: Penguin, 1988).
12. Gandhi to Maffey, Sabarmati, April 14, 1919, *CWMG*, 15, p. 218.
13. Speech at Mass Meeting, Ahmedabad, April 14, 1919, *CWMG*, 15, p. 221.
14. Gandhi's Telegram to Maffey, Bombay, April 21, 1919, *CWMG*, 15, p. 246.
15. Gandhi to Maffey, Bombay, May 30, 1919, *CWMG*, 15, p. 334.
16. "Disappointment," *Navajivan*, 21-9-1919, *CWMG*, 15, p. 163; next quote, ibid., p. 164.
17. G's *A*, p. 476.
18. Punjab Letter, October 17, 1919, *Navajivan*, 2-11-19, *CWMG*, 16 (August 1919– January 1920) (1965), p. 263.
19. Punjab Letter: "Amritsar's Love," Lahore, November 17, 1919, *CWMG*, 16, pp. 296–98.
20. Gandhi's Speech at Khilafat Conference, Delhi, November 24, 1919, *CWMG*, 16, pp. 307–308; next quote, ibid., pp. 309–12.
21. Amritsar, December 27, 1919, *The Voice of Freedom. The Speeches of Pandit Motilal Nehru*, ed. K. M. Panikkar and A. Pershad (London: Asia Publishing House, 1961), pp. 3–9.
22. Bapu to "My Dear Child" (Esther Faering), Delhi, January 16, 1920, *CWMG*, 16, pp. 486–87; and next quote, ibid.
23. Bapu to "My Dear Child" (E. F.), *CWMG*, 16, pp. 499–500.
24. Bapu to "My Dear Child" (E. F.), January 25, 1920, *CWMG*, 16, pp. 506–507.
25. Bapu to "My Dear Child" (E. F.), February 1, 1920, *CWMG*, 17 (February–June 1920) (September 1965), p. 3.
26. Ibid., pp. 3–4.
27. Bapu to "My Dear Child" (E. F.), February 4, 1920, *CWMG*, 17, pp. 12–13.
28. Bapu to "My Dear Child" (E. F.), Lahore, February 5, 1920, *CWMG*, 17, p. 13.
29. Bapu to "My Dear Child" (E. F.), Lahore, February 10, 1920, *CWMG*, 17, p. 22.
30. Bapu to "My Dear Child" (E. F.), The Ashram, February 22, 1920, *CWMG*, 17, p. 43.
31. Bapu to "My Dear Child" (E. F.), Bombay, March 17, 1920, *CWMG*, 17, p. 93.
32. Bapu to "My Dear Child" (E. F.), Bombay, March 21, 1920, *CWMG*, 17, p. 108.
33. Bapu to "My Dear Child" (E. F.), On the Train, March 30, 1920, *CWMG*, 17, p. 298.
34. Bapu to "My Dear Child" (E. F.), The Ashram, May 9, 1920, *CWMG*, 17, p. 402.
35. Bapu to "Dear Devdas" (Gandhi), Bombay, May 20, 1920, *CWMG*, 17, p. 436.
36. "What Shall We Do Now?" *Navajivan*, 23-5-1920, *CWMG*, 17, pp. 439–40, and next quote, ibid.

37. Gandhi to Viceroy Chelmsford, June 22, 1920, *CWMG*, 17, pp. 502–503.
38. "Non-Co-Operation," *Navajivan*, 4-7-1920, *CWMG*, 18 (July–November 1920) (November 1965), pp. 6–7, and next quote, ibid.
39. Letter to the Press (pre-July 1920), *Young India* (hereafter *YI*) 7-7-1920, *CWMG*, 18, p. 12.
40. M. K. Gandhi to "Sir" (Chelmsford), August 1, 1920, *CWMG*, 18, p. 104.
41. "Position of the Congress," *Navajivan*, 8-8-1920, *CWMG*, 18, p. 123.
42. Speech at Subjects Committee, Calcutta Congress, September 5, 1920, *CWMG*, 18, pp. 232–33.
43. Ibid., p. 234.
44. "Upper House" (Gandhi) to "My Dear Lower House" (Henry Kallenbach), August 10, 1920, *CWMG*, 18, p. 130.
45. M. K. Gandhi to V. J. Patel, "Report on Draft Instruction for Congress Organizations," September 22, 1920, *CWMG*, 18, pp. 279–84.
46. "Necessity of Discipline," *YI*, 20-10-1920, *CWMG*, 18, pp. 360–61.
47. "Non-Co-Operation," November 23, 1920, *CWMG*, 19 (November 1920–April 1921) (March 1966), p. 16, fn. 1.
48. "Council Elections," *YI*, 24-11-1920, *CWMG*, 19, p. 21.
49. Gandhi to Students in Allahabad, November 30, 1920, *CWMG*, 19, p. 47, and next quote, ibid., p. 50.
50. Speech on New Congress Creed, Nagpur, December 28, 1920, *CWMG*, 19, p. 159, and next quote, ibid., pp. 161–62.
51. Speech on Creed Resolution at Plenary Session, December 28, 1920, *CWMG*, 19, p. 165.
52. Wolpert, *Jinnah of Pakistan*, pp. 71–72, and next quote, ibid., p. 72.
53. Speech on Non-Co-Operation Resolution, Nagpur, December 30, 1920, *CWMG*, 19, p. 187.
54. Speech at "Nankana Saheb," March 3, 1920, *CWMG*, 19, p. 397.
55. Speech at Mass Meeting, Cuttack, March 24, 1921, *YI*, 13-4-1921, *CWMG*, 19, p. 478.
56. Gandhi's Interview with Viceroy Reading, Appendix 3, *CWMG*, 19, pp. 536–37.
57. Jawaharlal Nehru's *Autobiography*, p. 69, quoted in Wolpert, *Nehru*, pp. 49–50.
58. "Non-Violence," *YI*, 28-7-1921, *CWMG*, 19, p. 439.
59. Wolpert, *Nehru*, p. 54.
60. "Gorakhpur's Crime," *Navajivan*, 12-2-1922, *CWMG*, 22 (December 1921–March 1922) (November 1966), pp. 386–87.
61. Gandhi to son Devdas, Silence Day, February 12, 1922, *CWMG*, 22, p. 397.
62. Mohan to "My Dear Child" (E. F.), Sabarmati Jail, March 17, 1922, *CWMG*, 23 (March 1922–May 1924) (March 1967), p. 99.

CHAPTER 11

1. M. K. Gandhi to Hakim Ajmal Khan, Yeravda Jail, April 14, 1922, *CWMG*, 23, p. 135.
2. Ibid.
3. M. K. Gandhi to "My Dear Friend and Brother" (Maulana Mohamed Ali), Poona, February 7, 1924, *CWMG*, 23, pp. 199–200.
4. Gandhi's "Plea for Patience," *YI*, 3-4-1924, *CWMG*, 23, pp. 350–51.
5. Gandhi to "Dear Motilalji" (Nehru), Bombay, August 30, 1924, *CWMG*, 25 (August 1924–July 1925) (May 1967), pp. 53–54.

6. Gandhi's Speech at Excelsior Theatre, Bombay, August 31, 1924, *CWMG*, 25, pp. 56–7; and next quote p. 57.
7. "All about the Fast," *YI*, September 22, 1924, *CWMG*, 25, p. 200.
8. Gandhi's Presidential Address at Belgaum Congress, December 26, 1924, *CWMG*, 25, pp. 470–72; and next quote, ibid., p. 477.
9. Ibid., p. 479.
10. Gandhi's Public Speech, Madras, March 7, 1925, *CWMG*, 26 (January–April 1925) (November 1967), p. 244; next quote, ibid., p. 245.
11. Gandhi's Speech in Rajkot, February 15, 1925, *CWMG*, 26, p. 152.
12. Gandhi's Speech at Public Meeting, Vykom, March 10, 1925, *CWMG*, 26, p. 265; and next quote, ibid., p. 267.
13. Gandhi's Talk to Inmates of Satyagraha Ashram, Vykom, March 11, 1925, *CWMG*, 26, pp. 269–72; next quote, ibid., p. 273.
14. Gandhi's letter to C. R. Das, before June 13, 1925, *CWMG*, 27 (May–July 1925) (March 1968), p. 229.
15. "Are We Ready?" *YI*, 18-6-1925, *CWMG*, 27, p. 257.
16. "A Domestic Chapter," *YI*, 18-6-1925, *CWMG*, 27, pp. 259–61; next quote, ibid., pp. 261–62.
17. "A Deceptive Speech," July 18, 1925, in *YI*, 23-7-1925, *CWMG*, 27, pp. 390–91.
18. Madeleine Slade, *The Spirit's Pilgrimage* (New York: Coward-McCann, 1960), p. 58.
19. Gandhi to "Dear Friend" Romain Rolland, November 13, 1924, *CWMG*, 25, p. 320.
20. Gandhi to Helen Haussding, June 2, 1927, *CWMG*, 33 (January–June 1927) (May 1969), pp. 420–21.
21. "From Europe," *YI*, 8-10-1925, *CWMG*, 28 (August–November 1925) (April 1968), p. 303; next quote, ibid., p. 304.
22. Gandhi to G. D. Birla, August 17, 1925, *CWMG*, 28, pp. 878–79.
23. "To American Friends," *YI*, 17-9-1925, *CWMG*, 28, pp. 186–87.
24. Gandhi's Interview to Katherine Mayo, March 17, 1926, *CWMG*, 30 (February–June 1926) (September 1968), pp. 119–20.
25. Ibid., pp. 120–22.
26. "How to Help?" *YI*, 15-4-1926, *CWMG*, 30, p. 293.
27. "From Far-Off America," *YI*, 6-5-1926, *CWMG*, 30, p. 415.
28. Gandhi to P. G. K. Menon, April 13, 1926, *CWMG*, 30, pp. 226–27.
29. Gandhi's Speech at Meeting of Missionaries, July 18, 1925, *CWMG*, 27, p. 439.
30. Bapu to Mirabehn, January 3, 1927, *CWMG*, 32, (November 1926–January 1927) (April 1969), pp. 503–504.
31. Gandhi's Speech at Public Meeting, Comilla, January 5, 1927, *CWMG*, 32, p. 511.
32. Gandhi's Speech at Gauhati, December 24, 1927, *CWMG*, 32, p. 452; and next quote, ibid.
33. The first quote is Bapu to Radha, March 28, 1927; the second quote, Bapu to Jamnalalji, March 28, 1927, *CWMG*, 33, pp. 202–203.
34. Discussion with Dr. Mehta, April 3, 1927, *CWMG*, 33, pp. 209–10.
35. Bapu to Mira, April 25, 1927, *CWMG*, 33, pp. 250–51.
36. Gandhi's Speech at Opening of Khadi Exhibition, Bangalore, July 3, 1927, *CWMG*, 34 (June–September 1927) (June 1969), pp. 101–104.
37. Bapu to Mira, July 4, 1927, *CWMG*, 34, p. 107.

CHAPTER 12

1. Gandhi to Jawaharlal Nehru, July 20, 1927, *CWMG*, 34, p. 207.
2. "Help Gujarat," *YI*, 11-8-1927, *CWMG*, 34, p. 282.
3. *Bhagavad Gita*, II, 27, quoted by Gandhi to son Ramdas, August 11, 1927, *CWMG*, 34, p. 331.
4. Gandhi to son Ramdas, August 15, 1927, *CWMG*, 34, p. 358.
5. "But What about Me?" *YI*, 18-8-1927, *CWMG*, 34, p. 363.
6. Viceroy's telegram, October 24, 1927, *CWMG*, 35 (September 1927–January 1928) (August 1969), p. 182.
7. Mohan to "My Dear Charlie," November 11, 1927, *CWMG*, 35, p. 228; and next quote, ibid., n. 1.
8. "Hindu-Muslim Unity," *YI*, 1-12-1927, *CWMG*, 35, p. 353.
9. Gandhi's Letter to Harjivan Kotak, Orissa, December 11, 1927, *CWMG*, 35, pp. 378–79.
10. Wolpert, *Nehru: A Tryst with Destiny*, p. 77.
11. Jawaharlal to Gandhi, January 11, 1928, Appendix 10, *CWMG*, 35, pp. 54–52; and next quote, pp. 543–44.
12. Gandhi's "Independence v. Swaraj," *YI*, 12-1-1928, *CWMG*, 35, pp. 455–57.
13. Bapu to "My Dear Jawaharlal," July 17, 1928, *CWMG*, 35, pp. 469–70.
14. Bapu to "My Dear Child" (Esther Menon), February 18, 1928, *CWMG*, 36 (February–June 1928) (January 1970), pp. 32–33.
15. Wolpert, *Nehru*, p. 81.
16. Gandhi to Motilal Nehru, March 3, 1928, *CWMG*, 36, 76; and next quote, ibid., p. 77.
17. Gandhi to Dr. B. C. Roy, May 1, 1928, *CWMG*, 36, p. 287.
18. Gandhi to "Dear Motilalji" (Nehru), May 8, 1928, *CWMG*, 36, p. 299.
19. "All's Well," *YI*, 9-8-1928, *CWMG*, 37 (July–October 1928) (February 1970), p. 147.
20. Gandhi's "Speech at Valod," *YI*, 16-8-1928, *CWMG*, 37, p. 152.
21. Bapu to "My Dear Jawahar" (Nehru), December 3, 1928, *CWMG*, 37, p. 150.
22. Gandhi to Dr. B. S. Moonje, December 16, 1928, *CWMG*, 37, pp. 231–32.
23. Gandhi's Speech on Resolution on Nehru Report, Calcutta Congress, December 26, 1928, *Amrita Bazar Patrika*, 27-12-1928, *CWMG*, 37, p. 270.
24. "Curse of Assassination," *YI*, 27-12-1928, *CWMG*, 37, pp. 274–75.
25. Gandhi's Speech on Resolution on Nehru Report-II, December 28, 1928, *CWMG*, 37, pp. 284–85.
26. Ibid., pp. 287–88.
27. "The Congress," *YI*, 10-1-1929, *CWMG*, 37, pp. 326–28.

CHAPTER 13

1. "Scheme for Boycott of Foreign Cloth," *YI*, 24-1-1929, *CWMG*, 38 (November 1928–February 1929) (March 1970), pp. 388–89.
2. Bapu to son Devdas, February 9, 1929, *CWMG*, 39 (February 1929) (September 1970), pp. 432–33.
3. Bapu to Chhaganlal Joshi, February 9, 1929, *CWMG*, 39, p. 434.
4. "What Did I Do in Delhi?" 24-2-1929, *CWMG*, 40 (February–May 1929) (September 1970), pp. 25–26.
5. Bapu to Mirabehn, March 4, 1929, *CWMG*, 40, pp. 74–75.
6. Speech at Public Meeting, Calcutta, March 4, 1929, *CWMG*, 40, p. 78.

7. "The Bomb and the Knife," *YI*, 18-4-1929, *CWMG*, 40, pp. 259–61.
8. "Interview," May 1, 1929, *The Hindu*, 3-5-1929, *CWMG*, 40, p. 315.
9. "Who Should Wear the Crown?" *YI*, 1-8-1929, *CWMG*, 41 (June–October 1929) (October 1970), pp. 239–41.
10. "Interview with Mr. Jinnah," *YI*, 15-8-1929, *CWMG*, 41, p. 289.
11. Wolpert, *Jinnah of Pakistan*, p. 108.
12. Gandhi's Telegram to the Indian National Congress, Lahore, August 19, 1929, *CWMG*, 41, p. 303.
13. "My Limitations," *YI*, 12-9-1929, *CWMG*, 41, pp. 378–79.
14. Wolpert, *Nehru*, p. 98.
15. Jawaharlal (Nehru) to "My Dear Bapuji," November 4, 1929, *CWMG*, 42 (October 1929–February 1930) (December 1970), Appendix 2, pp. 515–17.
16. Bapu to "My Dear Jawahar," November 8, 1929, *CWMG*, 42, p. 116.
17. Vallabhbhai (Patel) to "Bapuji," November 11, 1929, *CWMG*, 42, Appendix 3, pp. 517–18.
18. "My Position," *YI*, 14-11-1929, *CWMG*, 42, pp. 150–51.
19. Gandhi's Telegram to Sarojini Naidu, November 14, 1929, *CWMG*, 42, p. 162 and fn. 2.
20. Wolpert, *Nehru*, p. 104.
21. Gandhi's Speech at the Congress, Lahore, December 31, 1929, *CWMG*, 42, pp. 341–43.
22. Wolpert, *Nehru*, p. 106.
23. Draft Declaration for January 26, 1930, *CWMG*, 42, pp. 384–85.
24. Mohan (Gandhi) to "My Dear Charlie" (Andrews), February 2, 1930, *CWMG*, 42, p. 444.
25. "Some Implications," *YI*, 6-2-1930, *CWMG*, 42, pp. 450–53.
26. Ibid.
27. "Salt Tax," *YI*, 27-2-1930, *CWMG*, 42, pp. 499–500.
28. "History of Salt Manufacture," *YI*, 27-2-1930, *CWMG*, 42, p. 503.

CHAPTER 14

1. M. K. Gandhi to "Dear Friend" Lord Irwin, March 2, 1930, *CWMG*, 43 (March–June 1930) (January 1971), pp. 2–7.
2. Gandhi's Statement on the Arrest of Vallabhbhai Patel, March 7, 1930, *Gujarati*, *CWMG*, 43, p. 24.
3. Speech at Prayer Meeting, Sabarmati Ashram, March 9, 1930, *YI*, 12-3-1930, *CWMG*, 43, pp. 30–31.
4. Interview, March 11, 1930, *CWMG*, 43, p. 38.
5. Speech at Prayer Meeting, March 12, 1930, *CWMG*, 43, p. 60; next quote, ibid., p. 61.
6. Speech at Bareja, March 13, 1930, *CWMG*, 43, p. 69; next quote at Navagam, ibid., p. 70.
7. Bapu to Mira, March 17, 1930, *CWMG*, 43, p. 89.
8. Speech at Borsad, March 18, 1930, *CWMG*, 43, pp. 100–101.
9. Bapu to "My Dear Jawaharlal" (Nehru), March 19, 1930, *CWMG*, 43, p. 103.
10. Wolpert, *Nehru*, p. 110.
11. Speech at Ras, March 19, 1930, *CWMG*, 43, pp. 103–105.
12. *YI*, 20-3-1930, *CWMG*, 43, pp. 110–11.
13. Interview, *The Hindu*, 25-3-1930, *CWMG*, 43, p. 118.
14. Speech at Buva, March 23, 1930, *CWMG*, 43, p. 120.

15. Speech at Broach, March 26, 1930, *CWMG*, 43, p. 126.
16. Speech at Prayer Meeting, Sajod, May 27, 1930, *Navajivan*, 3-4-30, *CWMG*, 43, p. 140; next quote, ibid., p. 147.
17. Speech at Bhatgam, March 29, 1930, *YI*, 3-4-30, *CWMG*, 43, p. 149.
18. "Remember 6th April," *YI*, 3-4-1930, *CWMG*, 43, pp. 170–71.
19. Statement to Associated Press, April 5, 1930, *CWMG*, 43, p. 179; next quote, ibid., p. 180.
20. Speech at Dandi, April 5, 1930, *CWMG*, 43, pp. 181–184.
21. "To the Women of India," *YI*, 10-4-1930, *CWMG*, 43, pp. 219–20; next quote, ibid., p. 221.
22. "Arrests and Brutal Justice," *Navajivan*, 13-4-1930, *CWMG*, 43, pp. 245–46.
23. Bapu to Mahadev, April 13, 1930, *CWMG*, 43, p. 250.
24. Gandhi to "Dear Motilalji" (Nehru), April 14, 1930, *CWMG*, 43, p. 258.
25. "The Black Regime," April 21, 1930, *YI*, 24-4-1930, *CWMG*, 43, p. 297.
26. Bapu to Mira, after April 24, 1930, *CWMG*, 43, p. 319.
27. Bapu to Mahadev, April 25, 1930, *CWMG*, 43, pp. 321–22; next quote, ibid., p. 322.
28. Speech at Chharwada, April 26, 1930, *Navajivan*, 4-5-1930, *CWMG*, 43, pp. 330–32; next quote; Ibid., p. 333.
29. M. K. Gandhi to "Dear Friend" Lord Irwin, May 4, 1930, *CWMG*, 43, p. 389–93.
30. Wolpert, *Nehru*, p. 111.
31. M. K. Gandhi to "Dear Friend" Lord Irwin, May 18, 1930, *CWMG*, 43, pp. 411–12.
32. Tendulkar, *Mahatma*, 3 (1930–1934) (1952), pp. 50–51.

CHAPTER 15

1. Bapu to Prema (Premabehn Kantak), July 30, 1930, *CWMG*, 44 (July–December 1930) (May 1971), p. 18.
2. Wolpert, *Nehru*, p. 114.
3. Ibid., p. 115.
4. Letter to T. B. Sapru and M. R. Jayakar, August 15, 1930, *CWMG*, 44, pp. 81–83.
5. Bapu to "Mani" (Maniben Patel), January 22, 1931, *CWMG*, 45 (December 1930–April 1931) (July 1971), p. 111.
6. Bapu to Mira, January 25, 1931, *CWMG*, 45, p. 115.
7. Bapu to Narandas Gandhi, January 26, 1931, *CWMG*, 45, p. 124.
8. Interview with Associated Press of India, January 26, 1931, *CWMG*, 45, p. 125.
9. Tendulkar, *Mahatma*, 3, p. 66.
10. Gandhi's Speech to Congress Leaders, Allahabad, January 31, 1931, *CWMG*, 45, pp. 133–34.
11. Speech at Motilal Nehru's Funeral, Allahabad, February 6, 1931, *CWMG*, 45, pp. 157–58.
12. Bapu to Gangadharrao Deshpande, February 10, 1931, *CWMG*, 45, p. 169.
13. Gandhi to Viceroy Irwin, February 14, 1931, *CWMG*, 45, p. 176.
14. Lord Irwin's version of Gandhi's Interview, February 17, 1931, *CWMG*, 45, pp. 185–88.
15. Gandhi's Report of His Interview with the Viceroy, February 17, 1931, *CWMG*, 45, pp. 188–91.
16. Telegram to Perin Captain, February 17, 1931, fn. 2, *CWMG*, 45, p. 192; next quote, February 18, 1931, ibid.
17. Gandhi's Report of Interview with Viceroy, February 18, 1931, *CWMG*, 45, p. 197.

18. Viceroy's Version of the Interview, February 18, 1931, *CWMG*, 45, pp. 193–95; next quote, ibid., p. 195.
19. Gandhi's Report of the Interview, *CWMG*, 45, p. 199; next quote, Viceroy's Version, ibid., p. 195.
20. Viceroy to Secretary of State, Appendix 4, *CWMG*, 45, pp. 429–31.
21. Speech at Council of Muslim League, Delhi, February 22, 1931, *CWMG*, 45, pp. 216–17.
22. Viceroy's Version of Interview, February 27, 1931, *CWMG*, 45, p. 235, fn. 1.
23. Viceroy's version of Interview, March 1, 1931, *CWMG*, 45, p. 240; next quote, ibid.
24. Gandhi's Note to Nehru, March 2, 1931, *CWMG*, 45, p. 242.
25. Viceroy's Version of Interview, March 3, 1931, *CWMG*, 45, p. 243.
26. Ibid., p. 244.
27. Viceroy's Version of Later Interview, *CWMG*, 45, pp. 244–45.
28. Gandhi's Statement to Press, March 5, 1931, *CWMG*, 45, pp. 250–51; and next quote, ibid., p. 255.
29. Irwin to Gandhi, March 6, 1931, *CWMG*, 45, p. 268, fn. 1.
30. Wolpert, *Nehru*, p. 126.
31. Gandhi to "Dear Friend" (Irwin), March 23, 1931, *CWMG*, 45, p. 333.
32. Gandhi's Speech at Karachi Congress, March 26, 1931, *YI*, 2-4-1931, *CWMG*, 45, pp. 348–49.
33. Ibid., pp. 350–51.
34. Gandhi's Speech on Kanpur Riots, March 27, 1931, *CWMG*, 45, p. 353.
35. Wolpert, *Nehru*, pp. 128–29.
36. Gandhi to C. F. Andrews, May 5, 1931, *CWMG*, 46 (April 16–June 17, 1931) (August 1971), p. 89.
37. Sir Malcolm Hailey's Note of May 20, 1931, Appendix 7 (A), *CWMG*, 46, pp. 417–19.
38. Bapu to Nanabhai I. Mashruwala, June 6, 1931, *CWMG*, 46, p. 335.
39. Mira's quote is from *CWMG*, 47 (June–September 1931) (September 1971), p. 49, fn. 2; the other quote, Bapu to Mira, is June 24, 1931, ibid.
40. Gandhi to Muriel Lester, released by Reuters, July 5, 1931, *CWMG*, 47, p. 101.
41. Interview to Reuters, S.S. *Rajputana*, September 4, 1931, *CWMG*, 47, p. 391.
42. Interview to *The News Chronicle*, September 11, 1931, *CWMG*, 47, p. 420.
43. Speech at Friends House, September 12, 1931, *CWMG*, 47, p. 2, fn. 1; next quote, ibid., pp. 2–3.
44. Speech at Federal Structure Committee, September 15, 1931, *CWMG*, 47, pp. 13–15; and next quote, ibid., p. 18.
45. Speech in Lancashire, September 26, 1931, *CWMG*, 47, p. 69.
46. Interview with Ramsay MacDonald, September 30, 1931, *CWMG*, 47, p. 96; next quote, ibid.
47. Speech at Meeting of Friends of India, October 7, 1931, *CWMG*, 47, p. 115.
48. Speech at Minorities Committee Meeting, October 8, 1931, *CWMG*, 47, p. 115.
49. Ibid., p. 119.
50. Bapu to Nehru, after October 16, 1931, *CWMG*, 47, p. 173.
51. Speech at Nottingham University College, October 17, 1931, *CWMG*, 47, p. 175; next quote, October 18, 1931, ibid., p. 183.
52. Talk at Oxford, October 24, 1931, *YI*, 12-11-1931, *CWMG*, 47, p. 228; next quote, ibid., p. 232.
53. Speech at Pembroke College, November 1, 1931, *CWMG*, 47, p. 263.
54. M. K. Gandhi to P. M. MacDonald, November 14, 1931, *CWMG*, 47, p. 302.
55. Madeleine Slade, *The Spirit's Pilgrimage*, pp. 147–48.

56. Ibid., pp. 150–51.
57. Speech at Public Meeting, Bombay, December 28, 1931, *CWMG*, 48 (September 1931–January 1932) (November 1971), p. 448.
58. Gandhi's Telegram to Viceroy, January 1, 1932, *CWMG*, 48, p. 472.
59. Gandhi to Willingdon, January 3, 1932, *CWMG*, 48, p. 487.
60. From Verrier Elwin's *The Tribal World of Verrier Elwin*, pp. 65–68, in *CWMG*, 49 (January–May 1932) (January 1972), Appendix 1, pp. 531–33.

CHAPTER 16

1. M. K. Gandhi to Sir Samuel Hoare, March 11, 1932, *CWMG*, 49, p. 190; next quote, ibid., p. 191.
2. Wolpert, *Nehru*, p. 140.
3. Sir Samuel Hoare to M. K. Gandhi, April 13, 1932, *CWMG*, 49, Appendix 3, pp. 534–35.
4. Mohan to "My Dear Charlie" (Andrews), April 7, 1932, *CWMG*, 49, pp. 275–76.
5. Bapu to Mira, April 8, 1932, *CWMG*, 49, pp. 278–80.
6. Bapu to son Devdas, April 24, 1932, *CWMG*, 49, pp. 359–61.
7. Bapu to Bhau Panse, June 30, 1932, *CWMG*, 49, p. 116.
8. M. K. Gandhi to "Dear Friend" (P. M. MacDonald), August 18, 1932, *CWMG*, 49, pp. 383–84.
9. Discussion with Vallabhbhai Patel, *CWMG*, 51 (September 1–November 15, 1932) (August 1972), Appendix 1, p. 457.
10. M. K. Gandhi to "Dear Friend" (MacDonald), September 9, 1932, *CWMG*, 51, pp. 31–32.
11. Bapu to son Devdas, September 13, 1932, *CWMG*, 51, p. 51; and Bapu to Ba, September 13, 1932, ibid., p. 52.
12. Bapu to Mira, September 15, 1932, *CWMG*, 51, pp. 56–57.
13. Gandhi's Statement to the Press, September 16, 1932, *CWMG*, 51, pp. 62–63.
14. Gandhi to Sarojini Naidu, September 19, 1932, *CWMG*, 51, pp. 70–71; and next, ibid., p. 71.
15. Gandhi to Rabindranath Tagore, September 20, 1932, *CWMG*, 51, p. 101; next, ibid.
16. Bapu to Mira, September 20, 1932, *CWMG*, 51, pp. 102–103.
17. Gandhi's Interview to the Press, September 20, 1932, *CWMG*, 51, p. 117.
18. Ibid., p. 118.
19. Discussion with Dr. B. R. Ambedkar, September 22, 1932, Appendix 1(B), *CWMG*, 51, p. 459; next quote, ibid., pp. 459–60.
20. Bapu to Mirabehn, September 26, 1932, *CWMG*, 51, p. 143.
21. Resolution at Hindu Leaders' Conference, Bombay, September 25, 1932, Ibid., p. 139.
22. Statement to the Press, September 26, 1932, *CWMG*, 51, pp. 139–45; quote from p. 145.
23. Wolpert, *Nehru*, p. 142.
24. Statement on "Untouchability"–2, November 5, 1932, *CWMG*, 51, p. 347.
25. Letter from C. F. Andrews, November 10, 1932, Appendix 17, *CWMG*, 51, p. 442.
26. Statement on "Untouchability"–13, December 30, 1932, *CWMG*, 51, pp. 304–305; next quote, ibid., p. 309.
27. "Appeal to Sanatanists," January 4, 1933, *CWMG*, 51, p. 358; next quote, ibid.
28. Bapu to "My Dear Horace" (Alexander), January 5, 1933, *CWMG*, 51, p. 365.

29. Gandhi's Talk with Supt. M. G. Bhandari, January 24, 1933, Appendix 6, *CWMG*, 51, p. 491.
30. Gandhi to "Dear Hariji (Kunzru), January 31, 1933, *CWMG*, 53 (January–March 1933) (December 1972), p. 200; next quote, ibid.
31. Dr. Ambedkar's "Statement," *Harijan*, 11-2-1933, *CWMG*, 53, pp. 260–61.
32. Gandhi's "Statement on Fast," April 30, 1933, *CWMG*, 53, pp. 74–75.
33. Bapu to Mirabehn, May 2, 1933, *CWMG*, 53, p. 85.
34. Bapu to Jawaharlal Nehru, May 2, 1933, *CWMG*, 53, p. 96; and next quote, ibid., fn. 1.
35. Wolpert, *Nehru*, p. 150.
36. Talk with son Devdas, May 27, 1933, *CWMG*, 53, p. 177.
37. "Breaking of the Fast," Appendix 6, *CWMG*, 53, pp. 444–45.
38. Gandhi's Speech at Leaders' Conference, Poona, July 14, 1933, *CWMG*, 53, p. 265.
39. Gandhi's Trial in Poona, August 4, 1933, *CWMG*, 53, pp. 341–42.
40. Ibid., p. 342.
41. Gandhi to "Dear Sir" (Home Secretary, Bombay), August 14, 1933, *CWMG*, 53, p. 353.
42. "The Breath of My Life," August 23, 1933, 5.30 P.M., *CWMG*, 53, p. 366.

CHAPTER 17

1. First quote, "Interview to Associated Press of India," September 2, 1933, *CWMG*, 55 (April 23–September 15, 1933) (August 1973), p. 392; next quote, "Advice to Friends," ibid., p. 393.
2. Jawahar to "My Dear Bapu," September 13, 1933, Appendix 14, *CWMG*, 55, pp. 457–58; next quote, ibid.
3. Bapu to "My Dear Jawaharlal," September 14, 1933, *CWMG*, 55, pp. 426–29; next quote, ibid.
4. Bapu to "My Dear Jawaharlal," November 1, 1933, *CWMG*, 56, (September 16, 1933–January 15, 1934) (November 1973), p. 167.
5. "Two Cruel Cases," *Harijan*, 3-11-1933, *CWMG*, 56, p. 177.
6. Bapu to "My Dear Agatha" (Harrison), November 16, 1933, *CWMG*, 56, pp. 232–34.
7. Speech at Public Meeting, Raipur, November 24, 1933, *CWMG*, 56, p. 278.
8. Speech at Public Meeting, Tinnevelly, January 24, 1934, *CWMG*, 57 (January 16–May 17, 1934) (January 1974), p. 44.
9. Ibid.
10. Rabindranath Tagore's Statement, *Harijan*, 16-2-1934, *CWMG*, 57, Appendix 1, pp. 503–504.
11. "Bihar and Untouchability," *Harijan*, 2-2-1934, *CWMG*, 57, p. 89; next quote, ibid., p. 87.
12. "Superstition v. Faith," *Harijan*, 16-2-1934, *CWMG*, 57, p. 165.
13. Speech at Bihar Central Relief Committee, Patna, March 18, 1934, *CWMG*, 57, pp. 289–90.
14. Bapu to "Bhai Vallabh" (Patel), May 10, 1934, *CWMG*, 57, p. 477.
15. Bapu to Mira, June 20, 1934, *CWMG*, 58 (May 18–September 15, 1934) (March 1974), p. 94.
16. Bapu to Vallabhbhai (Patel), July 2, 1934, *CWMG*, 58, p. 139.
17. Statement on Bomb Incident, June 25, 1934, *CWMG*, 58, pp. 108–109.
18. Gandhi to "My Dear Bidhan" (Dr. B. C. Roy), July 15, 1934, *CWMG*, 58, p. 190.

19. Bapu to Mira, on the Train, July 25, 1934, *CWMG*, 58, p. 244; and next quote, August 7, 1934, ibid., p. 298.
20. Bapu to Agatha (Harrison), August 7, 1934, *CWMG*, 58, pp. 299–300.
21. Interview to the Press, August 16, 1934, *The Hindu*, 16-8-1934, *CWMG*, 58, p. 316.
22. Bapu to Vallabhbhai (Patel), August 19, 1934, *CWMG*, 58, pp. 329–30.
23. Bapu to "My Dear Jawaharlal," August 17, 1934, *CWMG*, 58, p. 318.
24. Bapu to "Dear Vallabhbhai" (Patel), before September 5, 1934, *CWMG*, 58, pp. 403–406.
25. Bapu to Harilal, September 19, 1934, *CWMG*, 59 (September 16–December 15, 1934) (November 1974), p. 27.
26. Bapu to son Harilal, October 3, 1934, *CWMG*, 59, pp. 111–12.
27. Bapu to son Harilal, April 12, 1935, *CWMG*, 60 (December 16, 1934–April 24, 1935) (December 1974), p. 410.
28. Bapu to Narandas (Gandhi), May 5, 1935, *CWMG*, 61 (April 25–September 30, 1935) (May 1975), p. 37.
29. Bapu to Narandas, June 27, 1935, *CWMG*, 61, p. 246.
30. Speech at Kitchen Meeting, Wardha, February 22, 1935, *CWMG*, 60, pp. 251–52.
31. "The Extent of Medical Aid," *Harijan*, 5-4-1935, *CWMG*, 60, pp. 384–85.
32. "Let Us Pray," June 6, 1935, *CWMG*, 61, p. 137.
33. Bapu to "Bhai Vallabhbhai," December 11, 1935, *CWMG*, 62 (October 1, 1935–May 31, 1935) (October 1975), p. 170.
34. "Problems Confronting a Sanitary Worker," 27-10-1935, *CWMG*, 62, p. 70.
35. "A Fatal Fallacy," *Harijan*, 11-1-1935, *CWMG*, 62, pp. 92–93.
36. Statement to the Press, Bangalore, June 2, 1936, *CWMG*, 63 (June 1–November 2, 1936) (January 1936), pp. 5–7.
37. Bapu to "My Dear Jawaharlal," July 8, 1936, *CWMG*, 63, p. 127.
38. Bapu to "Dear Jawaharlal," July 15, 1936, *CWMG*, 63, pp. 144–45.
39. Bapu to "My Dear Jawaharlal," August 28, 1936, *CWMG*, 63, p. 249.
40. Talk with Jawaharlal Nehru, October 5, 1936, *CWMG*, 63, p. 347.

CHAPTER 18

1. Interview to Pandit Indra, March 20, 1927, The *Hindu*, 21-3-1937, *CWMG*, 65 (March 15–July 31, 1937) (July 1976), p. 11.
2. Wolpert, *Nehru*, p. 222.
3. April 1937, *CWMG*, 65, p. 63, fn. 1.
4. Message to Associated Press of America, April 12, 1937, *CWMG*, 65, p. 75.
5. Gandhi's Speech to Seva Sangh, Hudli, April 20, 1937, *CWMG*, 65, p. 119.
6. Ibid., p. 121.
7. Gandhi to "Dear Shri Jinnah," May 22, 1937, *CWMG*, 65, p. 231.
8. Wolpert, *Jinnah of Pakistan*, p. 153; and next quote, ibid.
9. Bapu to "Bhai Vallabhbhai," October 9, 1937, *CWMG*, 66 (August 1, 1937–March 31, 1938) (October 1976), p. 212.
10. Bapu to "My Dear Jawaharlal," November 18, 1937, *CWMG*, 66, pp. 296–97.
11. "Storm Signals," *Harijan*, 20-11-1937, *CWMG*, 66, p. 300; next quote, ibid., p. 301.
12. "A Message" for Lord Lothian, January 20, 1938, *CWMG*, 66, p. 344.
13. "Our Failure," March 22, 1938, *CWMG*, 66, pp. 405–406.

14. Gandhi's Speech at Seva Sangh, Delang, March 28, 1938, *CWMG*, 66, p. 447.
15. Statement to the Press, April 22, 1938, *CWMG*, 67 (April 1–October 14, 1938) (December 1976), pp. 36–37.
16. Bapu to "My Dear Jawaharlal," April 25, 1938, *CWMG*, 67, p. 47.
17. Joint Statement to the Press, April 28, 1938, *CWMG*, 67, p. 50.
18. Speech at Islamic College, Peshawar, May 4, 1938, *CWMG*, 67, pp. 63–65.
19. "Robber" (Gandhi) to "My Dear Idiot" (*Rajkumari* Amrit Kaur), May 7, 1938, *CWMG*, 67, p. 69; and next quote, ibid.
20. Ibid.
21. Bapu to Mirabehn, May 12, 1938, *CWMG*, 67, p. 80.
22. "Robber" (Gandhi) to "My Dear Idiot" (Amrit Kaur), Juhu, May 16, 1938, *CWMG*, 67, p. 84.
23. Bapu to Amritlal (A. T. Nanavati), May 2, 1938, *CWMG*, 67, p. 58.
24. Bapu to Mirabehn, May 3, 1938, *CWMG*, 67, p. 60; next quote, ibid., pp. 60–61.
25. Bapu to Balwantsinha, June 11, 1938, *CWMG*, 67, pp. 116–17.
26. Ibid.
27. "Is Violence Creeping In?" *Harijan*, 13-8-1938, *CWMG*, 67, pp. 245–46.
28. Wolpert, *Jinnah of Pakistan*, p. 162.
29. Statement to the Press, January 31, 1939, *CWMG*, 68, p. 359.
30. S. C. Bose's Statement, *The Hindustan Times*, 5-2-1939, *CWMG*, 68, Appendix 4, pp. 487–88.
31. "The Jewish Question," *Harijan*, 27-5-1939, *CWMG*, 69 (March 1, 1939–July 15, 1939) (July 1977), pp. 289–90.
32. Interview to *New York Times*, March 23, 1939, *CWMG*, 69, p. 77.
33. Bapu to "My Dear Agatha" (Harrison), May 20, 1939, *CWMG*, 69, p. 285.
34. Speech at Kathiawar Political Conference, Rajkot, May 31, 1939, *CWMG*, 69, pp. 312–14.
35. "Tyrant" (Gandhi) to "My Dear Idiot" (Amrit Kaur), June 19, 1939, *CWMG*, 69, pp. 358–59.
36. Tyrant to Idiot, June 23, 1939, *CWMG*, 69, p. 369.
37. Cable to General J. C. Smuts, July 7, 1939, *CWMG*, 69, p. 399.
38. Gandhi to "Dear Friend" Hitler, July 23, 1939, *CWMG*, 70 (July 16–November 30, 1939) (September 1977), pp. 20–21.
39. Statement to the Press, Simla, September 5, 1939, *CWMG*, 70, pp. 161–62.

CHAPTER 19

1. Wolpert, *Nehru*, p. 256.
2. Gandhi's Statement to the Press, September 15, 1939, *CWMG*, 70, p. 177.
3. Wolpert, *Jinnah of Pakistan*, p. 171.
4. Hindu-Muslim Unity. On the Train to Wardha, September 28, 1939, *CWMG*, 70, pp. 212–14.
5. Message to British People, October 3, 1939, *CWMG*, 70, p. 229.
6. Statement to the Press, Segaon, October 18, 1939, *CWMG*, 70, p. 267.
7. Wolpert, *Nehru*, p. 257.
8. Congress Working Committee Resolution, October 22, 1939, *CWMG*, 70, Appendix 13, pp. 419–20.
9. Bapu to "My Dear Jawaharlal," October 26, 1939, *CWMG*, 70, p. 297.
10. Hindu-Muslim Unity, October 30, 1939, *CWMG*, 70, p. 318.

11. Bapu to "My Dear Jawaharlal," November 4, 1939, *CWMG*, 70, p. 328; next quote, ibid.
12. Wolpert, *Jinnah of Pakistan*, p. 176; next quote, ibid.
13. Wolpert, *Nehru*, p. 266.
14. Statement to the Press, December 9, 1939, *CWMG*, 71 (December 1, 1939–April 15, 1940) (January 1978), pp. 18–19.
15. Statement to the Press, February 6, 1940, *CWMG*, 71, p. 188; next quote, ibid.
16. When the British Withdraw. On the Train to Wardha, March 3, 1940, *CWMG*, 71, p. 298.
17. Discussion at Working Committee, Ramgarh, March 15, 1940, *CWMG*, 71, p. 338; next quote, ibid., p. 339.
18. Wolpert, *Jinnah of Pakistan*, p. 182.
19. Ibid., pp. 184–85.
20. Wolpert, *Nehru*, p. 272.
21. My Answer to Quaid-e-Azam, Sevagram, March 26, 1940, *CWMG*, 71, pp. 371–72.
22. An English Suggestion, Sevagram, April 29, 1940, *CWMG*, 72 (April 16–September 11, 1940) (March 1978), pp. 26–27.
23. Of What Avail Is Non-Violence? April 30, 1940, *CWMG*, 72, pp. 29–31.
24. Bapu to Amrit (Kaur), May 15, 1940, *CWMG*, 72, pp. 69–70.
25. Gandhi to Linlithgow, May 26, 1940, *CWMG*, 72, pp. 100–101.
26. Bapu to Amrit, June 9, 1940, *CWMG*, 72, p. 159.
27. Bapu to "Dear Prema" (Premabehn Kantak), June 10, 1940, *CWMG*, 72, p. 168.
28. "Both Happy and Unhappy," Sevagram, June 24, 1940, *CWMG*, 72, p. 195.
29. Bapu to Prema (Kantak), June 25, 1940, *CWMG*, 72, p. 203.
30. Gandhi to Linlithgow, Birla House, Delhi, June 3, 1940, *CWMG*, 72, p. 212; next quote, ibid., pp. 212–14.
31. "To Every Briton," July 2, 1940, *Harijan*, 6-7-1940, *CWMG*, 72, pp. 229–31.
32. Discussion at Congress Working Committee Meeting, July 7, 1940, *CWMG*, 72, p. 237.
33. Gandhi's Speech at All-India Congress Committee Meeting, Bombay, September 15, 1940, *CWMG*, 73 (September 12, 1940–April 15, 1941) (April 1978), pp. 15–16.
34. Gandhi to Linlithgow, September 30, 1940, *CWMG*, 73, pp. 71–72.
35. Hallam Tennyson's title for his Life of Vinoba.
36. "Civil Disobedience," Sevagram, October 15, 1940, *CWMG*, 73, pp. 102–105.
37. Bapu to "My Dear Jawaharlal," October 21, 1940, *CWMG*, 73, p. 119.
38. Wolpert, *Nehru*, p. 279.
39. Instructions to Satyagrahis, January 12, 1941, *CWMG*, 73, p. 281.
40. "Communal Riots," Sevagram, May 4, 1941, *CWMG*, 74 (April 16–October 10, 1941) (June 1978), p. 26.
41. Statement to the Press, Wardha, April 25, 1941, *CWMG*, 74, p. 14.
42. Ibid., pp. 14–15.
43. Bapu to "My Dear Agatha" (Harrison), June 30, 1941, *CWMG*, 74, p. 132.
44. Speech at Sevagram, October 12, 1941, *CWMG*, 75 (October 11, 1941–March 31, 1942) (January 1979), pp. 8–10.
45. Ibid., pp. 6–7.
46. Ibid., p. 10.
47. Statement to the Press, December 20, 1941, *CWMG*, 75, p. 180.
48. Discussion at Working Committee Meeting, December 30, 1941, *CWMG*, 75, p. 188.
49. Speech at A.I.C.C. Meeting, Wardha, January 15, 1942, *CWMG*, 75, pp. 220–21.
50. Gandhi to Linlithgow, February 8, 1942, *CWMG*, 75, p. 299.

51. Linlithgow to Gandhi, February 20, 1942, Appendix 5, CWMG, 75, p. 456.
52. Gandhi to Linlithgow, February 26, 1942, CWMG, 75, p. 362.
53. Wolpert, *Jinnah of Pakistan*, p. 198.
54. Telegram to Cripps, March 25, 1942, CWMG, 75, p. 428.
55. British War Cabinet's Proposals, CWMG, 75, Appendix 6, pp. 456–58.
56. Gandhi's Interview with Cripps, March 27, 1942, CWMG, 75, Appendix 7, pp. 459–60.
57. Bapu to "Bhai Vallabhbhai" (Patel), April 13, 1942, CWMG, 76 (April 1, 1942–December 17, 1942) (July 1979), p. 31.
58. Wolpert, *Nehru*, p. 308.
59. Bapu to "Dear Jawaharlal," April 15, 1942, CWMG, 76, p. 40.
60. "Foreign Soldiers in India," April 19, 1942, CWMG, 76, p. 49.
61. Ibid.
62. Interview to *The News Chronicle*, May 14, 1942, CWMG, 76, p. 105.
63. Interview to Bombay Suburban and Gujarat Congressman, May 15, 1942, CWMG, 76, p. 107.
64. Gandhi to "Dear Friend" (FDR), July 1, 1942, CWMG, 76, pp. 264–65.
65. Franklin D. Roosevelt to "My Dear Mr. Gandhi," August 1, 1942, in *Profiles of Gandhi*, ed. Norman Cousins (Delhi: Indian Book Co., 1969), p. 227.
66. Bapu to "My Dear C. R.," July 5, 1942, CWMG, 76, p. 275.
67. Bapu to "Dear Jawaharlal," July 13, 1942, CWMG, 76, p. 293.
68. Ibid., pp. 293–94.
69. Draft Instructions for Civil Resisters, Bombay, August 4, 1942, CWMG, 76, pp. 364–65.
70. Introduction to Government Secret Circular, August 6, 1942, CWMG, 76, p. 374.
71. Interview to the Associated Press, August 6, 1942, CWMG, 76, p. 375.
72. Speech at the A.I.C.C. Meeting, August 7, 1942, CWMG, 76, pp. 377–81; quote from p. 380.
73. Ibid., p. 381.
74. Interview to the Press, August 8, 1942, CWMG, 76, p. 383.
75. Speech at A.I.C.C. Meeting, Bombay, August 8, 1942, CWMG, 76, pp. 284–96; quote from p. 389.
76. Message to the Country, 5 A.M., August 9, 1942, CWMG, 76, p. 403.

CHAPTER 20

1. Tendulkar, *Mahatma*, vol. 6 (1940–45) (Publications Division, Government of India), p. 181.
2. Gandhi to "Dear Lord Linlithgow," August 14, 1941, CWMG, 76, pp. 406–10.
3. Gandhi to "Dear Lord Linlithgow," New Year's Eve, 1942, CWMG, 77 (December 17, 1942–July 31, 1944) (October 1979), pp. 49–51.
4. Linlithgow to "Dear Mr. Gandhi," January 13, 1943, Appendix 1, CWMG, 77, p. 445; next quote, ibid.
5. Gandhi to "Dear Lord Linlithgow," January 19, 1943, CWMG, 77, p. 51; next quote, ibid.
6. Linlithgow to "Dear Mr. Gandhi," February 5, 1943, Appendix 2, pp. 446–48, quote from p. 448.
7. Gandhi to Linlithgow, February 7, 1943, CWMG, 77, pp. 58–60.
8. Gandhi to "Dear Sir Richard Tottenham," February 8, 1943, CWMG, 77, p. 61.
9. Madeleine Slade, *The Spirit's Pilgrimage*, p. 252.
10. Gandhi to "Dear Quaid-e-Azam" (Jinnah), May 4, 1943, CWMG, 77, p. 75.

11. Bapu to "Dear Agatha" (Harrison), December 29, 1943, *CWMG*, 77, pp. 213–14.
12. Gandhi to Khan Bahadur Ardeshir E. Kateli, January 6, 1944, *CWMG*, 77, p. 215.
13. Bapu to "Dear Manu," February 27, 1944, *CWMG*, 77, p. 239.
14. Gandhi to "Dear Dr. Jayakar," May 20, 1944, *CWMG*, 77, p. 275.
15. Bapu to "Dear Durga" (Desai), May 20, 1944, *CWMG*, 77, p. 276.
16. Bapu to "Dear Vanamala" (Parikh), July 10, 1944, *CWMG*, 77, p. 364.
17. Stuart Gelder's Cable to *News Chronicle*, Appendix 19, *CWMG*, 77, p. 474.
18. Gandhi's Interview to the Press, July 13, 1944, *CWMG*, 77, pp. 377–78.
19. Gandhi to "Dear Prime Minister" (Churchill), July 17, 1944, *CWMG*, 77, pp. 391–92.
20. "Brother" Gandhi to "Bhai" ("Brother") Jinnah, July 27, 1944, *CWMG*, 77, p. 393.
21. Gandhi to "Bhai Jinnah," August 23, 1944, *CWMG*, 28 (August 1–December 31, 1944) (December 1979), p. 44.
22. Gandhi's Talk with M. A. Jinnah, Bombay, September 9, 1944, *CWMG*, 78, pp. 87–88.
23. Ibid., pp. 88–89.
24. Barrister Yahya Bakhtiar to "Dear Professor Wolpert," Quetta, Pakistan, April 2, 1998.
25. Gandhi's Talk with M. A. Jinnah, September 9, 1944, *CWMG*, 78, pp. 88–89.
26. Ibid., p. 89; next quote, ibid.
27. Letter from M. A. Jinnah, September 10, 1944, Appendix 3, *CWMG*, 78, pp. 401–403.
28. Gandhi to "Dear Quaid-e-Azam" (Jinnah), September 11, 1944, *CWMG*, 78, p. 92.
29. Ibid.
30. Wolpert, *Nehru*, p. 337.
31. Gandhi's Speech at Prayer Meeting, September 11, 1944, *CWMG*, 78, p. 94.
32. Gandhi to "Dear Quaid-e-Azam" (Jinnah), September 19, 1944, *CWMG*, 78, p. 117.
33. Jinnah to "Dear Mr. Gandhi," September 21, 1944, Appendix 7, *CWMG*, 78, pp. 410–11.
34. Gandhi to "Dear Quaid-e-Azam," September 22, 1944, *CWMG*, 78, p. 122.
35. Gandhi's Interview to *News Chronicle*, September 29, 1944, *CWMG*, 78, pp. 142–43.

CHAPTER 21

1. Gandhi's Interview to Ralph Coniston, April 24, 1945, *CWMG*, 79 (January 1–April 24, 1945) (May 1980), pp. 422–23.
2. Bapu to Shantikumar N. Morarjee, June 4, 1945, *CWMG*, 80 (April 25–July 16, 1945) (September 1980), p. 253.
3. Bapu to "Dear Mannulal" (Shah), June 25, 1945, *CWMG*, 80, p. 367.
4. Wolpert, *Nehru*, p. 349.
5. Ibid., p. 347.
6. Gandhi to "Dear Friend" (Lord Wavell), June 15, 1945, *CWMG*, 80, p. 426.
7. Bapu to "Dear Jawaharlal" (Nehru), October 5, 1945, *CWMG*, 80, pp. 319–20.
8. Ibid., pp. 320–21.
9. Wolpert, *Nehru*, p. 354.
10. Gandhi to "Dear Friend" (R. G. Casey), December 24, 1945, *CWMG*, 82 (November 1, 1945–January 19, 1946) (September 1980), p. 215.
11. Bapu to "Dear Kaka" (D. B. Kalelkar), December 28, 1945, *CWMG*, 82, p. 287.
12. Wolpert, *Nehru*, p. 356.

13. Gandhi to "Brother Sachindra Narayan" (Roy), January 3, 1946, *CWMG*, 82, p. 340.
14. *Harijan* Revived, February 2, 1946, *CWMG*, 83 (January 20, 1946–April 13, 1946) (September 1981), p. 77.
15. Gandhi to "Dear Friend" (Wavell), February 10, 1946, *CWMG*, 83, p. 114, fn. 1.
16. G. E. B. Abell's Note on Interview with Gandhi, February 11, 1946, Appendix 2, *CWMG*, 83, pp. 418–19.
17. Ibid.
18. Gandhi to Abell, February 21, 1946, *CWMG*, 83, p. 162.
19. Bapu to "Brother Vallabhbhai," February 23, 1946, *CWMG*, 83, p. 173.
20. Statement to the Press, February 26, 1946, *Harijan*, 3-3-1946, *CWMG*, 83, p. 184.
21. Clement Attlee's Speech, March 15, 1946, Appendix 11, *CWMG*, 83, p. 432.
22. Wolpert, *Nehru*, p. 362.
23. Ibid.
24. Viceroy's Note on Interview with Gandhi, April 3, 1946, Appendix 14, *CWMG*, 83, p. 437.
25. "Why One More Burden?" *Harijan*, 31-3-1946, *CWMG*, 83, p. 318.
26. Nature Cure Prescriptions, March 25, 1946, *CWMG*, 83, p. 320; next quotes, ibid., pp. 320–21.
27. Bapu to Kanu (Gandhi), March 26, 1946, *CWMG*, 83, p. 322.
28. Gandhi's Talk with Agatha Harrison, May 3, 1946, *CWMG*, 84 (April 14, 1946–July 15, 1946) (November 1981), p. 97.
29. Bapu to "My Dear Amrit" (Kaur), May 15, 1946, *CWMG*, 84, p. 155.
30. Speech at Prayer Meeting, May 17, 1946, *CWMG*, 84, p. 162.
31. Statement of Cabinet Delegation & Viceroy, May 16, 1946, Appendix 7, *CWMG*, 84, p. 475.
32. Wolpert, *Nehru*, pp. 360–61.
33. Gandhi to "Dear Friend" (Wavell), June 12, 1946, *CWMG*, 84, p. 321.
34. Gandhi to "Dear Friend" (Pethick-Lawrence), June 12, 1946, *CWMG*, 84, p. 324.
35. Gandhi to "Dear Sir Stafford" (Cripps), June 13, 1946, *CWMG*, 84, pp. 330–31.
36. Cripps to Gandhi, *CWMG*, 84, p. 331, fn. 1.
37. Talk with Norman Cliff, June 29, 1946, *CWMG*, 84, pp. 385–86.
38. Wolpert, *Nehru*, p. 370.
39. Bapu to "My Dear Jawaharlal," July 17, 1946, *CWMG*, 85 (July 16, 1946–October 20, 1946) February 1982), pp. 5–6.
40. Bapu to "Brother Vallabhbhai," July 21, 1946, *CWMG*, 85, p. 35.
41. Wavell's Note on Interview with Gandhi and Nehru, August 27, 1946, Appendix 2, *CWMG*, 85, p. 515.
42. Sudhir Ghosh to "Dear Bapuji," September 7, 1946, Appendix 3, *CWMG*, 85, pp. 517–18.
43. "Antidote," September 2, 1946, *CWMG*, 85, p. 234.
44. "Congress Ministries and Ahimsa," September 6, 1946, *CWMG*, 85, pp. 266–67.
45. Bapu to "Dear Lily" (Lilavati Asar), October 7, 1946, *CWMG*, 85, p. 428.
46. Discussion with Co-Workers, October 18, 1946, *CWMG*, 85, p. 481.

CHAPTER 22

1. Talk to Refugees, November 7, 1946, *CWMG*, 86 (October 21, 1946–February 20, 1947) (August 1982), p. 96.
2. "To Bihar," November 6, 1946, *Harijan*, 10-11-1946, *CWMG*, 86, p. 81.
3. Talk to Relief Workers, November 7, 1946, *CWMG*, 86, p. 100.

4. Bapu to "Dear Vallabhbhai," November 14, 1946, *CWMG*, 86, p. 118.
5. Discussion with Sarat Bose and Others, November 24, 1946, *CWMG*, 86, p. 158.
6. Wolpert, *Nehru*, p. 376.
7. Gandhi's Note on the Constituent Assembly, December 3, 1946, *CWMG*, 86, pp. 184–85.
8. Extracts from Letter to Suhrawardy, December 3, 1946, *CWMG*, 86, p. 185.
9. Bapu to "Dear Agatha" (Harrison), December 5, 1946, *CWMG*, 86, p. 196.
10. Bapu to "Dear Manudi," December 2, 1946, *CWMG*, 86, pp. 178–79.
11. Bapu to "Dear Jaisukhlal" (Gandhi), December 12, 1946, *CWMG*, 86, p. 220.
12. N. K. Bose, *My Days with Gandhi*, p. 109, in fn. 3 of December 17, 1946, in *CWMG*, 86, pp. 238–39.
13. Letter from Dr. Sushila Nayar to N. K. Bose, December 22, 1946, Appendix 5, *CWMG*, 86, p. 490.
14. Speech at Prayer Meeting, December 17, 1946, *CWMG*, 86, p. 239.
15. Bapu to "Dear Manudi," December 20, 1946, *CWMG*, 86, p. 245.
16. Extract from Diary, December 20, 1946, *CWMG*, 86, p. 248.
17. Silence-Day Note to N. K. Bose, December 23, 1946, *CWMG*, 86, p. 255.
18. Bapu to "Dear Jaisukhlal" (Gandhi), December 23, 1946, *CWMG*, 86, p. 256.
19. Bapu to "Dear Vallabhbhai," December 25, 1946, *CWMG*, 86, pp. 263–64.
20. Bapu to "Dear Vallabhbhai," December 26, 1946, *CWMG*, 86, p. 270.
21. Pyarelal, *Mahatma Gandhi: The Last Phase*, vol. 1 (Ahmedabad: Navajivan Publishing House, 1956), p. 479.
22. Note to Nehru, December 30, 1946, *CWMG*, 86, p. 287.
23. Talk with Friends, December 31, 1946, *CWMG*, 86, p. 294.
24. Bapu to "Dear Parasuram," January 2, 1947, *CWMG*, 86, pp. 299–300.
25. Extract from Diary, January 2, 1947, *CWMG*, 86, p. 302.
26. Ibid., fn. 1.
27. Speech at Prayer Meeting, January 4, 1947, *CWMG*, 86, p. 311.
28. Bapu to "Dear Mira," January 6, 1947, *CWMG*, 86, pp. 314–15.
29. Bapu to "Dear Rajendra Prasad," January 8, 1947, *CWMG*, 86, p. 327.
30. Bapu to "Dear Ramdas," January 10, 1947, *CWMG*, 86, pp. 334–35.
31. Ibid.
32. Note to Manu Gandhi, January 19, 1947, *CWMG*, 86, p. 371.
33. Ibid.
34. Speech at Prayer Meeting, January 26, 1947, *CWMG*, 86, pp. 396–97.
35. Bapu to "Dear Satisbabu" (S. C. Mukerji), February 1, 1947, *CWMG*, 86, p. 414.
36. Bapu to "Dear Manilal," February 1, 1947, *CWMG*, 86, p. 415.
37. Talk with a Doctor, February 1, 1947, *CWMG*, 86, p. 417.
38. Speech at Prayer Meeting, February 1, 1947, *CWMG*, 86, p. 420.
39. Bapu to "Dear Vallabhbhai," February 2, 1947, *CWMG*, 86, p. 420.
40. Speech at Prayer Meeting, February 3, 1947, *CWMG*, 86, p. 425.
41. Bapu to N. K. Bose, February 7, 1947, *CWMG*, 86, p. 442.
42. Bapu to "Dear Vinoba" (Bhave), February 10, 1947, *CWMG*, 86, pp. 452–53.
43. Vinoba to Bapu, February 25, 1947, *CWMG*, 86, p. 453, fn. 2.
44. Note to Manu, February 10, 1947, *CWMG*, 86, p. 454; next quote, ibid.
45. Bapu to "Dear Ghanshyamdas" (Birla), February 15, 1947, *CWMG*, 86, pp. 465–66.
46. "Advice to a Congress Worker," February 17, 1947, *CWMG*, 86, pp. 470–71; next quote, ibid., p. 471.
47. Bapu to Manu, "A Note," February 18, 1947, *CWMG*, 86, p. 473.

48. February 24, 1947, *CWMG*, 87 (February 21, 1947–May 24, 1947) (February 1983), p. 16, fn. 1.
49. Speech at Prayer Meeting, Patna, March 5, 1947, *CWMG*, 87, pp. 44–45.
50. Speech at Prayer Meeting, March 23, 1947, *CWMG*, 87, p. 146.
51. Interview with Lord Mountbatten, April 1, 1947, *CWMG*, 87, p. 180,and see ibid, pp. 199–200.
52. Wolpert, Nehru, pp. 384–85.
53. Speech at Prayer Meeting, April, 1, 1947, *CWMG*, 87, p. 187.
54. Ibid., p. 183.
55. Speech at Prayer Meeting, April 2, 1947, *CWMG*, 87, p. 189; next quotes, ibid.
56. Speech at Prayer Meeting, April 3, 1947, *CWMG*, 87, p. 195.
57. Talk with Refugees, April 4, 1947, *CWMG*, 87, pp. 200–201.
58. Speech at Prayer Meeting, April 7, 1947, *CWMG*, 87, p. 225; next quote, ibid., n. 2.
59. Speech at Prayer Meeting, April 14, 1947, *CWMG*, 87, p. 280
60. Ibid., p.282.
61. Letter to Saraledevi Sarabhai, April 21, 1947, *CWMG*, 87, p. 322.
62. Discussion at Hindustani Talimi Sangh Meeting, April 22, 1947, *CWMG*, 87, p. 331.
63. Talk with Rajendra Prasad, Bhangi Nivas, May 2, 1947, *CWMG*, 87, p. 396.
64. Speech at Prayer Meeting, May 2, 1947, *CWMG*, 87, p. 398.
65. Talk with K. S. Roy, May 3, 1947, *CWMG*, 87, pp. 402–403.
66. A Talk, May 4, 1947, *CWMG*, 87, pp. 406–407.
67. Speech at Prayer Meeting, May 7, 1947, *CWMG*, 87, pp. 432–33.
68. Letter to Lord Mountbatten, May 8, 1947, *CWMG*, 87, pp. 435–36.
69. Wolpert, *Nehru*, p. 396.
70. Ibid.
71. Interview to Suhrawardy, May 12, 1947, *CWMG*, 87, pp. 458–59.
72. Ibid., p. 460, fn. 1.
73. Gandhi to Suhrawardy, May 13, 1947, *CWMG*, 87, p. 460.
74. Talk with Dr. B. C. Roy, Sodepur, May 14, 1947, *CWMG*, 87, pp. 467–68.

CHAPTER 23

1. Talk with Socialists, May 27, 1947, *CWMG*, 88 (May 25, 1947–July 31, 1947) (May 1983), p. 14.
2. Talk with a Co-Worker, May 29, 1947, *CWMG*, 88, p. 33.
3. Talk with Manu Gandhi, June 1, 1947, *CWMG*, 88, p. 50.
4. Ibid., p. 52.
5. Speech at Prayer Meeting, June 3, 1947, *CWMG*, 88, p. 67.
6. A Letter, June 3, 1947, *CWMG*, 88, p. 63.
7. Walls of Protection, June 8, 1947, *CWMG*, 88, pp. 101–102.
8. Gandhi to Nehru, June 9, 1947, *CWMG*, 88, p. 113.
9. Talk with Visitors, June 9, 1947, *CWMG*, 88, p. 116.
10. A Letter, June 15, 1947, *CWMG*, 88, p. 159.
11. Talk with Manu Gandhi, June 15, 1947, *CWMG*, 88, p. 159.
12. A Letter, July 12, 1947, *CWMG*, 88, p. 320.
13. Letter to Jaisukhlal (Gandhi), July 15, 1947, *CWMG*, 88, p. 340.
14. A Letter, July 20, 1947, *CWMG*, 88, p. 378.
15. Speech at Prayer Meeting, July 29, 1947, *CWMG*, 88, p. 461.

16. Talk with Congress Workers, Lahore, August 6, 1947, *CWMG*, 89 (August 1, 1947–November 10, 1947) (September 1983), p. 10.
17. Speech at Prayer Meeting, Patna, August 8, 1947, *CWMG*, 89, p. 18.
18. Interview to Suhrawardy, August 11, 1947, *CWMG*, 89, p. 28.
19. Bapu to "Dear Vallabhbhai" (Patel), August 13, 1947, *CWMG*, 89, p. 35.
20. Wolpert, *Nehru*, pp. 4–5.
21. Ibid., p. 405.
22. "Miracle or Accident?" August 16, 1947, *CWMG*, 89, pp. 48–49.
23. Ibid., p. 49.
24. Letter to J. Nehru, August 24, 1947, *CWMG*, 89, p. 83.
25. Mountbatten to Gandhi, August 26, 1947, *CWMG*, 89, p. 116, fn. 1.
26. Bapu to "Dear Vallabhbhai" (Patel), September 1, 1947, *CWMG*, 89, pp. 126–27.
27. Bapu to "Dear Vallabhbhai," September 2, 1947, 2, pp. 133–34.
28. Speech before Breaking of Fast, September 4, 1947, *CWMG*, 89, p. 154.
29. Advice to Young Men, September 5, 1947, *CWMG*, 89, p. 156.
30. Message to Shanti Sena Dal, September 5, 1947, *CWMG*, 89, p. 156.

CHAPTER 24

1. Statement to the Press, September 9, 1947, *CWMG*, 89, p. 166; next quote, ibid., p. 167.
2. Speech at Prayer Meeting, September 10, 1947, *CWMG*, 89, p. 167.
3. Ibid., pp. 169–70.
4. Speech at Prayer Meeting, September 17, 1947, *CWMG*, 89, p. 195, fn. 2.
5. Speech at Prayer Meeting, September 18, 1947, *CWMG*, 89, p. 200.
6. Speech at Prayer Meeting, September 21, 1947, *CWMG*, 89, p. 213.
7. Speech at Prayer Meeting, September 24, 1947, *CWMG*, 89, pp. 230–32.
8. Ibid., p. 233.
9. Speech at Prayer Meeting, September 25, 1947, *CWMG*, 89, p. 243.
10. Speech at Prayer Meeting, September 28, 1947, *CWMG*, 89, p. 253.
11. Ibid., p. 255.
12. Speech at Prayer Meeting, September 30, 1947, *CWMG*, 89, p. 261.
13. Speech at Prayer Meeting, October 2, 1947, *CWMG*, 89, p. 275.
14. Bapu to "Daughter Amtul Salaam," October 6, 1947, *CWMG*, 89, p. 293.
15. Speech at Prayer Meeting, October 19, 1947, *CWMG*, 89, p. 366.
16. Ibid., pp. 366–67.
17. Gandhi to "Dear Friend" (Lord Mountbatten), October 23, 1947, *CWMG*, 89, p. 389.
18. Speech at Prayer Meeting, October 26, 1947, *CWMG*, 89, p. 413, and fn. 1.
19. Ibid., pp. 413–14.
20. Wolpert, *Nehru*, p. 413; next quotes, ibid., pp. 414–15.
21. Ibid., p. 418; next quote, ibid., p. 419.
22. Wolpert, *Jinnah of Pakistan*, p. 352.
23. Speech at Prayer Meeting, November 2, 1947, *CWMG*, 89, pp. 458–60; next quote, ibid., p. 461.
24. Wolpert, *Nehru*, p. 420; next quote, ibid., p. 421.
25. Speech at Prayer Meeting, November 5, 1947, *CWMG*, 89, pp. 480–82.
26. Ibid.
27. "Outside His Field," November 7, 1947, *CWMG*, 89, p. 493.
28. Note to Jawaharlal Nehru, Addendum, *CWMG*, 89, p. 520.

29. Fragment of a Letter, November 15, 1947, *CWMG*, 90 (November 11, 1947–January 30, 1948) (April 1984), p. 36.
30. Speech at A.I.C.C. Meeting, November 15, 1947, *CWMG*, 90, pp. 38–40.
31. Ibid., pp. 41–42.
32. Ibid., pp. 42–43.
33. Fragment of a Letter, November 26, 1947, *CWMG*, 90, p. 109.
34. Speech at Prayer Meeting, November 26, 1947, *CWMG*, 90, pp. 112–13.
35. Ibid., p. 113.
36. Wolpert, *Nehru*, pp. 423–24.
37. Discussion at Constructive Workers Committee Meeting, December 11/12, 1947, *CWMG*, 90, pp. 215–21; quote from p. 216.
38. Ibid., pp. 218–20.
39. Speech at Prayer Meeting, December 13, 1947, *CWMG*, 90, p. 233.
40. Speech at Prayer Meeting, December 16, 1947, *CWMG*, 90, pp. 244–45.
41. Bapu's "A Letter," December 17, 1947, *CWMG*, 90, p. 248.
42. Speech at Prayer Meeting, December 25, 1947, *CWMG*, 90, pp. 297–99; quote from p. 298.
43. Speech at Prayer Meeting, December 29, 1947, *CWMG*, 90, pp. 318–19.
44. Ibid., p. 319.
45. Bapu's "Fragment of a Letter," December 30, 1947, *CWMG*, 90, p. 325.
46. Speech at Prayer Meeting, January 2, 1948, *CWMG*, 90, pp. 346–47.
47. Speech at Prayer Meeting, January 4, 1948, *CWMG*, 90, p. 357.
48. Ibid.
49. Speech at Prayer Meeting, January 7, 1948, *CWMG*, 90, p. 378.
50. Speech at Prayer Meeting, January 8, 1948, *CWMG*, 90, p. 386.
51. Speech at Prayer Meeting, January 12, 1948, *CWMG*, 90, p. 409.
52. Manuben Gandhi, *Last Glimpses of Bapu* (Delhi: Shiva Lal Agarwala & Co., 1962), pp. 116–17.
53. Speech at Prayer Meeting, January 16, 1948, *CWMG*, 90, pp. 435–36.
54. Ibid., p. 437.
55. Speech before Breaking Fast, January 18, 1948, *CWMG*, 90, p. 444, fn. 1.
56. Speech at Prayer Meeting, January 20, 1948, *CWMG*, 90, p. 464.
57. Speech at Prayer Meeting, January 20, 1948, *CWMG*, 90, p. 465, fn. 1.
58. Manu's *Last Glimpses*, p. 223; next quote, ibid., p. 224.
59. Speech at Prayer Meeting, January 21, 1948, *CWMG*, 90, p. 473, fn. 1.
60. Manu's *Last Glimpses*, pp. 284–85.
61. Ibid., pp. 289–301.
62. Remarks on Way to Prayer Meeting, January 30, 1948, *CWMG*, 90, p. 535.
63. Manu's *Last Glimpses*, p. 308; next quote, ibid., p. 309.

CHAPTER 25

1. Wolpert, *Nehru*, pp. 429–30.
2. Manu's *Last Glimpses*, pp. 312–13.
3. Ibid., pp. 330–31.
4. Wolpert, *Nehru*, pp. 431–32.
5. Nathuram Godse's Statement in Court, from *Rex versus Godse*, published by *The Word Quarterly: Gandhi Murder Trial*: "Official Account of the Trial of Godse, Apte, and Others for Murder and Conspiracy, with Verbatim Reports of Speeches by Godse and Savarkar." (Glasgow: The Strickland Press, n.d., but after 1950), pp. 49–50.

6. My wife and I walked with Vinoba in southern Maharashtra in late December of 1957.

7. G. Ramachandran, "The Core of Gandhi," in *Mahatma Gandhi: 100 Years*, ed. S. Radhakrishnan (New Delhi: Gandhi Peace Foundation, 1968), pp. 320–21.

8. S. Radhakrishnan, "Introduction," ibid., pp. 1–2.

9. Wolpert, *Nehru*, p. 433.

10. Professor Yogendra Yadav, quoted by Celia Dugger, *New York Times*, July 18, 1999, p. 4.

11. "Gandhi's Voice Summoned to Condemn India's A-Tests," John F. Burns, *New York Times*, May 24, 1998, p. 3.

CHAPTER 26

1. Martin Luther King, Jr., *Strength to Love* (New York: Harper Row, 1964), pp. 165–69.

2. David Levering Lewis, *King: A Biography*, 2nd ed. (Urbana: University of Illinois Press, 1978), p. 99.

3. Homer A. Jack, "Mohandas K. Gandhi and Martin Luther King Jr.," in *Mahatma Gandhi: 100 years*, ed. S. Radhakrishnan (New Delhi: Gandhi Peace Foundation, 1968), p. 135. Hereafter *MG:100*.

4. Ibid., p. 137.

5. Reported by Alister Doyle, *Los Angeles Times*, January 15, 1999, Section D., p. 12.

6. Nelson Mandela, "The Sacred Warrior," *Times*, December 31, 1999, V. 154, no. 27.

7. Nelson Mandela, "Gandhi: The Prisoner: A Comparison," in *Mahatma Gandhi: 125 Years*, ed. B. R. Nanda (New Delhi: Indian Council for Cultural Relations, 1995), pp. 5–6. Hereafter *MG:125*.

8. Einstein's tribute of February 11, 1948, quoted in Sarojini G. Henry, "Gandhi and Albert Einstein" in *Gandhi Marg*: Journal of the Gandhi Peace Foundation, 15, no. 3, October–December 1993, p. 336.

9. Quoted in N. Radhakrishnan, *Gandhi: The Quest for Tolerance and Survival* (New Delhi: Gandhi Smriti, 1995), p. ix.

10. U Thant, "Non-Violence and World Peace," *MG:100*, pp. 372–74.

11. Kenneth D. Kaunda, "Mahatma Gandhi Will Not Die," *MG:125*, p. 20.

12. Bill Mauldin's cartoon first appeared in the *Chicago Sun-Times*, April 5, 1968, and was reproduced in *Profiles of Gandhi*, ed. Norman Cousins (Delhi: Indian Book Co., 1969), p. 205.

13. Johanna McGeary, "Mohandas Gandhi," *Time*, December 31, 1999.

14. Mairead Maguire, "Reflections on the Fiftieth Anniversary of Gandhi's Assassination," in *Fellowship*, 64, no. 7–8, July/August 1998, p. 4.

15. Rajmohan Gandhi, *The Good Boatman: A Portrait of Gandhi* (New Delhi: Viking, 1995), p. 446; next quote, ibid., p. 459.

16. Horace Alexander, *Gandhi through Western Eyes* (London: Asia Publishing House, 1969), p. v; next quote, ibid., p. 187.

17. Judith M. Brown, *Gandhi: Prisoner of Hope* (New Haven and London: Yale University Press, 1989), p. 394.

18. W. Norman Brown, *The United States and India, Pakistan, Bangladesh*, 3rd ed. (Cambridge, MA: Harvard University Press, 1972), p. 95; next quote, ibid.

SELECT BIBLIOGRAPHY

The most important primary source materials for Gandhi's life are published in ninety volumes of the *Collected Works of Mahatma Gandhi*, by Delhi's Publications Division of the Government of India's Ministry of Information and Broadcasting, by "kind permission" of Navajivan Trust, Ahmedabad, volume 1 in January 1959 to volume 90 in April 1984. Most of Gandhi's literary works have been reproduced in those volumes of his *Collected Works*, but several of his important books were published earlier and remain in print, accessible to the general reader. These include: *Gandhi's Autobiography: The Story of My Experiments with Truth*, trans. By Mahadev Desai (Washington, D.C.: Public Affairs Press, 1948); his *Hind Swaraj and Other Writings*, ed. A. J. Parel (Cambridge: Cambridge University Press, 1997); his *Satyagraha in South Africa*, trans. by V. G. Desai (Stanford: Academic Reprints, 1954); his *Sarvodaya (The Welfare of All)* (Ahmedabad: Navajivan Publishing House, 1954); *Gandhi's Speeches & Writings* (Madras: Natesan, 1922); *Young India, 1919–1922* by Mahatma Gandhi, 2nd ed. (New York: B. W. Huebsch, 1924); *Indian States' Problem* (Ahmedabad: Navajivan Press, 1941); and M. K. Gandhi, *Delhi Diary* (Prayer Speeches from 10-9-47 to 30-1-48) (Ahmedabad: Navajivan Publishing House, 1948). Gandhi's secretary Mahadev H. Desai kept a daily diary during the first five years that he worked with Gandhi, seven volumes of which have been published: *Day-to-Day with Gandhi*, ed. N. D. Parikh, vols. 1–7 (Varanasi: Sarva Seva Sangh Prakashan, January 1968–January 1972). Gandhi's other secretary, Pyarelal, published three volumes of his records of Gandhi's activities, the first two entitled, *Mahatma Gandhi: The Last Phase*, vols. 1 & 2 (Ahmedabad: Navajivan Publishing House, 1956). Pyarelal finished volume 1 of *The Early Phase*, and his sister, Dr. Sushila Nayar completed volume 2 (Ahmedabad: Navajivan Publishing House, February 1965). Sushila Nayar subsequently completed two more volumes, *Mahatma Gandhi's Last Imprisonment: The inside story* (New Delhi: Har-Anand Publications, 1996) and *In Gandhiji's Mirror* (Delhi: Oxford University Press, 1991). The longest chronicle of Gandhi's life was written by D. G. Tendulkar, *Mahatma: Life of Mohandas Karamchand Gandhi*, 8 vols. (Delhi: The Publications Division, Ministry of Information & Broadcasting, Government of India, 1954).

Of the many biographies of Gandhi published since his death, the most balanced are Judith M. Brown, *Gandhi: Prisoner of Hope* (New Haven and London: Yale University Press, 1989); Geoffrey Ashe, *Gandhi* (New York: Stein & Day, 1968); Robert Payne, *The Life and Death of Mahatma Gandhi* (New York: E. P. Dutton, 1969); Dhananjay Keer, *Mahatma Gandhi: Political Saint and Unarmed Prophet* (Bombay: Popular Prakashan, 1973); Rajmohan Gandhi, *The Good Boatman: A Portrait of Gandhi* (New Delhi: Viking, 1995); Louis Fischer, *The Life of Mahatma Gandhi* (New York: Harper, 1950); and B. R. Nanda, *Mahatma Gandhi* (Boston: Beacon Press, 1958). The most insightful analysis into Gandhi's psyche is Erik H. Erikson, *Gandhi's Truth: On the Origins of Militant Nonviolence* (New York: W. W. Norton, 1969). The earliest, most sensitive introduction to Gandhi was first written in French by Romain Rolland, trans. by Catherine Groth, *Mahatma Gandhi* (New York & London: Century, 1924). Several other illuminating memoirs of Gandhi were written by his Western European disciples and contemporaries in London and South Africa as well as India, the best of which are Madeleine Slade, *The Spirit's Pilgrimage* (New York: Coward-McCann, 1960); Horace Alexander, *Gandhi through Western Eyes* (London: Asia Publishing House, 1969); C. F. Andrews,

Select Bibliography

Mahatma Gandhi: His Own Story (London: Allen & Unwin, 1930), and *Mahatma Gandhi at Work* (Allen & Unwin, 1931); the Reverend Joseph J. Doke, *An Indian Patriot in South Africa* (London, 1909); Henry S. L. Polak, *M. K. Gandhi: A Sketch of His Life and Work* (Madras: Natesan, 1918); Millie Graham Polak, *Mr. Gandhi: The Man* (London, 1931). The best work on Gandhi's youth and early manhood is by Professor Stephen Hay, whose "Gandhi's First Five Years," appears in *Encounter with Erikson: Historical Interpretation and Religious Biography*, ed. D. Capps, W. H. Capps, and M. G. Bradford (University of California, Santa Barbara: Scholars Press, 1977); also Hay's "Jaina Goals and Disciplines in Gandhi's Pursuit of Swaraj," in *Rule, Protest, Identity: Aspects of Modern South Asia*, ed. Peter Robb and David Taylor (London: Curzon Press, 1978); and Hay's "Jain Influences on Gandhi's Early Thought," "Between Two Worlds: Gandhi's First Impressions of British Culture," and "Ethical Politics: Gandhi's Meaning of Our Time," in South Asia Series, Center for South and Southeast Asia Studies, Institute of International Studies, University of California, Berkeley Reprint No. 359. The best work on Gandhi's experiences in London is James D. Hunt, *Gandhi in London*, revised ed. (New Delhi: Promilla Publishers, 1993); also see Hunt's *Gandhi and the Nonconformists* (New Delhi: Promilla, 1986). For Gandhi's two decades in South Africa, see E. S. Reddy and Gopalkrishna Gandhi, eds., *Gandhi and South Africa* (Ahmedabad: Navajivan, 1993); Maureen Swan, *Gandhi: The South African Experience* (Johannesburg: Ravan, 1985); Henry S. L. Polak, *The Indians of South Africa* (Madras: Natesan, 1909); Robert A. Huttenback, *Gandhi in South Africa* (Ithaca: Cornell University Press, 1971). The best book of photographs of Gandhi, including some of his most moving statements is *Gandhi: The Man*, compiled by Eknath Easwaran (San Francisco: Glide Publications, 1972). For Gandhi's early political activism in India, see Judith M. Brown, *Gandhi's Rise to Power* (Cambridge: Cambridge University Press, 1972), and her *Gandhi and Civil Disobedience: The Mahatma in Indian Politics, 1928–34* (Cambridge: Cambridge University Press, 1977). Ghanshayam Das Birla's memoirs include all the letters written by Gandhi to him as well as his to Gandhi in *Bapu: A Unique Association*, four volumes (Bombay: Bharatiya Vidya Bhavan, 1977). Shriman Narayan has edited *The Selected Works of Mahatma Gandhi* in five volumes (Ahmedabad: Navajivan Publishing House, 1968). Chandrashanker Shukla compiled the contributions of fifty-four people who, like himself, knew Gandhi in his *Incidents of Gandhiji's Life* (Bombay: Vora & Co Publishers, 1949). Prafulla Chandra Ghosh's Bengali memoir of Gandhi was translated into English by Dr. S. C. Sen Gupta, *Mahatma Gandhi as I Saw Him* (Delhi: S. Chand & Co. 1970). Sibnarayan Ray edited an excellent "International Symposium" on *Gandhi India and the World* (Philadelphia: Temple University Press, 1970). Another excellent anthology on *The Meanings of Gandhi* was edited by Paul F. Power (An East-West Center Book: Honolulu: University Press of Hawaii, 1971). For the centenary of Gandhi's birth, Dr. S. Radhakrishnan, in association with R. R. Diwakar and K. Swaminathan, edited *Mahatma Gandhi: 100 Years* (New Delhi: Gandhi Peace Foundation, 1968), containing memoirs and tributes from Gandhi's followers as well as world leaders. The following year, Norman Cousins edited *Profiles of Gandhi* (Delhi: Indian Book Company, 1969), another anthology of global tributes. B. R. Nanda edited a more comprehensive anthology of tributes in *Mahatma Gandhi: 125 Years* (New Delhi: Indian Council for Cultural Relations, 1995).

For more extensive study of this subject the following books are recommended:

Ahluwalia, B. K., and Shashi Ahluwalia, *Netaji and Gandhi* (New Delhi: Indian Academic Publishers, 1982).

Ambedkar, B. R., *What Congress and Gandhi Have Done to the Untouchables* (Bombay: Thacker & Co., 1945).

Select Bibliography

Bhattacharya, Sabyasachi, ed., *The Mahatma and the Poet: Letters and Debates between Gandhi and Tagore, 1915–1941* (New Delhi: National Book Trust, 1997).

Birla, G. D., *In the Shadow of the Mahatma* (Bombay: Vakils, 1968).

Bondurant, Joan V., *Conquest of Violence: The Gandhian Philosophy of Conflict*, rev. ed. (Berkeley and Los Angeles: University of California Press, 1969).

Bose, N. K., *My Days with Gandhi* (Calcutta: Nishana, 1953).

Bose, N. K., and P. H. Patwardhan, *Gandhi in Indian Politics* (Bombay: Lalvani Publishing House, 1967).

Chatterjee, Margaret, *Gandhi's Religious Thought* (New Delhi: Macmillan, 1983).

Chopra, Dr. P. N., *The Sardar of India: Biography of Vallabhbhai Patel* (New Delhi: Allied Publishers Ltd., 1995).

Chopra, Dr. P. N., and Dr. Prabha Chopra, eds., *The Collected Works of Sardar Vallabhbhai Patel*, 12 vols. (Delhi: Konark Publishers Ltd., 1990–98).

Choudhari, M., *Exploring Gandhi* (New Delhi: Gandhi Peace Foundation, 1989).

Dalton, Dennis, *Mahatma Gandhi: Nonviolent Power in Action* (New York: Columbia University Press 1993).

Desai, Mahadev, *The Gospel of Selfless Action, or, The Gita According to Gandhi* (Ahmedabad: Navajivan, 1946).

Devanesen, Chandran D. S., *The Making of the Mahatma* (New Delhi: Orient Longmans, 1969).

Engineer, Asghar Ali, ed., *Gandhi and Communal Harmony* (New Delhi: Gandhi Peace Foundation, 1997).

Galtung, Johan, *The Way Is the Goal: Gandhi Today* (Ahmedabad: Gujarar Vidyapith, 1992).

Gandhi, Rajmohan, *The Good Boatman: A Portrait of Gandhi* (New Delhi: Viking, 1995).

Gandhi, Rajmohan, *Rajaji: A Life* (New Delhi: Penguin, 1997).

Ghosh, Sudhir, *Gandhi's Emissary* (Bombay: Rupa, 1967).

Green, Martin, *Gandhi: Voice of a New Age Revolution* (New York: Continuum, 1993).

Harrison, Irene, *Agatha Harrison: An Impression by Her Sister* (London: 1956).

Hunt, James D., *Gandhi and the Nonconformists* (New Delhi: Promilla, 1986).

Iyer, Raghavan, *The Moral and Political Thought of Mahatma Gandhi* (New Delhi: Oxford University Press, 1973).

Iyer, Raghavan, ed., *The Essential Writings of Mahatma Gandhi* (New Delhi: Oxford University Press, 1996).

Jha, D. C., *Mahatma Gandhi The Congress and The Partition of India* (New Delhi: Sanchar Publishing House, 1995).

Juneja, M. M., *The Mahatma and the Millionaire* (Hissar: Modern Publishers, 1993).

Kripalani, J. B., *Gandhi: His Life and Thought* (New Delhi: Publications Division, 1970).

Mansergh, N. and E. W. R. Lumby, eds., *The Transfer of Power*, 12 vols. (London: Her Majesty's Stationery Office, 1970–83).

Mashruwala, K. G. *In Quest of Truth* (Ahmedabad: Shravana, 1983).

Menon, V. P., *The Transfer of Power in India* (Calcutta: Orient Longman, 1957).

Minault, Gail, *The Khilafat Movement* (New York: Columbia University Press, 1982).

Moon, Penderal, ed., *Wavell: The Viceroy's Journal* (London: Oxford University Press, 1973).

Moore, R. J., *Escape from Empire* (Oxford: Clarendon Press, 1983).

Nanda, B. R., *Gandhi: Pan-Islamism, Imperialism and Nationalism* (Delhi: Oxford University Press, 1989).

Select Bibliography

Narayan, Shriman, ed., *The Selected Works of Mahatma Gandhi*, 5 vols. (Ahmedabad: Navajivan, 1968).

Nehru, Jawaharlal, *An Autobiography* (London: John Lane, 1936).

Oldfield, Josiah, "Gandhi as I Knew Him," *John O'London's Weekly* (March 29, 1930), pp. 1000–1004.

Parekh, Bhikhu, *Colonialism, Tradition and Reform* (New Delhi: Sage, 1989).

Parekh, Bhikhu, *Gandhi's Political Philosophy: A Critical Examination* (London: The MacMillan Press, 1989).

Patel, C. N., *Mahatma Gandhi in His Gujarati Writings* (New Delhi: Sahitya Akademi, 1981).

Philips, C. H., and M. D. Wainwright, eds., *The Partition of India* (London: Allen & Unwin, 1970).

Prasad, Rajendra, *Autobiography* (Bombay: Asia, 1957).

Puri, Rashmi-Sudha, *Gandhi on War and Peace* (New York: Praeger, 1987).

Pyarelal, *The Epic Fast* (Ahmedabad: Navajivan, 1932).

Ray, Baren, ed., *Gandhi's Campaign Against Untouchability, 1933–34: An Account from the Raj's Secret Official Reports* (New Delhi: Gandhi Peace Foundation, 1996).

Reddy, E. S., and Gopalkrishna Gandhi, eds., *Gandhi and South Africa* (Ahmedabad: Navajivan, 1993).

Rothermund, Dietmar, *Mahatma Gandhi: An Essay in Political Biography* (New Delhi: Manohar, 1991).

Roy, Ramashray, *Self and Society: A Study in Gandhian Thought* (New Delhi: Sage, 1984).

Rudolph, Lloyd R., and Susanne H. Rudolph, *The Modernity of Tradition: Political Development in India* (Chicago: University of Chicago Press, 1967).

Sareen, T. R., *Subhas Chandra Bose and Nazi Germany* (New Delhi: Mounto Publishing House, 1996).

Sharp, Gene, *Gandhi as a Political Strategist* (Boston: Extending Horizon, 1979).

Sheean, Vincent, *Lead Kindly Light* (New York: Random House, 1949).

Stern, Elizabeth (pseud. Eleanor Morton), *Women in Gandhi's Life* (New York: Dodd, Mean, 1953).

Tagore, Rabindranath, *Mahatma Gandhi* (Santiniketan: Visva-Bharati, 1963).

Tendulkar, D. G., *Abdul Ghaffar Khan* (Bombay: Popular Prakashan, 1967).

Upadhyaya, J. M., *Mahatma Gandhi: A Teacher's Discovery* (Ahmedabad: Navajivan, 1969).

Watson, Francis and Maurice Brown, *Talking of Gandhiji* (Calcutta: Orient Longmans, 1957).

Wolpert, Stanley A., *Tilak and Gokhale: Revolution and Reform in the Making of Modern India* (Berkeley and Los Angeles: University of California Press, 1962).

Wolpert, Stanley, *Jinnah of Pakistan* (New York and Oxford: Oxford University Press, 1984).

Wolpert, Stanley, *Nehru: A Tryst with Destiny* (New York and Oxford: Oxford University Press, 1997).

Wolpert, Stanley, *A New History of India*, 6th ed. (New York and Oxford: Oxford University Press, 2000).

Woodcock, George, *Mohandas Gandhi* (New York: 1971).

INDEX

Index

Index

Index

Index

Index